The Divine Interlude

The Divine Interlude

A Novel

by

O. Talmadge Spence

"A Romance Contemporary Christian Chronicle"

The Divine Interlude

by
Dr. O. Talmadge Spence

ISBN: 1-889893-31-5

Printed in the United States of America

Ambassador-Emerald, International

1 Chick Springs Road, Suite 203
Greenville, SC 29609

16 Hillview Avenue
Belfast, Northern Ireland
BT5 6JR

www.emeraldhouse.com

DEDICATION

To Our Unborn Great Grandchildren

ACKNOWLEDGMENT
To
My Friend and Brother in Christ,

Noel

THE SONG OF THE ANVIL

Upon the Anvil hammers rang
    As godly men were born.
For soon the scaffold's noose would hang
    The remnant saints all torn.

The Anvil rang again, again
    More godly men were born.
A sovereign God decreed their end
    As remnant saints were torn.

The song the Anvil hammers sung
    Did reach God's Throne above;
And remnant after remnant, strong,
    Sustained God's truth and love.

The Anvil speaks of history,
    Recording every deed.
As man did hope in victory
    For life and children's seed.

The holy remnant children flee
    Across the pages there.
Their so-journ faces you can see
    Baptized with blood, but fair.

The Hammer speaks of circumstance—
    The day by day we meet.
The Hammer speaks of providence—
    God's mercy quite complete.

But there's God's Hand that guides the Heat,
    And holds the Hammer there;
He bends o'er Anvil on His Seat,
    And views with holy care.

He sits by His crucible-mold,
  Refining men who dare.
He guides the Heat, His carriage, bold,
  To see His Image there.

There's Fire and Heat much needed now
  To break man's stubborn will,
And in each vessel to endow
  And Holy Spirit fill.

'Tis God, 'tis God that holds it all
  And beats His vessels so;
'Tis God, 'tis God Who lifts the Fall
  And lets His children go.

The Hussites came and marked their name
  At burning stakes aflame.
Swiss Brethren came, maintained the same—
  The roll call gives no blame.

Dear Ulster, too, marked not a few
  Who struggled with great hope.
Dear Ulster, too, both strong and true,
  Rejected every pope.

Waldensians, Moravians
  Return again, again
To Pilgrim lands with Puritans;
  They measure man to man.

The French, The Czech, Bohemian,
  They march through history.
Aristocrat, barbarian,
  Christ is their victory.

The Holy Club, the Bogomils,
  They all mark clear the path.
Another group so often thrills;
  Each time a bloody bath

Anabaptist, too, and Quaker,
    They share a certain mark;
The stigmatism of Shaker
    Leaves reputation dark.

And sometimes here and sometimes there,
    In Roman Catholic shame,
We read of martyrs who did share
    The Holy Jesus fame.

Their doctrine was not always clear;
    They wrestled with the truth.
Their movement often seemed not near
    To Protestant's clear proof.

But now and again, we would see
    Amidst their own foray,
A longing just to be set free
    From popes of yesterday.

Paulicians, Priscillians;
    Franciscan, Dominic —
Like Lutherans, like Puritans
    Reformed in battle, thick.

But Reformation could not stay
    The Roman powers there;
An exodus, without delay,
    Must break the yoke they bear.

The inquisition brought a scar,
    Their bloody bodies, bent.
But each received his judgment bar
    To go with angels sent.

They laid their bodies on the rack;
    Their bones were stretched too far.
They weighted rope, then back to back,
    They plunged them with a jar.

For some simple faith to be kept,
　　These remnants pressed their plea.
For some pious eyes which had wept,
　　Perusing on the knee.

This "Little Flock," oft' hidden there
　　Away from public eye,
Held much in common in their prayer,
　　And raised a mighty cry.

The Separatist, the Stranger,
　　Dissenters were all there;
The Covenanter in danger—
　　"Kathari"—all do share.

They all sought the right to exist;
　　Believing it of God.
Their pious manner did persist
　　To seal each name in sod.

Not all of us now would agree;
　　Or help perpetuate
Their faith in Christian pedigree.
　　Some, even desolate.

God heard their every prayer, betimes;
　　He called them "Jewels," too.
The sounds of heaven heard like chimes;
　　Angels "carried" them through.

No organizational tool,
　　Or some committee chaired;
No ecclesiastical fool
　　Into its precincts dared.

They oft' lacked a leadership head;
　　Great love they had for truth.
They often faced an unknown dread,
　　But lived without reproof.

Often some doctrine seemed a pet,
    Endeared above the rest.
But central to the Cross they set
    Their faith on Christ, their Guest.

The song the Anvil hammers sung
    Did reach God's Throne above;
And remnant after remnant, strong,
    Sustained God's truth and love.

The Anvil rang again, again;
    More godly men were born.
A sovereign God decreed their end
    As remnant saints were torn.

Upon the Anvil hammers rang
    As godly men were born.
For soon the scaffold's noose would hang
    The remnant saints all torn.

—O. Talmadge Spence

Chapter One

The Land

(January-September, 1947)

There was a heavy fog hanging over the Bay of Fundy, but the trees and the grasses were gloriously green. At last, I had found the "Land of Evangeline" and it would be mine until the end of all my earthly days.

As soon as I, Gabriel T. Parsons, stepped off the Bluenose from Boston and touched the very tip of the southern end of Nova Scotia, I knew this was the land of my Evangeline, too. Since a child in the second grade, as my readings of books expanded into numerous other subject matters and foreign places, I had fabricated, by human vision, an unknown geography somewhere on earth; and now I had found it exactly as I envisioned. Every wave that the bow of the ship pierced across the Bay of Fundy sang, repeating its onomatopoeia, "russsh, russh, rush," "Rush across the Bay, rush!" The delight was on!

This was the trip to the home of a girl named Evangeline Marguerite Peters whom I met exactly eight months and ten days before in the year of 1947. I met her in January, in the beautiful surroundings on a campus of the Bible Christian College. We were both in the freshman class of studies there,

1

and I fell almost instantly in love; yes, at first sight. However, I carefully sought a proper introduction to her through a mutual classmate, Dave Lawtell. For the intervening semester months, we dated in the dating parlor of this conservative college. I had just completed two years in the United States Navy, the last two years of World War II in the South Pacific. Every day in the Navy I thought of God, but I did not know Him. Our first date, however, was to attend a basketball game there at the college, where I quietly told her I wanted to marry her. I do not think, at that time, she believed me. Yet, I still thought of God and was beginning to believe I wanted to know Him.

All through that first semester together, she told me of her childhood in the Land of Evangeline. She had Christian parents; she went through all of her experiences in that Land; she loved that Land. Now, so did I. She was as beautiful and cultured as the Land; she was a young lady of graceful poise with a classical simplicity that amazed me against the backdrop of a post-war energetic and casual society of the American forties and fifties, endeavoring to recover from the sacrifices and losses of the War itself. She also had a beautifully-trained voice both in speech and music.

Now, I was dockside at Yarmouth, passing through the area where welcoming friends greeted with delight those descending from the Bluenose. The earlier fog had lifted, and the terrain was greener than I even thought earlier. Evangeline was there with her father and her older sister, Louise Louisia. It was a good greeting and a good meeting for us all. They were friendly, reserved, and I was congenially received.

Her father was a quiet and gentle man whom I, a few hours later, understood to be a firm man in the greater things of life. His face was clear and his eyes were blue, slate blue, and although shorter in stature than myself, he seemed always taller after that first impression. His physical distinction was when he smiled; his eyes actually brightened and the worn creases of his face became more prominent. He carried the usual "New Scotland" (Nova Scotia) salt-polished face, like a browned rubbed-antique of noted worth. He also had, and it continued on through his entire life, a unique manner in conversation when he would respond in agreement to me and others with the word "yeah," while inhaling or sucking in the air instead of the usual unnoticed exhaling manner of my own acquaintances. Some said many Nova Scotians did that, but I never heard it like Mr. Peters.

I also met Mrs. Louise Louisia, Evangeline's only sister, and from that moment on I thought of her by both names. I had been told she married a handsome officer in the Royal Canadian Air Force. She was of a much stronger nature than Evangeline. At times she seemed a little course but not uncouth in it. But Louise Louisia was definitely a contrast with a mind of her own, a business of her own, and a life of her own.

We left the docking area, the four of us, and proceeded up the southwest shore of the peninsula, away from Yarmouth town, towards a very yellow house, somewhat uphill, across the road from a beautiful lake with an outlet back down into the Bay. Mrs. Louisia dropped us off from her automobile, as we said, "Good bye; see you soon!"

Before entering Evangeline's very yellow house, it being a clear day now, up more of the hill from the house, I could see the winding overflow of the lake going down to Fundy Bay and almost to the town of Yarmouth itself. This could have been no farther than about eight miles back to the dock of my arrival. Now, I could see clearly, without any fog anywhere, that the very green grass of the Land of Evangeline was even more green and more glorious. It suggested, for the first time to me, in these few moments of acquaintance there, the thought that "God must be a Great Barber, too, who cares daily and directly for such beauty. Both trees, grasses, and all greeneries are cut evenly in proportion to each other, and especially in Nova Scotia." I thought of the beautiful passage in the Bible, "Sing unto the Lord with thanksgiving;... Who covereth the heaven with clouds, who prepareth rain for the earth, who maketh grass to grow upon the mountains," The Book of Psalms, chapter 147, verse 7 and 8. I would later remember this again when Evangeline and I were to visit the Highlands in the north of old Scotland itself. It was also the first time I remember since childhood of being glad that God chose green instead of orange or red for His growths in the soil.

I took Evangeline's hand in mine as the only act of affection during this time of the acquaintances with her father and sister. The purpose of this first trip to her home, and my first trip to this Land, was to request permission for the hand of Evangeline Marguerite in marriage, and for her father's blessing of clear willingness to do so. All of this had to be right.

Evangeline and I agreed to this procedure on her brief visit to my home, when I introduced Evangeline to my own parents, Bishop and Mrs. T. H. Parsons, in Washington, D.C. This came after we left the spring semester at the college. My father and mother, with simple love, received Evangeline Marguerite to their hearts with delight. My dear father asked me in privacy, after Evangeline went to the kitchen with mother, and as a smile came on his face,

"Gabriel, is this the lady you have sought from childhood?"

I responded: "Yes. This lady encourages my heart to desire to live a better life in the future, Dad; and I believe she is that lady."

Evangeline had confirmed to me her love when we left the semester, prior to this visit with father and mother.

So, we planned for me to go to Yarmouth in late August. Of course, I would be bringing a ring of my promise and a token of our engagement to Evangeline if her father said "yes."

Her father gave me his permission and blessing, but only after he had posed two questions and a sorrow. "Gabriel, is there any insanity in your family?"

I immediately responded without realizing the full impact of the question: "None that I know of, Mr. Peters."

The second question demanded a greater personal knowledge than the first.

"Can you support my daughter with your financial means?"

I would have never imagined Mr. Peters' being impressed with my long-term ability, financially, to answer such a question with a promise. I was not a man of means. However, I responded slowly with deliberation: "With all my heart and strength I will endeavor to take care of Evangeline until I die."

I seemed to pass the two questions adequately, without any responsive commendation to me at all, but his third remark was the most shaking of all.

"Evangeline is my last daughter, of only two, and her mother is dead. I would greatly miss her if she would leave me now, all alone."

After an eternal second of time, I heard,

"Gabriel, you have my permission and blessing to marry Evangeline. She has told me much about you. I am satisfied."

My fiancée of only a few seconds, Evangeline, was having a problem in the kitchen, where she had deposited herself during my talk with her father, while endeavoring to boil potatoes for our supper. The problem was compounded by her desire to hear every word of the conversation between her father and me. After three attempts in three different pots of potatoes, burnt by too much heat and too little water, she gave the cooking up as our conversation ended. I went to the kitchen to tell her the good news which she had already heard. Mr. Peters simply eliminated the problem of the bad cooking by taking us out for supper to a delightful seafood meal and an equally lovely place up the road around the lake at the Greentree Inn. It is still there and even greener.

I gave my Christian testimony to Mr. Peters that I had become a Christian, April 17, 1947, just four months previous to meeting him, under the able ministry of Dr. Robert J. Jonathan, Jr., president of the college we attended. I gave Mr. Peters my natural age as twenty-one; but I emphasized my spiritual birth as only four months old. He understood my language, for he had already been informed that I had become a Christian before I met Evangeline. I gave him the verse that indicated how I came to Christ as, "Or despisest thou the riches of his goodness and forbearance and longsuffering; not knowing that the goodness of God leadeth thee to repentance?" Romans, chapter 2, verse 4. It was the goodness of God that led me to repentance.

Mr. Peters remained the same until his death — a quiet and gentle man with an unusual firmness. He was not changeable, by almost anyone. He kept his smile; he was a man of means with Scottish thrift in all of his funds, which sometimes made one think he was stingy. However, I found out he was not. He married later to a second wife who was a genuine Christian. Her name was Vera. He preceded her in death. My love for them both increased through the years; they taught me many things about life, and I will return to some of those thoughts later, as well as the wonders of the land of my Evangeline.

Evangeline's mother was undoubtedly very unusual. She died previously, at the age of fifty-three, and therefore I never met her. All pictures and descriptions and friends revealed her to be a beautiful lady, and her daily life was loved deeply by Evangeline. She considered her mother as a godly Christian artist, an unusual organist, and an outstanding teacher. She died in 1946; I always wished I had met her. One of her last requests was that Evangeline would go to the Bible Christian College in Groveland, Georgia, for her spiritual well-being in life. Her mother and father had followed the testimony of this college with great respect. They had financially supported this Christian institution for a large number of their years. The simplicity of all of these observations identified Primitive Christianity in a twentieth-century place and time.

Evangeline had already finished her formal training in voice at the Acadia Conservatory of Music as well as being a protégé of Kathryn McKenna, a greatly respected voice teacher in the Maritimes and all of Canada. At her formal, final public recital, presented in Yarmouth, a representative sent from the Juilliard Music Conservatory was present to finalize an invitation for her to go there to study voice. However, the request of Evangeline's mother, whom she held so dear, along with the encouragement of her sister, Louise Louisia, strengthened Evangeline to go to the Bible Christian College instead. Evangeline prepared for departure from her beautiful land in the fall semester of 1946 and came to the college where

I met her.

Evangeline's mother, Mildred Joye, was the only child of Captain John Prince, a highly respected sea captain between the Maritimes and the West Indies. Later in his marriage he resided at Yarmouth, owning a large mansion home at the top of a hill overlooking the Bay of Fundy and situated with eminence above the Bay. He and his wife, Ellen Mae, were a most unusual couple: one, being skilled in the dignity and craft of ship and navigation; the other, in culture, breeding, and refinement of a Christian persuasion. Mildred Joye had been the sole student aboard Captain John's ship, and she was personally reared in an excellent and broad culture to respect life in a God-fearing way, also, with breeding, culture, and etiquette.

Evangeline's mother was actually born on the island between the coast of Maine and Nova Scotia called Westport. The only way I became acquainted with how to get to her island-home was to proceed up the west coast of Nova Scotia to Digby; to go back down the neck by St. Mary's Bay to Long Island; and then to Briar Island. Then with a second ferry, in those days, from Briar Island you could go out into Fundy to Westport. Finally, it became one ferry to Westport.

Mildred Joye Prince was raised, as a young girl, between the training of that recluse-island and aboard her father's ship. She attended the Christian Church there, a modest-framed, white clap-board wooden church just north of Gull Rock. Mr. McArcy McGee Peters and Mildred Joye were married in this church, and Captain John marched down the aisle with his daughter on his arm with great dignity and pomp. Later on, Mr. Peters purchased Gull Rock and had a sheep ranch there. This, of course, was in their earliest days of marriage. Afterwards, they moved to Yarmouth. I don't think the sheep ranch worked out too well.

In Yarmouth, afterwards, Evangeline went to a one-room school house, near the river that ran between the lake of her home and the Bay. However, the training of her home and her dear mother gave her the artistry of voice and life. Mr. Peters gave her the discipline and the financial means needed to live by.

During the time of gaining permission for marriage, Mr. Peters and Evangeline took me, for six days, through the ever-increasing beauty of the Land of Evangeline. Of course, for that short time, we could only see the southern extremity of that glorious land; but in the future we would go back to the land again and again. We only went as far north as Meteghan and Weymouth on the west side of Nova Scotia, and then back down to the southeast by Argyle, Port Clyde, and Barrington Passage.

Farther inland, we saw natural lakes secluded by winding roads and timberland. There were many beautiful settings always revealing certain other lakes and rivers winding themselves back to the Bay of Fundy. The floral lupines were everywhere. It always seemed to me, every time we would return to Yarmouth, the lupines were always in bloom. We stopped at many tiny but colorful lunch places and the more lavish supper places. I could not get my heart full of the land, the beautiful green land of fog, rain, storm, and calm. We went to the historic lighthouse at Forchu, and back to Yarmouth, always back to Yarmouth, and the quaint shops with unusual and strange items, at least to me. Fascination was the word for the things, and reverence for God was the result.

What a wonderful time Evangeline and I had. We also read the Bible and prayed together, but even more so privately. Of course, we sang and sang all kinds of good songs. I composed a variety of song forms from the humorous to the sublime. I still have them, every one. The first of over forty ballads dedicated to Evangeline was entitled "Ma Chère."

Only in the succeeding years, with returns to this land, did the impact of the Land of Evangeline really come to fruition with its natural and spiritual value to me. This was added to the proper proportion of my love and identity with my earlier wonder, dreaming as a child about some land on earth that carried with it the simple, the beautiful, and the clean, clear geography of my heart's desire. Having lived in about 20 different houses in my youth, I could see another reason why

I loved the Land of Evangeline. I believe it was the rain and the storm and the fog and the sunshine green splashing all around everywhere in great profusion that gripped my heart so much. The tides would rise eighty to ninety feet in places, so high that their vertical actions turned over generators lying on their sides in the concrete dams. In earlier days, I loved Washington, D.C., but for an entirely different reason; yet I will return again and again to The Land of Evangeline.

However, The Land of Evangeline leaves Yarmouth and rises to its dynamic story at Grand Pré. Although it is hard to exactly pin-point this unusual land, its center is Grand Pré. Some even include a part of another province of Canada, New Brunswick, but Grand Pré is actually the center. Of course, Acadia is a larger portion of that identity totally surrounding Evangeline's Land. Longfellow's classical epic poem is set forth as "a tale of Acadie." In this word we include not only the former French colony in southeast Canada, that ceded to Great Britain in 1713, but also all geographies that pertain to New Brunswick, Prince Edward Island, Cape Breton Island, and Nova Scotia. Of course, the French dialect trims the word Acadia to Cajun with the first syllable, "Ca," the total abbreviation of "Acadia," and "jun," the abbreviation of "Injun" for "Indian."

The monument at Grand Pré, sculptured by Henri Hebert, stands with its honor to Evangeline, herself. There is a two-fold meaning in her statue there: one, it honors a historical event; and two, a literary beauty.

The former honor commemorates the French Acadians who were expelled from the Grand Pré area in 1755. Many of them, after troubles at sea, in their forced flight, finally settled in Louisiana, in the deep south of the United States. However, all the struggle in Acadia includes a time from 1613 through 1755. Cajun food, in New Orleans, marks a typical cuisine art they took with them. Evangeline and I would one day eat of this cuisine in a visit to a Conference held in New Orleans

The latter honor communicates a literary beauty. We are indebted to Nathaniel Hawthorne for telling the story to Henry Wadsworth Longfellow of the romance of Gabriel Lajeunesse and Evangeline Bellefontaine. His epic poem of romance arose from an accurate history of the eighteenth-century banishment of French Nova Scotian farmers who had refused to swear loyalty to their English rulers.

Longfellow picks up his narrative just after the couple had their engagement party in the Acadian village of Grand Pré, when suddenly the couple were accidentally separated and were forced to embark on different ships bound for the American Colonies. Seeking her fiancé, Evangeline eventually finds the Louisiana farm where Gabriel and his father had settled, only to learn that she unknowingly passed Gabriel on the Mississippi as he, "moody and restless," had set out to hunt in the western hills. For years Evangeline follows his fading trail until finally, as a Sister of Mercy in Philadelphia, she finds him, an old man, dying of the plague in the poorhouse. They are buried in nameless graves in the midst of the noisy city.

I have read, as a complaint, several times in several places, of Longfellow's epic story being "a single-minded devotion to an ideal," in contrast to a compliment, that it was Longfellow's "most successful contribution of metrical romance to American literature." However, I do not think idealism should be thought of as a complaint. Another critic extended a commendation of the epic as the most "flawless story of its period," with all "the colorings of the English landscape school of painting." Unfortunately, it is regrettable that it was not published until 1847.

This explains why, from my youth, and now my marriage, and through the person of Evangeline, "I knew this was the land of my own Evangeline, and it would be mine until the end of my earthly days." I came to believe, later, in my Christian life, that God not only directs His children, spiritually, but also naturally and physically and geographically to an appointment in life where a host of similarities come together with the leading of the Holy Spirit and the Holy Scriptures for the life of the believer in the Lord Jesus Christ, even if it is a wilderness. However, the knowledge of that principle was only infantile at this point in my life.

The simplicity of my own childhood; my utterly guileless mother; the simple preaching of my earthly father; many summers up on the Blue Ridge Mountains of Virginia; the beauty of nature from my one-summer serious visit to the John Felix farm near the Blue Ridge Mountains; and then all the other returnings to those mountains which kept their richness alive in my heart; along with Evangeline herself; her deceased mother, Mildred Joye; her father, Captain John Prince; and his wife, Ellen Mae; at least in hearing about them — all came to the forefront as I commenced my adult life in the good providence of God in all of these things in the Land of Evangeline. The idealism and romance and geography, and my new-found life in Christ, were only a prelude to it all. One day I would look back, in the midst of a divine interruption, and see clearly the grand providence of the goodness and grace of Almighty God.

For the time, however, I returned to my home in Washington, D.C., only comforted to know that I would see my Evangeline once again, with our engagement sealed with a ring, returning to the Bible Christian College within a month, the place where we first loved.

Chapter Two

The Learning

(October 1, 1947)

Somewhere down the road of life the conduct of man must demand a teacher who not only teaches, but who is also the observer of the one taught. This is especially true for some of the complexities of life and religion. Man knows nothing but by books or teachers who taught books or teachers who wrote books. Where primitive Christianity prevails, the complex questions may not arise as often. However, it is equally important to have a teacher for the primitive as well. But God did not intend for the primitive to remain too simple or naïve, and yet the simplistic principles behind the primitive must continue. God has no problem in being simple or profound. No one should deliberately seek the primitive to make it easy. This is unacceptable with God. Easy Christianity is simply impossible since the Cross is the central truth of the Gospel, very deeply wrought in the heart of God.

So, a teacher speaks of his student, and now the spokesman of this narrative is spoken by another.

Gabriel and Evangeline returned to the college, knowing it

12

had completely moved from a small, beautiful southern campus in Groveland, Georgia, to an enormous campus of impressive and stately buildings on at least two hundred and fifty acres at Grandville, North Carolina, just beyond the state-line of South Carolina. It had become known now as the Bible Christian University, with its appropriate new academic status. The student body had over-doubled from 1,800 to 4,000.

Gabriel had formerly read and believed as a child of a world-view of things in what he called 6-point type, remembering the small type of encyclopedic studies. He did not recall ever believing that knowledge was a large group of separated islands of thought according the names of the subjects of majors and minors, like mathematics, science, arts, etc., each a divided specialty. Everything man ever came to know was all on one continent of thought, knowledge, and truth; and then that entire epistemology was under God. Gabriel had believed in God since he was five years old.

However, now before his eyes he would see the world-view of thought in one spot, in an opportune learning laboratory supported by the riches of Biblical truth and grace through the Gospel. This time he would be seeing the truth and beauty of it all in at least 12-point type, a much larger dimension than he had ever dreamed of or was accustomed to before.

He had also learned some things from the darker side of life, that although all words in the dictionary retained the same definition, no matter what size the type might be, yet by what is known to men on earth, it is often true that in the larger presentation of that same word, man often applies the word with a change in the definition itself. This had something to do with the difference between denotation and connotation, or semantics. But more accurately, it was quite often man's cheating on the definition in a real world of sin to accomplish his own end in his own effort. The old illustration applies: they would endeavor to fit a square peg, or theory, into liberal, round holes. Once the difficulty arose that it would not fit, they would go down under the table, and with a can of "squirt," whatever that was, "squeak" drops here and there. Most people then concluded the square did indeed fit into the round hole.

Some called the "squirt" pragmatism; others, psychology; and still others, expedience. A minority called it compromise.

Would things change here in the University, too? Would the Gospel now be a commercial bit for the market, or would it indeed retain the same definition as before in a smaller ministry to the soul? Gabriel inquired of the Lord early after his conversion, "what does it really mean and what does it include when the Bible reveals 'Jesus Christ the same yesterday, and to day, and for ever?'" The Book of Hebrews, chapter 13, verse 8. Formerly, Gabriel had only learned things in 6-point type in his earlier childhood years. It was his prayer, for Evangeline and himself, that they would really understand the world-view without a new dictionary, or a change in the human use of the words defined therein. The world-view of God's creation and redemption had difficulties, but there were sanctified paradoxes built into the complex universe as well as in the heart of a deep Savior.

However, Gabriel must keep faith with his integrity given by grace; his honesty and truth were the only guardians. His heart must be his friend as he enters into the deeper understanding of all of life. All definitions must be applied as they are; and the paradoxes are not to be understood as contradictions, as was the pattern of Greek philosophy, and now, also neo-orthodoxy, but rather as the Bible teaches: two seemingly opposite presuppositions held in one, singular entity of absolute truth.

These words are set forth in no way to remotely imply only an intellectual Christianity, but rather to set forth the strong foundation upon which the individual Christian gains the Primitive Christianity needed for the time, whether he ever heard or understood the depth of them before, or learns more later. No matter whether man ever knows the answer or not, it would be true anyway. Even though some people are honorably simple, yet the complex remains. Others are more complex, and yet they may be having problems with the simple.

Here is an example of a college moving to the university status: the primitive growing and accepting the entire epistemological challenge to the full maturity of the world-view. Gabriel and Evangeline were now standing on the threshold of an endeavor to accept equally the full brunt of this paradox for the good of their testimony and the ministering to others. Gabriel must pursue the questions arising from his heart, which seem intellectually native to his own nature and childhood. He then, during this training and preparation period, through his love for Evangeline, must set forth his conclusions with a loving heart and a gentle communication of the same to her. It was Gabriel's hope and prayer that this would finally forward a proclamation of the Gospel to others through his ministry.

All of these things, in the balance of the paradox, should cause a good relationship between the simplicity of the primitive with the knowledge of the learned and his theology. Evangeline wholeheartedly claimed the simplicity of things. All things should finally yield some wisdom beyond the great divisions of twentieth-century espousements of the church. Without that wisdom, the chasm between Primitive Christianity and the profound Reformation Christianity would become an ecumenical climate to be destroyed. Without the Biblical paradox there would be only a human synthesis of all things rather than a genuine distinction between truth and error. Since this is true, there could possibly be a better laboratory forthcoming in Biblical growth into the large and the universal need here at the University. It was Gabriel's prayer that this would be true.

In Groveland, Georgia, the college was richly blessed to have the world-view of Christianity and the individual Christian life. Of course, the liberal arts educational entities may be a Biblical base through natural theology to strengthen the maintenance of a stronger stand for Christ in the world. The president had been offered impressive opportunities in history, fine arts, the dramatic arts, and as a secular professional writer; but he chose to be a preacher of the Word of God in a university context. He was a forthright, strong fundamentalist. As Gabriel thought about his friend who led him to Christ, he wondered what it would be like to have a twelve-year-old

Samuel heart with a fifty-year-old Solomonic mind. But at the instant of that thought he wondered if he, Gabriel, would ever grow spiritually in Christ Jesus with just the simple grace of God being his motive and will and his mind.

Gabriel was amazed and encouraged how the president and founder of the University, even in the beginning days, could see the need, in germ thought, to maintain such a broad inclusion of so many areas of life on a solid Christian base, including a strong emphasis upon evangelism and revivalism no matter what profession, calling, or occupation a student might have. The presence of the cultural program and the strong presence of preparing pastors, teachers, missionaries, and Christian administrators appeared to be a proper environment for God to do a good work in all categories.

In making the move from Groveland to Grandville, the cultural program became somewhat enlarged, but not out of proportion to the spiritual ministry of the divinity students. The cultural program really became more significant than before. Gabriel had never heard of Discipline and Deportment placed together in a context of Culture; and yet, in this University they were.

"Sacred Encores" was another cultural program in the college from the earliest days, presented each Lord's Day afternoon on some dramatic Christian theme to keep alive certain historical events either in the Bible or church history.

"The Artist Visitor" was presented several times within the calendar of the University year, and it, too, was initiated in the early days of the college. These were usually outside artists who were invited with their own artistic theme, and they were sometimes called upon to participate in some theme in which the faculty and students would also be involved through extra-curricular programs. These were classical in nature, and allowed the students to view the outside world in a hopefully honorable artistry. Although not all of the visitors were Christians, yet each individual would have an affinity with the testimony of the college. "The Artist Visitor" brought what was known as the "Art Seasons," which brought to the forefront seasonal varieties of the classics for such an occasion.

Nature was often involved in accompaniment to these themes.

There was also "The Classic Series." From the beginning days of the college, the staff, faculty, and students always participated directly in drama and opera. Sometimes only a portion of an opera would be emphasized in a small ensemble of voices and instruments. This "Classic Series" would set forth the narrative of a tale or story from classical literature or music. After Gabriel reviewed this large proportion in the study of culture he concluded concerning his God: "He hath made everything beautiful in his time:.." Ecclesiastes, chapter 3, verse 11.

The changes from the college days to the University status did not seem to change the Christian and Biblical center of the institution. There was a natural enlargement of several of these ingredients under culture, but mainly it was the proper advancements which brought the earlier educational levels simply to a higher plateau. Film-photography and the Art Gallery were added, which were natural extensions to the other five elements in the cultural program.

So, finally, seven cultural presentations were now in place for the University future with excellence in culture being ever urged by the Christian students of the University who were being brought into a new world, the World-View, for the Christian in the twentieth century. Gabriel had thought for some time that there was a danger in making only an exclusive "spiritual diet," so called, thus causing the student body to assume that God was not in nature and culture, but more so in strictly religious exercises and appearances. This would be a human fallacy. The World-View included all of the honorable experiences of life. Gabriel had read that modern man is capable, by the age of seventy-five, to have had fifteen trillion experiences in a lifetime. What an extravagant offer from God to a creature so small.

With five ingredients of culture, properly rendered in the earlier years of the Groveland college, through foresight, the 6-point type would be enlarged, in emphasis, to become 12-point. The move to University status in Grandville would

18

maintain the same, earlier dictionary. In the University, the same meaning of culture would survive, while bringing the Christian's life and culture to its full dimension of what God had in mind when He created nature and man, and then provided redemption for man, after the fall, as well.

Gabriel and Evangeline were indeed grateful to see the strong undergirding emphasis made upon the divinity students and that each semester commenced with revival services for the first three days before student registration. All students were obligated to attend these services. Chapel speakers extended a rich blessing from the Word of God, daily. From the beginning the president instituted these first three days believing that the students should seek God in prayer and Bible study concerning His will for their lives. This was important, prior to their selection of courses and academic programs leading to a degree, for their calling, profession, occupation, craft, skill, or other purpose in life, both male and female.

Gabriel and Evangeline were deeply moved by the University's spiritual stability and aims even in the face of the update changes in the publicly observed ingredients and progress on the new campus. Gabriel sought out Evangeline for her response after the first day of classes.

Evangeline met Gabriel in the Student Center with a rapture of human spirit.

"Oh Gabriel, isn't it tremendous and awesome?"

Gabriel knew he should wait before answering her because he had already learned concerning her zeal of joy; she would ask a question and keep right on talking and hinder your response.

"Have you ever seen such buildings? Have you seen the new drama facility? I have already counted sixteen fresh approaches for my Christian life for the future."

"Yes, yes, yes," Gabriel responded. "Allow me to soberly enumerate them. There is the 'Deportment Diet,' where you eat your words in honesty as you stand before the Dean with a discipline problem; there is the Lord's Day 'Sacred Encores,' where you may pray seated with your eyes wide open in spiritual refreshment. There will also be coming soon the 'Artist Visitor,' who will bring an outside viewpoint of the masters and the models that we may observe, beautifully, the 'Art Seasons' of the year from nature. Finally, in each semester, "The Classic Series" of some drama or opera will lead us into a fresh dimension in public, artistic studies of the literary narratives of both literature and music. Of course, our new University status has brought new dimensions to culture: first, film-production, and an art gallery of strictly religious art."

"Oh Gabriel, you always elaborate with your fine presentations to me. You are quite dramatic yourself, in your own way, and without being 'stagey' about it. I was simply sharing my sincere delight with my husband-to-be."

"Yes, Evangeline, and that reminds me, since you have brought up the subject of 'Husband,' I will need to make an appointment with Dean Perkins Monroe, who is still dean of men. He must present my request before the administration for permission for our hopeful marriage during the Christmas break. As you know, students must make this request at the beginning of the semester before a hopeful mid-semester marriage."

"Yes, I am aware of that, Gabriel, and I have been praying that the Lord would use their permission-response to confirm, through them, the accuracy of our timing of the will of God. The date still remains for December 20 in my own heart."

"Yes, Evangeline, I have also been praying before the Lord. My Navy days, at the close of the War, caused me to realize the goodness of God in sparing my life several times, and therefore I do not object to the discipline of this test in these days. But as we have conversed before, I believe the Lord desires me to proceed as quickly as possible in my education so we can move on. As you know the schedule is three years and three summers, at the most, as designated for my undergraduate program."

"Oh, there's the bell for my next class, Gabriel. Yes, I will remember your schedule, my beloved. I will see you in the Dining Common at lunch." (Evangeline proceeds to get her books and belongings together as Gabriel speaks.)

"We now have ten-minute breaks between classes in the University, but the time may come that we need fifteen minutes to get across this new campus to some places. Also, I understand that now in the University we are seated alphabetically. This is the plan for the Dining Common and Chapel as well as worship services. Don't forget that your name starts with 'P' just as mine does. From Parsons to Peters leaves open the three letters of 'b,' 'c,' and 'd.' Right now I cannot think of a proper noun beginning with 'Pb,' 'Pc,' or 'Pd,' but you never can tell when some name could come up in our world in this succession."

"Good-bye, Gabriel, I will see you in one hour."

"Good-bye, Evangeline: from Mr. Parsons to Miss Peters. Keep the alphabet straight every day now until December 20. Then we will never be concerned about another proper noun coming between us. I can predict that only the name of Parsons will survive. (raising his voice as Evangeline departs) Don't forget our three o'clock appointments each time this semester to meet in the Dating Parlor. I have already secured permission for this daily delight."

"All right Gabriel, I will see you then."

Gabriel and Evangeline continued delightfully studious until the three o'clock hour, and both arrived at the Dating Parlor together.

"The new Dating Parlor is beautiful, Evangeline, almost as beautiful as you are."

"Yes, Gabriel, I know you think that of me, and I am very glad to know your heart still speaks of it."

"The interior decoration of this spacious room," Gabriel responded, "is becoming to a new Christian University in the twentieth century. I am amazed that the president has been able to bring this large, visible testimony together for the training of our practical and academic environment. We will never forget these days, the memories, and times of study. One day we will not have this opportunity again."

"Yes, Gabriel. (pause) They beautified the entire room with historical and cultural settings. I want us to rotate our dating places in each of the sixteen sections."

"That's a good thought, Evangeline, because our purpose in meeting together at these times is to go through all our classes and share observations that will help our prayerful and hopeful balance from this source of such a variety of ingredients for our Christian World-View and future ministry. This is not an end within itself, but we will seek every beautiful and truthful thing for that which is ahead of us for the glory of Christ and the good of others."

"I know that this is regularly on your mind, beloved Gabriel, isn't it?"

"Yes, from the second grade I was attracted to a sight, in a very simple search of a world-view. Of course, my father's simple belief is that man did fall in a universe which God did create, and not outside the universe. My reading of books brought the horizontal world to a unit in my boyhood mind. Between the Bible and the books my boyish life commenced. Evangeline, at that time I was not a Christian, but as I have said before, a consciousness of God began at the age of five. Fifteen years later I would become a Christian, in the last semester of the Bible Christian College in Georgia, where we met."

"I know, Gabriel, and that is one of the things I have noticed about you, which I need in my own Christian life if I am to be a helpmeet to you in your later ministry. Evidently, God desires to use this root in your heart. A world-view deals with the world, and you must get ready for that emphasis for the glory of Christ. I have heard you often pray for the world. I don't think I have ever heard that kind of prayer prayed before by anyone I knew."

"Well, everything is not clear to me, yet, dear Evangeline. I must not anticipate anything before its time as far as a definite ministry is concerned. In the meantime, my own heart needs to witness concerning Christ and Him crucified. I must admit, however, and to you, my dear, our generation has not come to a Biblical balance about such a scope of the Christian faith. There have been great and pious men who saw this distinctive in the Bible, and their own lives were affected by it as well as others."

"Gabriel, do you think many people have this view as you do?"

"I do not know; I am only learning from my own hunger at this time. My recent conversion to Christianity has caused me to re-address and rearrange my former studies of the books into a serviceable place with the Lord Jesus. In recent days I have wondered how much I might have to throw away entirely if it cannot be converted to the Lord Jesus, too. I spent this last summer, after leaving your very yellow house and after our engagement to each other, in meditation and prayer over new Christian books of church history and the divines and their writings.

"I know there are others who served their Lord in a very small place with a simple ministry and a simple, primitive people. In still others, where the balance of sight is not seen and understood, it seems that all of their 'stars of eternal hope' are going away from each other, and far more darkness is being manifested as time goes on in their lives. This darkness accompanies even professing Christians, in our time, because man is using Christianity for his own horizontal benefits such as health, prosperity, and material success. I do not even know if Christianity should be used for those purposes at all. There is a new definition of Christianity being born in the earth."

"Are you suggesting, beloved Gabriel, that stars should all come together and act in the opposite direction and bump into each other?"

"Oh no. That would not bring anything but a final destruction of light itself in their own collision. Just today, in science class, however, a guest professor, Dr. John Rendle Wellson, explained that although all stars are indeed getting farther and farther apart, including their respective solar systems, yet all of the stars are at least going in the same general direction. They are not in a state headed towards collision. In the days of the Judges it is said, 'the stars in their courses fought,' Judges, chapter 5, verse 20. What a magnificent God, even when the stars fight for Him, they fight in orderly courses."

"Out in the universe, what do you think we are certain

about, Gabriel?"

"Well, since God created the universe, we are certain of law, order, design, purpose, and beauty in the universe. This is not just a machine, because there are many more complications involved which man has not discovered. It is simply the direct providence of God that superintends the universe personally. Yes, a universe. It is a personal operation by God, our Father. His care is so simple, dear Evangeline; and there never has been, and never will be "pandemoniumism" in the universe to destroy His authority and power. Evidently, God maintains a lot of space between the stars. In miniature, it may be illustrated in a similar manner by the fact that we do not see many ships on the ocean when we take a voyage to another continent. The ocean is so vast the ships do not clutter or cluster together in conflict with each other."

"If I am following you, Gabriel, can you accept such complicated theories and thoughts like that from scientists?"

"Oh no, we never wholeheartedly accept man-answers concerning God-questions. Man is still lingering with little information in the midst of huge questions; but the Bible does reveal that the sun, moon, and stars were given to us for signs and seasons, and we do respect the Wise Men of the Bible, called the Magi, for there is a human knowledge of the stars that God respects. He made it so. Of course, a false Magi becomes, as revealed in the Bible, also, the Satanic force of Magicians and other parts of the occult. There is a difference between the study of astronomy and astrology; the former is a valid study; the latter is a satanic study. Therefore, without accepting human speculations and satanic divinations, we should always be looking, in our own human knowledge, for unity in the universe."

"That's good, Gabriel. When you mention the universe, you are making it simple for me."

"Yes, and that, once again, is what we must endeavor to do in our preaching and teaching the Gospel of the Lord Jesus. So many do not understand the simple truth, and therefore the depths of later revealed doctrine in the Holy Scriptures are

read too early, without the time of the season in life being ready
for it. The first season is for the truth which is needed for
salvation and peace with God. You have to be a child, first.
Although God created the first two human beings full-grown
and mature, yet He no longer uses that plan for the future
replenishing of mankind. We all start out as infants to the
whole universe."

"The idea of a 'universe,' Gabriel, brings it all together."

"We are fortunate indeed to have been given a 'universe.'
That indicates it is not a 'multi-verse,' or a 'plural-verse,' or an
'anti-verse' or a 'chaotic-verse.' The fall of man is here; sin is
here; and chaos and inequities are present; but thank God,
Evangeline, we live in a universe. If stars are used by God to
fight against God's enemies and sin and chaos, as revealed in
the Bible, we should look for congruity between the farthest
star and the closest flower. It was Victor Hugo, I believe, that
said that God made stars to serve the planet earth; He made
the planet earth to serve the body of man; God made the body
to serve the soul of man; and, He made the soul of man to
serve the God of man. After that, the providence of God
commences the principle all over and over again down through
history. We conclude that God is in history in at least two
ways: He is in history in His creation and providence; He is
also in history because of the incarnation and virgin birth of
His Son, Jesus of Nazareth, in a time, space, history world."

"I realize it is imperative for you to see things according to
the knowledge you speak of, my dear Gabriel, but always
remember there are many, many people like me who only see
the simple, the beautiful, or the ugly, whether viewing nature
or the universe. In that flower you spoke of, we always need
to be reminded of the unity of the universe."

"Oh, I have not forgotten that, my dear one. As I have
told you before, Evangeline, my love was born to you because
everything about you lives in the simplistic Land of Evangeline.
From your very eyes to the islands surrounding Nova Scotia,
your beautiful simplicity has brought much into my heart and
life. I have already told you before, on several other occasions,
we need to keep the truth and hope of Primitive Christianity

alive in this world. However, we must never forget Reformation Christianity in the preaching and building of Christian lives through some complex Christian truth. There are Creeds and Councils, unfortunately, that must define and defend Biblical truth as history unfolds itself in a fallen world, yea, even an apostate world."

"What would you give in a narrative form that would illustrate that, Gabriel?"

"In the Old Testament this dichotomy could be viewed through the examples of Moses and King David. In the former we have the primitive walk with God in the truth and history of the Wilderness Wanderings of the children of Israel. In the days of King David we see the move towards reformation of the nation in the midst of the complications of David's own family and the apostasy among the later kings and peoples. The reformation of the people brought a golden time in spite of the protestations necessary and the reformation changes demanding courageous attention among the people. In King David's day, culture, music, dignity, and beauty of life flourished. In other words, my dear Evangeline, historical life does not always keep simple in a fallen world."

"Is the matter of concern," responded Evangeline, "in your heart a result of the puzzle involved in the world-view of things? or the defense of the Gospel against the ignorance prevailing in our world? I do not equate ignorance with simplicity, Gabriel, and I know you do not either."

"Both, I suppose. Your implication is correct in the matter of ignorance, Evangeline, and I am glad your beautiful heart does not put stock in ignorance as a way to keep simple. Neither do I believe that the intellectual mode is to be equated with the acquisition of knowledge for the sake of pride. Each of us must remain true to our perspective and respective gifts which came from God. I would be the way that I am if no one was here but God and me. I must be that way, or possibly I should say, I should be that way.

"But concerning your question about a puzzle in the universe, we, probably, as Christians need to see that there is more to life than what we personally see and understand. The very transcendence of Almighty God demands an extremely complex series of structures and systems, and especially in the development of the incorporeal elements of angelic life. Sir Isaac Newton and his Newtonian principles have been criticized by the skeptics, who were also scientists, but did not believe that the universe was like a perfect machine. Some of these things need to be cleared up by Christian scholars, because there is a solution there."

"What would you suggest as a solution, Gabriel?"

"It appears to me, at this point in my life, that it is only a puzzle in this regard; not that it is either true or false. However, God never intended for Christians to become the prestigious scientists of the world, per se, and certainly not of the universe. The complexity was to keep us humble: no finite creature in a state of immanence could ever go too far in the knowledge of God's universe. So, rather than our seeking only a solution to the puzzle of the universe and the God-questions, we, as evangelizing and born again Christians, should contribute more to the paradox that I continue to speak of in its relationship to the doubt and denial of critics of Christianity. It is quite ironic, but medical science says we know more about the heavens than we know about the human brain. You would think we would know more about our own brain than about God's heavens. There are three human responsibilities in life: first, to get our individual self right with God; second, to keep the heart right in spirit through communion with God; and third, to live in a right relationship with our fellowman and society."

"That's good, Gabriel; if the paradox does not hinder us from discharging our responsibility to others in honoring our Lord. We must know more about our mind and heart for the Lord Jesus than the galaxies. I am sure that we have the Word of God for that, and not the scientists."

"You are very right, Evangeline. We must only seek knowledge for the sake of the Lord Jesus. All else is pride. Man should know by now that the perfect machine simply does not exist, but the universe, by its laws, is indeed precise. However, the fall of man and evidences of the fall do reside in the universe. Therefore, when and if a problem in Christian doctrine and the Christian practice arises, we must seek God for an answer, or believe that it is only a God-question and not a man-question. Instead of believing there is chaos everywhere in the universe, as the modern scientists believe, more accurately we should acknowledge there is a puzzle everywhere in the universe and even in the Christian's life; but God is easily able to solve all puzzles. Since God is not primarily making Christians scholars of science, He seeks obedient, spiritual creatures for His glory. The Sage of Jerusalem brings to the front God and creation, 'That which is crooked cannot be made straight,' in Proverbs, chapter 1, verse 15. Solomon mentions it again in chapter seven, verse 13. Thomas Boston, one of our Puritan divines, has given us an excellent book on this puzzle and places God in charge of the entire matter of puzzles and honorable problems in nature and life. I believe the title of his book was *The Crook in My Lot*."

"Yes, dear Gabriel, there is a "crook in my lot," too. Is it not wonderful that our salvation is by free grace alone?"

"Yes, Evangeline, we shall close our time together for this afternoon session. My heart has been refreshed by your heart today. (a pause, as Gabriel seeks the eyes of Evangeline.) Yes, my dear. I am so glad that God gave you to me, and your interruptions, as you think of them, are always appreciated. Please continue to do that in the years ahead. I do not desire to go any further than I should in these things. I am only learning, my dear."

"Yes, Gabriel, I understand your heart in all of this."

"We live in a generation that does not desire much except the casual and the carnal. People do not want to think too much. You can hear the words going around: 'you speak too deep for me.' Is that it? Or, is that spoken by one who is living too shallow in his life? Others say, in our generation, 'You should never take yourself too seriously.' I really do not understand this language. We are talking about God, atheism, agnosticism, and the apostasy, and we say things like that."

"Have Christians back through history been concerned

with these things, Gabriel?"

"The Christians of several centuries ago were writing as if they were concerned far more than I am. They present the very 'finest of the wheat' from the Word of God. (another pause) Dear Evangeline, you have brought all of our observations of a paradox today to an end. I realize, today, that God must make a paradox of the primitive truth of the Gospel and bring also the complexities of His puzzles into a resolve and a harmony where both entities are saved in one blessed union. This thought is prompted by loving you. There is something very staggering and humbling in the account of primitive Christianity, as set forth in the Book of Acts, and we must harmonize that beauty with the later Pauline Epistles in which such depth is revealed concerning God, Who into history came through the incarnation of His Son, the Lord Jesus Christ. Of course, God in history, and in the history of fallen man, brings man into the depth of both the distress of sin and the eternal rest of grace. The primitive days of Acts have led us through a history that today stands deep into the beginning of a very complicated apostasy. (pause)

"I will cite only one more observation for today with you.

"Matthew Arnold is considered one of the hinges on the door of modern thought of man which the English-speaking world, a century ago, turned from Christianity to Modernism. He was considered to be a fair-minded and articulate exponent of the Liberal view. Like the growing tendency of our generation, he thought of himself as a Christian; he absorbed a classical education from a famous Christian father. He had the highest respect for Christianity, but did not believe in historic or apostolic Christianity, which was clearly revealed in its early days. Note the Book of Acts, chapter 2, verse 42. Much that he believed was rooted in the bold, rebellious French Revolution, but he wrote his part as a learned first chair appointed professor in English literature at Oxford in 1857. This prestigious chair spoke out in 1882 as Matthew Arnold delivered a famous lecture from a beautiful quotation of King Solomon in which he proceeded to apply its wisdom to the state of education at that time. He spoke against the former tide in education that 'we must leave the wisdom and classics of our former days. We must substitute other studies for them.'

"He spoke of a model already set in his time that a man by the name of Sir Josiah Mason actually founded a college at Birmingham, England, to 'exclude mere literary instruction and education' of those classics. Arnold predicted that in a hundred years from his time there would be only a few of what he called 'eccentrics reading the classical letters and almost everyone will be studying only the natural sciences.' His 'hinge' was on the door of education; but dear Evangeline, the other hinge will come from the door of the so-called Christian church in removing itself from historic Christianity." (a long pause)

"Well, my dear Gabriel, we only have fifty-four more times to meet in the Dating Parlor before the last one and then our Christmas break to be married. If all of them are going to be like this first one, I do not really know what will ultimately be my Christian life. However, I will not forget your heart of grace and your mind of Christ. Your ministry is mine by service and love, and you may count on my desire to understand you from my primitive viewpoint. There is no conflict, my dear Gabriel. In closing our time together, I want to read from the Psalms of 'Blessed is the man,' and then you conclude with prayer. This Psalm is dedicated to you today."

"Yes, that is Psalm One, and there are two men in it. I only pray that I will be the man of your first verse, 'Blessed is the man that walketh not in the counsel of the ungodly…'"

Evangeline completed the reading of the entire Psalm; Gabriel closed with prayer, praying that God would bring the two of them together in marriage, December 20, but also in a greater understanding of the ways of God with their own ways of married life, in a world-view relationship with all of life. Gabriel requests God to forgive him of any inequities in his thinking about God on that first day in the new University.

At supper, that evening, in the Dining Common, they sat side by side at their appointed table places in their respective alphabetical order of "Parsons" and "Peters."

Chapter Three

The Permission

(October 1 - December 17, 1947)

The fall semester at the Bible Christian University started late because of the tremendous efforts involved in the building of the new campus. When Gabriel and Evangeline arrived for the opening of the semester, October 1, 1947, they sought the course schedule three days later, as the administration reserved revival services first. Gabriel took twenty-three credits for the semester; Evangeline, seventeen. They were in love and engaged. Gabriel had already requested Dr. Perkins Monroe, dean of men, to present his request before the administration, believing them to be prayerful and mature in the matter. If permission was granted, it meant that Gabriel and Evangeline could return to finish out the fall semester of 1948 as well as enter the spring semester, of 1949, married.

Dr. Monroe had been a friend to Gabriel at the time, the very day, he was saved by grace back in the college at Groveland, Georgia, April 17, 1947. Gabriel's somewhat quiet but precocious childhood marked his need of the will of God rather than just himself making a choice. Also, his time in the Navy revealed his need of discipline in life. Therefore, he did not object to another test concerning his marriage awaiting permission from the administration. Dr. Monroe also encouraged him in the Lord, privately, after the morning that the president, Dr. Jonathan, preached the Chapel message on "God's Severity and Grace."

At first, Gabriel was offended by the message. It seemed directly pointed at him. He went to Dean Monroe's office and firmly spoke of the fact that he was thinking he would simply leave the college. God gave Dr. Monroe wisdom, and he realized Gabriel was under the conviction of the Holy Spirit to be born again. Dr. Monroe calmly replied: "Gabriel, you do not want to leave today, do you?"

After other words, Gabriel's heart began to change towards the chapel message and the president, and that night, about 8:45, in his lodging on campus, he dropped to his knees with a broken and contrite heart and was gloriously saved by grace. His roommate was present and also encouraged him to stay in college. His name was Ron Ryan from Canada. Gabriel then realized the necessity for his being offended in the morning after Chapel. He was a sinner, and in reality, his offense was also against the God of the Word that was preached.

In contrast to that "offense," as Gabriel thought of it, there was Professor Pratt Whitley who was a Speech teacher. This was the first class that Gabriel attended in which all the new students were requested to give their name, their address, and a brief testimony of their being saved. Gabriel was caught off guard as Professor Whitley informed the class that there was a new student who had entered the second semester of the school year and he desired him to come forward and give his testimony. Gabriel came forward reluctantly but resolutely and greeted the class, gave his name and home town, and then respectfully stated that he was not a Christian, but was there to study music. Gabriel also respectfully stated that he hoped his not being a Christian would not affect his academic acceptance by the University. After the class was over, Professor Whitley graciously assured Gabriel that it would not affect him as a teacher, but that he would be praying for him to accept the Lord Jesus as his Savior. Gabriel left the class without "offense" and held in his heart a gratitude to Professor Whitley for his wisdom towards him.

When the University commenced its first fall semester in Grandville, North Carolina, Gabriel had been saved almost five and a half months. In these months Gabriel had sought God earnestly to guide him all the way through life. He increased His reading of the Bible and other appropriate books suitable to his needs for God. He had known Evangeline only four months after his arrival in the college unsaved. The meeting of Evangeline began at about the same time God began to deal with Gabriel's soul. But his seeking God to guide him all the way through life began to be answered immediately in the sending of Evangeline into his life.

Now that Dean Monroe had notified Gabriel of the decision of the administration to grant permission for his marriage during the Christmas break, Gabriel and Evangeline would proceed in their plans for December 20. So, having prayed much about the marriage, it was planned to be consummated two months from Dean Monroe's response, October 20. They had two months more at the University, and they were intensely involved in their daily studies and their daily discussions at three o'clock. Another new dimension would now open in their Christian life, and in their search for God's will for their entire lifetime together.

The Bible had spoken unto their hearts in this matter, revealing marriage as God's taking two people and making them one, by God, Himself, joining the couple together. Then God would seal the union with a warning in the words of Jesus: "What therefore God hath joined together, let not man put asunder," Matthew's Gospel, chapter 19, verse 6b.

The parents of Gabriel thought of their son, in childhood, as a good, quiet, obedient son, and probably too studious for his practical good. At times, Gabriel was too firm in some of his directions, and his parents were concerned about it. But they considered him a good boy and trusted the outcome. They did not know he was unsaved until he told them at about the age of fourteen. He read the Bible and many other books, and they assumed him to be saved. Although he was baptized in water at the age of ten years old, it was only an act on Gabriel's part, an endeavor to do something to fulfill his longing heart for God. He was never baptized again.

He grew up fearing God, from age five, and from that time on there were a number of times in his young life when he became God-conscious: through spiritual awakenings, guilt, and fearing hell. He knew he sinned. At times his conscience screamed in his soul against his inner thoughts and sins. This was particularly true in the thoughts of his mind without a great number of overt evils. He took two dimes from his sister one time; he took a quarter from the bedroom dresser while his father and mother were asleep. However, those things were cleared up by Gabriel's own acknowledgment. He saw a dirty dog one day on a farm involved in an ugly sex act which caused him a sick stomach, but he never saw pornography until, accidentally, one day, in a book on the bunk of a Navy mate. He was so shocked and was sick to his stomach; he never viewed such sights again. He was eighteen years old at that time.

However, although in a public place, years later, in a foreign country and the environment of a plush hotel, he did view a five-to-ten-second television segment, at which he was so shocked that he had to quickly flee the very room. He had never taken the position that a television, as an invention, was evil. Gabriel prayed unto God about this shocking experience in an open world, and then prayed for the world again. The burden of this experience did not pass from his mind as a burden until God lifted it six days later. Gabriel's victory came from Psalms 6 and 4, in that order, on the floor on his face before the Lord. He always remembered the incident as a sin of defilement instead of a sin of volition, but he believed a satanic test came into his life from the experience of it.

Gabriel could not remember when he did not believe in the Bible as God's infallible, inspired, and inerrant Word. Although those very theological terms were not in his vocabulary then, he believed it to that capacity and depth without knowing the theological words. When he later studied the terms, he simply acknowledged them in the affirmative as what he had always believed.

His God-consciousness began to leave his life about two years before he entered the Navy. For four years, then, he entered into thoughts in which he concluded he was irredeemable, thinking he possessed a nature and disposition outside of God's grace, but not outside of God's goodness and mercy. He could see and did acknowledge that God was good and merciful to him. But now Gabriel was gloriously saved by grace through the death and shedding of the blood of Calvary by the Lord Jesus Christ, God's Son. He found out that his natural and general disposition was depraved as everyone, but Christ died for all mankind, and he was a man. Then, the Bible became his guide for life and he was seeking to fulfill the plan and will of God for his life. Gabriel did see a difference between the sin nature and the human nature, however; this brought respect for natural gifts God gave creatures.

Seventy-seven days had now passed in the fall semester at the Bible Christian University, and Gabriel and Evangeline had pursued their studies with diligence. Their hunger was intense; their grades were high. But most of all, they were saved by grace, and the good providence of God had brought them together; and Gabriel had a spot in God's earth, the Land of Evangeline, as a natural beauty for his earthly journey to heaven. The Blue Ridge Mountains of Virginia and North Carolina were introductory natural beauties that challenged Gabriel's mind and imagination for the Land of Evangeline. Gabriel could not get over what God called Ezekiel's wife, speaking thusly, 'the desire of thine eyes'; and God mentions it three times in Ezekiel, chapter 24, verses 16, 21, and 25. God even associated it with His own nation, Israel. What a great God to speak of Evangeline in such a manner.

They had met together in the Dating Parlor fifty-five times, Monday through Friday, at three o'clock, for their one-hour discussions, coordinating all their studies and thoughts learned in the first seventy-seven days of the fall semester of 1947, with

Evangeline's beautiful simplicity and Gabriel's active mind. Now, in three days they would be married in Gabriel's home church in Washington, D.C. Saturday they would be in Gabriel's home with his parents. Dad Peters was coming for the marriage, and several other distant relatives, with one relative who lived in the Washington, D.C., area. Sunday, Gabriel and Evangeline would be in worship hearing his father preach. Although he was not the pastor he was the invited speaker. Monday, of course, would be the day of marriage, December 20, 1947, 4:00 PM.

After this last three o'clock session in the Dating Parlor of the University, they would be leaving campus for Gabriel's home on an overnight bus to Washington, D.C.

Their conversations begin:

"Well, my beloved Evangeline, we have come to our last discussion before our marriage. These seventy-seven days with you in the University will be cherished throughout my lifetime. As a Christian, I am now ready to marry you, my dear Evangeline."

"And I, you, Gabriel. I am overcome with your love for me and my happiness in heart and the blessings of God upon us both."

"The University, at this time, was in the divine plan of God for our lives, Evangeline. I can see it clearly: because of you the Land of Evangeline is mine through all my days on earth. I intend to marry you, and you only, no matter how death treats us. This is because you are mine given by God, and when I write any future letters to you, if and when we are absent from each other, I will, in remembrance of this last meeting, conclude all my letters to you as, simply, 'Always, Gabriel.'"

"Gabriel, my darling, how thoughtful for your love to think so far ahead."

"The simplicity of it all is prompted because on Monday, our vows will speak of our love 'until death us do part,' and in my heart I see no release for me until I die."

A long pause proceeds as tears fill their eyes, but no other emotion is manifested.

"Gabriel, these have truly been 'hallowed walls' for you and me."

"Yes, dear, we have sat in each of the sixteen sections of this Dating Parlor."

"Yes, beloved Gabriel, in each section over three times. I figured it up; three times in each section with seven to spare."

"What did you decide to do with the seven to spare? No! let me guess. You have been choosing the Scottish section more often; is that correct, my dear?"

"Yes, Gabriel, it was the nearest thing to Nova Scotia and the Land of Evangeline. I thought you would be pleased."

"Yes, I am, and I was. I thought something like that was happening in your decisions from time to time in this room. You have overcome me, Evangeline. (a pause) Evangeline, as you said, these have been 'hallowed walls' for us. So many of my inquisitions of thought have been resolved this semester. The seven forms of culture, including discipline, the chapel speakers, the 'Visiting Artists,' the special events, the students, teachers, deans, burdens of examinations, the simple achievements, new friends, the great variety of song forms, science, physics, mathematics, languages, speech, theology, sermons, prayers, love, pain, the world, the lost, the saved, the hopes, despairs, sleep, work, the place of enemies next to the place of paintings, architecture, literature, and all else have begun to fill our one continent of knowledge. And all of these things must be understood in the continuity of a singular history and in only one universe into which God sent His Son, the Lord Jesus.

"Thank God for our esteemed president and companion in the Christian way. Thank God for his large vision in this place. Vision is our earthly view of what we would like to do for our Savior in our Christian life. Dr. Jonathan did just that. I trust that he will have a long life on this earth to spread the Gospel through this multi-faceted testimony. Your land, Evangeline, is the counterpart of this vision. Your land, Evangeline, is the most wonderful place in the world for simple beauties of the Bay, the sea, and the land. As a complement in God's arrangement of nature to me, this University is the most wonderful place in the world for an acknowledgment of the complex, the multiplicities, and the questions of life itself. It is lovely to be in your land, Evangeline; and it is safe to be on the acreage of this University land. Piece by piece, it all fits the puzzle and acknowledges the problem accountable in a singular world-view. And God has come into history; God is in all lands of the world, through providence, goodness, and mercy, seeking souls by His amazing grace. He has given them lands as beautiful as yours and mine, Evangeline. Jesus is exalted, souls are saved, revivals come in all the lands of earth, and we must proceed with it all, in a single view, and lead everybody we can, 'upon whom the ends of the world are come,' First Corinthians, Chapter 10, verse 11."

"Dear Gabriel, my beloved, for you surely to be my husband, my head, my lord, as Sarah said it, will be such a privilege. I love thee for all these thoughts and words that I have heard in such a brief period of history as only twelve months. I think I am growing in God and grace, from the simple to the sublime, and I want to walk on with you through all my life."

"As we are learning, dear Evangeline, we need both the simple and the sublime, as well as the profound, and every other blessed opportunity in our vision of what we think of Christ in our earthly view together. You are embellishing me in my own heart and life, and soon we will be wed. It is the mistake of many who think that only evangelism is the key to the ministry; or, only church administration is the key; or, methodology, or money, or missions are the means. It is the message and the man that God uses. In these two, all other means are found. I think, dear Evangeline, I have at least found out why I was born and saved by grace."

"Why, dear Gabriel? Why?"

"To simply get people to think, to get people to think, simply think and, sometimes, maybe, deeply think of their Lord."

A time of reflection passes between Gabriel and Evangeline.

"Evangeline, we knew something of the 6-point type of life; I think the 6-point has been raised to 12-point, too, here at the University. The wonder of this miracle in this place is that the definitions are still the same as they were in the dictionary of my early childhood and humble, simple Christian parents."

At their last supper on campus that evening in the Dining Common, they sat side by side at their appointed table places. Tomorrow they would eat breakfast and lunch alone in the Student Center. They needed the hours remaining to discuss their marriage before boarding a bus to Washington, D.C., through the evening and night, to see Gabriel's parents. Poems and notes were by their supper plates, from those who had sat with them that semester, wishing their forthcoming marriage the best.

Gabriel and Evangeline found out, in their last table appointment, that there were no "Pbs," or "Pcs," or "Pds" between Parsons and Peters.

Gabriel and Evangeline left the next day for their Washington, D.C., wedding and the commencement of their lives for Christ. Gabriel had the loving permission from the heart and will of Evangeline; he had received the blessing permission from Dad Peters; and he received the discipline permission from the administration of the University. But more than anything, God had given the heavenly permission, too, when he allowed him to fall in love with Evangeline. Gabriel knew now the duty, discipline, and the delight of this precious will of God in his marriage. The reason it was the will of God was that it was right for these two, for the will of God will also be beautiful, because that follows whatever is right.

Chapter Four

The Vows

(December 20-25, 1947)

The marriage took place in Gabriel's home church, 1015 D Street, Northeast, in Washington, D.C. His father, Bishop T. H. Parsons, had pastored this church in Gabriel's boyhood. The current pastor, Dr. Frank C. Clarke, graciously yielded to Gabriel's choice of his father to conduct the wedding ceremony in the National Church.

Previously, Bishop Parsons had pastored also in northern Virginia, and planted churches in East End Richmond, Schuyler, Gold Mine, Buckingham, Maple Grove, Newport News, all in Virginia. He also planted two other churches in Maryland. Later on, his father pastored larger and more prestigious churches in Norfolk, Memphis, and the National Church, Washington, D.C. In retirement, he planted a final church in Ohio.

Most of the newly planted churches were up, on, or near the Blue Ridge Mountains, quite near to the Blue Ridge Parkway. In fact, Gabriel, as a boy of twelve years, spent a full summer on the John Felix farm during the building of the Blue Ridge Parkway. He almost daily accompanied the crew of workers

39

as they cleared the land across these beautiful mountains. The "CCC boys" as they were called (The Civilian Conservation Corps), were working the crisscross roads over the Blue Ridge, east and west as the Parkway was north and south. Of course, he also had time to explore streams, springs, lakes, and timberland roadways, up and down hills. His favorite and only horse died and he wept. His life was spared during a thunder and lightning storm, while lightning burnt the double-barrel shotgun he was curiously holding in his hand.

Gabriel observed and read about nature. He loved the beautiful Parkway, and would, later, in his Night Institute, bring the students up here for outdoor Bible teaching and preaching, both for young Christians and unbelievers, too. A number of these were people who lived on Capitol Hill. In Virginia, the Blue Ridge Parkway, passing on down through North Carolina, is also called the Skyline Drive because some of the mountains are higher and nearer the sky. These mountains will finally proceed down into South Carolina and end up in the Smoky Mountains of Georgia.

Evangeline's land in Nova Scotia did not have mountains like Virginia's Blue Ridge system, but there was an antithetical affinity of similarity between them. Both had regular fog and glorious greeneries, winding roads and lakes, and similar rural scenes. However, the contrast came between simplicities and complexities in the two geographies. On the Blue Ridge, Mount Mitchell, and its chain, had the highest peaks east of the Mississippi River. There were more dangerous snakes and animals in the habitat of Virginia and North Carolina areas. More sheep were raised in the Land of Evangeline, whereas the emphasis on the Blue Ridge was goats, goat's milk, and goat's milk fudge.

Of course, Washington, D.C., itself, to Gabriel, was one continual learning center after another. He had the opportunity of several Federal Government programs for special students. There was not an emphasis upon enabling the illiterate in his time; they cultivated the literate. He skipped the third and the fifth grades in elementary school; he had teachers who were interested in his learning ability. Early he had been chosen for the Music Appreciation School led by Walter Damrosch and Hans Kindler. He was a newspaper boy with the Washington Post for the Senate and House of Representative buildings; he met senators and congressmen, including Senator Robert Taft, Jr., who was instrumental in his being a page for the Senate for summer months. Bishop Parsons also had a number of friendly contacts and acquaintances with political men on Capitol Hill, including Congressman George A. Briceson.

Gabriel attended a regular one-day a week, for over a year, actual observation of the restoration of Colonial Williamsburg, and met two of the Rockefellers, whose philanthropy was instrumental to this restoration. He was editor of his elementary school newspaper. Peabody Music Conservatory was attended in a special program for young people during World War II, and Gabriel attended there for one year in the night program. He was a boy messenger for the government during the last two years of high school, and played first trombone in a semi-classical musical ensemble. From high school he entered the United States Navy at seventeen. After his return home and undergraduate work in the Bible Christian University, he attended studies at the Georgeton Theological Seminary, in the northwest section of Washington called the Georgetown Area.

The church on D Street was an older and smaller church which followed the early gothic style of architecture. Later, the church would be sold and a larger and more contemporary style chosen on a piece of property four blocks closer to the nation's Capitol, at Sixth and Maryland Avenue, Northeast. Both churches were located on Capitol Hill.

Gabriel and Evangeline were pleased with the church and ceremony arranged by his father. Gabriel was particularly pleased with the church because it was a reminder of the size and architecture of Evangeline's church as well as the rural churches in Nova Scotia.

The wedding was as simple as it could be, and beautiful above measure. The veil, gown, and flowers of Evangeline were excellently made for her five-foot seven-inch, beautiful form. Her hazel eyes and long, dark brunette hair enhanced the beauty of her poised personage. She stood beside Gabriel's stately six-foot one-inch, slender height. A singular stained-glass gothic window marked the background above both the chancel and the podium. It was quietly formal. A male, trained singer, who was the church choir leader, gave an offering to the Lord of his classical gift of song. The sister of Gabriel assisted in the preparations. Gabriel's mother was present in her proper pew. Evangeline's mother was greatly missed. Thirty-two candles modestly banked the chancel. Christmas decor was evident. Dad Peters was there, too. David Lawtell, who introduced Gabriel to Evangeline, was an usher; the musical ensemble leader of earlier time, LeVon Gilbertson, was best man; and a young man, Sonny Alberts, who grew up with Gabriel, was the other usher. A little flower girl served representative of one of the local church families to complete the wedding party. Gabriel's mother wept a little but without distraction; she was experiencing Christian joy.

Bishop Parsons gave a clear Christian ceremony and message, in his usual simple dignity, but with a little more smile than usual for a sermon. A double-ring token of vows were forthcoming and the packed audience of the church observed in simplicity. Gabriel and Evangeline gave their vows and responded to the recessional cue from the organist. The singular, pronounced human element was Gabriel's nervousness in the fear of God. He placed the ring on Evangeline's right hand at first, but retrieved it to the left hand as Bishop Parsons gave his third prayer. However, Gabriel accurately memorized and recited his vows in stentorian syllables, every word of the Old English long form. Evangeline trusted Gabriel's father, Bishop Parsons, with his encouraging comfort, to assist her with each deliberate word.

All went well; God's Word was there; and God's presence. Friendliness and love filled the hearts of the departing friends as rice rained on the couple and the bridal bouquet flew to another.

The Reception took place at Gabriel's home. Within another hour the bridal couple left and were now alone. The winter sun had set and Gabriel and Evangeline were driving towards nearby Alexandria, Virginia, almost attached to Washington, where they would spend their first night of marriage.

"You were lovely today, my dear Evangeline, even more so than any day I have known you."

"Yes, my beloved Gabriel. It is because we are now one, for a part of the strength of your soul is now with me. I have never known a day in my life like this in earthly blessings."

"It is true, my beloved Evangeline, we are now one. It does not take even the birth of a child in our life to prove this; we are already one, together. The child that the Lord may give us later will only be a testimony to others of what we have known all along."

A pause persists, then joyous laughter takes over for a number of minutes, with still several other outbursts. Then quietness comes.

"Where are we going for our honeymoon, my darling? We have been so full of other pressing and precious things, we never discussed it."

"No, I wanted it to be a surprise to you."

"Oh, I should have known; where then?"

"We are going, in wintertime, to the Blue Ridge Mountains and the Skyline Drive. We are going to take it exactly the way it is in the winter."

"Oh darling, I believe I knew it all the time. It will now be the other side of my Land of Evangeline. I long to see it with you."

"We will stop in nearby Alexandria, Virginia, tonight, at the luxurious Abraham Lincoln Hotel. Then, tomorrow night, we will lodge in the more modest, but beautiful Martha Washington Hotel in Fredericksburg, Virginia. Then the third night we will be up on the Blue Ridge Mountains and lodge at Green Meadows. The fourth night we will come down a ways from the mountains to lodge in the Luray House at Luray, Virginia, very close to the Luray Caverns, which we will visit. The fifth night we will stay at Cabin Peak Lodge, back up higher on the Blue Ridge Mountains. That will be Christmas Eve. And finally, we will return for our sixth night's lodging back in Washington, D.C., at the corner of North Capitol and K streets, Northeast, just about next door to the National Capitol Building. That will be Christmas Night, and the lodging has been given to us for the night by a friend. Our first Christmas day will be ours alone."

"You really have outlined it well, my Gabriel, 'Lord' (playfully). "Let's see if I can remember: the plush Abraham Lincoln Hotel; the more modest, but still beautiful colonial Martha Washington Hotel; then, the spacious Green Meadows up on the Blue Ridge, emphasizing the "glorious greeneries" of Nova Scotia; then the Luray House, near the Luray Caverns; then Christmas Eve, back up on the mountains to Cabin Peak; and then finally, Christmas Night, back in Washington next door to the Capitol. Is that right?"

"Yes, Evangeline, that is right."

"All of these details seem to indicate to me, Gabriel, that you must have something special in mind and meaning in this, my darling. Is that right?"

"Yes, Evangeline, that is right. The six nights are planned with entirely different evenings of historical decor and lifestyles. These would represent the possibility of six different kinds of places and lifestyles from which God may lead us into the fulfillment of His will for our lives together in His vineyard. The Abraham Lincoln Hotel might be representative of some luxurious place to minister, like he sent Daniel. The Martha Washington Hotel would indicate that God's will may be a bit more native to my background, colonial, beautiful, but not extremely pretentious. Yet, God may lead us to a place like Green Meadows, the nearest thing I know to your breeding and beauty, quite similar to the Land of Evangeline, but not as high as our mountains. God may send us into the caverns of darkness and the unknown. That would indicate we labor and love in the hidden and hard places of our world. But God might send us to a place like Cabin Peak, where the dangerous heights and storms and cold prevail, where apostasy dwells; and we would be called upon to stand at all cost, at all cost!"

"Oh, Gabriel, Gabriel! What a thoughtful series of possibilities in our obedience and service for the Lord. I only trust I will be enabled to follow you on any course. I am understanding more and more of your heart, mind, and potential surrender to God; but I tremble without your headship and comfort and love. I truly want to follow you, dear Gabriel, as you follow God. I have no calling for myself; only now to trust you in your calling and obedience. I can see, as the Bible reveals it; I am to be your helpmeet. I will, with all my heart, give you a Ruth-heart, as ultimately it was a gift to her Boaz so long ago. 'Whither thou goest, I will go; and where thou lodgest, I will lodge: thy people shall be my people, and thy God my God; where thou diest, will I die, and there will I be buried: the Lord do so to me, and more also, if ought but death part thee and me.'"

Gabriel immediately responded: "The Book of Ruth, chapter 1, verses 16 and 17."

The depth of these things caused Gabriel to turn aside the automobile into a beautiful park to stop. It was now night, almost half-hour past seven o'clock on their very wedding day. Gabriel turned towards Evangeline near tears.

"Oh, Evangeline, darling Evangeline! I must acquiesce here and confess to thee this wedding night that my nature and disposition is not always calm and deliberate with purpose as you have heretofore known me in all these precious months. I have experienced, since a child, great pent-up angers and fears in the strength of my pride. After being saved by grace, I have seen these deep marks in me. I desire tonight to beg God to turn that strength into a life for His glory. I have known of your strength as well. We must dedicate ourselves to always keep the unity of the spirit in the bond of peace towards each other, and you must assist my weakness in every crisis..." (Evangeline interrupts Gabriel)

"Stop, my darling; stop awhile and just listen to me. I, too, although I have been thoroughly genuine with you in our full acquaintance and courtship, know there are hidden ways in me that will rise up, too. You will sometimes have to proceed in the "taming of the shrew" in me. I know it will come. God has given us this present, true love, in our actions together, which has made captive of these dispositional traits at this time, but your confession brings me to the further need of true submission to the will of God and in your leadership of our lives, and especially me."

"Evangeline, my darling, I pledge to lead according to my understanding from God, with all my heart. This is why I told you before that I would always sign my letters to you, when we would be temporarily absent one from the other, with 'Always, Gabriel.' That is what I more fully meant back when I told you. 'Always' includes whatever and whenever and however things arise between us; we will humbly return to 'Always.'"

Gabriel and Evangeline embraced and spoke lovingly and cherishingly to each other. Then, Gabriel proceeded to drive on to the Abraham Lincoln Hotel, in Alexandria, the plush hotel. While driving, the renewed, light heart of Evangeline spoke.

"Gabriel, Gabriel, you did not tell me what we will be doing during the daytime of December 21, 22, 23, 24, and Christmas Day."

"That is simple, Evangeline. We are going to play together, love each other, sing romantic songs, eat different foods, including a hot dog. We are going to run and skip and have two Italian spaghetti dinners, and just plain have fun. We will laugh; we may cry, shout (pause). Then, we will love again. Will that be all right?"

"Yes, Gabriel, yes, yes!"

They entered the Abraham Lincoln Hotel and after gaining their luxurious room, went and ate a sumptuously prepared, rich food plate, in courses, in the plush, lush restaurant on Gabriel's modest financial means. He thought, fleetingly, of his promise to Dad Peters. But for this night, it would commence with extravagance, without thrift. They were so in love that they neglected to see all of the beautiful decor, in detail, which Gabriel had thought to be such an important part of this night and next morning. But, it did not matter; they saw enough to know what Gabriel had planned and whom he loved. Next morning, when they had breakfast at Hotel Lincoln, they noted the decor a little more.

The Martha Washington Hotel, at Fredericksburg, was, strictly speaking, a perfect Southern colonial hotel, but less pretentious in size and luxury, yet beautiful throughout. They noticed the decor even more here than they noted at Hotel Lincoln.

Green Meadows, on top of the Blue Ridge Skyline Drive, was filled with the decor associated with those early days in America when nature was so magnificent and plentiful and spacious in the virgin-land of America. At Green Meadows, yes, "gloriously" Green Meadows, sculpture and paintings combined themselves with hills, rivers, pasture, timberland, horses, carriages, and great plantations noted in the South. This was truly nearer to the Land of Evangeline, yet a bit more rugged, but still "gloriously green." They noted the decor here on this evening in greater detail, more than the two places the two nights before. However, they kept holding hands and looking into the eyes of each other, making up for the extra time they spent perusing the beauty of the decor itself.

The Luray Caverns and the surrounding valley-view led to the Luray House. They then were for awhile absorbed with the caverns as Evangeline thought deeply about the dark places of the earth God might send them. However, after their exit from the caves of that place, they returned to their love and life, and entered the Luray House for refreshment, rest, and love, which Gabriel had by now called "the classical joy of life."

Cabin Peak, was entrenched in their thoughts as Evangeline once again reminded herself of Gabriel's purpose in bringing her there. God might lead them into even deeper hardships and sorrows. She remembered that the Bible speaks of those saints who "wandered about in sheepskins and goatskins; being destitute, afflicted, tormented;...they wandered in deserts, and in mountains, and in dens and caves of the earth;..." Of course, Gabriel added: "Hebrews, Chapter 11, verses 37 and 38."

Cabin Peak was the least beautiful, over-rugged, with a wilderness garment, the least convenient, and worse than Gabriel thought it would be. He apologized for his choice of this and the night's burden for her. He had been there several times as a young boy and did not remember it so rough and rude. The blankets were insufficient; Gabriel and Evangeline had to sleep tight to keep warm, and it was a single bed.

But Gabriel's humor survived by quickly quoting two passages from the Bible. "Again, if two lie together, then they have heat: but how can one be warm alone? Ecclesiastes, chapter 4, verse 11." Gabriel also quoted: "For the bed is shorter than that a man can stretch himself on it: and the covering narrower than that he can wrap himself in it. Isaiah, chapter 28, verse 20."

Evangeline did not respond to him at all. But she did hug him tighter.

Tomorrow night, Christmas night, she thought, they would be back in Washington at a special apartment provided by a friend.

Chapter Five

The Flesh

(April 17 - July 10, 1949)

In early January, Gabriel and Evangeline returned to their intense studies at the University. They were determined to complete their work together at the earliest possible time: she in music; he with a double-major in music and speech. However, it was obvious that Gabriel would widen the academic spectrum, later, with history, theology, Bible, and languages, with possibly a later emphasis in seminary and graduate schools, in more history and philosophy.

Gabriel, however, knew that before his own human agenda was fulfilled, God might give His own direction according to His own will. This was an established pattern for Gabriel, as was sought before, in his first semester in the University. He first asked Evangeline to marry him; then, Dad Peters; then, the administration's permission for the mid-semester marriage. He had already received the permission of His Lord, earlier, concerning their marriage. The principle would remain the same, in his heart, for all his entire lifetime. He, as a young Christian, began praying about God's will for his old age, too, during a time when he was assistant to four unusual men who failed in their later lives.

Besides this, God had given him a beautiful earthly land in his love for Nova Scotia, the Land of the Evangeline, his wife. God had also directed Gabriel in the selection of lodgings for their honeymoon through Christmas night.

His return to the University was a resolve of the first magnitude: both for the academic acquisition of the scientific method of knowledge; and then, in the empirical method of knowledge, he must always pursue, on his own, for his spiritual needs. Gabriel would choose other places of learning and study, from time to time, that he believed to be fitting into the will of God and providence for his life, as he would fulfill different ministries. At this point, Gabriel had not received a divine calling directly to the ministry from God. He believed that his natural gifts, as sought for in natural theology and the goodness and mercy of God, had brought him thus far, and that God's direct calling would be forthcoming later. But Gabriel was clear that he would indeed serve God with his Evangeline by his side.

His thirst for knowledge was intense, since his second grade of public school. The human instrumentality of his second-grade teacher, Miss Anna Cole, had sparked his learning interest immensely. She was a large woman, and her appearance would not be drawn to the beautiful. But when she spoke and taught, she was consumed with delight. Later, Gabriel said she was a most beautiful teacher. She opened up his understanding in the second grade and visited his parents to encourage them about their son. She made Gabriel the editor of the elementary school weekly newspaper; she encouraged his poetry and music which had already begun to appear in his life.

His first poem was "The River of James," which was one of over twenty rivers in his childhood life until he went into the United States Navy. These rivers started with the Potomac River near Washington, as well as the James River from northern Virginia down to Jamestown and the first English settlement in the new world. He had visited that area a number of times as a child. Seven of the twenty rivers became special to the childhood of Gabriel, although he knew them all. Miss Cole would speak of other things in her regular disciplined daily lessons. She taught "contemplation," "imagination," "visual art," all things in "nature," "rest," and many other interests in simple life.

Another teacher in Gabriel's boyhood, who remained unmarried, was Miss Charlene Sherman, an outstanding music teacher in high school. She gave him his first musical instrument and placed him in the school orchestra and band concerts. Gabriel made a special trip back to see her after his honorable discharge from the Navy and his acceptance of Christ as Savior. He gave her several copies of his cantatas and expressed deep appreciation for the blessing she had brought into his life through music. She used to call him "Junior," probably because of his short stature compared to the other students in the high school, and due to his young age. He witnessed to her of Christ and his Christian faith. Gabriel regretted that he never witnessed to Miss Cole; he was never able to locate her.

Gabriel's undergraduate work had not been as a divinity student. He did not pursue the courses of the preachers in the University. Later, he believed that God was in this directing of him from his youth in the large exercise of reading programs. He believed he read 100 books a year as a young boy and man. This reading load increased upward to about 275 books a year in his adult life.

The presupposition in the heart of Gabriel was simply to deal with the resource of his influence and to help people, small or great, in their different attitudes about the world, religion, nature, and especially Christianity. He was simply practicing the teaching of what he was learning concerning natural theology and revealed theology in the light of his world-view of all knowledge and history. His love for music and life was drenched with history, and after his conversion to Christianity, the magnificent teachings of the grace of God in the Sonship of the Lord Jesus Christ made all of history alive. Jesus, in His birth, came into history. Because of creation and providence, God was in all history. His greater concern was for Biblical history, as it was the key to all other histories. The Bible was the Book of books to him. Gabriel was impressed with John Wesley's dedication: "In 1730 I began to be *homo unius libri* (a man of one book), to study (comparatively) no book but the Bible." Gabriel found this quotation in Wesley's *Journal*, May 14, 1765.

Upon their return to their studies at the University for the second year, Gabriel and Evangeline, now married, rented a modest two-room apartment in a large twenty-room house where several other University couples lived, too. The husband of one of the couples became an outstanding fundamentalist in later years, and his wife was an unusual pianist. This was the first actual acquaintance, personally, on a day-by-day relationship, that brought Gabriel to be knowledgeable of Fundamentalism. Gabriel's father highly respected a number of fundamentalists. Bishop Parsons was a faithful reader of the books authored by fundamentalists. He respected their clear and strong stand for the Word of God and the Lord Jesus Christ. He believed the fundamentalists identified the apostasy in their generation, wherever it appeared. Two other couples from the University were there in the community house as well. Their lives were a contrast to the first couple.

This large, four-story house was situated on a rather large acreage on Old Shady Donnon Road. The fourth floor was one room under the peak-roof of an old colonial-styled, white, multi-columned front. This was called the "Look Out." This became Gabriel's special study room because nobody else wanted it.

He would return to the first-floor apartment where one of the rooms was walled, with two sides glassed in. This was a solarium, a blessing to Gabriel and Evangeline. Such a room kept the entire apartment bright.

On this particular day, Gabriel returned again from the "Look Out," before supper time, and commenced conversation with Evangeline. It was obvious he was on a serious note.

"I have been doing a lot of thinking, Evangeline, and I need to talk to you."

"I know, dear, I have known this for some time."

"You, my beloved Evangeline, have been growing in grace and going on with the Lord. I don't think that I am making the spiritual progress that I should. Our early days of marriage have been wonderful to me. I have nothing but a glad heart, and a happy consciousness with you as my dear wife. Please accept that completely. Today is April 1, 1948, and I have enjoyed 102 glorious days with you in our blessed union. So, my darling, the words I must speak are not because of you at all."

"I know that, Gabriel; I know your love for me is steadfast; I could not be more happy than I am with you. But you speak on, dear."

"I get the observation that you are growing in grace, and I am not. There's no jealousy in this, dear; rather to the contrary, I am encouraged and edified by your Christian life. It is possible that I am entering into a struggle or war between the flesh and the Spirit. Romans, chapter 7, identifies my heart exactly. Let me read this. ' I find then a law, that, when I would do good, evil is present with me. For I delight in the law of God after the inward man: But I see another law in my members, warring against the law of my mind, and bringing me into captivity to the law of sin which is in my members. O wretched man that I am! Who shall deliver me from the body of this death?' Did you hear that, Evangeline? It all boils down to this: while I am conscientiously praying to know and do the very will of God, and please Him, I am also wanting to do my very own will through all my desires, which is after the 'flesh'!"

"Gabriel, I, too, have wondered about this in your life, although I have not seen any open rebellion, outwardly. Possibly, if anything, you appear more morose, at this time in your life. I think, Gabriel, in my own case, it might be more simple. My vow to you became my own personal victory, in Christ, for the same thing. I vowed to follow you, believing you were following Christ. That choice was a crisis to me, because I have had a will, too. I may be more simple than you, but my will has been just as strong. I know you know that. However, the clarity of my dedication, which I agonized in

54

prayer about before our marriage, solved the problem of my
heart. The true direction was straight ahead of me with you.
Therefore, I am looking to Christ that you will obey God in
this very matter you are seeking Him about. I believe God
answered my prayer instantaneously in my home during our
engagement period before the fall semester began, while
awaiting permission from the University administration
through Dean Monroe. I simply committed all of this to God
in prayer and Bible reading at that time. God purified my
heart for this matter, then and there."

"But Evangeline, that compounds my own problem and
responsibility. I am, in some ways, having to seek and do the
will of God for my own need, as well as consider you, too. I
am having to seek the will of God for two people."

"Oh no, Gabriel, we are only one! Remember?" (a long
pause).

"Yes, Evangeline, that is true. (another pause) However, I
thought, possibly, when God made us one, there would be a
greater equality of knowing the will of God between us,
although I knew of my headship in marriage and that it is
imperative for me to be the head. I simply feel that the greater
responsibility in my struggle remains mine. I suppose this is
the problem — me!"

"Possibly we should consider this a blessing between us.
Otherwise, the struggle about the will of God could become
an ongoing controversy between us in our marriage if we were
not one. There could be a controversy of two opinions, causing
two clashing concepts of spiritual growths. It must come out,
rather, that the seeking of the will of God for you, Gabriel,
would also be for me, following your obedience to God in your
own heart. I know that this is easier for me to say, than, in the
future, for me to practice. I will still depend upon your sharing
things with me concerning similar struggles as you meet them."

"That may be at least a key, my darling, in this matter; and
I will endeavor to do that as I understand to do it. So, I invite
your simple obedience to your husband as was your
surrendered will in your vows to me. My own vows did carry
the greater responsibility, undoubtedly, so I will seek God in

that direction. I have come to believe that the will of God in everything is revealed through the agreement of three primary matters: consistent readings from the Holy Scriptures; the work of the leading of the Holy Spirit in harmony with the Scriptures; and then the good providence of God bringing circumstances into our lives which open the doors for us to then actually do the will of God as revealed and confirmed by the Word and the Holy Spirit."

"Oh Gabriel, no three selections could be chosen better than that; stick with that understanding, my beloved. In my more simple way, I could only add, as your wife, things which should support your selections. Things like prayer, advice, encouragement, a warning if I saw it, and most of all, my love for you in what you must do for God."

They have a prayer together. Gabriel returns to his studies.

The schedule that Gabriel planned and hoped for was to finish his degree at the University, along with Evangeline, in three years and two or three summers. He would then hopefully proceed, immediately, in music and speech, proceeding to languages, history, philosophy, and theology. He believed that his natural gifts, and providence, had indicated this direction, so he accepted natural theology to be his tutor in leading him to revealed theology. The end of these plans led Evangeline to have an interruption to her own academic program, but she would finally go on and finish her masters and doctoral program as well.

This should not be concluded without Gabriel's presupposition. He knew that revealed theology was the most important way for God to speak. That is the reason why he had deliberately turned to the will of God, which must be supported by revealed theology, the Holy Scriptures, the Holy Spirit, and providence. Gabriel knew that nowhere in nature is grace revealed; but God's mercy, goodness and benevolence were there. Later, he would say he could find just as many miracles, or unusual providences, in his life, before he was born again, as appeared afterwards. The distinction, however, was they were miracles of a different kind. Gabriel concluded that too many people only seek their natural way, sometimes supported by natural theology; but he believed that man must see God behind and in nature and the natural way, and that behind the natural way was a spiritual reality. Therefore, this is a correction for anyone who takes the natural assumption of only a human way of life.

A letter arrives at the Old Shady Donnon Road address from Gabriel's best man at his wedding, LeVon Gilbertson. He opened the letter and read it to himself and remained silent.

"Who is it from, Gabriel?" questioned Evangeline.

"It is a letter from LeVon."

"Oh? We have not heard from him since the wedding. What did he write about?"

"Well, as you may recall, he professed Christ as his Savior before I did, while I was yet in the Navy. He was not in the War, he missed it about a year, and after college he went to a denominational seminary and responded so well to the denomination and their distinctives that he is now a pastor and a delegate to the 'First Quadrennial Conference on Evangelism' scheduled in Memphis, Tennessee. He wants me to be his guest for this important occasion. I am to be an official guest, present for the sake of observation only. This is the first meeting of this kind in the history of his denomination. Other denominations are planning similar fellowship meetings in their own denominational groups on evangelism. LeVon's denomination is one of seven who will be meeting with their seven bishops selected for the introductory session. My presence there will only be for this opening, evening session. I know very little about his present ministry; we grew up together and had a mutual interest in music for a short time before my conversion to Christianity and Christ. He desires me to be an observer with him and give an appraisal, afterwards, of the agenda. Also, he wants me to consider the ministry for my life in his denomination."

"Gabriel, is this a providential circumstance of God in bringing this invitation into your life?"

"I don't know, Evangeline. I grew up in my father's home, in a denomination, and he was greatly honored by them, at least among the more conservative group. I have thought of this often: both the matter of my father's blessings and honor to his conservative character, and his heartbreaks and controversies. To me, there seems to appear too often in the denominations a lack for a burden for the fundamentals of the Gospel, at times, yet, also, a greater attraction for the ecclesiastical and political system. This is often a demanding emphasis that affects loyalty to Christ and His Word. For many it becomes to them a greater emphasis and energy for the structure in a system rather than a joy and delight for the Savior and the Scriptures."

"I have sensed that in your previous conversations as well, my dear."

"Well, LeVon says that this general conference is for the summer of 1954 in Memphis. He has been in the ministry, himself, since 1944, shortly after he was saved. He was only an assistant to a pastor until his seminary training was completed in the spring semester of 1948. He is now pastoring a prosperous denominational church in Tennessee."

"Possibly you could go, dear, if you believe you should. It will be after your final summer studies for graduation in 1954."

"That is some time from now, dear. I wonder why such a meeting is slated for such a distant date? Evidently, it is a most important occasion, and they are desirous of an extended planning and advertisement for their audience. Possibly, I will have completed my doctoral work in early June, before their schedule of August, if the Lord wills it for me. We will pray together, Evangeline, about this. Maybe I should view more kindly the denominational view of Christianity."

"My darling Gabriel, I know you recall my testimony back in Nova Scotia. I was born in a liberal denominational church, and only heard the clear, pure call of the Gospel one time, when two American evangelists, in the providence of God, were invited to our church for a weekend series of services in song and sermon. They were brothers in the same family. Both the music and the preaching moved my heart to accept the Lord Jesus as my personal Savior. In four sermons in three days, I became a novice in the Lord, but established in accepting the 'Good News' forever. I came, on the last night, to the prayer room, and my faith was made firm in the Lord. Their names were Harry and Henry McMillan. My father asked the pastor, after the series of services, why we did not hear the Gospel preached like that regularly from the pulpit? His pastor answered:

'Religion is a private thing; and we should be wise in preaching it.'

"He then asked my father,

'Did you not think they preached too plain? Did you not think it was too emotional in the appeal?'

"Dad only responded:

'My daughter, Evangeline, was gloriously saved by grace, pastor; and her life is beautifully changed.'

"The pastor responded not another word. Of course, we considered another church, but there was no difference. Father thought we should stay and do all we could to change the message. He did have an influence and the pastor was removed, appropriately, after another year. But the condition remained the same."

"That confirmation from your heart, dear Evangeline, was involved in my love of you at first sight. I knew you knew the Lord; you were a Christian rather than a religionist. In my readings I have always distinguished between the Reformation and Protestantism, per se. They are very similar, but their contributions in church history were not the very same. The Reformation gave the greater emphasis upon Justification by Faith and full redemption by grace. Protestantism, as a movement, proceeded down into history, but seemed to be more a development of theological systems and ecclesiastical structures, and denominational identities. Finally, their distinctives and differences became greater than the fundamental Gospel principles. All of the denominations proliferated with a different, alternate theological system in contrast to Roman Catholicism. I wish to speak kindly about this because some of the theological systems were a great blessing and necessary to the ongoing work of the Gospel in history, and in my own life."

"Knowing more about your heart and mind, my darling, I believe I am beginning to understand that I must enlarge Evangeline's 'theology,' too. I believe what you are saying is a balanced acknowledgment of both the Reformation and the Protestant influence rather than a denial of either. Is that correct?"

"Yes, you have lovingly heard me; I did not think I concluded it as well as it should be concluded, but it does indicate the track of truth I must pursue. If you can understand my heart and mind, I know I have something of the best audience I will ever meet, which is in you, my dear Evangeline. I will write LeVon, and let him know that I am considering his invitation for the Conference. I knew him better before he was saved than my knowledge, personally, since his becoming a Christian and a minister. We will certainly think and pray about it, dear."

Chapter Six

The Reckoning

(July 10, 1949)

Gabriel's life between April 17, 1947 and July 10, 1949, was filled with intense studying and the forming of his Christian faith. However, during that time, and at the same period, he began to enter into his own personal struggle with the flesh. July 10, 1949, marked the end of that particular struggle in which he had viewed himself in Romans, chapter 7.

Gabriel resolved his faith in the matter by distinguishing the difference between justification by grace through faith, and sanctification by crucifixion through a crisis as revealed in the New Testament, by Calvary's same 'access' to the blood of Christ. Gabriel saw the struggle and war of the flesh in Romans to be also won by grace through the reckoning, yielding, and obedience to God as revealed in Romans, chapter 6. But justification by grace through faith, in Romans, chapter 5, verses 1 through 11, and sanctification by a spiritual crucifixion, Romans, chapter 6, verses 1 through 14, were each a crisis experience in the aorist tense in the Greek verb. The aorist tense is uniquely a Greek momentary action, or punctiliar crisis.

However, both of these truths resolved in an ongoing,

continuing process in his need and growth. In justification by faith, the aorist tense of Romans, chapter 5, verse 1, led immediately into the abiding in the Christ life in the present tense and perfect tense, as an ongoing of the Christian life in growth. Sanctification, similarly, experientially, began in the aorist tense, Romans, chapter 6, verses 1 through 14, with seven such tenses underlining the crisis: "justified," "dead," "baptized," "buried," "raised." "planted," "crucified," and "destroyed."

These, punctiliar completed actions led to a process, a quest, so that the Christian "also should walk in newness of life"; the Christian life was to be a daily walk. This was clear, therefore, to Gabriel, that neither a sinner nor a Christian could draw a conclusion that God would accept a sinning practice in the justified by faith life, or, a sinless perfection in a sanctified practice. God had it revealed in such a balanced paradox that no flesh, identified as Christian, could conclude from these truths a licentious practice or a legalistic practice.

The full benefits of redemption, for a Christian, theologically, were a crisis plus a process to heaven, and the glorification of the Christian body. Even in Creation, God had used the crisis plus the process through the six solar days. God, by fiat said, "Let there be light," yet, He "planted a garden," "made a woman," etc. This crisis plus process was all done in solar days, six only. When creation was finished in six solar days, the providence of God took over and sustained it all. God was no longer creating; He was only governing and preserving those created things with His providence.

This doctrine and prayerful practice, involving the doctrine of sanctification, became a conscious act and part of faith on July 10, 1949, when Gabriel returned back to his own spiritual acceptance of Christ, as Jacob returned back to Bethel. Gabriel saw the truth of this return to his own "Bethel," the place of the first divine depositum of justification by faith that led him to repentance and conversion to the Lord Jesus Christ.

As Gabriel went back to his Bethel of saving grace, he realized that every spiritual need would be met there; and there he finalized his struggle in his wrestling, in Old Testament type, with the Angel of the Lord at Jabbok. A spiritual crucifixion was illustrated in Jacob's crisis of the Lord's pulling a bone out of joint and restoring it back, which yet left him with a shrunken thigh for his crucified walk. This did set forth to Gabriel the mark of spiritual crucifixion in the process of his daily walk with the Lord, which should continue all the rest of his earthly life.

All of this took place in a crisis place, Jabbok, between his first Bethel and his second El-Bethel; but it was all a part of the divine depositum of God's amazing grace granted to him at his first Bethel, and he was only drawing upon that depositum. This was not "a second, definite work of grace," as some erroneously espouse it, as an "entire" sinless perfection, but simply was the ongoing work from regeneration's grace. Now, Gabriel was drawing upon that depositum, as an "access by faith into this grace wherein" he already stood, Romans, chapter five, verse two. At the first Bethel, "the Lord stood above," at the top of the ladder, bringing salvation to Gabriel, personally. Before the second El-Bethel, the Lord was on earth wrestling with Jacob. All of these gracious provisions were provided for by the very righteousness of the Lord Jesus in Gabriel's life: in the former, the imputed righteousness of Christ was extended to Gabriel; in the latter, the imparted righteousness of the Lord Jesus was granted unto him.

Thus, at the evening-time of July 10, 1949, we see Gabriel and Evangeline in this quiet victory in their repose in grace.

"Today is another marked day on the calendar of our hearts, together, Gabriel. Your own heart has been filled with the rich blessings of God, and therefore my own heart responds and rejoices to the overflow. I suppose we could at least follow through with that joyous text in Psalm, chapter 23, verse 5: 'my cup runneth over.' This is so applicable for you today, my darling. I might add: 'your saucer, your wife, receives from the overflow, too,'"

"I believe, Evangeline, that 'your own cup runneth over,' possibly before you met me. Your testimony before me has manifested a spiritual resource that I did not see in my own life in past times."

"Dear Gabriel, I have had my struggle, too, through my Christian life, but when I fell in love with you, I definitely sought a consecration before the Lord, then, that I did not have before. But because of God's blessing to me of my husband, I sought the Lord in thanksgiving. I believe that was possibly the greatest Christian victory over the flesh of my Christian life. I have spoken of this to you before."

"Yes, I remember that now. I see again, the simplicity of your faith, my dear. I do believe that true primitive Christianity, many times, by-passes the intellectual struggle of the mind by proceeding straight through to the heart, by grace. I heard once of a man with a very severe cold, who went to the pharmacist for a cure. Upon his arrival the pharmacist asked him, 'Did you bring your prescription?' The man replied: "No! but I brought the cold.' So many of us struggle to get the prescription when we ought to simply go to Jesus for the cure and the victory. My twenty-seven months, increasing each month after I was saved, made the struggle deeper. However, for over a year, at the beginning of my conversion to Christ, I simply rejoiced in the Lord for my salvation. But I want to make it clear that not everyone struggles the same way to victory through Christ concerning the flesh. I was like Jacob; others may be like Isaiah, who 'saw the Lord high and lifted up,' and God's holy 'train filled the temple,' Isaiah, chapter six. This may account for some of the difference in the presentation of the doctrine of sanctification, in which we emphasize our own personal reception of it, in our own experience, above the Biblical doctrine itself. Also, some may call it 'rededication,' or 'consecration,' or 'blessing,' 'revival,' 'restoration,' 'separation,' 'more grace,' or other.

"The main thing we are concerned about in this subject is that the grace of God will break the power of the flesh in all of our lives. We are living in a time when Bible doctrine is not as important as so-called Christian experience. In fact, both in evangelism and charismatism there is not only a false definition of these two subjects preached and taught now, but both are involved in too much experientialism. The time is too subjective; doctrine is not considered seriously or objectively important in our time. Therefore, I realize, personally, that we must not give center-stage to any kind of 'higher life' or 'deeper life' expectancy from this true Biblical doctrine of sanctification. What we need is a Bible answer for our 'desperate life' in Christ. We must never aggrandize or over publicize the 'crisis experience' of holiness against the greatest neglect which is in the 'quest of the process in the life of holiness.' It is that holy life we seek, which is only in the holiness of God Himself. Our nature, within itself, will never be any kind of a nature but what it is: having sinned in all the past; falling short of the glory of God always in the present. God did not send His Son to change the nature of sin to make it something other than what it really is — sin. The work of God's grace in sanctification to the believer is never further than the present tense, and this imparted righteousness is subsequent to His imputed righteousness in the New Birth; at least experientially."

"How would you appraise this in your own life as in this answer to prayer for you today, my dear?"

"The greatest truth I believe I have learned in these recent months concerns the Cross of Jesus. I had formerly limited Calvary, I believe, to the conversion of saving grace and then the abiding life which should follow. I think I thought of the Cross, in this saving grace, as of a glorious, beautiful Savior. My own personal struggle with the flesh of my pride and will has brought me back to take another view of the Cross again. I see now, more clearly, that our beautiful Savior was also a Warrior. There is a sense in which the Cross is also, as the hymn declares in 'The Old Rugged Cross,' an ugly shame against Jesus Christ. That is what that hymn is all about. The battle of Gethsemane is not the place of redemption, in the Garden, but it introduces us to the battlefield of the Cross where Jesus' blood was shed for us to be saved. The ugly agony in the Garden is a prelude to our own agonizings in prayer. The beauty prevails at the first: in Romans, chapter 5, our Lord Jesus is revealed to us 'while we were yet sinners, Christ died for us.' What a beautiful salvation; it is for sinners. Yet, in Romans, chapter 6, the Christian, not the sinner, must be crucified with Christ; that the body of sin, the ugly part, might be destroyed, or 'rendered inoperative.' The crucifixion in Romans, chapter 6, is not the wooden Cross of Jesus, but the spiritual Cross which is ours, indeed. We do not believe, because of the eternal purpose of hell, that sin is annihilated, but crucifixion with Christ renders sin inoperative as a power in our life, so that 'henceforth we should not serve sin.' Sin is no more Lord; we are no more slaves! Christ is Lord of our lives! Christ renders the 'old man' inoperative so that we do not have to live after the flesh, but rather after the Spirit. We were slaves before the new birth; but we are now sons of God, and should not continue as slaves to sin. Thank God for this great truth!"

"But it does not mean we will trust ourselves to be holy; does it, Gabriel?"

"No! No!, dear Evangeline. We will trust Him for His holiness. But we must not underestimate His provision for us in this struggle. It must be adequate and thorough. We must remember that sanctification in our lives goes no further than the present tense in our quest in following 'after holiness.' It is always true; we must draw upon His grace. What came to pass for me today is that we saw the need to 'go forth, therefore, unto him without the camp,...' '...that he might sanctify the people with his own blood.' However, the verse we will need for tomorrow is, 'follow peace with all men, and holiness, without which no man shall see the Lord: Looking diligently lest any man fail of the grace of God; lest any root of bitterness' come back and we be defiled again. Both of these passages are in the Book of Hebrews: first, Chapter 13; then, Chapter 12, respectively."

"Gabriel, I want to rest with you, in the simple words you have given me today, in God's wonderful grace."

"Yes, my beloved Evangeline; I love you, too. There will be other struggles for other days. Let us continue to reckon it so, yielding daily, through obedience to His Word. Let us pray now."

It is a mistake to conclude at this time, in the lives of Gabriel and Evangeline, that only "spiritual matters" occupied their minds all the time. Their horizontal happiness and joy continued throughout their daily delights in nature, in music, in decor, in food, in looking for streams and flowers, fountains and hills, and the "glorious greenery" of the soil and fruition like the Land of Evangeline and the Blue Ridge Mountains. Besides, Evangeline is now with child; oh, what a prospect for their future lives! These spiritual matters only mark their days of simple faith and earnest studies. They will both need all of this, soon.

Gabriel proceeded with graduate school and seminary completion of studies for his Master's degree in history and his doctoral program in theology. He finished all by June, 1954. LeVon Gilbertson, through these intervening years had become one of the superintendents of his denomination. He was appointed his home state conference, Tennessee. He kept in regular contact with Gabriel, commending him for his academic achievements and inquiring further of his family background. LeVon had also heard that Evangeline had finished her undergraduate degree in music, too. Their first child, a boy, was born, and they named him Joseph Paul. LeVon inquired greatly concerning Gabriel's Th.D. doctoral dissertation work which was entitled "The Problem and Paradox of the Christian's Body, Somatology."

Chapter Seven

The People

(August 23, 1954)

Rev. LeVon Gilbertson arrived in Memphis, Tennessee, to attend, as a state superintendent and delegate, the newly formed "First Quadrennial Conference on Evangelism," August 23, 1954. Seven denominations are meeting as a Fellowship, for the first time, and Dr. Gabriel T. Parsons is with him as an officially invited guest to the Conference. LeVon is twenty-seven years old; Gabriel is twenty-eight. The Hinton Conventional Center is the largest complex of its kind, with auditorium and adjacent facilities, in Tennessee.

The receptionist in the large foyer of the Hinton Convention Center has just placed a tag on the lapels of LeVon and Gabriel. LeVon was waiting for him as Gabriel came separately from his new home in the Georgetown area of Washington, D.C. Ten thousand people pre-registered, including Gabriel, and most of them had already gathered into the large central auditorium. This was the night of introductions to be extended with three other day and night sessions yet ahead. Gabriel would only be present for the first night as an observer. Enthusiasm and cheerfulness prevailed for the prompt commencement of the evening organizational meeting of formal introductions of the purpose of the Convention. The organ music proceeds above all the other voices. The printed programs are being read by many, as others cheerfully talk of the Convention itself. There will be two sessions during the evening with an intermission for personal fellowship and refreshments. Seven chairman-bishops of the seven historic denominations will be introduced in their several capacities and offices. The key-note speaker initiates the purpose of the first evening together, including introductions of the succeeding speakers as well. Three more days will involve all the boards, seminars, workshops, and leadership lectures. Gabriel has never attended such a large audience of Christians for such a purpose before. The Conference carried with it an ecumenical flair that did not distinguish individual faith. Gabriel is there by invitation of LeVon Gilbertson, and he seeks to profit from this practical occasion. LeVon commences his own enthusiastic conversation. Over the vast auditorium the organ music still prevails.

"Well, Gabriel, here we are at last. It has been sometime now since your wedding, and you appear married and still in love. I am happy for you; so is my wife. She thought it was a beautiful ceremony. (a pause) I am glad you have come for this occasion with me. This is our 'First Quadrennial Conference Fellowship on Evangelism.' Besides my own denomination, six others have gathered with us to form a 'Fellowship for Christian Evangelism.' There are some two million members from around the world identified with the churches of these denominations represented here tonight."

"What are the names of the denominations present, LeVon? I apologize for my ignorance in coming as your guest tonight. I have not known of the actual details. You spoke something of it in your correspondence as an organizational meeting of denominational persons and programs for evangelism."

"Well, the denominational identity is not as important any more as it used to be, but each still has its own theological distinctive. More and more, since World War II, we are a

Fellowship of denominations of similar theological persuasions because of a new dynamic movement of the Holy Spirit in the earth. This unity has become a greater force of importance and delight for all of us. (a pause, as the crowd is tightly moving into the auditorium) I am glad you came, Gabriel. Your scholarly appraisal will be good for me, and I trust we will also contribute blessing to you. I did not go into detail about the Conference itself because I wanted your most objective view and appraisal of it all. I invited you as an outstanding young scholar and friend among my acquaintances, and desired, most sincerely, your input of these things."

"Thank you, LeVon. Are you stating that the agenda for the Fellowship has already been formed without an agreement concerning your denominational and theological positions?"

"Oh no, Gabriel. This is the very first time, corporately, we have come together like this. There have been behind-the-scenes preliminary meetings of smaller boards with their respective leaders, but this is the first time to truly present such a possibility of such a Fellowship. There will be three more days in lectures of the details of study which have gone into the prospect. Most of our church members do not know the details of the purpose of this meeting, but it will be introduced in due time. A larger dialogue concerning our doctrine will take place in the days ahead. However, this hope of such an evangelistic program is most important to the leaders of these denominations. (pause, amidst the sounds) Let us try to find our seats; my section is near the front. Your seat number is on your lapel tag. We are fortunate for my denominational seats to be so close to the stage and podium. Ah, here we are; I'll lead the way to our seats." (many are standing or sitting with the general conversation buzz of an auditorium; the organ continues to prevail in the overtone of the voices.)

Suddenly, as LeVon and Gabriel are seated, the multitude of people are electrified with the applause from the mass crowd. The enthusiastic audience has now turned to the right portion of a large stage as seven distinguished looking men come to the center, raised podium area. All wear conservative suits with individually prominent, colorful neckties, and although conservative, each suit is a different shade of black or blue or gray. A pastel shirt is associated with the color of the suit. The applause continues for ten minutes, with one of the gentlemen on the stage coming forward to endeavor to quiet the applause while acknowledging the commendation of the audience. Finally, an eighth, and younger man, steps forward from the left side of the stage and raises the familiar song, "Amazing Grace." After only one stanza, the audience returns to their applause as the first of the seven men makes his way to a set of three chairs behind the podium itself. He now stands behind the podium. The song leader then announces, ecstatically, into the microphone, "We welcome Bishop William Jason Fagin, from Franklinville, Georgia."

The applause erupts again, even louder, as Bishop Fagin, at the podium, raises both of his hands. This increases the applause as LeVon shouts to Gabriel, "Isn't this exciting?" but turns back quickly to the podium, not really expecting an answer.

Another five minutes would pass before the speaker responds, "I am glad to see all of you here tonight."

The audience vocalizes back to him, "Yeah," as applause quickens to a stop.

A quiet calm comes, as the speaker waits through the silence. He then speaks with clear tones.

"Church bishops, general secretaries, leaders, delegates, and guests. We embark tonight upon a most dynamic dialogue to seek the possibility of an International Fellowship in Christ which goes beyond any such event before in the history of our denominations. The remaining years of the 1950s will signal many such meetings of other groups of denominations around the world. Every protestant denomination will enter and seek this dialogue towards a common, kindred fellowship beyond and besides denominational and theological persuasions. This will be done in the hope to unite our differences and distinctives, at least, to bring about such a Fellowship for the exclusive goal of the evangelization of the whole world." (applause erupts, even more fervently).

This time when Bishop Fagin raises his hands, silence immediately falls upon a hushing audience. The bishop continues.

"There is evidence among us as leaders that other denominations will be called upon to gravitate to the nearest denominational affiliate theological entity into a fellowship such as we are introducing also tonight, for the evangelization of the whole world. (grave silence prevails) In this our hopeful series of discussions, it has become my privilege and task, as urged upon me by my denominational brethren, to be the Presidium-Chairman of Decorum of this Board of dialogue, composed of us, the seven Bishops and the seven General Secretaries seated before this podium. These brethren, composing a board of fourteen men, do initiate tonight our First Quadrennial Conference of the Seven historic International Pentecostal denominations around the world. (short applause)

"Each of our denominations has pursued this hope through its individual annual conferences, separately, and is here tonight supported by this hope, unanimously. But we have agreed, throughout all our denominational conference boards, to come together at this time with the express purpose of the evangelization of the whole wide world. (applause erupts again, in open spontaneity, but ceases when Bishop Fagin raises his hands.) The Agenda of this evening is being carefully monitored and recorded by the seven denominational General Secretaries that I have mentioned before, seated here before us at the front. We are making history tonight; history for the evangelization of the whole wide world!" (the audience in full force stands to their feet shouting, "Hallelujah," "Glory to Jesus," with "Amens" scattered everywhere. Sprinkled through the auditorium are a few, here and there, of those who are not disposed to rise to their feet, evidently because they are simply endeavoring to understand more clearly what is being developed in these words, including Gabriel)

Bishop Fagin concludes his key-note message with a final resolve.

"And now, as Presidium-Chairman of Decorum, I am honored to introduce Bishop Carter H. Cranwell, from Oklahoma, and we welcome, in our audience, the delegation from his denomination. Let them stand!" (about one-seventh of the audience stands in the section designated. Bishop Cranwell proceeds to the podium)

"Bishop Cranwell is Chairman of Denominational Polity," added Bishop Fagin.

"Ladies and gentlemen, leaders and laymen, all brothers and sisters in the Lord, we welcome you to this great day! Hallelujah!" (brief applause) "We represent the seven oldest, historic pentecostal denominations in the world. We have held this distinctive for fifty years and more. We have deliberately withheld our usual announcement of denominational identity so that we may join together today to consider a unity for the evangelization of the world for Christ. We will make all these identifying denominational titles later in the Conference in the hope of our individual goals for Christ. But behind the scenes, all of the protestant denominations of the world are in the process of dialogue with a great longing of heart, since World War II, to do something about the problems of the world and to heighten evangelism to our top priority. Plans are being made to stir dialogue among all protestant church leaders; to encourage fellowships to commence with their nearest denominational and theological distinctives; to enlarge the perimeter of our distinctives to the distinctives of other denominations; and to form a dynamic force in bringing all of us together for the total evangelization of the world (no applause; a pause).

"There has survived in church history, since the Protestant Reformation, fourteen great theological systems: to Calvinism, four; to Lutheranism, two; to Wesleyism, two; to Arminianism, two; to Baptist, one, to Pentecostal, two, and to Pelagianism, one. If we will work together, and humble ourselves, we could immediately extract an evangelistic force, for this purpose alone, and reduce the 987 different denominations, outside of Roman Catholicism, to fourteen fellowshipping groups. The primary need of this Conference, in the very outset, is to quell anyone from thinking we are bent on a course of compromise in our holy, Biblical distinctives. We will never compromise an inch away from our historical testimony, our hopes, and our prayers." (applause reaches its peak in response to these last statements.)

Bishop Cranwell raises his hands in a shaking fashion, as to the Devil. "No! No! We, as men of God's choosing will never compromise! We will hold the fort; we will keep the faith. And one of the immediate positions we must state: we will not have Romanism in this Fellowship; we will not include so-called Christian cults like Mormonism, Jehovah's Witnesses, Seventh Day Adventists, or the presence of Armstrongism among us; or any such like. We simply believe it is time for the true protestant, historical denominations to get together instead of getting further apart. Whatever is protestant, we want to unite for the evangelization of the entire world for Christ. Now! Let, Us, Do It." (applause).

Bishop Cranwell quickly turns and walks strongly to his seat away from the podium. Each of the other bishops congratulate his words amidst the dying of applause.

"Our next speaker is the Chairman of Evangelism in this First Quadrennial Conference on Evangelism. He has exciting good news of where evangelism is headed in our century. Listen now, carefully, to Bishop Carl Synans Keifer of Santiago, Chile. He is the presiding bishop of evangelism on the international front, and he is presently stationed in Santiago." (applause as Bishop Keifer approaches the podium.)

"Ladies and gentlemen, the largest pentecostal church in the world is located in Santiago, Chile. I have been there. I am now there. The membership, of that one church, has reached 28,000 pentecostal Christians. This is a significant index to the future wonders God desires and will be doing with us as pentecostalists. But that particular emphasis will be forthcoming through our later speakers, tonight. My heart is greatly encouraged to inform you that great world-wide evangelists are standing in the wings of this great spiritual drama. Great men of God are beginning to appear on the international scenes of the world. I am sure, by now, that you have heard about the rising ministry of Dr. Willie Wheyman. He started from his own non-pentecostal denominational roots in the South and then began to lead our national youth crusades to national evangelism. He is now the leading evangelist of all of our hearts. He preaches the simplest Gospel possible; he makes the Gospel easily available and believable; you may simply take a walk from the second balcony of the stadium, and a sinner's prayer awaits you. He is on a number of impressive national boards, fellowships, seminaries, and has just returned from his first successful crusade abroad. Souls by the multitudes are coming to Christ. He is already on the launch pad for the souls of the world by the end of this century. He has an international Gospel for an international audience. He is even loved by other religions, and political men of nations are attracted to him as a person. Other evangelists are learning from him and his example. I know of no denomination in which there is not respect for him among the leaders, as well as many of the local church pastors and congregations. The news media has pushed him to the front, for some strange reason we cannot humanly explain, something very, very rare for our time. We pray he will lead us into the twenty-first century with the greatest success of any American evangelist we have known in the history of the United States. Evangelism is now our first priority. Who in any of our churches could possibly be against the evangelism of lost souls? We do not want to get stuck with some pet doctrine to delay or hinder the evangelization of the whole world.

"As Bishop Cranwell, magnanimously, stated, there will be no compromise with our theological beliefs, but we must place all our beliefs on the line for evangelism. There is nothing higher than souls! Let us use all of our doctrines to support evangelism. Television is an instrument that can be used, and, ultimately, it will carry programs to the end of the earth. This will open up film-productions for Christ. We must catch and use the evangelistic gospel song, with all of the manifestations, physically, that God has given us as His pentecostalists. We must broadcast these evidences everywhere we go. We must evangelize in every lifestyle and culture in existence and leave their convictions and principles to themselves for their own satisfaction, rather than legislate some kind of religious appearance to them. Let's get out of here and catch the fish; we'll clean them later! We are not against peoples' styles, cultures, distinctives, dress, whatever they may be; we are interested only in their souls. Will everyone of you young ministers accept this major challenge tonight—a challenge of a lifetime of evangelism for Christ, without your own convictions of how to do it?"

The young ministers and young laymen stood as one person amidst the supporting applause from the auditorium. This continued along with an outpouring of "Hallelujahs" and "Glorys," echoing across the audience. The organ joined the shoutings with a singular excerpt of "Glory, Glory, Hallelujah; His truth is marching on," with many of the audience joining in on the last phrase. Bishop Fagin returns to the podium. He raises his hands once again which subsides the restless crowd. A deep silence comes.

By the time the Bishop had come to the podium a one-hundred voice choir had already come to position on the stage, and the organ and piano had given an impromptu resolve as the musical introduction extended.

Bishop Fagin extends, joyously to the audience, "The choir will now introduce the theme song of the Fellowship, an original composition for this occasion, and for our future Quadrennial Conferences and crusades. Listen; you'll learn it quickly."

The piano and organ once again repeat their dominant seventh chord with a long hold. Four musical parts swell to the first phrase.

"The Whole World needs Jesus;
    The Whole Word needs a Friend.
The Whole World needs Jesus;
    Someone on Whom they can depend.
In times, like these, when love must find a home (long hold),
    The Whole Wide World needs Jesus."

Six stanzas are added with a return to the refrain as the great crowd joins in, easily learning it quickly at the end of each stanza, "The Whole Wide World needs Jesus." Much enthusiasm is generated in each succeeding refrain. Each time, the song leader turns to the choir and then back to the audience with great exuberance for the refrain.

As the song concludes, Bishop Fagin returns to the podium to introduce the third speaker.

"Ladies and gentlemen, before our mid-evening break for refreshments and fellowship, it is my delight to introduce to you, Bishop Elmer Edward Michaud, Chairman of Musical Ministries, and speaker also for this Quadrennial Conference." (a pause, with emphasis) "Bishop Michaud." (a brief applause)

"Ladies and gentlemen, as we look back across the history of church music, England and the United States of America, by far, have made the greatest contribution to its treasury. Many of these songs have been translated into many languages of the world. The time has come for the church to realize, also, the great contribution, to this legacy, of the songs of the pentecostalists. With that in mind, it is also time for the entire church of Jesus Christ to make its greatest selections of Christian music for the best potential in reaching the souls of men. This great potential resource of evangelistic music is to be selected for the direct purpose of lost sinners. We have been told that there are almost one hundred different song forms in music from the masters and their models in the classical and the traditional style. These have mainly resulted from Italy, Europe, and England, and even back to Russia. However, the American repertory of music has proved to be the more fitting and suitable for the lost masses, by reducing the various forms down from the oratorios, cantatas and anthems to the human Gospel Song. The English hymn had its day.

"In today's world, for the sake of evangelism, we need to totally emphasize the Gospel Song in its rightful place in the twentieth century. This is the experiential song of our own pentecostal experience. We need the guitar to assist us, since it has become a symbol of musical understanding around the world. We are aware of the fact of the stately and lofty earlier music, strictly composed for worship and reverence and form. However, we as pentecostalists, have seen the importance of evangelistic music, with feeling, emotion, for the Holy Spirit to be able to work more freely through our songs and through us. We have had fifty years of experience in this type of music, and God has used it successfully through this channel of blessing to the churches. A new music must now come to the united denominational spectrum. We are in need of a contemporary Christian music for our time. Along with a new-pentecostalism, appropriate for this generation, we need a fresh, new selection of music for the young people of the world.

"The other protestant denominations have led us in neo-orthodoxy, neo-evangelicalism, but we, as new-pentecostalists, need to contribute to the visible Body of Christ a new selection of music for the new generation of young people. We must seek out evangelistic music, not just for worship and reverence — music that sounds like a funeral parlor — but music to move the whole wide world. We believe that we are on the edge, just before us, of a new breed of composers, with a fresh format of songs, for the freedom and moving of the Holy Spirit in this opportunity of a world-wide audience. Pentecostal composers who will be heard around the world are already coming to American prominence. Through our songs, millions of people are going to feel God's presence and be saved. God is going to enlarge our choice of the pentecostal guitar and tender and soft voices of song to reach the souls of men. Even the drum is going to come back and be used of the Lord.

"These means will break down walls and barriers, and open the hearts of many people for God to bring an awakening to the world, in victory and triumph, as we emphasize the power of the Holy Spirit needed in the last days before the coming of Christ. The power of the Holy Spirit is what we need; and the pentecostalists have that, particularly. Come and join us, all of you young people; come and join us! And for the old saints who still mark our pews, do not fold your hands and live in the past. Help us hold the new song up! Let the Holy Ghost take away our old ways and scruples so that He may do a "new thing" in the earth. Let us go forth in power, in power and spirit! Hallelujah!" (the audience stands on their feet again; "hallelujahs" are heard reverberating en masse across the crowd. At this point, many are shouting and praising God, even running the aisles, in an enlarged force beyond the earlier responses.)

Bishop Fagin, finally, is able to further the Conference through the ecstatic shouts of victory. He raises his hands, shaking them as the audience begins to subside.

"Beloved people of God, what a challenge for all pentecostal singers, choirs, quartets, and ensembles for the neo-evangelism of the future! Hallelujah be to God, Hallelujah!" (after another wave of praises, the audience returns to their seats as Bishop Fagin commences his announcement.)

"Denominational leaders, delegates, guests, and friends, you have heard three of our speakers for the evening; there are three more to come. We are going to take a twenty-minute intermission for your convenience, fellowship, and refreshment; but return promptly when you hear the music raised again at 8:25. May God bless you, and let everybody say, 'Amen'" (and all joining in) "AMEN!"

LeVon urges Gabriel to come with him into one of the private, reserved anterooms where refreshments will be served for the denominational leaders and their guests. Everyone is exceedingly friendly and calls out to LeVon as he passes through the crowd. A few introductions were made, in passing, of Gabriel to others. The crowd continues to move, pressingly, towards the many exits from the auditorium, pushing each other gently, but with great excitement of spirit. Finally, LeVon reaches an exit and he leads Gabriel to the reserved room down a hallway. They enter and are immediately served a cold drink and half-sandwiches with tasty cracker-and-cheese pieces and cake. The paper plate is most unusual with many colors and the words "First Quadrennial Conference on Evangelism" embossed. They are finally seated in an alcove of the rather large, impressive room.

"Well, Gabriel, you have seen tonight a great outpouring of inspiration and challenge for the future of evangelism. It is the greatest renewal of God's people I have ever witnessed. As a child, and I did not know you then, I was reared in a cold, staid, formal church with a pipe-organ and stained-glass windows. Now, in my life, the Holy Ghost has broken up that old formal way and given us liberty and freedom in our worship and witness. The old English hymns were so cold; I never did understand what the words really meant. I do not know if you have ever seen anything like this before; probably not. However, I wanted you to come. I did not, formerly, in our correspondence, go into all of this. I simply wanted you to come. What do you think?"

"First, you may, or may not recall, that my own dear father is in the ministry, and has been for twenty-six years."

"Yes, I remember that, Gabriel. You always spoke of him with the highest regards, when you did speak of him at all. In our years in the musical ensemble, I guess our thoughts were not along this line. Of course, I remember your father in your wedding service, too."

"Yes. (pause) I was going to say in response to your question of my thoughts: first, I never thought of the church I grew up in as you so vividly described yours. It was not, as I remember, cold, staid, and formal. I thought of it as warm, friendly, and most worshipful. Every English hymn taught me more about the great doctrine of the Lord Jesus Christ, the Holy Trinity, the Holy Spirit, and the greatness of the Father in the universe. For a number of years, early in my life, I would hear the Gospel preached through my father, in the power and anointing of the Holy Spirit, as deep conviction of the Holy Spirit came upon me with fear. I thought that the Holy Spirit was taking the Word of God to the entire audience in this same manner. To me, being a sinner, conviction was brought; to believers, I thought the Holy Spirit brought consecration and humility."

"Oh, is that so, Gabriel? Well, that sounds interesting and different. Of course, you were not saved then, were you Gabriel?"

"No," responded Gabriel.

"Neither one of us was saved during either form of church service as young boys, Gabriel. Does that mean that neither kind of worship service, in those days, could evangelize our souls?"

"No, that's not true for me. In my case, I should have accepted Christ earlier than I did. I certainly had the opportunity to do so; and the Holy Spirit certainly punctuated the Word of the Bible in those early worship services."

"Well Gabriel, this is why I wanted you to come to this Conference. You were always the studious person, and you only entered our musical group, before either one of us was saved, as you would often say, to bring another chapter in your knowledge of a semi-classical repertory. I have always thought of you as a different friend, a scholarly person; and I have never known you to lie. With that admiration and confidence in you, as an ongoing friend in my life, I remember your first letter to me before your wedding. You desired me to be your best man; you wrote vividly of your 'conversion,' you called it a 'conversion,' to Christianity and Christ. I had never heard of one becoming a Christian exactly like that. I wanted, in this Conference, to receive an appraisal from you, for I did not believe you would lie about it.

"This Conference is an emphasis upon a renewal or new thrust for the Christian, which some call an awakening! You have always, since the first of our acquaintance, been a person of reasonable and good attitude. When I put reasonable, scholarly, honest, good spirit, and now 'conversion,' together, I think of you. You have pleased me by coming tonight. I know that it is almost time for the three remaining speakers to proceed according to the agenda, but I want us to get together as soon as possible, at another time, a fixed appointment, for you to give me your candid opinion. (the organ could now be heard from the auditorium). Oh, there's the cue for us to return to the Conference. I regret to say that, as a superintendent-delegate, I will have to meet and participate in an after-service with brethren of my own denomination to prepare for tomorrow's meetings. All of the denominations present will be preparing for the same. But I want to know: will you promise me that I may contact you later? and we will indeed get together, as I have desired? Please, my dear friend, will you meet with me, Gabriel?" (again, a serious pause).

"Yes, LeVon. I certainly will."

They returned to their reserved seats as Bishop Fagin was approaching the podium again.

"Ladies and gentlemen, it is time for our fourth speaker, Bishop Huett Thomas Malls, Chairman of Evangelistic Methodology, of our First Quadrennial Conference for Evangelism. Bishop Malls."

"I am privileged and honored to speak to you tonight on the subject of 'The Methodology of Christian Evangelism.' Since 1942, four major Christian organizations and institutions have come into existence with something of a final burden for this century with a two-fold goal: one, to participate in an evangelical scholarly dialogue with our more liberal Christian brethren; and two, a total denominational thrust for the world-wide evangelization of unchristian neighbors. Piloting organizations have been at work in the total coordination of Christians everywhere, and especially in a total denomi-national unity. (a pause)

"In 1942, there was born the National Interaction of Christian Evangels, NICE. This was a bringing together of all who would be identified with the basic evangelical truth of the Bible. This was a conservative movement from the Christian world; they interviewed each potential denominational or personal candidate for membership. Even certain Christian organizations were contacted. Their base was Washington, D.C. This would be an organization dedicated to evangelical evangelism. This was clearly to be understood as an organization, not as separatist fundamentalists, who were so unloving and too harsh. NICE is an organization of nice evangelical evangelism.

"In 1947, and as a part of the entire evangelical spectrum, there was a companion organization of The Evangelical World Seminary, TEWS. This was a bringing together of thirty of the world's leading evangelical scholars from around the world, who were a part of the original British Evangelicals at the end of the Victorian Age and the Princeton theologians. Here again, it was not to be the voice of the separatist fundamentalists, because they were too technical concerning the 'inerrancy' of the Holy Scriptures. This was believed to be the greatest aggregation of scholars since the Reformation, if not the first century of Christianity itself. These leading scholars would agree to a conservative interpretation of the Bible and be willing to dialogue with the more liberal theologians of the world. Many books have been written by these scholars as a result of this impressive seminary. They made claim that they would recall the voice of the conservatism of the former strong days of seminaries and the scholarly in thought. Their geographical base would be San Francisco, California. This would become an organization dedicated to apologetical evangelism.

"These first two organizations would then be supported by the commencement of an international, multi-lingual Christian magazine, published fortnightly, under the title of Contemporary Christianity (CC). This publication was dedicated to missionary and apologetical evangelism, accompanied with scholarship articles espoused by the two previously mentioned organizations, as well as the total presentation of all the dialogues involving the liberals as well, but not a flair for fundamentalists.

"Finally, through the world's leading young evangelist, Willie Wheyman, with a direct relationship with NICE, TEWS, and CC, these four entities would be dedicated to mass evangelism. Wheyman would be a member of each in the quartet of evangelism ministries and would serve as a board member, or a chairman in one or more of them.

"With these four forces in place, dedicated to The Great Commission of Christ, every method possible will be employed for the evangelization of the whole wide world. The methods of missions, monies, means, motive, and men will be launched in our time to forward the force of evangelism around the world. We will launch it to the top of the charts of politics, sports, entertainment, and religion. We will be known for Love instead of controversy; life instead of the old stagnations; uniting instead of dividing, and simplicity in the application of evangelism rather than intellect, conviction, and separatism.

"All of these forces will be willing to dialogue instead of debate, to agree instead of only differ. We will use historical research of the methods of the revivalists of the past to bring to the front every effort for presuppositional evangelism. We will go to every place man is, and where he is, and every nation, in their culture, loving them instead of changing them. We will push straight on into the twenty-first century. We will be bold as the Bible declared us to be; to boast of our Gospel as Paul declared himself to do; and, to be a Christian conqueror of the world's masses as John, the Beloved, told us to be in the Book of Revelation.

"God is now preparing us to be international evangelists who will no longer be tied to the old fears, fads, fashions and faults of the Christian past. Martin Luther, and all the reformers, used doctrine; we will use Spirit, the Holy Spirit. The modern evangelist will see the larger scope; gain respectability for his manner in his message; and we all will see God in these things very soon. We are praying for it; we are planning for it; and we will use every means to that end. *Contemporary Christianity* will be our publication as an international mouthpiece.

"Our slogan will be, 'Real Christianity for a Real World; a Christianity Needed for Our Day and Time.' With these means and methods, we will move through the world like a spiritual cyclone, and we believe millions will begin to follow our banner and call for Christ. Will you tonight, everyone of you, accept this fourth challenge in our First Quadrennial Conference for Evangelism? Go and glow with us on this adventure for Christ into the twenty-first century!"

A standing ovation to the speaker resounded with enthusiasm to join these Christian forces in the opportunities ahead. Bishop Fagin joins in with his exuberance as he once again raises his hands for the announcement of the fifth speaker.

"Denominational leaders, delegates, and guests: our next speaker is Bishop Alexander Gregory Vinson, Chairman of Scholarship for the First Quadrennial Conference for World Evangelism. Bishop Vinson."

The leading pentecostal historian and scholar approaches the podium with deliberate care, holding four books in his hands. His heavy, articulate voice, touched with a warmth and calm, academic deliberation, brings a hush to the general audience. There commenced a touch of oratory and academic authority to the minds of those present. There was a simple brokenness in him without the loss of his continuity.

"Dear friends of pentecostalism. Over fifty years of pentecostal truth have passed experientially among us, since we were on the other side of the railroad tracks. From our former background and founding fathers, we fled away from cold formality and technical theological molds. We longed for a higher land and a deeper sense of Almighty God. The Holy Ghost baptisms and anointings, graciously given by the Lord, were beautifully received by His people as they were slain under the Spirit and were humbly reduced to the floor of our churches. We have sung our inspired songs and prayed our weakened prayers. We commenced in lowly straits in lowly places and planted our churches wherever we could, and even went across the railroad tracks, in the poor and sick recesses of society, to sing, pray, and preach. We took not only the Gospel but healing and health, and went away from those early days with miracles and spiritualities. That was our doctrine; that was our practical doctrine.

"We have now come to the fifth decade of the twentieth-century and have entered across the railroad tracks, and God has given us a prosperous land in the earth. We still preach, pray, sing, and see the manifestations of the Holy Spirit among us. The Lord has, in this decade, increased our understanding of His power and given us prophets in our services; and we will stand still until the Holy Spirit comes through the gift of prophecy. The prophecies are increasingly speaking of greater miracles to attend the preaching, with healings, the glossolalia, and spiritualities accompanying. This is what we are now beginning to see; this is our doctrine; this is why the Lord sent us in this generation. We are just beginning to see the secrets of the Holy Spirit among us. The great fundamental core of Biblical principles has done its work; but there yet remains the final outpouring of the Holy Ghost, the latter rain which Job, Moses, Joel, and James spoke of in God's Word, when the heavens will crack wide open with a profusion of signs and wonders, even reaching to the moon and the heavens being shaken, as we have been shaken in our shoutings in our churches. This is our doctrine; this is our testimony.

"All the way through the Bible, as the scholars have uncovered, from the first mentioning of the Holy Ghost, there was to be an enlarging and increasing emphasis and presence of the Holy Ghost. Then, the Day of Pentecost came into history. But prophecy also concludes with a greater manifestation and demonstration of the Holy Spirit. We are to be 'in the Spirit on the Lord's Day'; the Spirit is to call, 'Come up hither and see the things which shall be hereafter'; we are yet to be 'carried away in the spirit into the wilderness'; and then we will come to know and hear, 'the Spirit and the Bride say come!' This is our doctrine; this is our teaching.

"Whereas history is indeed replete with the great emphasis of those who would preach Christ, we are called upon, also, to preach the Holy Spirit! This is our doctrine; this is our text. Thank God for the manger; thank God for Calvary; but what about the pentecostal Upper Room? This is our doctrine; this is our text!

"We are no longer in the years of history; we are in the climax of God's mighty deeds, the climax of His great power; all of it! That is our doctrine; that is our history!

"The Bible continues to have its place in all of our lives;

that is as it should be and will continue to be. However, strict doctrine and strict theology must now yield to the added importance and simplicity of the teeming millions of earth, so that they may be reached, too. Fresh insights into our methodology must come, just as the later laws of physics, science, mathematics, and the arts have all been extended in understanding and knowledge. We must now include social studies, human counseling, and pragmatism and individualism in the world under the Gospel. We must no longer think of ourselves as a closed-doctrine of only a former day. God wants us now to understand more of the humanity of Jesus' love and Judean lifestyle. He wants us to know of His humanitarian sympathy for every man. We are in great straits, and the greater the straits, the greater the need of the power of the Holy Spirit in man. God now seeks to magnify signs and wonders before the whole world. A signs ministry confirms the Gospel. Thank God; this is our doctrine; this is what we pentecostalists believe.

"God desires to heal more people, and we have been led to have more faith. He desires for the past curse of monetary prosperity to be lifted. Prosperity is a blessing received out of the Hand of God through His miracles. Yes, there are those in the past that could not handle prosperity and therefore their 'unfaith' hindered them. We have an international mission to fulfill; we have the urgent need to live in such a lifestyle that we will be enabled to proceed around the world, unfettered with the daily cares. This is our doctrine; this is our privilege as God's people.

"As Bishop Malls urged, as Chairman of Methodology, on this glorious Quadrennial occasion, we need means, missions, monies, a manner, and a man for this coming World Conquest; so we need more pentecostal scholars with practical scholarship to clear our lives of the debris of poverty and sickness. Jesus told us to make friends with Mammon, which is money. This is our pentecostal doctrine; this is our privilege. (with brokenness and tears)

"I offer, as a humble suggestion, in closing, four rather new publications of books to help us in these matters and in our hope of lost souls, in bringing them to Christ. First, a book on methodology authored by Dr. Bob L. Southey, at the beginning of this century. The book is entitled, *Evangelism on Fire.* The second book, by Dr. Thomas E. Benney, *Revival Roads to the Multitudes.* Then, and even more meaningful, the book written by Dr. Nathaniel Hills Howard, *The Positive Power of God Without the Negatives,* and another book I would suggest by the same author, *The Magic Positive Story.* And finally, a recent Christian author, Dr. Cleveland Woodlief Powers, *Winning Others by the Power of Positive Thinking and Influence.* There is only a short time left, beloved (spoken brokenly), we must use all fire, all roads, positive faith without negatives, and the influence of our total personality, to publish, preach, using every dollar possible, and all other means for this hour of evangelism. This must be our doctrine; this must be our faith. We must do this by the year 2000. I leave a tried and worn, old text from the Old Testament as well as a fresh and open text of the New Testament and then retire to my hotel room, after our benediction to pray.

"First Samuel, chapter 13, verse 19, beginning:...'Now there was no smith found throughout all the land of Israel: for the Philistines said, Lest the Hebrews make them swords or spears; But all the Israelites went down to the Philistines, to sharpen every man his share, and his coulter, and his axe, and his mattock...they had not a file for the mattocks, and for the coulters, and for the forks, and for the axes, and to sharpen the goads.'

"First Corinthians, chapter 9, verse 21, beginning:... 'To them that are without law, as without law,... that I might gain them that are without law. To the weak became I as weak, that I might gain the weak: I am made all things to all men, that I might by all means save some'"

"We must be humble enough to give up our prejudices and scruples of the past, and our dead doctrines and interpretations, so that the Holy Ghost may use us, too, as 'made all things to all men, that...by all means...we might save some.' This must be our doctrine; this must be our love."

The mood and moving of human spirit in the audience has fled all applause, as the hearts of many seem broken, too. Quite a number are kneeling at their seats, while others are standing somber and sober.

Bishop Fagin returns to the podium for the sixth speaker.

"Dear hearts, we have now come to our last speaker for the night. We close our first evening of the First Quadrennial Conference on Evangelism of the seven historic pentecostal denominations by introducing, our beloved brother, Bishop Jinson Whitehead Simons, Chairman of Finance. As he comes, let us all stand for a silent prayer." (after one moment, Bishop Fagin prays) "Our Father, take charge of the closing of this Conference tonight. Anoint Bishop Simons to bring this auspicious body to Thy Throne and our needed challenge. Amen."

Dr. Simons readies himself for his message.

"Dear beloved Christians, all of our speakers have given us the desire of God's heart for His pentecostal people in this our First Quadrennial Conference on Evangelism. More and more the pentecostalists are being believed as The Third Christian Force in the world today, as well as being the fastest growing movement in the world. The pentecostalists now transcend all denominations of those being both saved and baptized in the Holy Ghost. We were born into existence at the beginning of this century, yet in fifty years we are the third force. Mainly, at this point in the 1950s, God is using Spirit-filled Christians in the denominations.

"At the beginning of our own pentecostal fellowship, we are seeing evidence of other mainline denominations attending our meetings, and many of them are being baptized in the Holy Ghost. I believe this indicates God is seeking pentecostal Christians to use for His glory.

"In the future, we believe this will be the pattern God will follow. God will certainly keep strong the pentecostal denominations and their respective leaderships, but He will be using the 'personality-stars' which are shining in the pentecostal heaven of hope. The pentecostal denominations must now take on the role of mother and father of those individuals God has chosen as His star-evangelists. God has made them individual pentecostal personalities for salvation and healing in the new-evangelism for this time. We must see this leading of the Lord for the future. We are God's pentecostalists, all of us. We have been given a number of distinctives as our speakers have made clear. Among the gifts that the Gospel will also give to evangelism in our time are: the continuance of the healing lines; the manifestations of praise, shouting, and the glossolalia; fasting and prayer; and, the special gift of prophesying and revelation through tongues. There are already beginning to appear what we should understand as the prophetical personalities of pentecostalism. We must revere and encourage these men before us. We have been given the distinction, and earlier than other denominations, the gift of women preachers, pastors, evangelists, as well as women being used of God with prophesyings and tongues.

"We have pioneered in these distinctions of our pentecostal, independent leaders, too. Now I use the word 'independent' advisedly; but nevertheless we acknowledge God's selections in these things. The Bible not only speaks of the church at Jerusalem, a holy catholic entity, but also the church at Antioch, finally different and distanced from Jerusalem. And yet, Peter and Barnabas both came to Antioch with a great sense of oversight. So, we must expect for the future our brethren and our sisters to be used of the Lord, individually, as well as their identification with our churches, corporately. As this increases, the pentecostal personalities could be serving the churches and the pastors and other denominational leaderships. Let us keep this truth in mind: there is the Body of Christ; and there are the individual members in the Body of Christ. Leadership and pastors must yield to God's preference of the use of the evangelistic personality instead of just the local church.

"These introductory remarks now must lead us to finances. There is one gift of the Holy Ghost which we have not heard much about, even after fifty years in existence, as pentecostal people. I do not know if it has been ignored or if by oversight we have not seen it. Are we afraid to take this gift to our pentecostal claim of the Gifts of the Spirit? I wish to speak of this in closing this great Convention. I must actually name it so that it will not be forgotten. This gift, itself, is mentioned only once; and the passage is found in First Corinthians, chapter 12, verse 28. It is there in the center of the verse; it is a one-syllable word. It is the gift of 'helps.' Did you catch it? It is the gift of 'helps.' We need the Greek word to underline it. It is the word *antilempsis*, literally meaning, 'so as to support.' It is used in First Thessalonians, chapter 5, verse 14, 'support the weak.' This is found in Vine's Expository Dictionary. Hort, in concluding his studies, defines the ministration as 'anything that would be done for poor or weak or outcast brethren.' I am sure all of us know what 'support' is. We refer to it in our time as 'alimony support,' 'welfare support,' with the meaning of financial and monetary support. This Greek word yields to 'money-helps,' or financial helps, from our financial prosperity and blessing from God. At the center of our belief in prosperity theology, recently confirmed to us through our pentecostal prophets, is the Gift of Helps. The Vatican has known of this Gift for the Church through many years. We must come to know this, too. We have for too long believed that poverty was a way to piety, virtue, and humility. That is not true. We need to do away with that kind of belief. More and more, God is giving us outstanding businessmen, pentecostal businessmen, full-Gospel men. They are coming with great wealth, and we need to see them as a gift of 'helps' to an otherwise fledgling church. There is presently a group of businessmen who call themselves 'The Fulfilled Gospel of the Fulfilled Businessmen.' They, too, are reaching each other around the world.

"Our scholarly bishop extended this very subject, with a broken heart, in the previous message. As God leads us internationally, we must go with the 'support' of His gift of 'helps.' Great days are coming; great opportunities for evangelism; television is untapped yet; we must capture the airways. The entire electronic medium could easily produce an electronic church. If the people cannot or will not come to the church, we will take the church to them. Already, one of our leading pentecostal personalities has commenced requesting the sinner and the believer to place their hands on the television set to receive salvation, healing, or any other answer to prayer. For too long, too many have thought of the television set in the home, with its two antennas on top, as the two horns of the devil. Well, we just got him saved and God will use the devil-box. (several 'Amens' and 'Glory' ejaculations of praise came from the audience.) It will take millions and millions of dollars to initiate such potential resource, and it will take millions more to sustain these ministries. Just as we have heard of other gifts of the Spirit, let us pray for 'helps,' in the plural, that many, many might be used of God to financially support the ministries so contingent upon us.

"As the opening session of our First Quadrennial Conference on Evangelism comes to a close for tonight, I invite you to join Bishop Vincent in prayer, in your hotel room, as he will be praying in his. Pray for the Gift of 'helps' for the hope and challenge of the World-Wide evangelism opportunities before us. We close with the piano and organ playing 'Just As I Am,' and let us think of these words applied to a different purpose than usual. May the personal pronoun, 'I,' be understood of your obedience to be a pentecostal businessman to 'support' the weak and the work. Bishop Fagin, give us the benediction."

LeVon speaks to Gabriel under the prayer that he will have to leave as he mentioned before. He mentioned that he was glad that Gabriel came, and he apologized for his abrupt departure to his responsibility as a superintendent and his board meeting for the organization of the following days of sessions. He urges Gabriel to remember his promise for them to get together soon to talk about the Convention. And Gabriel confirms it again. LeVon closes their last words just before slipping out of the auditorium with.... "Gabriel, I have something very special to request of you at the end of our future get-together and talk. It concerns an opportunity for you to give a lifetime ministry in our denomination. Your scholarly

knowledge and good spirit would make a great contribution
to us. Pray with me about that, too."

Gabriel gave no audible or other reaction or response at
all, but left trembling in his soul.

They both left the auditorium together, but Gabriel left for
the parking lot of the Hinton Convention Center with a deep
aloneness. He was determined he would drive straightway
back to his Georgetown home in Washington, D.C., from
Memphis, throughout the night, instead of selecting a motel
until morning. Gabriel's heart and mind needed the trip back
home to think and pray and meditate and ponder the powerful
evening of words. Thus he did for the hours on the road.

Upon his arrival back home, he took Evangeline in his arms,
held her tightly, spoke of his love for her as if he had been
away from her for half an eternity, and then went for a few
minutes to pray silently with his son, Joseph Paul, who was
now five years old. Afterward Gabriel retired to bed, holding
Evangeline tightly in his arms, reminding himself of how they
did sleep tight at Cabin Peak on their honeymoon. There were
no words uttered by Gabriel concerning the meeting with
LeVon at the Convention Center, but Gabriel said again and
again, "Evangeline, I love you." Evangeline understood all of
the silence. They slept only about two hours late; there was
no classes that day. Gabriel had graduated, even from Graduate
School. And now he must be a man of God or play the fool for
people.

Chapter Eight

The Waiting

(September 13, 1954)

The August 23, 1954, First Quadrennial Conference on Evangelism by the seven historic pentecostal denominations was only eleven days past when Gabriel received a telephone call in the evening from Rev. LeVon Gilbertson. Still excited from their last meeting, LeVon announces his desire to set an appointment together as Gabriel promised. After a discussion of dates, LeVon said his schedule agreed for Friday, September 13, 1954. Gabriel urged LeVon that since he was determined to make the trip to him by automobile, he and Evangeline would be host and hostess of the visit, providing the Friday evening supper and resting bed. Gabriel also suggested that LeVon stay over Sunday, returning leisurely on Monday, the 16th. LeVon thanked him for the invitation, but responded he would have to be in Kingsport, Tennessee, by Sunday afternoon, two o'clock, to preach in one of his churches for a dedication of a new evangelism facility. Gabriel had wanted him to hear his father, Bishop Parsons, preach in nearby Washington that Sunday. But LeVon was happily ready to come for Friday, departing Saturday, whenever their visit and conversations were completed, and said that he would accept the gracious hospitality supporting their serious talk. Of course, also, he wanted to see Joseph Paul Parsons, now five years old, a regular little man of the Parsons house.

After the telephone call arranged everything and concluded, Evangeline immediately talked with Gabriel about the supper she should prepare for LeVon's coming, and of possibly giving some fresh decor to his room. Gabriel agreed.

Gabriel and his young family were enjoying their new home in Georgetown, D.C., after their move from the Old Shady Donnon Road mansion, near the University in North Carolina. They moved to the Washington, D.C., suburbs, near the Georgeton Theological Seminary, for his history and language majors in his Master's Degree, as well as the completion of his Doctorate in Theology.

Another reason for moving back into that area was that his mother, Vera, had died and left a financial birthright to him. His father, Bishop Parsons, was almost sixty years old, the presiding bishop in the Methodist Church of the state of Maryland. Although a portion of this gift was given to Bishop Parsons, yet his heart confirmed the larger portion to go to Gabriel. This totally unexpected income to his mother came from a person she befriended across some years when she was between thirty-five and forty years old. This friend died in late 1952. Gabriel's mother died rather suddenly in early 1953 at the age of fifty-two. This financial gift from his mother gave Gabriel the opportunity to purchase their new home in Georgetown. God had blessed Bishop Parsons with good health and means although he had had it hard in his early ministry. He had a home north of Gabriel, around the circumferential highway of Washington, D.C., in the Takoma Park area.

Also, Gabriel's family was delighted to be able to worship in a number of churches in nearby Maryland, where his father would regularly preach, as well as teach in workshops and conferences and special opportunities opened to him in his office as bishop. His state conference also had about twelve churches in the Metropolitan area of Washington. Gabriel thought this was also good for his son, Joseph Paul, to hear as much of his grandfather's preaching as possible. His father would often invite Gabriel also for special lectures on the Bible and historic or apostolic Christianity in the various districts of Maryland. This kept Gabriel in the proximity for his schooling during that period as well as near, geographically, to his father. His only sister had also died from a previous heart condition, one she had since birth. Gabriel, alone, would be the surviving member of the family of Bishop Thomas A. Parsons, D.D. Gabriel and his family, since moving back to the Washington area, had taken advantage of their residence in the nation's Capital and attended the various opportunities which Evangeline loved because of her husband, and there were many sites which Joseph Paul, even that young, could enjoy. Evangeline was awe-struck by the nation's Capital in contrast to the Land of Evangeline.

Also, the Blue Ridge Mountains were always nearby. With Gabriel's father in the Maryland suburbs, he now had access to his Maryland Conference. His headquarters and offices were located near the Reston, Virginia, Maryland line. When Bishop Parsons was invited to other denominational churches, which was frequent, he would only respond to the invitation of the conservative pulpits and peoples. He was well-known, in his own Methodist Conference, as a conservative, fundamental, Bible-believing preacher to all men. He was highly respected for his character and ethics as well. He had been of the Methodist movement since he was a child, but especially having affinities for John Wesley's Biblical message of heart and hope. Gabriel's grandfather was a lay-minister in the Maryland Conference before Bishop Parsons. Bishop Parsons had nine brothers and sisters and all of their names started with the letter "H." His father wanted all of them to go to heaven when they died. However, Vera, his wife, in some of the young discipline problems of the family, sometimes would remind him that "H" also stood for another place a person could go after death.

The 13th came and LeVon Gilbertson arrived in the

afternoon about 3:30. It was a pleasant September afternoon, and Joseph Paul was playing out on the front porch when LeVon arrived by automobile. LeVon joyfully picked up Joseph Paul and came straight on into the house. Gabriel was in his study, inside the front door straight down the hall to the right, and Evangeline was in the kitchen, having once again checked the decor for the guest room for LeVon. However, Gabriel and Evangeline had heard the commotion stirred by the voice of Joseph Paul ringing out: "Daddy, Daddy, Mister LeVon is here." They all met with jovial hearts in the front foyer of the house. As cordial greetings exchanged, Gabriel set the two ground rules of the visit: one, the entire evening was devoted for the enjoyment of each other; two, tomorrow was set for the appointed "promised talk." Joseph Paul wanted to know if the evening included popcorn. LeVon replied quickly to him, "yes." With that settled and all moving into the living room, happily, Evangeline excused herself, but reminded them that supper was almost ready.

Immediately after supper, Evangeline shared her lovely personality with Gabriel and LeVon with personal remarks and pictures of her marriage to Gabriel. When Gabriel excused himself to be with Joseph Paul and his personal needs for the evening, LeVon could not help but notice the special way in which Evangeline spoke of her husband. He was astounded by her respect for him. However, he had already noticed that in Gabriel towards Evangeline, too. This was now being set forth in her description of her love for Gabriel, as well as sharing the pictures reminding LeVon of their gratitude for his presence as best man in the wedding. LeVon was on the verge of tears but checked them. He only said:

"This is a precious home to me. The love here is singular in my experience as a pastor with people and superintendent with leaders. I meet so many, in these days, that when the honeymoon is over the marriage weakens and seems to be over, too. Do you know that abortions are beginning to appear frequently in our nation? Even the laws formerly binding marriage and home are being weakened now? I am becoming afraid for the families of tomorrow."

Gabriel returned with Joseph Paul; and LeVon, still burdened with his remarks to Evangeline, spoke to Gabriel.

"I was just observing to Evangeline concerning the weakening of the families in our nation and that there seemed to be love for marriage and honeymoon, but not a love in the married life and the home afterwards.

Gabriel, gently and with respected caution to LeVon, responded: "Yes, and we are also concerned with the conditions in the churches of our time as well."

"Yes, of course, responded LeVon." There was some pause and then smiles broadened in order to retreat back to the happiness of the visit with LeVon.

LeVon also retrieved his conversation, in its departure from their pleasantries, and found a half-way house of thought for inquiry.

A little later, before Joseph Paul had to go to bed, popcorn was indeed served. Joseph Paul had been given the minor authority to request popcorn to be served whenever it was appropriate for him to do so when guests were present. But he had been previously cautioned to request it when an appropriate time called for it. At this very moment he did request it, and after a brief word with him about it, Evangeline gave way as well. So within a few moments, with the assistance of his dear mother, of course, popcorn was served by Joseph Paul.

"Gabriel, what have you been doing in these years since you moved back to the Washington area? Of course, I know of your completion of your graduate studies at the University and now your seminary work here at Georgetown."

"Well, I can easily think of three things, and I will present them in priority order at this point in our lives together. First, my heart remains steadfast with the Lord Jesus Christ, and that increases the joy of my earthly life with my dear Evangeline. She is the greatest earthly thing God has ever given me since my birth and my parents. We still deeply love and respect each other, and Joseph Paul is right there in the middle of it all. (small laughter). Second, it has been good to be with my dear father at this time. Since the death of my mother, Dad has faithfully continued on with his ministry for the Lord in his denomination. We have been spiritually refreshed by hearing him preach again. He continues to amaze me in the un-academic sincerity of his love for the Bible. I believe his ministry is blessed with a personal, but simple, anointing of the Holy Spirit. And third, while I was completing my doctoral studies, an opportunity opened for me to be given the privilege of evening lectures, four nights a week. One of my professors, and our academic dean, Dr. Beauchamp Paulson, requested me to give these lectures as a Night Institute at the seminary. Several senators and congressmen in our government, with several of their staff members, had heard me deliver four lectures a little over two years ago. This was in connection with a functional public forum seminar for our day. The lectures, at that time, were "Primitive Christianity for Reformation Times and Our Time."

"They then sought out Dr. Paulson concerning those lectures, expressing that the lectures had met a need in their busy lives. They wanted to know if it was possible to hear a series of lectures on the subject. When Dr. Paulson approached me about the matter, I responded that I would be delighted to further those studies and lectures. Well, much to our surprise, we have maintained this schedule of twelve-week quarters, four times a year, for two years, with a one week break between the quarters. The first class I met with, beginning at 6:45, in the evening, requested that we have a one-hour class period, which gets me back home by 8:00."

"Gabriel! Gabriel! This is an unusual opportunity for you on Capitol Hill. And the subject matter is most unusual for this time in history. What would you possibly deal with from such a subject of history for people like these government officials in this generation?"

"Please excuse me Gabriel," interrupted Evangeline, and she excused herself to LeVon. "It is 8:30, darling Gabriel, but Joseph Paul must go to bed. May we have our regular prayer for him now?"

"Thank you, Evangeline. Yes, we will simply pause right

now and sustain this practice with our son and for our son. We have always, at least one of us, LeVon, kept his bedtime as a time for prayer for him. Sometimes we sing or read a poem or tell a story, and then pray. But since LeVon is our guest tonight, Joseph Paul, we will have him to pray for you. Would you like that, son?"

"Yes, Daddy; yes."

LeVon proceeded in prayer for Joseph Paul, especially, after which he and Joseph Paul embraced. After words of "good night" to Joseph Paul, the conversation between LeVon and Gabriel resumed. Evangeline made preparation for the sleep of Joseph Paul.

"Gabriel, just what would you lecture to the Capitol Hill people from your chosen subject?"

"Well, it had been an old presupposition in my own heart, since my conversion, so I simply thanked the Lord for giving me this opportunity to develop it more completely. The students, with several being rather prestigious people, and others as assistants to them, all live in a radius of twelve blocks of the Capitol which is called Capitol Hill. They live in the nearby, old apartment sections, restored, north, south, east, and west of the national Capitol. These buildings can be no higher than forty feet on the Hill, or they might obscure the view of the Capitol Building itself. Their time is of essence. They must squeeze in almost everything.

"So, they proposed the schedule and I conformed. Many of them are not Christians but are often from such a background. Some are of other religions as well. Others are atheists or at least agnostics; still others are even dabbling in the occult. They are practically unchurched, and some of the problems simply arise out of their work load. They have little confidence and belief in what is going on concerning religion and Christianity in our day. I believe that they see that the historic definition of the New Testament is being lost, at least from their perspective. All I am endeavoring to do is present God and historic Christianity as a plausible, credible presuppositional thought. I am simply hopeful to just get them to think there is the possibility of a true God, and that He created the world and mankind. This was indeed the presupposition that the Apostle Paul took to the Greeks on Mars Hill, the Book of Acts, chapter 17."

"Are many attending such lectures, Gabriel?"

"God gave us about two hundred students the first quarter which has now increased to about three hundred. You must keep in mind that it takes three quarters to complete the course, with one-quarter in the year only for the introductory principles. Therefore, this provides two different audiences who can only spare a quarter for the introductory principles; but there is the three-quarter course, including the introductory principles as well, with a further in-depth presentation. But in both arrangements the number of students is about the same. I should keep you cognizant of the fact that these are simply people who are interested in taking the course rather than work for the credits."

"That's great, Gabriel! What do you share with them, my brother?"

"I am simply endeavoring, through the Word of God and human books, to present three periods of history in my subject title: first, the very early period of Primitive Christianity and the simple faith and doctrine of that first century in knowing God; and, second, to set forth something of the depth and complexity of the knowledge abused in the one thousand years of the Dark Ages, which did burst forth in Reformation Christianity. The third period is marked Remnant Christianity in which God has raised up certain remnant movements in church history to take a stand for historic Christianity whenever a people's hungering for God was threatened with extinction from the public access. My presupposition is that in all history there must be access to the paradox of both of the two major sides of Christianity, actively working in every generation, to know what Biblical and apostolic Christianity is truly about in our own time. It is the definition of New Testament Christianity that I am concerned about in these lectures."

"How's that, Gabriel? I do not fully understand."

"The final point of the presupposition is that Christian faith, for every individual in history, must include all people, whether they be simple, lowly, or even poor; and it must include all people, whether they be intellectual, scholarly, or even rich. The fundamental simplicity of the Gospel is only worship and the doctrine of grace through faith; that is all! And wherever there are the intellectual and the scholarly in history, they must humble themselves to the primitive principle of only worship and the doctrine of grace through faith; that, too, is all!

"However, from that crucial point of regeneration, the new birth, or justification by faith, all Christians must then grow towards an orthodoxy and an orthopraxy that reaches for the deep things of God as revealed in His infallible Word. The simplest summary of this entire presupposition is revealed in the simplistic Manger, and in the complexity of the Cross. However, the joy and victory of it all is that no one has to pursue and know all of the depth and complexity of the Cross of Jesus, because He paid it all without our knowing it all.

"Our priority pursuit of the Gospel only lies in being born spiritually alive again and growing in the grace of the Lord Jesus in the spiritual life of that spiritual birth. I am called upon to use the wisdom of the knowledge of it all in order to bring people back to the Manger, but then on to the Cross. There will always be Man-questions versus God-questions, but no one has to know the complete answers to the God-questions. The Christian is to keep a simple, primitive, obedient heart all the way through his entire life, even if he is endowed with an intellectual gift from God. Only then will the fruit of Christian scholarship be a blessing to all of us. The loss of the plausibility and credibility of the existence of God is the greatest loss of lost men. We will always need to simply worship God; we will always need simple grace through faith."

"But, Gabriel, what are you doing to get them to listen to what seems to me to be a philosophical dissertation?"

"The only answer I could possibly suggest to that is, I am relying upon the fact that God's Word says God's Holy Spirit will illuminate and bless and lead all men into the truth they need in order to know God."

"But Gabriel, it is almost unbelievable to think that any

soul could be saved without the singular method of direct evangelism. All we are doing is introducing all people to Jesus Christ. That is the whole key to what I have been taught and have practiced in Christianity. And here you come along and say that the simplicity of thought in the Gospel is to lead us to think of Theology and Christianity as first being plausible and then credible, leading us on into the theology of the Cross. I do not understand you, Gabriel."

"But my dear friend, LeVon, you must keep in mind that we are living in the time of an apostate Christianity. We cannot easily unravel the erroneous cheap gospel and easy-believism in the minds of the mass public, because they are the ones that have taken the apostate Christianity into their thinking. So, we must go back to a primitive condition, and present the original, simple, pure definition of the Gospel of the Lord Jesus Christ as it was done at the first. We have to reason with people; we have to make plausible the simplest thing to them; and we must get them to see the credibility of God and His Son, and their own urgent need of God. No one will seek God except those who believe they need Him. That is the primitive Christianity we must deal with now. We must see that the apostasy has brought a new, neo-definition of the Gospel which is not the same Gospel as was given to us in the Primitive Christianity of the days of our Lord on earth."

"I think I am beginning to understand you in this, Gabriel, that the very reasoning and thinking of man is also lost and needs to be saved. (a considerable pause). My, what a different need you present. (another pause) What do you think, in the light of this, is the will of God for the rest of your life?"

"Well, first of all, I want to establish that I do not think of myself as some outstanding person, LeVon. I just simply have found myself, observing the public presentation of a worldly and popular gospel, and I cannot but see we are truly losing the New Testament definition of Christianity in our time. The burden has increased in my heart and mind. Since July 10, 1949, I have been waiting on the Lord to know what He would have me do. That day is still marked on my calendar: I was in great need for the Lord of my earthly life that day; and I am still waiting for God to call me, to know, begin, and finish His will, in my generation. LeVon, I am waiting, only waiting on God. (a pause) The Night Institute of these two years has certainly alerted me to the reality that there are some people we will never reach for Christ unless we are enabled by the Holy Spirit to resolve for them some doubts about the basic truths of historic Christianity."

"Gabriel, do you think of these dissertations as being effective for our time, to be received by many more people?"

"My dear LeVon, I do not think of these lectures as anything other than Biblical messages absolutely necessary for the evangelism of souls. I find people who are hungering for God, but do not know how to know Him. I am only starting there where they are and proceeding to hopefully get them to think. There is something about the modern man, now, that is at a loss to understand the phenomenon that is taking place in the Christianity, so-called, of our time. Modern man does not understand the meaning of modern Christianity, so-called, as is presently presented to him." (a long pause)

Certainly, Gabriel had come to the conclusion that their hopeful, nothing-but-pleasant evening would have resulted in favor of his guest; but in reality, it had ended with a number of serious considerations between them. However, Gabriel was comforted by the fact that God had laid the questions raised as all of LeVon and not Gabriel. Gabriel was only responding to questions he had never planned with answers he never thought would have arisen first that evening with LeVon. Gabriel had fully intended to be a host to his friend in the home of Gabriel, Evangeline, and Joseph Paul.

The evening was over. Both retired, after another prayer. They departed for rest as Gabriel smiled and said:

"Let us rise early, 6:30, if you will; I will cook; Evangeline is giving way for our day together. After our breakfast, I will show you a secret place, my *ben most bore*. Good-night, LeVon; rest well!"

"Good-night to you, Gabriel. You have already given me much to think about, even though it is different from any discussion I have ever known concerning Christianity."

However, the night was not over for LeVon as he did lie awake on his bed to ponder and ponder and ponder, waiting for the morning light and Gabriel.

Chapter Nine

The Institute

(September 14, 1954; October, 1951 - October, 1953)

At the 6:30 morning breakfast, Gabriel made his special "Blue Ridge Cheese Omelet" for LeVon and served it with the "Parsons' Patty Sausage." LeVon took coffee; Gabriel took tea. They both seemed unusually hungry. This particular "Omelet" and the "Parsons' Patty Sausage" are commemorative of Gabriel's complete flop in trying to prepare breakfast for Evangeline on Christmas morning in the Washington, D. C. apartment while she remained in bed. He took too much time in teasing Evangeline while she was still asleep. But Gabriel perfected the breakfast in the later years but continued to remember it by the names given to the first effort.

Afterwards Gabriel took LeVon to the third floor of his home, up around and to the third floor after ascending two rather ornate staircases from the first floor. This old Georgetown home was a part of the original "Threlkeld's Addition," and the house itself was built before the Civil War. In the course of the ongoing years since the Civil War, this stately and unique Italianate flat-front brick, three-story, plus basement, Victorian house had needed regular alterations in

105

its maintenance.

"Upon their entrance to the third floor, led by Gabriel, LeVon was taken aback as he saw a beautiful long room, running the entire length of the roof line of the house. Of the five thousand square feet of the home, this third floor occupied almost eight hundred square feet. The room was filled with the decor of paintings, tapestries, and beautified maps of the Land of Evangeline. It was all there, its history, in art forms, scottish plaids, scenes of Grand Pré, pictures of Gabriel and Evangeline in their wedding, their wedding certificate, the Bay of Fundy, Westport Island, Briar Island, the Ferry, the Bluenose, Gull Rock, Digby, and Evangeline's very yellow house of her birth. The entire room was now without any partition except for an alcove of another eighty square feet used as an entrance to all of its unusual beauty.

"Gabriel, this is no mere attic; it is just beautiful! What is going on here in this room?"

"Evangeline did it and made a surprise of it for me on our fifth wedding anniversary in 1952."

"It is beautiful! A lot of thought was lovingly put into it." (pause) "And there's the very yellow house, and all the greeneries in glorious green."

"Yes, LeVon, we want to keep our natural love and our spiritual faith, 'until death us do part.'" (a long pause while LeVon continues to look, including every inscription, until he is satisfied)

"This is the place of 'My Watch'" said Gabriel.

"Yes, and much of your huge library is here. I saw the other part, I presume, in your study downstairs, at the entrance to the home itself. I looked in on that while you were preparing breakfast."

"This library here only concerns history, three histories: World Civilization, Church History, and Remnant Christian History. The Land of Evangeline is situated, as you can see, LeVon, interwoven more in the midst of the room and spaced between the bookshelf sections, along with, of course, remembrances of the Blue Ridge Mountains. My study, downstairs, is dedicated to only the Bible, God's Word, theology, languages, Biblical history, and other subjects. Bible history is the only history inspired and revealed by God. This history, here in this room, concerns man's history, even church history as lived by man. Every Christian's life must have revealed doctrine, as the first, foundational floor of life. This assures us of our salvation 'by grace, through faith,' so we may have saving, orthodox truth. Every Christian's life must also have revealed narratives, histories, stories, to set forth the saving power of God in man's personal, private practice of the Christian life—called orthopraxy. Then, too, every married couple, as Christians, must have a private life in their love for each other, a land of their roots and love in beauty."

"Yes, I think I understand, Gabriel. Every born again Christian must know Primitive Christianity and Reformation Christianity. You are really endeavoring to live for Christ, together, in love, and for others to do the same, before their Lord."

"I thought this would be a good place for us to have the 'talk' you requested and I promised. Have a seat anywhere and be comfortable, LeVon."

The two sat down and simply remained silent for several minutes. There in "The Watch," LeVon had taken about forty minutes to let the meaning of the room sink down into his mind and heart.

"Gabriel, already, since arriving into your lovely home, I have realized several important distinctives that have paved the way for our talk. First, the beauty and simplicity of your home, family, and spirit here speak loud against the age in which we live. I have not witnessed anything like this anywhere I have been. Second, the early conversation of last evening brought me to the need on my bed last night to ponder and ponder what you said. In recalling to you the brief conversation I had with Evangeline about trends in our country — my burden at that time being abortion and divorce — you responded that the church, also, had brought concern to your heart. Well, it is not usual in our time to speak against the church much, because of the optimism and positive attitudes which are beginning to attract the leadership of the churches, as well as many of its people. And this is especially true because of the post-war desires to regain all lost hopes during World War II. Then, when you mentioned your own ministry of the last two years in the Night Institute and spoke of a direction in a ministry of dealing with people's thoughts and their thinking as a basis of leading them to Christ, I was astounded. What kind of evangelism do you identify this to be?"

"Well, my dear friend, I have not actually named it as a method of evangelism; that does not seem to be too important, for I think that word 'method' is too limited, as well as what is being meant, in our time, in using the word 'evangelism.' What I believe regeneration is suppose to do, according to the Word of God, is not only to save us, but change our entire life and way of thinking. I think of this truth as a 'conversion.' That is the best word I can think of: a 'conversion' to Christianity. I believe modern Christianity tends to isolate the Gospel into a 'new concept' entirely, and it should not be done in that way."

"But so that I might be able to identify this for my own understanding, what kind of evangelism do you believe it should be called?"

"My thoughts have been along the line of 'presuppositional apologetics for conversion evangelism,' or reaching the sinner in the actual context in which his own present presupposition is in his own heart. Every person in the world, because of his birth, culture, and daily practice of life, has been forming a basic presupposition of his own heart. Everything he does passes through that heart-presupposition, and his heart-eyes has that kind of viewing-glasses towards everything else. We are seeking to speak, 'a word in season to him that is weary,' in the presupposition of his own sinful heart that a Christian conversion might result, LeVon. (a pause) In other words, we are seeking to find the presupposition of an individual or movement or crusade, and meet that presupposition with the appropriate truth that individual identity stands in greatest need of. I regret that this sounds so complicated, but the matter is truly simple. Jesus had the great advantage of looking into the hearts of any crowd or individual and reading the need of that heart and the truth of that heart like we would read an ordinary book."

"Presuppositional apologetics for Conversion evangelism, Gabriel? Well, that immediately gets us into the kind of language which is obvious in your subject of 'Primitive Christianity for Reformation Times and For our Day.'"

"I suppose it does sound a bit philosophical or intellectual, but I do not know of any other way to get to the need of the human heart in the horrifying maze of current theological thought and practice in evangelism."

"What would you say is the basic root, in its most simple language to me?"

"LeVon, this is the real question, as you have identified it. The answer to that is what drove me into my own ministry of presupposition for my life with Evangeline. And that bottom line, of necessity, must be understood as the basis of Primitive Christianity. Allow me to place it that simple, for I return to this in almost every lecture in the Institute. It is this: 'All evangelism must be, in our time, based upon a conversion to a singular end. That end is to exalt the Lord Jesus Christ in everything that we do. Period.'"

"Gabriel, you mean that is it? The whole point, period?"

"That is it, LeVon, my friend. We have lost that presupposition. The moment of evangelism is not the end; the salvation of the soul is not the end. Not even the precious truth concerning the Elect, which I reverently respect if it is not in the 'hyper-position' of a person's theology. Allow me to say again: Evangelism has as its only purpose that a man is saved by the free grace of God for the purpose of exalting the Lord Jesus Christ, in everything, and forever. This would include our eternal service to God in a glorified state, with our election and predestination having been brought to its own blessed fruition."

"Gabriel, Gabriel, there is no harder task for a Christian leader or a Christian layman to do than change the modern thoughts of this generation on the method of evangelism to accept and believe that."

"LeVon, I believe you are correct. (a pause) No, nothing

short of leading souls through the door of the simplicity of changing the high-powered talk of 'Evangelism Methodology' back to the early table-talk of the modest homes of the evangelism in the Book of Acts. After the Day of Pentecost, and we believe it was for about eight years, all the Christians did was go to Solomon's Porch in Jerusalem to hear the Apostles, and then return to the homes of their offered hospitality, with free meals and lodgings, and continue stedfastly in the apostle's doctrine, breaking of bread, in prayers, in one accord, from house to house. They had public church in the morning and home church in the afternoon I suppose. This simple presupposition brought about the good and sanctified revolution that turned the world upside down in the time of Primitive Christianity."

"Gabriel, what I appreciated about your being with me at the First Quadrennial Conference on Evangelism, and to this very moment, is that you have not lambasted me or the Conference with condemnation first, but you have sought out, with wisdom, a way to speak to me for the sake of your heart. I believe that is a part of that Primitive Christianity you talk about, too."

"LeVon, LeVon, my dear friend, the only motive we must keep is to help others to understand the Word of God. We will not win this war, against this apostasy, with only militancy; we must seek wisdom and magnificence. It is too late; time is of essence, now. I do pray you are right about me, for I realize what is at stake in the hope of winning souls for Jesus, against the backdrop of what is powerfully going on in the false and hopeless end of modern, modern methodology; and they are two extremely different things."

"What would you give as examples in the past?," responded LeVon. "Give something akin to your heart, Gabriel, and of this time? I know you do not think that you are the only one in the world with this Primitive Christianity in a reformation intelligence."

"Yes, I hope your kind words are right and I receive them from you, my friend, as from the Lord. (a pause) I know there have been many back in history who saw a multitude of changes in the definition of Christianity as the apostasy of Rome developed a deeper and more subtle 'neo' in order to survive in its own power. In answering you, LeVon, I do not mean, at all, that I would commend all of the groups I will name. But first, I believe, as I have alluded to them before, there have been only three kinds of so-called Christianity in history, past: Roman Catholic Christianity; Ecumenical Christianity; and Remnant Christianity. The first, Roman Catholicism, was growing during the primitive period and reached its full apostasy at the Council of Trent, in the same century, but in reaction to Martin Luther and the Reformation. In the second, there has always been the hope of an ecumenical movement either against Rome or a return to Rome. We can see this in Constantine, Erasmus, the Anglican Church, the Cults who try to identify themselves as Christians in their time, by either joining in with Rome or against Rome. There are many more like this. And, in the third, the remnants are many: the Moravians, the Waldenses, the Hussites, the Bogomils, the Ana-Baptists, the Huguenots, the Reformers, the Puritans and Pilgrims, the fundamentalists, etc.

"It is the firm conviction of my heart in studying these that probably all of them longed for a return to Primitive Christianity. They did not get back to any historical re-enactment of it because you cannot go back into history itself. But a person may have the love of the spirit and youthfulness of that first century in Christ Jesus. The Bible reveals it. These unpretentious, modest, and sometimes immature movements stayed total destruction and a great loss. Some of them are questionable. However, like Ephesus of old, Jesus rebuked the surrounding situation by stating, you 'have left your first love,' and requested the church to repent or He would remove their candlestick. So, it seems clear that Primitive Christianity and Reformation Christianity are our best representations in church history for what we need. A number of the remnants were insufficient to the time; some ended up even as heretics. The orders of Romanism, such as Cluny, the Dominicans, the Franciscans, etc., were friars for Romanism; but there were a few, even in Romanism, who hungered for reform. They are not perfect models, but the presupposition of them cannot be improved, as far as I know."

"Gabriel, Gabriel, Gabriel! This is a revolution."

"Yes, I suppose some would call it that. But for Americans we had a time in the birth of our own nation when two revolutions were going on at the same time; one was good and successful; the other was bad and failed."

"When was that, Gabriel?"

"The American Revolution and the French Revolution. The word 'revolution' should not be considered to be the very same as the word "revolt, anarchy, etc. It can be also used as an honorable word, indeed."

"Gabriel if God sends a clear separation between all the popular, current methods of evangelism to the Christian denominations in this century, it could be the greatest revival in history. (a pause) But my dear friend, Gabriel, I cannot see our pentecostal denominations, presently, even remotely headed in that direction. I believe we have tasted of the 'new wine,' which you would say is not the 'old wine,' and most leaders, laymen, and churches have come across the railroad tracks to never return."

"LeVon, you have been in my prayers that God would use you as a puritan in a decaying system, to hopefully bring a return back to early Christianity. I am acquainted with some of the history of the early pentecostalists. They were headed in a different direction in those days. Their longing for the Holy Spirit centered around a clean, pure, godly life instead of the Gifts of the Spirit. They were hungering for purity, not power!"

"You are correct in that conclusion, Gabriel, and we have not arrived at this point except through much debate, controversy, and sorrow with many of those early pentecostalists. Possibly, we could be rightfully accused of never publicly acknowledging what those early pentecostalists sacrificed that we might be where we are today. The 1950s will be the deciding decade of the actual direction we will take. I am deeply troubled by your statements and your studies."

"Be of good courage, LeVon; do not allow your possible

influence for the truth to be lost. I do not desire to simply condemn and deplore you; I desire to entreat and pray for you. I saw your enthusiasm at the Conference, and I would like to believe, today, your motive is for the souls of men. However, I am confident that modern evangelism, itself, and of itself, does not have a scriptural motive behind all of it, and we cannot get there without the truth."

"I had also come to visit you on this appointment, not only to know your heart and belief concerning our Conference, but to hope that you might consider choosing my denomination for the ministry. It was your scholarship and Christian life that motivated me to hope for that. It may be that I desired your ministry among us for a human reason alone. I do not believe the Lord would have me urge any further this hope of my heart upon you, but I would appreciate it very much if you would consider several places in our state conference and others who might would welcome your presentations of lectures, messages, and writings, because of your hope of magnificence with your militancy. Would you consider such an acceptance if I assured you I would be seeking opportunities and places where wisdom would prevail? I must admit, at this time in my life, I do not embrace your thinking about all of this as you do."

"At this moment, I am thinking of my esteemed Dr. Robert J. Jonathan, Jr., president of the Bible Christian University and my studies. He was the kind of man who endeavored to encourage and assist a young student who was seeking right with the truth of the Holy Scriptures. I will certainly promise you that if and when you might contact me, I will be very prayerful and hopeful that I could be a blessing. I will be cautious, because I believe the Bible urges clearly the need of our separation from the apostasy in all their fellowships. I know of no other position to take."

"What do you think is on the horizon, now, Gabriel?"

"Well, it is only my personal thoughts. Personally, I claim nothing but a desire for the leading and understanding from the Lord. I am nothing in it all. My present ministry, although unusual in the Night Institute, is yet in the Hands of the Lord for the future. However, it appears to me that the 1950s will set in place something of a permanent direction and purpose for the Christianity of the time. In your Conference, Bishop Malls, Chairman of Methodology of Evangelism, gave his friendly view of four great influences born in the middle 1940s and early 1950s. I fear that these four influences will, in reality, be foes of historic Biblical Christianity instead of friends. You will remember them, I'm sure: 'The National Interaction of Christian Evangels,' of 1942; 'The Evangelical World Seminary,' of 1947; the religious periodical, *Contemporary Christianity,* of 1952; and, the evangelist, Dr. Willie Wheyman. All of these agree that methodology is the main quest for the future evangelization of the world."

"Gabriel, it is not necessary for you to respond to everything you heard in our Convention to communicate your heart to me. You have answered my request in a better way than I had thought to guide our time together with an outline of questions directly resulting from our beloved bishops. It may be that I would like to call upon you for that. I may. Possibly, you could send that to me through our future correspondences together. I do ask you to pray for me; I am in a place of indecision about all of this. In fact, I am consumed with great enthusiasm and excitement about what I am doing in my ministry. I want to be honest with you, my friend. My heart is indeed dedicated to evangelism as I understand it."

"Yes, LeVon, and I am, too. Sobering things stand before us. I only urge you to keep a daily 'Watch Out' in your position in the secret of your heart. The secret things passed through my heart here today in this room are the only secrets my beloved Evangeline does not bear. Although I do not care if she knows them, they are mainly burden-secrets, confidence-secrets and encouragement-secrets. To tell the secrets of the 'Watch Out' of my heart could either bring me to bitterness or to pride. Therefore, I promise you, I will bear this meeting we have had with confidence, and I do not want to be your enemy. Rather, I will be praying for you as a friend. I trust you will build a place in your life, your *ben most bore,* which simply translated means 'a secret hole.' Go to that secret place, regularly, and 'Watch' in these days through care and prayer. Let us seek a conclusion that will not only glorify Christ, but keep ourselves in the love of Christ. (a pause) I love you, LeVon."

After an embrace and prayer, both Gabriel and LeVon descended both of the beautiful staircases, back to Evangeline and Joseph Paul. There was a precious departure from LeVon, with ever-conscious hearts that the forces of that day would not bring the loss of a precious friend. They departed a sorrow of joy.

Chapter Ten

The Return

(1954 - 1956)

Back in July of 1949, Gabriel was graciously delivered from a struggle of the flesh through the power of God. His victory comforted him through his study of the example of Jacob across the river Jabbok. In reality, the scriptural pattern, to Gabriel, was leading him back to his personal Bethel. The meeting of the Angel of the Lord, which Gabriel understood to be the pre-incarnate manifestation of the Lord Jesus Christ in His provision for Jacob in his struggle of the flesh, meant that the Lord Jesus would lead His servants in all times of their own personal history and walk with Him. At Bethel, this was an Old Testament theophany of God's Son. The victory of that wrestling struggle put Jacob on the road back to Bethel. This, too, exemplified to Gabriel there was always a need to return to the primitive time of his first love for Christ, as well as the primitive 'first principles' of his conversion to Christianity. Of course, this would emphasize the first 'Bethel,' as a signal type of regeneration, to always be the true point of reference for salvation by grace through faith in the Lord Jesus. No other experience, act, ceremony, baptism, or other would be allowed in Gabriel's mind to be paramount or primary to anyone's conversion to Christ and Christianity.

So, Gabriel's struggle of the flesh was behind him. The Biblical truth of that was centered in Romans, chapter 6, in his 'reckoning,' 'yielding,' and 'obedience' to Christ in a surrender that would place the flesh behind him, always there, but not as dominion and lord of his life. Going back to Bethel was a full return from twenty years of life in which Jacob was deceived and failed in his relationships with God. Jacob desired a full return to the principles of Bethel. So, this was Gabriel's plan before the Lord, too.

He had come to see that he was viewing the contemporary people of his generation identifying with twentieth-century Christianity when he attended the First Quadrennial Conference on Evangelism at the request of LeVon Gilbertson. He saw and heard the testimony of the neo-pentecostal bishops and the seven historic pentecostal denominations in their second and third generations. In reality, however, to the earlier pentecostalists, the call to holiness in the Christian's life, not the Gifts of the Spirit, had been the reason for the pentecostal teachings of the Holy Spirit in their time.

Gabriel, through all his readings, began to see that like any other truth down through history the new definition of Christianity would substantially lose the first Primitive Christianity meaning, just as the later generations of pentecostalism had lost the meaning of the early, first generation of pentecostalists. In fact, Gabriel knew that the neo-pentecostalists were simply another part of the neo-christianity espoused by the other major protestant denominations. Gabriel could identify the pulse of the upbeat heat in neo-pentecostalism in their methodological zeal for evangelism, having already been conditioned to the Gifts of the Holy Spirit in a new definition, and he knew this was to be their modern direction. He realized the neo-pentecostalists had allowed extant revelation to be accepted in visions, dreams, tongues, impressions, demonstrations, and audible voices, so-called, by the popular pentecostal evangelists of the second and third generations.

There was no historical evidence that there was any common definition between the earliest pentecostalists, in the true remnant, and what was going on now among the neo-pentecostalists. Definitions of pentecostalism, gifts, manifestations, and ecstatics were always in a subjective state of experiential definition, continuing on and differing more with each generation. The later neo-pentecostalists, in fact, were beginning to openly attack and intimidate the Biblical, more fundamental, early remnant within the earlier pentecostalists. There had been excesses found among the earlier pentecostalists, but there were strong men who would deal with them, wisely, prudently, firmly, and cast the excesses aside. This was particularly seen in the local churches, conferences, and board meetings behind the scenes. The later neo-pentecostal historians would not include that other side in their histories.

There were many in the earlier days who took a true stand against the unfundamental rejection of the old landmarks of true historic Christianity among them. It was in the 1950s that Gabriel saw the departure of the pentecostalists from their legacy and their more modest heritage and birthright. There were bishops in those earlier days who took their stand, were crucified in their reputation, or downgraded out of the appointment of their pastorates by enemies within their denominations; and those earlier bishops died of broken hearts, just as in the days of Baptist, Methodist, and Presbyterian soldiers of the Cross before them. Gabriel's dad, Bishop T. H. Parsons, had given his life to the preaching and teaching of the Word of God and had seen certain pentecostal heresies taking his own denomination.

A great number of methodists were indeed in the First Quadrennial Conference on Evangelism. They had come to that Conference, having departed the methodist church to join the neo-pentecostalists, and had become members of one of the seven pentecostal denominations. The 1950s marked the decade of change to compromise and neo-pentecostalism from that section of Christianity which had the last, true affinities with Reformation Christianity.

Gabriel, from his studies, believed that all major denominations, formerly related to Reformation Christianity, were also in process of departing from their historical positions and, undoubtedly, there would be neo-presbyterians, neo-baptists, neo-methodists, neo-Lutherans, neo-calvinists, neo-wesleyans, etc., who would ultimately become a part of the ecumenical movement back to Rome. At least, Gabriel was going to study these movements and see if his present appraisal was true.

Just two years before that First Quadrennial Conference on Evangelism convened, Gabriel was given an opportunity from God to have his Night Institute, urged by Dr. Beauchamp Paulson, because he, too, was watching the demise of the historic and apostolic Christianity of Biblical principles in the seminary itself. This was beginning to appear across America and would reach its fruition in the 1960s. Gabriel's doctoral dissertation on "Primitive Christianity for Reformation Times and For Our Day," had been a leading of the Holy Spirit, he believed, and would be related to his future ministry.

He was actually giving these lectures as he was concluding his own research and writing to finalize his dissertation for the Georgeton Theological Seminary. Dr. Paulson, in his discernment of the time, saw its value and urged Gabriel to proceed. However, after two years, Gabriel and Dr. Paulson realized the waning of true interest, which often deteriorated into an argumentative situation of the students within their own backgrounds after some of the night classes. Yet, it was an excellent window through which Gabriel was to see the changes in contemporary Christianity which were coming to the schools, denominations, and the churches. Gabriel was thankful that he had had that window of sight along with the conclusions of his own dissertation, and that the students of the Night Institute were open to his lectures. They respected him, but gave argumentation to others concerning the disturbing sessions. It was a blessing that God granted respect between the teacher and his students.

The second year of the Night Institute concluded the eight

quarters by the last of August 1954, and it was agreed to have a pause from the new fall quarter, which would have been the beginning of a third year. The previous third quarter had suffered some decline in the enrollment, although it was substantially good. Dr. Paulson and Gabriel agreed to this change. It was their hope that this quarter-break and a time of reflection might even stir up more interest for a later return to the Institute sessions.

So, Gabriel and Evangeline, with Joseph Paul, would return for his studies again at the Bible Christian University in Grandville, North Carolina. Only because of his heart's pull for accurate research on the times in which he lived was he constrained to further his studies, possibly for a Ph.D. This was to take him into other disciplines besides English Bible, theology, and history. Evangeline, continually seeing the weakness of contemporary music, believed she should further her studies — perhaps for her Master's degree in musicology. Her undergraduate studies had been as a voice major and a speech minor. Both Gabriel and Evangeline believed that these studies were necessary if they were to follow the Lord for the purposes of their ministries in these times.

Most of all, however, Gabriel wanted to seek meetings with the president.

Now that they had moved back to the University and were situated in Grandville, in a different rented home, Gabriel made an appointment with Dr. Jonathan. It was only to be an acquaintance appointment and a renewal of their friendship. Of course, they had maintained a good relationship in their correspondences with each other, yet this meeting was necessary. For that particular day, the president's time was limited, and Gabriel never desired to impose himself.

Gabriel had kept his lovely home in Georgetown, a home of historic importance in its architecture and legacy of existence. Georgetown had many homes such as this registered in the Historical Society surrounding Washington, D.C., both in Virginia and Maryland. He would only rent the first floor out, and only to a special couple who held Gabriel in high regard. They had attended three quarters in the Night Institute. The second and third floors were locked up with all of the furnishings of Gabriel and Evangeline.

The first floor study library had been moved to the second floor. The "Watch" room, "The Land of Evangeline," as it was described, remained exactly as they left it. They were sure to preserve their "primitive love" for each other through the companionship of this little place "up high" in the house. They were fortunate, they believed, to have found such a fine couple to keep, care, and live there. Because of its location and legacy, they received a good price on the rental, and to say the least, their finances would become strained in their move back to the University. The last year in Georgetown, just prior to their departure, Evangeline had their second child, a lovely girl. Soma Jeanne was born January 2, 1954, the year they made their return to the Bible Christian University for further studies.

The meeting of Gabriel with the president was indeed a rich blessing to both of them. Although it was brief, they sustained a lasting friendship until the president died. He lived to preach his last sermon into the time of the later ministries of Gabriel. Their conversation at this time brought them both up-to-date in their respective ministries as well as the conditions of the various religious movements in the world, and especially within the protestant churches and Romanism. After the personal greetings between each other subsided, they were seated in Dr. Jonathan's study with its unusual and unique decor. His love for all the arts obviously continued in his busy life until the end of his days. Gabriel had kept up his correspondence with him and continued to give a somewhat detailed report of the Night Institute and the First Quadrennial Conference on Evangelism in Memphis, Tennessee. Dr. Jonathan was always current with the developments of the fundamentalists and the apostate movements.

So, once again, Gabriel meets him in his study. They had been in conversation for several minutes.

"Yes, Gabriel, these type of conferences and crusades on

122

evangelism are convening all across our nation. The Bible has prepared us, and the Holy Spirit desires to enable us in the forthcoming battles ahead for all Christian leaders in all fields of calling and administrations. We must remain true to the Lord Jesus, no matter where truth leads us."

"You are correct, as usual, my esteemed brother," responded Gabriel. "I think of you often, when I think of the battle, for I have followed your agenda of travels, teachings, and the leading of the University testimony. I pray everyday for this place; that its historic Christian witness will never perish in the earth. The new methodology of evangelism must be checked, and you are a remarkable influence in not only the pulpit but complementing the message of grace with another distinct and unusual influence in the seven aspects of culture as founded so carefully here. You apply the same principles with the singular affinity of the Gospel of the Lord Jesus Christ."

"Gabriel, of course, I receive your refreshing correspondences to me from time to time, and now your return to the University here is an indication of your own dedication for the future. Has God settled your life with a personal calling to the ministry at this point in time?"

"No, my dear brother. One of the main reasons for my return at this time, to 'my Bethel,' is to know God's direct will for a definite ministry for my life and that of Evangeline with me."

"I trust that your Bethel-return will be enriched of the Lord to be your 'El-Bethel'; and that the 'God of Bethel,' and the 'God of the House of God,' will direct your house, in the land of your own Evangeline, through all the days of your entire life. I have been following your agenda, too, and you have pleased me, my dear son in the faith. You are becoming quite a respected, young scholar. Even Senator Charles Baker has heard good reports of you on Capitol Hill in Washington. For him to make such remarks is a commendation within itself. Although I know him well, he does not profess to be a Christian. However, I think he wants everyone else to be."

"I have only heard of him through Dr. Paulson, one of my professors in the seminary; but I believe we could truly say that God has blessed our unpretentious ministry in the Night Institute. I believe contact was made with appropriate individuals on the Hill who are in dire need of God in these troubled times."

"I'm sure, my friend, Gabriel." (pause)

"I thank God for you, my brother; you have often assisted me, as a Christian, with your wide background and discernment of people and things."

"I know your heart, Gabriel, and I prize your friendship. Keep your primitive spirit with the Lord and launch out into the deep. Also, I have wanted you to do two things for me out there in the future. I have been thinking of this for several years. One is to attend our First World Congress on Fundamentalism. We are planning this out in the future. I want you to be one of the night speakers or lecturers for our need and time in the sessions. Also, I want you to be an overseas lecturer for our new faculty for summer foreign study formats abroad, and it would be most appropriate to follow through with your recent studies in the Night Institute for an international audience. These lectures will be technically translated into at least six other languages as you deliver them in English. This will be a summer extension study from the University here. I hope to be with you for this initial overseas establishment of the University studies. We have set no dates at this time. What do you think, Gabriel?"

"Well, my dear brother, I did not expect this. You have honored me. I came back here to receive studies for my own need, and you have placed me in the giving position. I must admit we will be straining the words of our Lord, in Paul's writings, 'It is more blessed to give than to receive.' I think, in my case, of being the giver I will be in more trouble than a blessing."

"I am sure the Lord would be pleased with your ministry in this matter. Keep in mind, however, that both the door of the possibilities of World Congresses on Fundamentalism, in different foreign countries, as well as the possibility of regular summer extension studies abroad could become a permanent schedule each year. We believe that God could use these specialized opportunities to meet the battle against historic Christianity and the apostasy. I definitely believe you should head up theology and history in our series of lectures. It appears, as is true in each of our other selections for professors, that you are well suited for such an opportunity and battlefield. This is not a nice request; it is a desperate request. Will you do this, Gabriel?"

"I fear that I must bow, humbly, to your request, my dear brother. I do not know of anything that I, personally, have done to seek this. I must accept this moving of ocean waves to my shore as drawing me into a definite calling for my life. I don't see how I can reject you, dear brother. I am believing that the scriptures led me back to 'my Bethel' and that the Holy Spirit is leading, in another way, through you. The problems and circumstances of our time, and especially this particular time in my own life, demands obedience in my heart. I trust you see my ministry and ability suitable for such a task better than I might see it today."

"Let us pray, Gabriel; I want to pray for you especially for this task."

He prayed and Gabriel departed.

Gabriel, later, would always acknowledge that this prayer period brought a much-needed, but quiet infilling of the Holy Spirit as he said "yes" to the open door of this invitation by the president..

"I will keep in touch with you about all developments in these things, for it is only in the stage of planning and inquiring for dates, places, and other details. It may be up to five years from now.

"Then it's settled, Gabriel, and as I told you on the telephone after you arrived back to Grandville, I will be taking you to a Chinese lunch today. It's about that time, and after I speak a word to my secretary, I will meet you down in the foyer. I'll only be a few minutes."

After the tasty oriental lunch and a fresh humorous time, Gabriel returned home to Evangeline. He reiterated the contents of this visit with Dr. Jonathan. Evangeline was greatly interested in the possibilities of an open door overseas, both in the Congresses and the University Extension Studies. She immediately was concerned about the children, and such opportunities as a permanent residence for the summer there, and travels to other lands for the family, and Gabriel and herself for the Congresses. Evangeline assumed that the entire family would go all the time to all the places, together. Gabriel endeavored to calm her hopefully adventurous heart with the fact that absolutely no details had been proposed regarding the thoughts she had about it. In fact, Gabriel did not remember that the name of Evangeline had even been brought up in the previous discussions.

Besides that, Gabriel had made a commitment to Dr. Jonathan without consulting Evangeline at all. It was all so sudden. This would be the very first time in their marriage that Gabriel made at least a mental decision which was not discussed with Evangeline. It appeared, from the little information received, that possibly there would be separations of him from his family that might be hard.

A strange and foreboding spirit accompanied Gabriel's heart that evening, and for several days, as Joseph Paul, Soma Jean, and Evangeline could not seem to do enough for Gabriel in their love and expectation of the days ahead. Of course, it was all prompted by the happy heart of Evangeline. Even Joseph Paul announced popcorn again for the evening, which custom he had been growing away from but had not completely discontinued.

So, Gabriel made his return to his honorable friend, and he was now to be introduced to the remnant movement of Fundamentalism. Would this return be "Bethel?" or, "El-Bethel?"

But one thing was sure: the selection of "Theology and History" was the right choice of subjects for the leading of God for years in Gabriel's heart and life. These are the two hinges on the door of primitive-reform Christianity.

Chapter Eleven

The Fundamentals

(January-November, 1957)

The studies for Gabriel's Ph.D. were completed in two full years, including three summers. Evangeline, also, had completed her Master's degree in musicology. The year was now 1957. At the time of their graduation they were both thirty years old. A third child was born August 8, 1955, a boy, and his name was Ariel John. Joseph Paul was eight years old; Soma Jeanne, three; and, Ariel John, two.

God had smiled much upon this family. Their tenth wedding anniversary would come December 20, 1957, which was the mid-two-year period of the recent graduate studies.

The concluding months of 1954 were something of a vacation at home in Grandville, although the family did visit their home in historic Georgetown with a make-shift apartment of four and a half rooms on the second floor. They were fortunate to have had something of a private entrance from the enclosed large vestibule of the home, which kept the first floor completely private. They could enter and exit without disturbing the couple on the first floor. Michael and Michelle Olsen still desired to continue their rental agreement for the future. They did not have children and planned to buy or build their own home later. They had become Christians and ascribed their conversion to the studies of Gabriel in the Night Institute, and were both successful in their respective businesses.

Fundamentalism did the most to stem the ecumenical tide of liberalism that was increasing in the denominations. Many unknowing individuals, who thought Fundamentalism might be a growing cult of dogmatism, yet realized the truth of the situation as they studied its history. Fundamentalism was still remembered from a scholarly origin and sponsored an evangelistic fervor according to the Holy Scriptures. There were a number of outstanding scholars in several fields of study, such as Biblical and critical analysis in Biblical languages. In fact, a number of students from these scholars were still leading in their respective denominations and ecclesiastical posts.

Although there are at least nineteen denominations originally represented in Fundamentalism, yet it is true that the three largest denominations were represented in the first generation of Fundamentalism by: Dr. J. Gresham Machen from the Presbyterians; Dr. William Bell Riley from the Baptists; and Dr. Bob Jones, Sr., from the Methodists. Dr. John Randall Wells, another Baptist, was representative of a first-generation fundamentalist and typical of that group. Dr. Walter A. Maier, a Lutheran, was a strong radio preacher who would be classified on the fringe of Fundamentalism. Bishops Thomas A. Melton and Hubert T. Spence were the only two early men of pentecostalism who stood for Fundamentalism in principles against the growing excesses and extant revelationalism of neo-pentecostalism. Of course, there were independent pastors and ministers who came from these and other denominations, but they were fewer in number. To this day, the writings of the second generation, in or out of Fundamentalism, mention these men in their writings of the historical birth of Fundamentalism. One noted writer on Fundamentalism placed Edward J. Carnell, originally from a fundamentalist background, who became the second president of Fuller

Theological Seminary, as committing suicide. Dr. Carnell lamented, in his later years, that Dr. J. Gresham Machen was, indeed, the father of Fundamentalism and that he regretted this from such a great man.

Fundamentalists gained some followers and support from all of the leading denominations for a time. Every denomination that still identified itself with the Protestant Reformation became a part of this solid testimony of the fundamentalists. Each individual minister or church that did carry spiritual sympathy with the movement contributed to its success in evangelism and revivalism. Fundamentalism transcended denominationalism, a local pastor, or a denominational leader. Many across the spectrum of denominationalism joined in when Fundamentalism was born in history. Gabriel's father, Bishop T. H. Parsons, attended the earlier meetings presenting himself as a fundamentalist, and was accepted as such.

We cannot really estimate the spiritual value and scholarly impact the early fundamentalists had upon its own movement and the world. Much of the old liberalism was defeated by them. However, there was a new enemy on the horizon, and there was no need for them to go back and shoot cannon balls at dead dogs, and think that this present neo-church could be met in the battle with peashooters. There was evidence that these new cubs would be old lions on the battlefield one day. Fundamentalists do not usually grasp, by a full homework, that which is needed to recognize new enemies when they come. They tend to place too much emphasis upon old enemies of the Christian Faith.

Fundamentalism still had a cutting edge against the apostasy, as well as an effective influence across many denominations in one way or another, even in the late 1950s after many neo-evangelicals had defected from historic Fundamentalism. Fundamentalism, they thought, was too strong. However, the movement was not too strong, although Gabriel believed there were some too militant in the second generation, like a loose cannon. But he met those who desired magnificence on the battlefield as he did.

This magnificent spirit was true from its birth until the rise of neo-evangelicalism of the 1940s. The neo-evangelicals withdrew from fundamentalists for three definite reasons: the doctrine of separation; their claim of the lack of esteem for academic Christianity; and because of the militancy of the fundamentalists against the apostasy without love.

The most important benefits which came from Fundamentalism, as Gabriel saw it from his studies, were:

First, the distinctive clarification of what indeed was the fundamental core-doctrines of the Bible for the salvation and redemption of the sinner. This greatly clarified and aided evangelism.

Second, Fundamentalism had already identified the apostasy that had entered the churches, called Liberalism or Modernism, which was contrary to the Word of God. This greatly aided the separation of Bible-believers from the apostasy.

Third, Fundamentalism gave a defense (an *apologia;* "answer," First Peter, chapter 3, verse 15) for the Bible in the context of the truths which the Liberals rejected. This greatly aided the clarity of the Christian testimony in the world.

Fourth, because of the fact that some Liberals had captured actual church properties and pulpits which had held for years the teachings of the orthodoxy of Fundamentalism, those pastors, and that part of the congregation who followed them through the Word of God, had to make an exodus and plant new, independent churches, conferences, and missionary enterprises. This greatly aided the immediate and necessary identities of the local churches as truly Bible-believing people.

Fifth, the Biblical fundamentalist's defense of the Faith occasioned the births of other Fellowships and Associations, such as the World Congresses, where those of like precious faith and mind could come together in strength. This greatly aided the fellowship needed in the entire Body of Christ on earth.

Sixth, successful evangelistic campaigns and revival crusades were initiated and sustained through the new churches born to Fundamentalism and the Bible. This greatly aided the hope of the next generations of peoples and churches to be planted and encouraged for survival in the world.

Seventh, new publications began to multiply, and other ministers of the Gospel found encouragement and direction for their own ministries and churches. This greatly aided others, outside of Fundamentalism, proper, to have access to their own Biblical needs and see the necessity for taking their stand against error and the apostasy.

Eighth, Congresses and Conferences were further formed to provide an enlarged access to Fundamentalism from various other geographies and places in the world. Missionary movements began their work on foreign fields. This greatly aided the furthering of the Great Commission into all the world.

Ninth, the theological trilogy of Biblical inerrancy, infallibility, and verbal-plenary inspiration of the Holy Scriptures was definitely necessary to distinguish the point of the battle to be defined. This aided greatly to protect and preserve the integrity of the Word of God in the hearts and minds of God's people and others in a changing Christian world.

Tenth, these teachings of Fundamentalism, through scholars, evangelists, and faithful pastors of the Word of God, identified, with greater clarity, the true purpose of the movement itself to others. This greatly aided confirmation that Fundamentalism was indeed a viable movement as other Christian remnants and movements had been back in church history.

Eleventh, because so many departures had been made from Primitive Christianity since its beginning in the New Testament, there was a needed return by the fundamentalists to the early teachings of historic Christianity. This aided greatly to the solidarity of relationships with historic Christianity running through Dogmatic Theology of the years, as well as through historic Remnant Christianity.

Twelfth, since it was believed that the Protestant Reformation was a classical, true return to the Word of God and its doctrinal teachings on a Biblical base, after the Dark Ages of one thousand years, the fundamentalists totally identified with the Reformation teachings which revived in their movement. This aided greatly to the true historical base and test for all theological systems which came from the Reformation. It was a call back to Reformation Christianity.

Thirteenth, the Authorized King James English Version became the Text of the fundamentalists, because it was believed that it was the most preserved English Text from the Greek Text which God preserved. This only Authorized Text in the English-speaking world became the source of a certain lineage of translations which held to literal translation.

This aided greatly to the needed question of "What is the Text of Christianity in our time?" without which there could be no answer to the second question, "What is the interpretation of that Text?" Gabriel noted in his studies that all of the Remnant Christian groups had had access to that lineage of Texts, including the Greek Text, which confirmed the Reformation Greek Text by Erasmus as well as Luther's translation of the German Text from the Erasmus Greek Text. Other languages had their translations from that Greek Text as well.

Fourteenth, both successful evangelism and revivalism were highly prized among the fundamentalists because souls saved and revived would widen the future witness for Christianity. This aided greatly to the continuance and victory of Christianity in the earth. Fundamentalists had been at the forefront in evangelism from its very beginning, and yet that evangelism was proposed through uncompromising convictions of Biblical truth from historic Christianity.

Fifteenth, doctrine was revered as the acid test of what were the fundamental teachings of the Gospel of the Lord Jesus. This aided greatly to proclaim that the foundation of Christianity was found in the doctrine of Scripture alone. In their first generation the fundamentalists had rejected the claim of the liberal that "the Bible contains the Word of God," and now gave a call to the belief that "the Bible is the Word of God."

Sixteenth, and last, it was clearly understood by fundamentalists that they were a movement in the earth, born of God; and as other good, remnant movements before them, they could fail, too, if they forsook the fundamentals of the Gospel and the Christian life. This aided greatly to the need of continued humility in Fundamentalism. Gabriel believed there were a number of fundamentalists who knew that fighting on a battlefield could produce an individual too militant, but Gabriel also knew that there was a magnificence to the call of the fundamentalists.

So, Gabriel truly identified himself as a separatist fundamentalist. From time to time he would be called upon, as all others should, to monitor the "ist" by the "als," while never desiring to be a part of only the "ism." This had been seen before in church history, many, many times, and always the "ism," only, would become "schism" to the testimony of Christ.

However, these dangers, as all other dangers in the Christian life, must never make cowards of those who dare to run the risk because of their love for the Lord Jesus and the souls of men. Though the bathwater of Fundamentalism must be thrown away from time to time, we must never throw away the voice of the cry of that infant movement. Sometimes, Gabriel, as a fundamentalist, would state, "We are prone to forget that all of the neo-movements of our time have some of the same sins and weaknesses as ourselves, but we are not in error with our Lord. This should not be a problem for anyone living and abiding in the grace of the Lord Jesus. However, false doctrine and the apostasy, God will not tolerate in those who profess His Holy Name." Once again Gabriel thought of his personal teacher, Dr. John Rendle Wellson, the pastor-teacher who stood upright as a fundamentalist.

Gabriel would indeed endeavor to keep his promise with Dr. Jonathan, but would do that with a burden he saw in the movement that he would presently tell to God in prayer. However, he would also pray daily that God would tell it to the fundamentalists' leaders, or the movement would fail in the earth in the future.

Chapter Twelve

The Doctrine

(January 16, 1958)

Primitive Christianity is marked almost solely by Worship and Doctrine. These were the great evidences of pure, simple Christianity of the first century: the regenerated heart immediately worshipped God; the soul had been saved by the teaching doctrine of grace through faith in the name of the Lord Jesus Christ. We cannot overestimate this great, simple fact. The historic Book of Acts actually happened in a time, space, history context.

The following simplistic description continued through the Book of Acts: "And they continued stedfastly in the apostles' doctrine and fellowship, and in breaking of bread, and in prayers.... And all that believed were together, and had all things in common;... And they, continuing daily with one accord in the temple, and breaking of bread from house to house, did eat their meat with gladness and singleness of heart, Praising God, and having favour with all the people. And the Lord added to the church daily such as should be saved," chapter 2, verses 42 through 47.

It is not possible, however, to pass this early historical

account without adding that great controversy came directly upon the Apostles and the early disciples who accepted the Lord Jesus as Savior. The message of the Gospel, itself, with its inherent truth against sinful man, caused controversy everywhere it went. However, out of it all, Seven Outpourings of the Holy Spirit are recorded in Acts; and Seven Satanic attacks are made against this fledgling church within the thirty years of time covered in this book. It is not possible to separate the controversy, the persecution, and martyrs from the Primitive Christianity of worship and the doctrine of being saved by "grace through faith" in the risen Lord Jesus Christ!

It was not legalism and negativism in the early Christians that caused the controversies and martyrs, but rather the pure "Good News" of the Gospel of the Lord Jesus itself, inherently. Man, as a sinner, is the root of the controversy, persecutions, and martyrdoms, in his rejection of the promised Messiah from the Old Testament. Gabriel saw clearly this controversy, persecution, and division. Also, he saw that this same reaction and rejection continues still against the church wherever the Gospel is taught according to the Holy Scriptures in any generation. Christ had brought a "sword" with His "salvation."

Of course, the Four Gospels of Matthew, Mark, Luke, and John, of eighty-nine chapters, would concern the time of the life of the Lord Jesus Christ, which contains a history of almost thirty-four years. The history in the Book of Acts would cover another thirty years from the Day of Pentecost through the first Roman imprisonment of the Apostle Paul. Most conservative scholars also believe Paul was released from the first imprisonment and continued missionary activity in other geographies after Acts, chapter 28. This brings the total years of recorded history in the New Testament to about the year 64 A.D., when Paul, after his second imprisonment, was beheaded, under Nero. Paul's testimony in Second Timothy, chapter four, marks his end.

The writing of the New Testament itself continues after the Books of Acts: James wrote his epistle about 45-48 A.D.;

and the Book of Revelation concludes in its writing about 96 A.D. All of the other twenty-five books of the New Testament were therefore written between 48 A.D. and 96 A.D. The total books in the Old Testament were thirty-nine; the total in the New Testament were twenty-seven. This would complete the Canon of sixty-six books in the entire Bible.

Gabriel viewed Primitive Christianity, therefore, as portrayed in the New Testament, covering particularly the first sixty-five years of the first century. Probably, the following books should be included, having been written within that time-frame: James, Matthew, I Thessalonians, II Thessalonians, I Corinthians, II Corinthians, Galatians, Romans, Luke, Philemon, Colossians, Ephesians, Acts, and Philippians. The writings of I Timothy, Titus, I & II Peter, Hebrews, II Timothy, Mark, Jude, I, II, III John, Gospel of John, and Revelation were possibly written to commence the second generation of Christianity, because Peter and Paul are urging the appointments of deacons and elders after churches have been born. But it was the firm conviction of Gabriel that all of the Books of the New Testament were written by those who had been eye-witnesses of those events in history, or verified and given apostolic authority by the apostolic eye-witnesses themselves. Gabriel believed the very writers of the Holy Bible were among the same men who canonized the final 66 books of the Bible instead of it being done in later church history by men or councils.

In that first generation of Primitive Christianity there was a "maranatha spirit" which was simply a Christian heart having a conscious spirit of watching, longing, and expecting the second coming of Christ in His resurrected, glorified Body, which He received after His resurrection and ascension back to heaven. Later on in history, after Reformation Christianity had commenced, this "maranatha spirit" was formalized into the doctrine of the Pre-millennial coming of Christ back to the clouds and then to the earth.

The Gabriel T. Parsons family had now returned to their

lovely home in Georgetown, after Gabriel's Ph.D. studies as well as the studies on "Fundamentalism." He returned to pursue his studies on "Doctrine," itself, with Dr. Beauchamp Paulson, the faculty dean of Georgeton Theological Seminary, the place of his Th.D. studies.

The timing of his return to Georgetown was directly for his family to meet together, in great joy, for their tenth wedding anniversary, December 20, 1957. They were returning to the "Land of Evangeline," as portrayed in the third floor room of their Georgetown home for that special date, and to also plan another trip back to Nova Scotia, the origin of Gabriel's Evangeline, his dear wife. Gabriel and his family must not forget this "root" of the land Gabriel loved, and which he sought from childhood. But the 1957 commemoration was to keep alive, on down through his children and children's children, the wonder of a God-given marriage with all of the ingredients of life in a fallen world under the grace of God.

Primitive Christianity, as Gabriel espoused it, may proceed on into the controversies of Reformation Christianity without destroying the joy and delight of a primitive love which can survive on down into the sorrows and vicissitudes of life. December 20 was to be a day of great joy for the Parsons family. His father, Bishop Parsons, was still with them as well. The third floor extended a room forty-two feet by twenty-six feet, portraying the birth of all of them. Even Bishop Parsons agreed to its beauty and purpose, in spite of the fact that he was not able to be with them for their anniversary. His ministerial duties called him away in church responsibilities for the Christmas Season.

However, this particular day was also marked with thanksgiving to God for the eleven friends of this family, eleven individuals who had become an integral part of this family. The eleven friends were Bishop and Mrs. Thomas H. Parsons, Gabriel's parents; Miss Anna Cole, teacher; Miss Charlene Sherman, music teacher; Dr. Robert J. Jonathan; Dr. Beauchamp Paulson; and the five members of the Gabriel-Evangeline marriage, Joseph Paul, Soma Jean, and Ariel John. These were the eleven unique friends of Gabriel's earthly pilgrimage with the Lord.

Of course, this list was not completely comprehensive of all friends of the Parsons family, and it was yet to be revealed of the coming of an unusual couple into this friendship in 1969.

However, on this glad occasion of December 20, 1957, the eleven friends were mentioned in thanksgiving to God for their lives together. Gabriel remarked, humorously, "We need another friend to be our twelfth disciple?" (they all smiled).

Ariel John returned: "What about making Dad Peters, the 'twelfth disciple,' Daddy?"

"Yes, my dear son, you are correct; and we need to pray for him in his present time of sickness, too."

Joseph Paul, on that special anniversary day, when everybody was to express themselves with a special word of thanksgiving, concluded the testimonials with,

"I want to thank the Lord for Mildred Joye today for being the mother of our dear mother, Dad's Evangeline. She must have been an unusual Christian as we see something of her in our dear mother and wife."

Gabriel paused before reading the Bible and closing with prayer, by saying,

"Yes, son, you, like Ariel, have filled our hearts with added joy to know that both Dad Peters and Mother Mildred Joye have been remembered today."

They all concluded the worship with "Amen." Evangeline's face was radiant!

It had come into the heart of Gabriel that God had, personally, given these Christians to him and his family. This was not only God's earthly resource of blessing to his testimony and ministry, but they also gave heavily freighted words for the teachings of Primitive and Reformation Christianity in relationship to the Lord Jesus. These Christians had influenced Gabriel for good and God. Gabriel rededicated himself to the task of speaking up for this legacy of Christian history in the future. This message was to be proclaimed to sinners and saints together, the atheist and the theist, and the confused and the converted ones.

Now it was January, 1958, but the wedding anniversary lingered in their memories. Gabriel had been a Christian for almost eleven years. His life with Evangeline had never failed; their love had not faded. To God be the glory! They had endeavored to bring up their children in a natural, easy home of Christian love, but with firm convictions and Biblical principles which must be respected and practiced. However, natural theology contributed much: flowers, decor, music, the third-floor room of "The Land of Evangeline," and a hopeful balance of Primitive Christianity and Reformation Christianity.

The time had come for Gabriel to contact Dr. Beauchamp Paulson at the seminary. He, like each of the other personal friends of Gabriel, gave a different contribution to Gabriel's life and ministry. Dr. Jonathan, at the University, ordained Gabriel to the ministry of the Lord Jesus Christ, July 10, 1957, during the time of his special studies on "Fundamentalism." Gabriel selected July 10th because that was the date in 1949 he made a full dedication to the Lord in his struggle of the flesh and the will of God for his life. It was the eighth year of that dedication when he was ordained. Gabriel was now thirty-one years old.

He met Dr. Beauchamp Paulson in the year of 1950 when he entered the seminary for Th.D. studies. Dr. Paulson was chairman and dean of the faculty, and the leading professor of a one hundred-year-old institution, founded in 1850, before the Civil War. This seminary was deeply entrenched in American Presbyterianism in its earliest days, but had become, in the first half of the twentieth century, an interdenominational institution. This is one of the reasons Gabriel selected this seminary. He had applied to several other seminaries, but they demanded the graduate to sign a doctrinal statement upon freshman entrance. He thought it was a presumption to request a student to promise that before he had been adequately taught their theological position.

Also, Georgeton Seminary was still conservative in its teachings of the Holy Scriptures. After the Civil War, this seminary had joined the more Biblically conservative Southern Presbyterian Church, just as there was formed the Southern

Baptist and Southern Methodist in the aftermath of the War. The Civil War divided these three major denominations, adopting the word "northern" or "southern," peculiar to their geographical struggle of the War. Of course, too, the Mason-Dixon line was drawn, just a few miles north, in the state of Maryland.

Dr. Paulson was a consistent man in his teachings and revered for his disciplined, solid lectures, and he gave the appearance of a man of dignity. However, although the seminary proceeded with strict standards for the faculty and students, yet, he, himself, in some areas of his life he was weak. After the death of his wife in 1930, he never married, but possibly should have done so.

However, Gabriel needed to have a number of talks with Dr. Paulson. He was the most different individual of all of Gabriel's acquaintances. It was clear that Dr. Paulson respected Gabriel, and was quite instrumental in the establishment of the Night Institute in the seminary and naming Gabriel to head the lectures, which he did for three years. Gabriel had also returned from time to time for a few other lectures in this relationship with Dr. Paulson.

Gabriel had arranged a one-hour appointment, at 2, on January 16, 1958, to see Dr. Paulson. This being only introductory in nature, the time would be limited. Gabriel had not visited him since his Ph.D. studies, although they had shared correspondences. A tentative program of Biblical and theological interviews was scheduled with him for the future. Dr. Paulson was looking forward to meeting his former young student, who had, by now, reached some reputation and respect for his own scholarship and travels. Possibly, Dr. Paulson saw something in Gabriel he had at one time envisioned for his own life and did not fulfill. Dr. Paulson was an entirely different person than Dr. Jonathan. But Gabriel needed both sounding boards in the hope of gaining the paradox of two men's different reactions to the generation of the apostasy. Dr. Jonathan was a genuine fundamentalist, but with the gifts of a man for any season of life and history. Dr. Paulson had the knowledge needed for his position in life, but he did not have the power of conviction as Dr. Jonathan.

Also, Gabriel desired to make another appointment with Dr. John Rendle Wellson, the guest professor, from time to time, at the Bible Christian University. His special field of studies was in theology and Biblical languages, which would be most helpful in the balance that Gabriel needed to bring his heart to full-circle before he took his stand for his permanent ministry. Dr. Wellson had the largest private library of any teacher he had ever known, and Dr. Wellson had personally encouraged Gabriel as his favorite student. Gabriel had a key to his private library at his church which he pastored, and they often had sessions over certain subjects that Gabriel would bring to him during the years that he studied at the Bible Christian University. When Dr. Wellson died, his library was left to Gabriel.

The time had come for the appointment, however, with Dr. Paulson.

"Well, my dear Dr. Paulson, I am so glad to see you again in the providence of God. This is my first time to see you, personally, for about three years or more."

"Yes, my esteemed Dr. Parsons. What a Christian joy for me. I still love you as Gabriel, but I now respect you as Dr. Parsons. Congratulations to you, my dear Christian companion in the Christian 'Way.'"

"Thank you. But 'no,' my brother, we must pick up where we left each other, when I was here as Gabriel. Your correspondences have maintained our friendship, and you continue to be both a help and a blessing to me in the ministry for Christ."

"Your correspondence questions have been more refreshing and intelligent than my answers. I still remember your special lectures among us here on "Primitive Christianity and Reformation Christianity for Our Time."

"Well, I was barely scraping theological and Biblical ground in my desperate search then, and I feel I am only seeing the fruit of that ground in a limited harvest now."

"You are a most assiduous Christian Teacher, my brother, still with a 'primitive Christian' spirit and a 'Reformation

Christian mind,' (a little laughter comes) as you would say of others."

"Well, your consciousness of these matters, Dr. Paulson, has not quite reached my consciousness or desire." (more laughter).

"Now, Gabriel, what are we to speak about at this time in our lives? I am keeping in my mind your hopeful interviews with me for the future."

"I believe the word is simply, 'Christian doctrine,' Dr. Paulson."

"Doctrine, you say?"

"Yes," responded Gabriel, deliberately.

"What kind of doctrine, my brother?"

"Just the subject of doctrine. (pause) We are living in a generation that is beginning to destroy the place of 'doctrine' in the Christian faith, the pulpit, and the private lives of Christians. May I give you three examples of this?"

"Yes indeed, Gabriel."

"The first example comes from a leading Christian historian of our time. His background comes from early pentecostalism; his father was a leading bishop in that denomination. This historian is a serious, prolific writer for pentecostalism. He is a man of academic letters. He is openly saying and writing that it is unfortunate that Martin Luther did not see in his own Reformation against the Roman Catholics the more important need of the Holy Spirit without doctrine. He observed that if Luther had seen the importance of the manifestation of the Holy Spirit in the church, as the modern Charismatics do, we would have had a mighty awakening, with evangelism and revivalism leading the world to Christ, rather than the great separation that finalized the days of the Protestant Reformation."

"You say he is a man of academic letters, writing this? It is impossible to read, seriously, the historic account of the Protestant Reformation and make this conclusion unless the person is biased to his own presupposition. Also, the Holy Spirit is subject to the Holy Word of God and would not work in a manner against the Holy Scriptures."

"Your immediate remarks are welcomed, my brother, as they are the very same conclusions I have drawn. However, the problem of our time enlarges as we observe regular statements made by the founder and president of the largest reputed Christian television network in the world which also carries adverse statements along the lines of the more primitive testimony. In a somewhat impromptu meeting on his network, live, he, a man without letters, simply brushes aside Bible doctrine by saying, 'I cannot get over it; how much time has been wasted with words and writings and preachings of the past over doctrine, so-called Bible doctrine.' Those conversing with him on the television, simply laughed in agreement over such a waste of history."

"I understand your concern, at this time in your life and studies, concerning the simple but great word of the Bible and Christian history, the word 'doctrine,' Gabriel. What do you conclude from this? (a pause) But, I believe, first, you had a third example."

"Yes, and the third is most serious. The first two were quoted from the neo-pentecostal spectrum: one of them a leading historian; the other a leading neo-pentecostalist businessman, considered a preacher, by some, who leads an international television network. However, my third example comes from the leading evangelist of our time, now internationally known, Willie Wheyman. He purports that he believes that a man could go to heaven without ever having known of a Bible or the name of Jesus Christ, if he, in his heart, wants to live a good life and loves God in his own way. He has also taken the position that the Romanist, the heathen, and the Jews, all have a special 'light' or have a special relationship with God as 'Jews,' and should not be thought of as needing the evangelistic 'Gospel' of the Lord Jesus to be saved. There about 20 years between these two observations made by Dr. Wheyman, so he cannot be accused of senility of life; he has consistently maintained these expressions."

"Yes, my brother, I am aware of this example, and I am greatly concerned where it could lead us."

"Yes, at the heart of this, with all three examples included, in what is happening in our generation with Biblical 'doctrine' greatly concerns me. All three of my examples, and there are more, are placing Bible doctrine outside the fundamental teachings of the Word of God. The Great Commission, given by our Lord, is a Commission into all the world, Jew, Gentile, Romanist, Heathen, and all, 'discipleizing' all 'nations' by 'teaching,' which as you know better than I, is a word translated in other passages of the New Testament for the word 'doctrine.' Do you really concur, my brother, that 'doctrine,' Bible doctrine, is still essential for a person's redemption and salvation?"

"Yes, Gabriel, I do; with all my heart and mind. It is revealed by God; it is true. (a pause) Sometimes, I have had great regrets that I have not stood stronger in behalf of 'doctrine'; it is absolutely imperative to do so now. You, one of my students, have taught me this."

"That, I consider to be a strong response to me by you, Dr. Paulson. Accompanying these present outrageous statements and unbiblical conclusions are extant claims to visions, dreams, audible voices, impressions, demonstrations, 'prophecies,' to say nothing of poor Biblical exposition and 'strange doctrine,' in huge outpourings of emotional and passionate proliferations. The loss of doctrine is a loss of the distinctive teachings of the Holy Scriptures; the additions of extant revelations, so-called, is an attack on the very authority and sufficiency of the Holy Word of God. The liberals had already subtracted from the Bible in their interpretations; and now the modern neo-pentecostalist does not mind adding to the Bible with his own so-called revelations."

"Is it in your heart, Gabriel, for our future interviews to pursue doctrine, my brother? I see you have concluded your heart, and undoubtedly your direction is set."

"Yes, that was what I hoped for in these opportunities with you."

"Then, I will welcome these sessions for my own needed benefit. (an intercom buzzer sounded) I regret that I must excuse myself now. Another appointment has been set in my administrative work with the seminary. I welcome these times together, my beloved friend. My secretary will give you an outline of my present schedule as a guide for you to arrange your appointments, as you can, in your own busy schedule."

Gabriel extends his appreciation for this introduction for subsequent times with Dr. Paulson. Gabriel particularly sought out Dr. Paulson, after studying Fundamentalism, because he considered Dr. Paulson a Christian brother, yet he knew he was not a fundamentalist. He would be identified as a moderate conservative, who would not necessarily accept the trilogy of inerrancy, infallibility, and inspiration, but would believe in at least two of them. Dr. Paulson would not have accepted extant revelations, but in a more loose fashion than Gabriel, he probably would accept impressions of the Holy Spirit as the heart was governed by the Bible. The test with Dr. Paulson would tell Gabriel just how far one could go before losing Primitive Christianity and Reformation Christianity; one or both? Also, how far one could go with such a friend.

The winter sun was beginning to set as Gabriel did wind his way through the traffic back home through northwest Washington to Evangeline not very far away. Also, he longed to see his three children who would indeed enter, God willing, a future generation where the primitive-reform Christian doctrine and life could be affected by new and strange ideas. However, many people would never know that the new and strange ideas were really 'doctrines' — 'doctrines' which were false!

Chapter Thirteen

The Remnant

(March 16, 1960)

After the doctrinal interviews with Dr. Beauchamp Paulson of the Georgeton Seminary, a very important turn of events came to Gabriel. It came in the year of 1960, the month of March. Dr. Paulson called Gabriel, this time, and requested an appointment with him for the sixteenth of the month.

Gabriel was in a time of planning a long-range series of meetings in a number of states in America, with lectures and sermons for seminaries and churches. He would only be able to plan Friday evenings through Sunday mornings in this schedule. The states requesting him to come included Pennsylvania, Ohio, Illinois, Kentucky, Oklahoma, Kansas, Texas, and California. A few of them were rejected by Gabriel, but acceptances had been received with an agenda slated for about two years.

Gabriel was once again involved in the Night Institute at Georgeton Seminary, as well as being featured as a special lecturer in the Day Seminary for four days of the week. The Night Institute also continued for four nights, always keeping Friday through Sunday open each week. He was fully salaried by the seminary and had been for over a year. So, he and his family still resided in their beautiful Georgetown home not too far from the seminary. Evangeline was also lecturing on music three days a week at the Georgeton University, a companion academic union with the Georgeton Theological Seminary, with their campuses adjacent to each other.

This was a most pleasant time for Evangeline; she was happily involved with Gabriel, the children, and their mutual work together. In fact, no series of circumstances could have been better planned for this quintet of people. Besides, Evangeline was still in love with Gabriel. The Georgetown area of Metropolitan Washington, D.C., was a very historic section and in the proximity of many advantages for the children in art, music, science, and recreational facilities and parks. It was her hope and prayer that this would continue, if it was the will of God. She was remunerated well for her teaching, too.

Joseph Paul was almost eleven years old; Soma Jeanne, past six years; and, Ariel John, not quite five years old. A single, young Christian lady, twenty-four years old, who had been attending the Night Institute that year and had her degree in Elementary Education, had accepted the private home teaching of the three children. She was an unusually gifted person, and Gabriel knew he was fortunate to have her as a formal teacher for his children. She taught for a four-hour period, each morning, Monday through Friday, on a ten and one-half month schedule to meet school regulations. The schedule of Evangeline did lend two mornings of the Monday through Friday schedule, in which additional assistances would be given if needed. The young lady was a genuine Christian, with continued respect for Dr. Gabriel Parsons, and believed this was the will of God for her to be there in the home. She had a beautiful countenance; her name was Juliana Queens. She had a keen mind and a conscientious heart. Her teaching reminded Gabriel of his second-grade teacher, Anna Cole.

The situation in Gabriel's home was still the same; that of a Christian couple whose love for each other was a Christian triumph in a time of the moral decay of many families. The

United States was entering a dangerous time. The youth had heard "Rock and Roll" music, and the Rock music festivals were in vogue with great immoralities, drugs, and the occult. Abortions were on the increase; divorces were high; and the churches were becoming more ecumenical and liberal.

Gabriel was already speaking of Remnant Christianity as a third essential study of influence for all Christians, ministers, and seminary professors. He had already established his urgency concerning Primitive Christianity and Reformation Christianity. He became aware of the importance of Remnant Christianity, such as the Hussites, the Moravians, the Reformers, the Huguenots, the Puritans and the Pilgrims, and Fundamentalists in the years in-between these two periods of the first and the sixteenth century. Gabriel has now come to his early prime in his ability to speak of the history written in God's Word and the history as recorded by man. Theology, Biblical languages, and history went hand-in-hand. He and Evangeline were approaching thirty-four years of age. Their preparation was behind them. Although the financial legacy from Gabriel's mother had been a great blessing to them, needless to say, it had become somewhat depleted. Their educational and family costs had taken a toll of their resources; yet a modest amount remained. Their home had been paid off, and they were now receiving an excellent salary together from their faculty positions.

However, it was Gabriel's lectures, across the nation and other places, that were strengthening their financial stability. At this time in his ministry, many seminaries, colleges, and churches were requesting his able sermons and impressive lectures. Even universities, more as an oddity, were extending some invitations to him. He was an able exegete for expository teaching of the Bible, but he used his exposition directly within the framework of Biblical theology. This brought the entire authority of the Bible down through Biblical history, as the way in which God unfolded His Word from the beginning. Gabriel also brought these studies to bear upon church history's three-fold movements: Primitive, Reformation, and

Remnant Christianity. Of course, then history would enter into prophecy, with some of the prophecy of the Bible having already been fulfilled in history. Passages in the Bible like the seven parables in Matthew, chapter 13, as well as the Seven Churches of the Book of Revelation, chapters 1, 2, and 3, caused Gabriel to realize that God required Christians to know history. There was a text that bore down upon the heart and mind of Gabriel with great force: "That which hath been is now; and that which is to be hath already been; and God requireth that which is past"; Ecclesiastes, chapter 3, verse 15.

Also, the Second Advent of the Lord Jesus Christ was yet ahead, evidently, not too far into prophecy from present history.

Gabriel would not back off from the whole truth and nothing but the truth. He saw all truth, natural theology and revealed theology, on the same continent of knowledge, a one-world of all things. He continued to persist that man must not separate any truth from all truth. His motto, printed on his bookplates in his library, in every volume, was *veritas supra omnis*, "truth above all." He pled for the Reformation plea: *homo unius libri*, "a man of one Book." He wrote more than twenty-five cantatas and oratorios with expressed Christian belief right up front. He sought for individuals he knew who loved the truth as he did, so that his knowledge would not be anything original with himself. He wanted the world to know that truth had clearly made its full entrance into the world of literature. He sought to be a loving, Christian gentleman, but he would not reject the accusation that there were times of anger in his life. He was a firm, strong speaker and he wanted to be. He had a mind that retained the things he thought important; with that kind of mind he chose to forget many things not vital to his calling and ministry. He chose what he wanted to remember. He was bent on the one goal of Biblical truth; he desired all other rivers of truth, goodness and righteousness to run into that one place. That which survived was just one continent of truth; no islands were permitted to float around or get divided from the main body of truth. He just kept coming back to that singular world-view, or universe-view, as he sometimes called it. The truth concluded itself:

Jesus is the Living Word; Jesus is the Written Word.

Gabriel believed that God ordained and encouraged men to have books and teachers to teach them. He believed Adam wrote the first book, undoubtedly, Genesis, chapter 5, verses 1 and 2. In fact, God who desired books, had that desire because God's own greatest revelation would be through a book, The Book, the Bible. This was the only infallible, inerrant, inspired Word in human history.

Gabriel had a large definition of what was a book? It easily included: inscription stones, ostraca, velum parchments, monuments, symbolics, sculpture, architecture, pictorial and alphabetic languages. Almost everything that man had produced, from ziggurats to myths, to legends, sagas, and formal script—all were set forth finally in books or previously in at least stone.

Now, the time had come for Gabriel to be tested in his ministry. The purpose for the above-mentioned human accomplishments was primarily given to set forth that Gabriel knew he was only a man, and man at his very best must be tested. He would emphasize in his teachings that a man could know, and knowledge could come to belief. But what man knows and believes must be finally "tested," by what man has been taught and learned, and then knew and believed, and then placed on trial, must survive with confirmation, for man to be able to say, "Now I see." This is why the final matter to Gabriel was the empirical method that passed through a God-led experience of life. Gabriel was neither led by emotion or mere subjective experientialism. But he believed man must experience all of his life.

So, the time had come for Gabriel, Evangeline, and their ministries to be tested. But this developed through the human instrumentality of Dr. Beauchamp Paulson, the more moderate dean of the faculty at Georgeton Seminary.

Tomorrow morning, March 16, 1960, Gabriel had been requested to meet Dr. Paulson at 10:00 AM in his seminary office.

The time arrived.

"Good morning, Gabriel; I am glad you were able to meet me today."

"Yes, and good morning to you, too, my friend. I trust you are doing well today."

"Yes, thank you. I need to accomplish two important things immediately in this appointment. First, I have been genuinely appreciative of both you and your dear Evangeline working with us, here in the University and you in the seminary. I could not be more pleased. (Gabriel nods a thanks) Second, we are living in awesome and treacherous times in the history of the world. The trends are being set for a grand change, everywhere."

"Yes, Dr. Paulson; and the most treacherous of all is that a new definition of Christianity is being erroneously taught and preached by so-called evangelists and denominations. 'Rock and Roll' music is beginning to destroy church worship with a contemporary Christian music, so-called. But the primary cause, my dear brother, is the change in the definition of historic Christianity."

"My dear Dr. Gabriel, you are correct, and you taught me that. Even in our own seminary and university I see the beginnings of these things affecting us. Of course, that 'primary' reason you speak of is why I have particularly called you today to this appointment. That is also why I sought earnestly before our administration for you and Evangeline to teach here in both of our institutions."

"You are running a risk, my dear friend, in having us, I am sure."

"Oh no! Not at this point, but I can see what is ahead. The 1960s will be extremely dangerous for moral and spiritual values as presented by conservative Christianity. (a pause) However, my next remarks will probably astonish you, but in my later years, and from your acquaintance and friendship, I have wanted to do the right thing in my time and life to the end of my days. In a short time I will be sixty years old; I will soon have to retire. I have been in this place for thirty-two years of service."

"And you have served it well, my brother."

"That is received with a good heart because you are the one expressing that to me. (a pause) On the other hand, there are many things I cannot tell you, and should not tell you about this old, prestigious place in Georgetown. Changes are ahead of us as far as the conservative, historic Christianity, as you call it, is concerned. I am torn between two choices: to recommend you to the administration to take my place as Dean of the Faculty; or,..." (pausing, near tears)

"Dear Dr. Paulson, there are some things here I do know about myself; and the condition here is everywhere I go. Your leadership has made the best of the coming change, and I respect it at this time, yet knowing a greater change is certain to come to pass. I believe I know your heart and concern, and I am glad I was here when you served in your capacity of leadership. I know you have grave responsibilities and burdens in this place."

"Gabriel, I have known that you know much about this institution here; I can tell by your lectures and what the students say; and you have received unusual respect from those who know you. In the spirit of that, and even by the spirit of your dear Evangeline, yet I know we are in a changing hour here in the seminary. The days will come when a new people will proliferate in America, and they will deliberately exclude truth, as you teach it, and as I have grown to love, more and more. You have been strength to me in these things."

"But Dr. Paulson, what is really on your mind and heart? I fear I interrupted your conversation because of your pause."

"Well, Gabriel, I am on several other seminary boards in our nation; and the problems are the same. Now and then, I become aware of a seminary that is still more conservative than most. I wanted to share the testimony of one seminary that is looking for a dean of the faculty who would also be president of the seminary. This institution started in 1898 and is sixty years old. It was founded by a presbyterian lawyer who studied abroad and who was ordained in the Southern Presbyterian Church. He married the daughter of the Governor of the state of North Carolina. His name is Dr. Franklin P. Nichols, a godly and intelligent man. He founded the institution somewhat later in his life, and after his death in 1915 was succeeded by a second president who died last year. The seminary is not under any presbytery, or General Assembly, but has an independent charter directly under a Board of Trustees. The Trustees are the sole authority and the seminary owns all of its properties. I have spoken to the Board of you, Evangeline, and your family, including your past studies and ministries. They immediately sensed an affinity with your life and Biblical presuppositions. They were especially moved in heart by your 'primitive-reform' emphasis in your teachings. I repeat: I would be sorrowed if you left here. But I will only be here a few more years, and I believe your future there would be a greater joy to you. It is in my heart to place your name here as my successor, or, to the institution to which I have referred. Now, my brother, my burden is lifted. I am open for any discussion from you." (a pause of deliberation)

"Dr. Paulson, your presentation is clear, and knowing your love for me I am not surprised that you think of us as you do. I am humbled by your thoughts and words today. I have simply pursued my ministry in a straight line — to teach, humbly, the truth for our time. I know you know I will need some time to pray, seek God, converse with my dear Evangeline, as well as my family. It must be right for them, too."

"Of course, my brother," responded Dr. Paulson. "I have a portfolio on the entire history and ministry of this seminary prepared for you to study. You may take it with you. It has averaged about five hundred students each year."

"What is the name and location of this independent seminary?"

"Antioch Theological Seminary, in Ocean View, North Carolina, not too far from your own alma mater."

"Yes, a good name, and an appropriate name for the time. I think I know just about where it is located. (pause) Do you have any other words, my friend, of your own personal advice to me?"

"No, my brother. I do not want to speak of any advice to you. I know I am prejudiced for you to stay here."

"Well, Dr. Paulson, our paths have crossed once more. You

have been most kind today to me. I must 'wrestle' this decision through; I only seek, with all my heart, for the will of God, with my name and family written upon that will. I want you to have a prayer with me now, as I leave. I know your time is needed in other matters for today, too."

Dr. Paulson and Gabriel stood, embraced, as Dr. Paulson poured out his heart in prayer, and Gabriel joined him in concert, "Amen," at several points in the prayer.

Now, Gabriel must go home and speak lovingly to his dear Evangeline and their three children. Gabriel did not want to color any of this matter from his own color chart of life.

After that, Gabriel will go to the "Watch Out," his *ben most bore,* his Land of Evangeline, and pray for the remnant around the world.

Chapter Fourteen

The Test

(1960 - 1969)

Antioch Theological Seminary was about twenty-five miles due east from the Bible Christian University. Only four miles farther east and you would be on the shores of the Atlantic Ocean. It was south of Wilmington, North Carolina, about five miles; farther south and you would begin approaching Greenbrook Gardens. The place of the seminary was Ocean View, an inlet town which had a population of eighteen thousand, both beautiful and convenient for a seminary student body of about five hundred. Shopping in nearby Wilmington was an asset, too.

Gabriel believed it was the will of God for him to accept this seminary post as the President and Dean of the Faculty. His entire family became excited about the ocean and the beautiful inland appearance of the array of boats and commercial watercrafts always marking the landscape. The children particularly enjoyed the area.

Evangeline was somewhat saddened about leaving her University lectures and studies, but she knew Gabriel would pray through to know the will of God with the guide of the

Bible. There was also a bonus-blessing in the decision, because when approached, Miss Juliana Queens consented to go with them in the move. That singular point brought a great peace to the heart of Evangeline.

Bishop Parsons, Gabriel's father, encouraged his son to go. He was the only positive spokesman in it all. He was in his late sixties now, with good health, and was one of two bishops his denomination selected to make a preaching mission to the foreign fields with their missionaries. He was once again honored for his faithfulness to the Word of God. Therefore, Gabriel and his family would not see Dad Parsons for almost a full year.

They sought to rent out the first floor of their Georgetown home and much to Gabriel's surprise, Michael and Michelle Olsen, the couple who rented it before when they went back to University studies, were now desirous to lease it again. They were an unusual couple who had been saved as a result of the first sessions of Gabriel's Night Institute at Georgeton Seminary back in 1953. They had both seen disappointing churches in the Metropolitan Washington area and had almost given up their search for the Lord in a church after their conversion to Christ.

The ministry of Gabriel brought a fresh Christian view of Christ to their lives, and they had been attending a Methodist church commended to them by Gabriel's father, Bishop Parsons. They had been waiting for several years to build their home in the Georgetown area, but had postponed it at this time because of the success of their businesses. However, they considered the delay a providence because they needed more time than they presently had to oversee the building of a new home. They had no children, but they were unselfish in every compartment of their lives together. Their desire to return to the first floor of Gabriel's home made a great convenience for both parties. Gabriel believed that God had worked this out, once again; this was His good providence in their lives for their move to the seminary.

Upon the arrival of the Parsons' family in Ocean View, the

Board of Trustees and their wives were present to greet them. It was about four o'clock on a beautiful afternoon and a lovely buffet was waiting for them in the faculty dining room. A stately, old colonial seminary Manse was already provided and furnished for them adjacent to the campus. The chairman of the Board, Mr. Boaz A. Broadman, with his quiet dignity, extended a formal appointment of charge to Dr. Gabriel T. Parsons and family. It was carefully announced that Dr. Parsons was to be the new President of Antioch Theological Seminary and Dean of the Faculty. This gave Gabriel administrative authority as well as academic authority.

As had been previously requested before Gabriel moved from Georgetown, Mrs. Evangeline Marguerite Parsons was to be Dean of the School of Fine Arts. She was to be one of five deans, including the schools of English Bible, Biblical Languages, Special Christian Care, and Historical Theology. President Parsons was to select his own agenda of lectures, and he would choose from the faculty list who would be deans and the teachers of classes for his first fall semester which had been set for September 3, 1960. The Parsons had arrived June 10, and had already set up interviews with each faculty member for the next immediate weeks. The faculty was set for twenty-eight members, besides a full time staff of 16. Forty-four individuals would serve five hundred students, besides six hosts and six hostesses for the schedule of special occasions. There were eighty-five days between the interview with Dr. Paulson and the actual arrival on the seminary campus. Gabriel and Evangeline had sought God in prayer, in the Holy Scriptures, and their own hearts to make this move. This first day brought joy and assurance to them. God had moved them to Antioch Theological Seminary, in Ocean View, North Carolina.

Gabriel's task was now to set forth the Deans. Much had been worked out prior to his arrival. He had already submitted all details to the Board of Trustees; every detail had been accepted unanimously. Dr. Paulson had assured the Board they were gaining a defender of the Christian Faith, a godly man. They could see both qualities at work in a short time.

The appointment of the Deans were as follows: Dean of the Faculty, Dr. Gabriel T. Parsons; Dean of English Bible, Dr. Kenly G. Grayham; Dean of Education, Dr. J. Lee Davidson; Dean of Biblical Languages, Dr. Daniel T. Ussher; Dean of Special Christian Care, Dr. Donald D. Dawson; Dean of Fine Arts, Dr. Evangeline Marguerite Parsons.

Gabriel made these presentations to each of the Deans privately, and then posted the complete list on the seminary's main bulletin board. However, he personally delivered both the list and the printed formal announcement to Evangeline with the children present in the Manse. With a rather formal dignity, he emphasized "Dr." when he read her name. Evangeline looked with surprise, as she broke out with a response:

"My dear Gabriel, what has happened with this announcement of 'Dr.'? I trust that this will not change me as a 'primitive' Christian before you."

"Dear Evangeline, we have been so busy in our move, I did not explain the details until now. I want to congratulate you at this time, before our children. You have been most earnest and consistent in gaining your Ph.D. in Music History. I know that I did encourage you along the way as you completed your dissertation at the Georgeton University. Dr. Paulson was given the privilege of calling me directly, and delivering to me the notification that your dissertation had been accepted and your degree was to be granted. There will be the public, formal presentation of the same at the end of this fall semester. We must make plans to return to Georgetown for this occasion. But, I included it in the printed list of our deans at this time before we begin our ministry here. As far as this human honor affecting a change in you as a 'primitive' Christian, it is too late. God has already made you one, my dear Evangeline."

After a prayer of thanksgiving, Gabriel arises from his knees and embraces Evangeline in total silence of abounding love and gratitude. The children slowly gathered around, enlarging the embrace.

The immediate major change by President Parsons in the format to the teaching plan was to install a World-View Cycle in the semester program. The schedule would be a class every hour on the hour, five days a week beginning at 7:30 AM for faculty prayer; 7:45 AM, student assembly; and then, 8:00 AM through 2:30 PM. The outline was as follows, according to the new cycle:

     8:00 AM - English Bible of the New Testament
     9:00 AM - General Education
    10:00 AM - Fine Arts
    11:00 AM - Historical Theology and Orals
    12:30 PM - Biblical Languages
     1:30 PM - English Bible of the Old Testament

The whole purpose is to educate the students that all majors are a part of Gabriel's World-View of knowledge before God. The student must realize this relationship of Natural Theology and Revealed Theology: Creation, Nature, and Redemption were all from God.

The entire cycle program would be directed by the president in getting the presupposition established in it. It was clear that the Bible program and History would permeate the entire background of all studies: Primitive, Reformation, and Remnant, in the light of the ecumenical time.

The pattern of Biblical theology was the framework upon which exegetical exposition of the Biblical context would be identified with history and prophecy. Gabriel believed strongly that Christians needed to know the text in the context and the context in the total content of all Biblical theology of all the contexts. He personally counted 2,081 contexts in the entire Bible, and each one of them was related by the divine selection and inspiration of the Holy Spirit. Gabriel would often put the matter in this perspective: "A text without a context is a pretext; but a context without the total Text of the Holy Scriptures is simply a floating island without a past or a future."

Finally, it was to be understood that Antioch Theological Seminary was, in reality, a non-denominational institution. Although it was founded by a presbyterian, yet he chose to establish the seminary through an independent Board of

Trustees. The seminary and all the property were in the hands of that Board, and Bible-believing students from any historic Christian background were cordially invited to attend. Every student was accepted to the seminary because he had signed his name to this distinctive, along with the Creed and regulations of the institution as well.

The seminary was born in the time of the fundamentalist movement at the beginning of the twentieth century. This was distinguished as a separatist, fundamentalist, independent seminary. This was to be maintained by the faculty, the staff, and the students. The seminary Handbook did set this forth clearly, without apology, and it included discipline and culture.

One of the special features that Gabriel brought to the seminary was the Friday afternoon "Question and Answer Forum" he arranged in the presence of the deans and the faculty. Gabriel would set forth about seven important paragraphs on a particular subject, and then give the deans the opportunity of questions to further clarify Gabriel's first outline. In the fall semester, Gabriel came to another Friday forum which he had particularly designed in the time of his early administration, establishing his historical base.

Gabriel addresses his audience.

"For another Friday, we welcome members of the faculty and deans of the schools: Dean Grayham, Dean Davidson, Dean Ussher, and Dean Dawson. We are once again glad to have another meeting together as we endeavor to pursue background material of our teaching studies. It has been our custom to post the subject ahead of time each week. Each subject is presented with the hope of considering an appropriate matter to assist us in our teaching of the Lord's Word of truth, and related subjects, in our generation.

"Today's subject concerns 'The Distinctiveness of Time with Consideration of our Creator, His Creatures, and History.'

"First, we would propose: When God created time, in which He did take six solar days, He, before the foundation of the world, drew a straight line of His sovereign will from time beginning to time end. God would then permit, in later history, all His creatures to exercise their own limited will from a point on that sovereign line.

"Second, that starting point, of God's sovereign will, after the fall of man, upon the birth of every creature, would lend itself to a will which might be exercised to the left or to the right of that line. This was to be God's liberty to the creature with human responsibility, and as a result of this, man would have to take his position as a liberal or a conservative, a libertine or a legalist, etc., in his will concerning natural and revealed theology.

"Third, God ordained that upon the line of His sovereign will, neither "pandemoniumism" would ever be allowed nor the possibility for a creature to take on deity. At Creation, the indwelling thoughts of God for the creature would be manifested with His outgoing thoughts in historical actions.

"Fourth, God ordained, also, that no creature's will would have an unlimited capacity for an unlimited amount of choices; and it would follow that the paradox would declare the affinities which are compatible for the seeming opposite forces; and the incompatible dichotomies of man's limited forces would result in a delusion of the creature from God.

"Fifth, these two opposite directions of 'left' and 'right' might function in both the sinful creature and the redeemed creature, whether it be manifested in natural theology or revealed theology. Man was expected, by God, to make choices and perform deeds in his lifetime of human experiences.

"Sixth, because of God's sovereign will of His straight line in history, through His providence, He would always retain integrity and safekeeping for the universe, that God may bring a specific will of His own to the checking, changing, and/or destroying of a creature's will or action that might be considered destructive to His sovereign will otherwise. God would personally rule the universe.

"Seventh, because of revelation of the Lamb of God slain from the foundation of the world, there had to be manifested from eternity, into a time, space, event, historic Christianity. Therefore, it follows that God must give the Written Word of

God in the Holy Scriptures. Through this revelation the saving power of the grace of God would be revealed to lost mankind. This was accomplished through the Crucifixion of the Son of God in His Substitutionary Atonement. This event would be supported through God's goodness and mercy through natural theology, and specific understanding would be given by the Holy Spirit through revealed theology.

"This seven-fold affinity becomes the Divine Paradox of the universe, and without this affinity, time would occasion the absolute destruction of a fallen world by fallen creatures themselves. This Divine Paradox is initiated by the infallible, inspired, and inerrant Word of Almighty God."

Dr. Grayham gives the first question.

"Dr. Parsons, would any fallen creature be able to form a paradox that would overthrow the Divine Paradox?"

"Dean, Dr. Grayham, the answer first is 'No.' One of the main reasons no creature could do this is that he, not being God, could never devise a paradox that would be outside his own immanence. Thus, any hopeful building of such a paradox would immediately fall into a limitation that would be a contradiction. That is the reason both the Greek's hope of a paradox, before Christ, becomes a fallacious contradiction, as well as the so-called paradoxes of neo-orthodoxy in the nineteenth century. Only God's paradox functions because He is both transcendent and immanent.

"However, we must realize that man ever seeks and longs for a singular formula that includes all possibilities in the universe. Some scientists, like Albert Einstein, reached larger possibilities with his $E=mc^2$, than the usual man of the past. But no man has, or ever will, devise a formula for the entire universe. Only God is capable of bringing such a formula to a conclusion."

Dr. Davidson gives the second question.

"Dr. Parsons, how would you describe the entire length of God's sovereign, straight line in all of history, in the way man's will and God's will relate?"

"Dean Davidson, man's will in history follows a pattern of four courses because of the way fallen man acts: first, most of his history drifts, just drifts, taking a longer time; second, there is man's history when God extends a catastrophe and interrupts man's drifting will, causing him to stop the direction he is taking, or get back to the sovereign line; third, man's will may simply be a trend, a point in time, or turning point in time, which is a gentle departure or return to God's line; and, fourth, man's will may reach such a climax that God makes His will known explicitly in a divine climax. All four courses are governed by the wisdom of God.

"The driftings can be seen in the Orient over many centuries; the catastrophe can be seen in wars, inventions, plagues, or suffering; the trends are witnessed by a patriot, one man, stirring a fresh hope or evil; and the flood is an example of a climax.

"In the days leading up to the Flood we have examples of all of these in a different way: first, 1656 years drifted from the days of Cain's killing his brother, Abel, to the days of the seventh from Cain, Lamech. Then, a catastrophe overtakes the human race with the 'sons of God' who went unto the 'daughters of men.' However, after that catastrophe of sin, God brings a climax with a Flood. Undoubtedly, there were earlier trends which 'the 'sons of God' adopted which led them into a compatibility with the 'daughters of men.' These patterns may be seen in other places of the Bible as well."

Dr. Ussher gives the third question.
"Dr. Parsons, are we to understand that there could be the possibility of any secondary actions of the will of man and God less than the four you have mentioned?"

"Yes, Dean Ussher, because of the universal mercy of God and the providential goodness of God, there are lesser, secondary actions in history. These I would place under the 'trends' I mentioned. These are simply actions instituted by man when he only initiates his 'trend' towards a willful action. My definition of a 'trend,' as I previously implied, would be a human 'point,' or 'turning point' that of itself is not good or evil. It is a 'trend,' 'a turning point' in the actions of man, himself.

"The Golden Age of King David, with such glories of worship, would be a good 'trend.' The 'turning point' towards a revival in Josiah's time is a good example, too. Of course, they were good trends. But there are trends with tendencies toward the worst. In the times of the Judges in the Old Testament, there was a 'tendency' to live without the rule of a kingly need; so, they did what each man thought right in his own eyes without a ruler pointedly guiding him.

"In the New Testament, circumcision was first a trend, tendency, after Christianity was preached after the ascension of Christ. Paul advised Timothy to be circumcised, but advised against it for Titus. In the case of the former, Timothy had a Jewish mother and a Gentile father. So, because of that Jewish extraction it was more becoming to obey the law of circumcision for the sake of not condemning the Old Testament ordinance of the matter. But this was not the pattern for Titus; there could be no compromise with circumcision because man was saved 'by grace through faith,' alone, without ceremonial law. The 'trend' of circumcision for the New Testament Church could not continue as a demand by the Jewish rabbis and law."

Dr. Dawson gives the fourth question.

"Dr. Parsons, in contrast to this enlightening presentation on the subject of time, what contrast would you give concerning eternity?"

"Dean Dawson, this is an appropriate question as we come to the end of our time for today. (a pause) Eternity is not as easy a question and answer as our thoughts on the difficulty of time. This is true because we only live in time in our present state and world. Time is man's best commodity; he can 'redeem' time, in a manner of speaking. That is why history is so important to preserve, to remember, to learn from and

164

improve the present tense of time. Biblical history is the revealed history God has given us, and He wanted us to read, literally, the historical sections of the Bible which occupy about three-fourths of Biblical content. Also, I believe God wanted us to have access to books, to read books, for we know nothing but by books. The books of World Civilization, Church History, Church Remnants, Reformation and Primitive Christian history. Next to the Bible, history is our best teacher.

"But eternity is less known. No thought could ever enter and confront the human, finite mind which is less intelligible to us than that of eternity.

"First, we need a hopeful definition of eternity. The revealed word study, itself, does not give a great light on the subject. Literally translated, it gives the rendering of 'unto the ages of the ages' as a definition. The emphasis there is something of the entrance thought needed to see eternity. Very little is gained by attempting to contemplate eternity as the absence of time. That leaves the whole subject open for other and myriad definitions.

"Possibly, we should immediately define eternity as a mode of existence of the eternal God. This is attested everywhere in the Holy Scriptures, including the fact that the Word is revealed respecting His character as well.

"Of course, too, this word 'eternity' is dedicated in the New Testament as 'the gift of God,' through God's Son, the Lord Jesus Christ, in the phrase of 'eternal life.' This concerns, in our time context, a certain quality of life; yet, one day, we shall enter into eternity with an eternal quality, extended, and forever. But in our definition, we must never allow the word, in both the Hebrew and Greek, to carry with it the entire definition of 'eternity.' And yet the glories of eternity and its mode are not fully revealed in the word alone. We must also follow the doctrinal and theological teachings of the word as well."

President Parsons closes the session discussion.

"Thank you, beloved deans. Your questions were far wiser than our answers. That is a true point to be remembered.

However, this kind of discussion is both edifying and necessary in these days when both history and doctrine are delegated to the background of our contemporary Christianity, as subjective, human experience has been pressed to the forefront. All of the questions in all of our hearts should always be poured out before God. It is good to think of every aspect of Him. Then we leave the questions and answers with Him.

"The Bible has an answer for every question and everything, but most of the questions man could ask are answered in Deuteronomy, chapter 29, verse 29: 'The secret things belong unto the Lord our God: but those things which are revealed belong unto us and to our children forever, that we may do all the words of this law.' Amen! The wisdom we need for these things can be understood in our discretion between what is a God-question and what is a man-question? It is the latter to which we have turned our attention today.

"Faculty and Deans, you are at liberty; good day."

The 1960s was a decade in American history marked with the greatest decline in the spiritual and moral values that the country had ever experienced. This included the pulpits, the evangelists, denominational churches and society as well. The decline was followed by a new (neo) definition of historic Christianity itself. Gabriel called 1963-1970, "The American Great Tribulation Period." "Rock and Roll" music reached the top of influence among young people who were now identified with a lifestyle of permissiveness, immorality, and improprieties. Fornication and drugs were rampant; Rock Festivals displayed public nudity; babies were born out of wedlock; babies were aborted; laws were changed to accommodate the public in their sins. It was clear: since man was sinning sins and breaking laws which man, himself, could not enforce by law, the law was changed or made to accommodate man's sin.

The 1973 "Roe versus Wade" decision resulted in 35,000,000 abortions in the next 25 years. An average of about 1.4 million women were having abortions each year, and forty-four percent of those had had one previous abortion. This opened other claims and definitions concerning the family, planned parenthood, with an increased acceptance throughout the medical profession for "medical abortions," as well as "euthanasia," or what was falsely called "mercy killings" for the desperately infirmed and aged. The home came into great jeopardy. Artificial insemination became a biological experiment as well as cloning a conception of child after an intellectual pursuit of the DNA. But all of these losses were simply the result of the apostasy which had come to the churches and the powerless pulpits of America. The historic landmarks of historic Christianity had been abandoned for a new-theology of a neo-church.

While evangelism and revivalism were being Biblically defined in the Seminary, this was followed by much prayer. The lectures of President Parsons were outlining the neo-christian forces in view of his continuing studies of the Bible in the light of the ecumenical movement, which was definitely following the neo-theology away from Biblical orthodoxy. Scriptural separation from the apostasy was being questioned by the neo-evangelicals. Apostasy was considered by Gabriel as the greater problem of the time; and once it was accepted, the church, the people, and the nation would most certainly be demoralized as well as be estranged from God.

There was a triumvirate group of sister-fellowships which was growing more and more into greater movements. They were: one, the charismatic movement became sister to; two, the neo-evangelical group headed by Evangelist Willie Wheyman which became a sister-fellowship to both the charismatic and Roman Catholic; and, three, Romanism was seeking dialogue and fellowship in a so-called "renewal" which Pope John, XXIII, espoused as a "new pentecost." A new global political and religious force was being born.

Chapter Fifteen

The History

(1947 - May 1, 1969 - 1989)

Dr. Gabriel T. Parsons accepted the appointment, as from God, to move to the Antioch Theological Seminary, June 10, 1960. In his very first year he set up a schedule of a Question and Answer series with his Deans. This was a time when there was to be a respectful exchange of questions from the deans and answers from the president. Already, in the early days of Gabriel being president, there was a good relationship between him and the other leaders in the seminary.

Since the study of history was so very important in the World-Wide View, as presented by Gabriel, the first series of questions by the Deans concerned Gabriel's presentation of time and eternity, with a large emphasis upon the creation of time as the basis upon which Almighty God brought history, time, and space to the forefront through Creation. Also, this would be urgently needed for the historic incarnation of God's Son in the flesh as the historic Jesus Christ of Nazareth.

So, Gabriel's background on this subject of time was essential to historic Christianity.

Gabriel considered time as being created by God, and man

is therefore only capable, in his present life, of time, space, event, with everything being completed in historical evidences. Next to the Bible, history is man's best textbook. If history is not recorded accurately, then there can be no true understanding of what has happened.

The beginning of historical records is not without problems. Because much history, at first, was written in the form of a saga, a legend, or a myth, many centuries passed before a true, factual history was actually fulfilled. The early archaeological artifacts, stones, ostraca, and other forms of books, and other evidences were so deeply rooted in the myth that liberal theologians of our day demand that the Bible, also, be interpreted by the same demythologizing as is done in other records.

The liberals of our day demand that the very same "scientific historical method" of the ancient writings be the method of interpreting the Word of God. The fallacy of this method, superimposed on the Bible, lies in the fact they do not believe the Word of God, the Bible, is the infallible Word of God. They treat the Bible just like any other human book, and they reject the objective, historical facts, preferring to follow the ancient manuscript method. They believe they must demythologize the Bible, too.

However, the secular historians, who came later, began to follow the literal, factual form of historical recordings. The father of such history is a Greek who is considered the "Father of History." His name is Herodotus (484? - 425 B.C.) Until the Jewish historian, Josephus (37? - 100 A.D.) came, the previous Jewish history followed the earlier form of the myth-history, too. Josephus learned from Herodotus the objective, factual history. Josephus' works are an excellent example as set forth in his Jewish Wars. After the days of Josephus, unfortunately, the Jewish historian returned to the earlier historical form of the myth. The Apocrypha, the Kabbala, and many of the traditional Talmud were of such a nature.

The conservative, separatist fundamentalist cannot afford to give up his belief that the Bible is the very Word of God, and he will not surrender his faith and mind to the mere human conception that the Bible only contains the word of God by some presuppositional interpretation based on the approach and assumption of modern scientific historical research. Although earlier history falls into the category of the myth, yet that cannot be the method for the Bible. Even in church history past, there have been historians who fell into the trap of the myth and prejudicial material.

Eusebius of Caesarea (263? - 340 A.D.), Christian theologian, historian, and bishop, fell back into such earlier historical writings. His affinities and partialities with Constantine (288? - 337 A.D.), a Roman emperor, caused a biased, ecumenical union which greatly furthered Roman Catholicism in the fourth century. This tended to a mythical or untrue presentation of the facts of the period surrounding Constantine. To this day, because of such departures from objective history, there are two entirely different histories set forth by the Romanist and Protestant. Now, the Roman Catholic history is so rooted in the claim of Apostolic Succession that Peter has been obscured and believed to be the first of 265 popes to the present time. Much Roman Catholic history lies also in the myth and mystery.

However, there remained a few other historical evidences marking the genuine purpose of historic records. The purpose of history and non-fiction is to declare a story, a narrative, or a tale as being the truth—factually true. Fiction, on the other hand, is a different matter: it magnifies a story, fictionally, using imagination with creativity for literature, but is not factually true. Gabriel believed there was a place for fiction but not to be purported as true history.

This is of such a consequence for the modern Jew that the *Wissenschaft des Judentums* drew its impetus from the instability of the history of Judaism in the nineteenth century. Its leaders were motivated in part by a conscious desire to interest young Jews, who were uncertain of their allegiance and Jewish history. This movement sought to go back in this uncertain history and seek out the truth. A number of notable Jews, such as philosophers and poets, brought back considerable evidences of historical truth.

New sources were found, as the contribution of the records from the *genizah*. A very notable one was found in Cairo. The word itself refers to a pious custom of preserving documents which bear the name of God or have been used for sacred purposes, usually with the eventual intention of burying them in the ground. It is not uncommon to see in Jewish cemeteries a grave-plot marked simply *Genizah*. The astonishing haul of manuscripts and printed texts known as the "Cairo Genizah' was recovered, however, not from a graveyard but from a synagogue, the Ben Ezra synagogue in Fustat, which is Old Cairo. This synagogue dated back a thousand years or so, and the vellum parchment and paper which were extricated from beneath floor-ground, discovered in the 1890s were of great historical importance. They included: Bible and Talmud, liturgy and poetry, legal and literary documents, personal and business letters, ranging in date from the tenth century and earlier, on down to the end of the nineteenth century.

Much local history attracted much attention, as Jews sought for their roots in the places where they were beginning to feel they belonged, and wished to demonstrate to their gentile fellow citizens that they too had an honorable past in their common land.

The apostasy of the twentieth century covers every area in which man functions: history, literature, architecture, art, music, physics, science, and monetary occupations and professions.

Modern physics and science are being studied now from the consideration of chaos. Where are the studies of law, order, design, purpose, and beauty? Drugs and Rock and Roll music must not be monitored at the bottom of the music staircase, because the bottom is saturated at the chaotic gutter of life. There was a time when man considered art a noble pursuit; he measured it from the top of form and freedom and nobility and beauty. Now, it is measured from freedom without form.

In music, they are now saying that form is only the scaffolding to the composition, and once that has been accomplished the scaffolding is taken away. So, form is needed as a scaffolding, only to be taken away when freedom has done its work. It is impossible for freedom to be taken as such. The problem with this modern illustration is that there is a misunderstanding about the place of the scaffolding form. Scaffolding, as such, is not involved here. It is the inner studs, rafters, joists, and joints which still bear the building; and with music there would be no freedom of decor of the building without the inner structure remaining the same all the time. So in music it is not the scaffolding that holds the freedom of the composition, but rather the construction of music itself that must survive.

What is left when we take away actual, factual history? There is nothing back there at all if we take history away; certainly nothing we could be sure about. No matter how many zeros you add to zero, you still have only zero, which mathematically speaking is nothing.

When Primitive Christianity is rejected, and Reformation Christianity is rejected, and Remnant Christianity is overlooked, man will find that the vital organs of Christianity have been destroyed. Even if man fills all that space with the protestant theological systems that they produced, he will simply continue to mutate systems and their various appendages.

In our fallen world, we do not have models and masters of Christians everywhere. We must look for them; they are rare.

One of the main discussions Gabriel did set forth during his presidency at Antioch Theological Seminary, as Dean of the Faculty, was a part of the Deans and Faculty's weekly meetings with him on Fridays for nine years. The purpose was to reveal the heart of their president in the light of his generation. In the first year great delight was manifested as Gabriel would propose the weekly subject for the Bulletin Board in advance of the meeting itself. All the twenty-eight members of the faculty would be present, and usually the five male Deans were present. Evangeline did not attend the meeting because of duties at the Manse. It was usually a Friday, three o'clock meeting, before the end of the day and week. Gabriel would open the meetings.

In the nine years under the leadership of Gabriel as president, the regular Friday sessions continued. Their purpose was to stir the heart and mind towards a greater relationship with God in the lives of His people than His people had considered. All through these years the student body, faculty, and deans continued their respect for President Parsons. However, the Board of Trustees was wavering as inroads and trends of the apostasy devoured the public view of natural theology and revealed theology. At the same time, the institutional church was experiencing a phenomenal growth numerically and financially with the new definition of Christianity.

In the nation, neo-pentecostalism had the largest growth, proportionately to the churches. This effect was seen clearly upon evangelism and the crusades of Evangelist Willie Wheyman, who regularly, at this point in his history, had liberals, Romanists, and Charismatics on his board and platform. The Evangelical World Seminary was becoming more charismatic than in its founding as a neo-evangelical movement of the Reformation. What scholarly stability they had was now giving way to the subjective experientialism of the charismatic gifts. Finally, in later years, TEWS would have the largest archives of pentecostal history and growth than any place in the world. The *Contemporary Christianity* (CC) magazine had reached world-wide proportion with translations of the fortnightly issue including fifty-two nations. The National Interaction of Christian Evangels (NICE) finally became the organization to include the Seventh-Day Adventists, Unitarians, and showed sympathy for Rome and the Pope.

The neo-pentecostalists, which ultimately became the Charismatic movement had penetrated all of Protestantism and Roman Catholicism by the 1970s. Contemporary Christian Music (CCM) had integrated Rock Music into the Gospel Song form, and the churches were literally filled with "the beat" of the world. On the threshold of the 1970s, Roman Catholic universities were opened for the neo-pentecostal message and song. This commenced the time when the neo-pentecostalism of Protestantism came into fellowship with the neo-pentecostalism of Romanism, and a union of both came under the title of "The Charismatic Renewal."

It is at this point, in 1969, that we hear of the trend of President Parsons Friday afternoon sessions increased to his beloved faculty and deans. The audience has been opened to all the students in attendance. There is a more gentle voice which now has accrued in these times together with a growth of forty-two faculty members and his six deans. Evangeline is also there sitting in the sixth chair arranged around the chair of the president and his lectern. Evangeline, in the ninth year, sat regularly now with the deans and shared her perspective in the question period. A hush falls upon the members of the session, who had faithfully served their beloved president and his leadership. This would be the last session of his presidency; the Board had requested him to resign, which he did. Dr. Parsons is now standing before the assembly, which have arisen to their feet with great respect.

Dr. Parsons gives the standing, opening prayer: "Our Heavenly Father thou art the beginning and the end of all things; Thy Son, the Lord Jesus, is the Alpha and Omega of the revelation of God. Therefore, we rejoice that the ending of a matter is better than the beginning of it, when Thou art there. For this day, we give thee thanks; and to this end Thou hast graciously brought us. Thou hast been good in all things, and bless now this last session to our beloved laborers, in Jesus' Name. Amen!"

Dr. Parsons indicates for the audience to be seated.

"Ladies and gentlemen, esteemed deans, beloved students, and friends: We have richly enjoyed your loyal hearts through all of these nine years together. (interrupting respectfully, the entire body arise to their feet and state as if conducted to a concert, "Amen, Beloved President!" There was no clapping of hands; simply an extended pause.)

"Thank you; you may be seated." (pause)

"Also, I wanted to acknowledge the presence of Mr. Boaz H. Broadman, the chairman of the Board of Trustees of this seminary. Mr. Broadman. (another pause; as Mr. Broadman stands briefly and is then seated again.)

"Our topic today concerns: 'The Contemporary Voices of Neo-Christianity in our World Today.'"

"We will set in order the agenda of presentation for this subject.

"First, a new or 'neo' definition of historic Christianity has finalized itself in our world. It originated from within the church institution itself rather than from an external source or enemy.

"Second, this neo-christianity is the composite amalgamation of four entities: The Charismatic Movement, the Ecumenical Movement, the Neo-Evangelical Movement, and the Roman Catholic Church.

"Third, at this exact point in our generation the full knowledge of the final manifestation of this neo-movement is not openly known by the grass-roots public or Christian audiences.

"Fourth, every Christian church, seminary, and ecclesiastical conference, convention, and congress must begin to address this drastic change and heresy to their respective audiences. The boards, trustees, directors, and pastors, in general, all have been aware of it for several years.

"Fifth, it should be clearly understood that this heretical change could destroy the public Protestant Ethic and the Reformation Spirit in the world if it continues unchecked by the solid teaching and preaching of the pure Word of God. This happened before at the close of the Puritan-Pilgrim Ethic which existed from 1626 to 1686, called the Biblical Commonwealth, and was instrumental in the birth of our beloved nation and the writing of her sacred documents.

"Sixth, it should also be clearly understood that neo-christianity, by its own new definition, will change the essence of a living Christian organism to a Christian organization and institution, only. An institutional Christianity should be defined as the human ability of a church to exist without the power of the Holy Spirit with the Holy Scriptures.

"Seventh, it was the emphasis on methodological evangelism that brought neo-christianity and its groups into a new-root for a neo-gospel. This root is beginning to flourish in the earth and will further develop its influence. It is believed by those who practice such evangelism that Biblical doctrine is considered to be a hindrance. As a result of this, the apostasy must grow in the earth.

"These seven observations must openly occupy our questions and deliberations for this our last meeting with you. (Dr. Parsons remains standing to receive the first question.)

Dr. Grayham gives the first question.

"Esteemed President Parsons, what should we understand as the actual meaning of the word *neo* in its relationship to our common English word 'new.'"

"Thank you, Dean Grayham. The word *neo* comes to us from the classical Attic Greek period in history when this word was thoroughly understood by the philosophers, and understood as a definitive borrowing from the meaning of 'new' or 'recent.' It is distinguished from another synonym, *kainei*, which means fresh in time; whereas *neos* means new in time, something really new in time, not heretofore known.

"In the case of Neo-Christianity, it applies to 'any interpretation of Christianity based on the prevalent presupposition or philosophy of that new time in history.' There would follow through the centuries since its origin among the Greeks, such schools as: 'Neo-Catholic'; 'Neo-Classicism'; 'Neo-Darwinism'; 'Neo-Gothic'; 'Neo-Platonism'; 'Neo-Romanism'; 'Neo-Romanticism'; 'Neo-Scholasticism'; etc.

"In all of these *neo* schools of thought the basic idea is to take an 'old' presuppositional meaning of a certain subject involved, as used before in its original meaning, and give it a 'new,' in time, presupposition which has not been used before in the old or original presupposition. This, in turn, is now used for a reinterpretation in the light and knowledge of a more modern time. It has become a universal and international practice to do this, even for ancient concepts, including 'Neocene' in evolutionism; 'Neo-Confucianism'; Neo-Melanesianism'; etc.

"What has happened in 'Neo-Christianity' is that modern man has taken the 'old' truth of Primitive Christianity, as revealed in God's Word, and given it a 'new' presuppositional base, for our modern time, as a new interpretation away from historic Christianity. This new interpretation is not according to the old interpretation that the Bible revealed and much of Dogmatic Theology in church history supported and confirmed for centuries. That modern continuity has now broken away from its past historic moorings. The best example of this in our time concerns 'The Jesus of the Gospel' versus 'The Gospel of Jesus.' In the former, we see the historic Jesus of Nazareth revealed as the incarnate Son of God; in the latter, we see Jesus merely as the highest form of man, the perfect men, but not God incarnate. In the former, we see historic Christianity; in the latter, we see modern or liberal Christianity. The Liberals use the exact same text in the Holy Scriptures but simply interpret it with their new presupposition of Jesus only as the highest man. This 'new' interpretation is then applied to every other context of Jesus.

"Dr. Parsons, our esteemed president: what would you say was the catalyst which commenced Neo-Christianity in all of its present ecumenical forms?"

"Yes, Dean Davidson, I almost anticipated this question in my last answer. (pause) All the way back in church history there have been other periods of a 'new-Christianity' with their own new presupposition. Anytime, anywhere, in church history, that any individual or Council changes the original presupposition of Primitive Christianity, or any Biblical truth set forth by a Biblical council, subsequently, and takes it away from historic Christianity, he is entering into a 'neo' presupposition with the interpretation of Biblical Christianity.

"The absolutes of the Bible are not liquid; they are stable, and must not be changed. This has happened before. Arius, of the fourth century A.D., endeavored to reject the hypostatic union of the full deity and humanity of the Lord Jesus, being only 'of a like substance with the Father.' That is an example of a 'neo-council,' first convening at Nicea. Fortunately, the presentation of Athanasius, a younger man, did set forth that Jesus was 'of one substance with the Father,' which was indeed in agreement with the New Testament revelation of Jesus, as the true, incarnate, God, and that belief was strictly held in Primitive Christianity. As a result of this defense, the original revelation in the Bible was kept according to the original revelation from God to man in His Word. The original presupposition was sustained. There is a certain lineage of Creeds and Councils which support the old definition.

"In our own time, for the sake of an unseparated world-wide evangelism, the methodology of this modern evangelism has compromised the Gospel and rejected the scriptural separation, as taught in the Bible, which is necessary if Christians are to be kept from compromise with the apostasy itself.

"In our own time, for the sake of an unseparated world-wide evangelism, the methodology of this modern evangelism, in these compromises, has been what we think of as neo-pentecostalism and neo-evangelicalism, neo-orthodoxy, and the ecumenical movement. This, also, has brought fellowship with Roman Catholicism, which in the time of the Middle Ages became neo-catholic, the longest continuing apostasy in church history. This was in contrast to the Old-Catholic Church of the early Fathers. The catalyst is for the sake of evangelism, world-wide. We must not sacrifice Biblical doctrine for souls to be saved, per se."

Dr. Ussher presents the third question.

"Esteemed president, where is the record or witness found concerning these directions and trends that you have knowledge of for your conclusions?"

"Thank you, Dr. Ussher; a needed question (pause). Since

1955, I have been on a schedule of travel lectures. According to my journal, in these fourteen years I have averaged about seventy-five series of lectures a year, which has thrown me into the camps of seminaries and universities where ecclesiastical leaders have heard my presentations. This has given me about 180 presentations. These leaders of the denominations, conferences, and professors have approached me concerning what was being discussed in their private meetings. All of these matters have been printed in the denominational union meetings and fellowships and may be secured upon request. An overwhelming majority have concluded with the optimism of methodological evangelism, the personalities involved, the NICE movement, TEWS movement, CC publications, as well as the Willie Wheyman Evangelistic Association.

"Here again, anyone who is following these leading organizations, regularly and seriously, will find in their publications the content I have presented. These matters are being discussed openly, but I do not believe the grass-roots of these representatives have become fully aware of the consequences of what is being thought and planned. Some of the leaders have actually told me that the common and local people are not as informed as they should be concerning what is happening to their doctrinal and Biblical position on these things. There have been many controversies in the denominations; a considerable number of leaders and pastors have already suffered from their remaining true to their convictions of the Bible. In many of these places I was invited as a guest, beginning with Bishop LeVon Gilbertson of the 'First Quadrennial Conference on Evangelism.'

"At this point in time, I do not know of any conference or official, other than the remnant to which I have referred, that has not become a part of ecumenical evangelism. We must keep in mind that ecumenical evangelism, without obedience to the doctrine of the Holy Scriptures, will bring more people and money into a local church. Compromise always has. It is no secret; but I am sure the grass-roots churches will soon be shocked to know how far-reaching an error is ahead of them.

But at that stage in its development, I doubt that it will make much difference. I have attended other conferences; I have written over twenty-five books; my own position is quite clear. I have been received most respectfully, and a number have agreed with my appraisal of the situation. Television has launched the neo-christianity around the world. Before God, I do affirm that the information I have set forth has been an accurate presentation of what is going on. That is the reason I have proceeded into further studies for some length of time. I believe the future will simply substantiate it more, unless God chooses and His people pray for a revival and a return to God and His Word."

"Dr. Ussher, did you have another question?"

"No, Dr. Parsons, I just raised my hand at your conclusion to affirm I knew your position and agreed with it. But I thought it becoming you to place your confirmation on record. I knew that you would probably be reluctant to defend this material, personally. I thought as a friend to these facts, I should let others present know of their verification. Thank you, very much."

"Thank you, my brother."

Dr. Dawson gives the fourth question.

"Dr. Parsons, our honorable president, my question concerns what you mentioned about the possibility of the destruction of 'The Protestant Ethic' because of this condition in our world that you mentioned. Would you expand further remarks on this?"

"Yes, Dean Dawson. First, I would like to make a gentle distinction between the Reformation and Protestantism. In the former, we are talking about Reformation Christianity established through Martin Luther, which is a movement of Bible Christians from the sixteenth-century slavery under Roman Catholicism who first desired to change or reform that Roman Church. In the latter, protestantism, we are speaking about a somewhat later development of the protestant distinctives of various theological systems. These distinctives began to proliferate into the various protestant denominations. This, then, established a variety of theological presentations which we believe became the ethic of Protestantism in the Body of Christ. Not all Christians pursued the faith of the basic Reformation movement which we believe was a direct sovereign work of Almighty God.

"'The Protestant Ethic' was established by the Biblical truth of those theological systems which came after the Reformation had done its work. This contribution brought us back in history to the clarification of historic Christianity. It brought back the genuine place of doctrine to the church. The Reformation brought us back to 'Justification by Faith'; to the infallible Word of God; the teachings of grace through faith. It destroyed the Romanist bonds and demands of a work righteous, sacramental system; it brought us back to Primitive Christianity.

"This modern apostasy will also mean the loss of 'the Puritan-Pilgrim Ethic'; the 'Bible Belt Ethic' in America'; 'The Constitutional Ethic' in America; and the moral and spiritual ethic in the people of the nation. We must see that apostate Christianity will affect the public proclamation of the Gospel and the loss of the true definition of Christianity in certain areas of life. However, the survival of the Gospel, itself, and God's people, themselves, will never be destroyed! 'The Lord God omnipotent reigneth!'

"I am sure I need to conclude this question with something of a definition of the word, 'ethic,' itself. This definition can either be applied to a group or an individual. 'Ethic refers to the body of moral principles or values governing or distinctive of a particular culture or group; or, a complex of moral precepts held or rules of conduct followed by an individual, as a personal ethic.'"

"Thank you," responded Dean Dawson. (pause)

"It has not been the pattern of these years here in the seminary for Dr. Evangeline Marguerite Parsons to be with us. (a gentle responsive laughter by the assembly.) She is the only

Dean who serves two educational institutions. She is the Dean of the Home School of our children, and she is the Dean of the School of Fine Arts here in the seminary. Would Dean Evangeline Parsons like to say something at this time in our last faculty-dean assembly?" (a pause, as the Deans, in concert, respond: "yes," and the faculty also joins in with the second "yes!")

"Dr. Parsons, our beloved president, as your wife and Dean of the School of Fine Arts for the last nine years in the seminary, I would like to share one matter on my heart, and then ask a two-fold question."

"I yield to Dean Evangeline Parsons as she has requested. Dean Evangeline." (with a slight bow from the president, the assembly laughs cordially. A pause.)

"First, I would like to express my appreciation and Christian love today to all of you who have served the Lord through these nine years, under my husband as president. My heart has rejoiced in Christ through you. Also, thank you for the respect you have given my husband, your president, through these years. Wherever we may be in future years, I wish you could still be with us. But if that is not possible we hope you will always be our Christian friends. Also, we pray that we will all be standing true to Christ for the future as well." (the assembly arises with a hearty 'bravo,' suitable for Fine Arts; Some weep; all agree, "Amen." Evangeline is somewhat overcome by their response; she blushes. A pause. The body is seated.)

"And now I would like for Dr. Parsons, my husband, whom I love, to once again, for my benefit and yours, give the answer to two questions, at my request.

"First, what is your definition of apostasy, and what is your definition of scriptural separation?"

The president replies after a deliberate pause.

"Apostasy means 'a falling away,' and it results when a person compromises his Biblical principles so as to mix truth and error in such a fashion within himself that he is comforted by the truth in that mixture, and yet is deceived by the error that he has, by compromise, embraced with it: God then, gives that man over to a delusion.

"Scriptural separation is first and foremost a scriptural separation unto the Lordship of Jesus Christ as the Lord of his or her life; and because that Lord constrains each Christian to be separated, in life and testimony, he or she personally separates from all fellowships with apostates and apostasies. (a sobering pause)

"At the close of this last session, I want to once again speak of our delight in having Mr. Boaz A. Broadman, chairman of the Board of Trustees, with us today. (Mr. Broadman stands as a motion of gratitude is manifested towards Gabriel.)

The faculty and deans stand to their feet as prompted by the raised hands of Gabriel. The president concludes:

"Faculty and Deans, you are at liberty. Good day."

Thus ends the last meeting of President Parsons with his dearest friends in historic Christianity. The first and the last series of questions dedicated to Gabriel's beloved faculty and deans have been purposefully presented, both series being on the subjects involving the history of man. The first opened up the subject of history by distinguishing time from eternity, as the commencement of history. The second dealt with the most recent history being set forth in the contemporary struggle against historic Christianity, which comes at the end of World Civilization towards the Second Advent of Christ.

So, from the beginning of time to the end of the time of man, Gabriel sets forth his agenda and inventory for his future ministry.

In the 1960s other protestant churches received the neo-pentecostal message of the glossolalia and gifts of the Holy Spirit, as defined by the neo-pentecostalist. New and extant revelation apart from the Holy Scriptures was being claimed through audible voices, dreams, and visions, so-called. The "prophet" of these heresies was appearing as a prominent feature of the neo and charismatic pentecostalists' meetings and conferences.

In the 1970s, Roman Catholics, by the hundreds of priests

and nuns, were "experiencing" the Holy Spirit baptism, the gifts of the Holy Ghost, so-called, as the other protestant churches had received in the 1960s. Even a few Cardinals of Romanism were involved and endorsing the movement. In Romanism, all of this phenomenon was identified back to a Romanist "baptism" sacrament, and instead of the Holy Spirit being identified in Regeneration, it was now understood by Romanists as a "renewal" of that which had been received in the "baptism-sacrament." It was a Roman Catholic doctrine rather than a historic Christian doctrine of the Primitive and Reformation Christianity.

By the 1980s all of the tags and labels formerly identified as pentecostal or protestant or Roman Catholic, were being identified under the singular term, "charismatic." This word was singled out from a Greek word in the New Testament, *charisma*, and limited to the meaning of "gifts." The Greek word of the New Testament is used in so many different, true doctrinal distinctives, but now the word had become limited, explicitly, to the "new-gifts," of which the *glossolalia* meaning "tongues," had become the most prominent.

The "Charismatics" had now become a conglomeration of religious concepts under a tag and label away from Primitive Christianity; it was an apostasy away from that historic work of God. This was also a departure from Reformation Christianity, so much supported in the spirit of Remnant Christianity back through church history. To Gabriel, it was unthinkable that the contemporary could forget Romanism, the Papacy, the Council of Trent, Mariolatry, and the Martyrs, to say nothing of Wycliffe, Tyndale, Huss, and Martin Luther. The contemporary Christian Church had lost its memory and turned its back on historic Christianity. Therefore, the historic principle would no longer be used to validate truth and doctrine and theology.

The four forces of the "National Interaction of Christian Evangels"; "The Evangelical World Seminary"; *Contemporary Christianity*, the religious fortnightly publication; and the World-Wide Evangelistic Crusades of Evangelist Willie Wheyman; along with a host of businessmen, institutions, politicians, and churches were uniting an influence around the world, on an international scale.

The 1960s and nine years of Gabriel's presidency at the Antioch Theological Seminary brought Gabriel Parsons to see the fruit of the seed sown for the future of the 1970s, 1980s, and the 1990s. His experience at this seminary was a miniature of history. The corporate leadership of the Board of Trustees began a respectful withdrawal from Gabriel's leadership in his plea for historic Christianity. Gabriel had appraised, with objective study and prayer, the loss of the Biblical, pure teachings of the Lord Jesus, the New Testament, and Primitive Christianity. He realized, in his own empirical studies of the contemporary forces, that the first century, the sixteenth century, and all histories of the remnants of grace, had now been discarded for a definition of Christianity that included liberals, Romanists, and others to change the meaning of Christianity in the twentieth century.

Of course, Gabriel always recognized that there was a remnant in the late twentieth century, as was true always in history, who would not compromise their historic faith. Very little homework in the field of history would be forthcoming again from the generality of the public institutional church. This had been one of the mainstays of the past ministers and churches before the apostate's time.

Above all, modern ecumenical Christianity had left the absolute authority of the Word of God, which the Holy Spirit had carefully guarded with Inerrancy, Infallibility, and verbal-plenary Inspiration.

The "First Quadrennial Conference on Evangelism" had identified fourteen theological groups, and said no "Romanist" would be a part of Evangelism. But now in sixteen years the Romanists were Charismatics with the ecumenical movement, and a part of the World-Wide popular evangelism of the time.

The "First Quadrennial Conference on Evangelism" included Pelagians, and the Unitarians, and Universalists, because there was inherent in the seven historic pentecostalists their tolerance of "The United Pentecostalists." This group believed in "Jesus, Only," which meant a rejection of the

Christian Trinity of the New Testament. They had remained as pentecostalists without doctrinal censure through the years of their movement from the beginning of the twentieth century.

The historic protestants had always taught from the Bible the total depravity of man, instead of the goodness of man as the Pelagians had held. Of course, the Unitarians and the Universalists were simply a modern extension of this belief in the name of Christian Liberalism and Modernism.

Evangelist Willie Wheyman had held a growing concept that the Jews and the Heathen had special light from God and, therefore, could come to God another way than through the Gospel of the Lord Jesus Christ. Later on, Willie Wheyman would actually take his concept to its logical conclusion and allow that a person could be saved and go to heaven without the Gospel, the Bible, and the name of Jesus.

The "First Quadrennial Conference on Evangelism" said they would not include in their evangelistic fellowship the cults, but now the "Jesus Only" pentecostalists and the "Seventh Day Adventists" were given acknowledgment to their considerations as any other Christian identity. The "National Interaction of Christian Evangels" (NICE) was seriously considering them for membership.

When the new-evangelicals broke with the Fundamentalists in the 1940s, no neo-evangelical would have ever suspected then such an ecumenical movement to be accepted. That was in the 1940s. Yes, the fundamental core of truth was no longer the center of public evangelism and revivalism.

Gabriel, as president of the Antioch Theological Seminary, gave nine years dedicated to the teaching of the pure Word of God in the context of historic Christianity. He accepted the challenge offered him by the Board of Trustees believing this seminary, like a Biblical laboratory, could have been a force to bring forth an apologetic defense to this small remnant of students and trustees. He believed the students who attended the seminary in those years would never get away from the truth taught.

In the first two years at the seminary, Gabriel noted that

the student body rose to 700. In the fifth year, 800; in the ninth year, 950. The faculty rose twenty percent, and still another Dean was added in Biblical Languages. However, the Board of Trustees was receiving pressure from the denominations that the students who graduated from Antioch Theological Seminary were too strong, too Biblical and bookish. They did not believe that the graduates were able to fit into the ecumenical evangelism of the time, or would be knowledgeable of the charismatic renewal of the time.

In 1969, in the ninth year of his leadership, President Parsons was asked to resign after several pleas for change in his presupposition for the seminary. Only Mr. Boaz A. Broadman, the chairman of the Board of Trustees, gave his dissenting voice and vote because of the respect and Biblical stand of Dr. Gabriel T. Parsons.

Gabriel could write many pages of this nine-year period. His dear father, Bishop Parsons, died in the second year of his being at the seminary, and one year after his return from the missionary preaching mission. Also, Gabriel's favorite teacher, Dr. John Rendle Wellson died in the fourth year of his being at the Antioch Theological Seminary. He had often invited him to speak and teach in the seminary during those first four years as president there. Gabriel missed him greatly.

However, Dr. Paulson, Dean of the Faculty at Georgeton Theological Seminary struggled on in his stand for the Bible, and it appeared to Gabriel he had become stronger in his position there.

Through all the years, Gabriel and Evangeline were still in love and in fellowship with God. The three children were growing in grace and in the knowledge of the Holy Scriptures, and they highly respected their dear parents. Joseph Paul was twenty years old, a Christian young man studying for the ministry; Soma Jeanne was fifteen, studying music under her mother; and Ariel John was fourteen, youthfully happy and even then contemplating a major in history for his college days. Miss Juliana Queens, still teaching their children in the Parsons' home, was growing in the dignity of the grace of God.

Gabriel and his family left the seminary at Ocean View, North Carolina, with added grace and stronger faith from this test God had sent to him. He had the respect of his students and Boaz A. Broadman, the chairman of the Board of Trustees. A large number of saints had substantiated their own testimony through the mails, and a large number of the graduates were out on the field planting independent, Bible-Believing churches for the glory of God with the testimony of a separatist fundamentalist. Most of all, Gabriel and Evangeline knew they were a part of Remnant Christianity, built upon the primitive-reform historical Christians.

The test brought them through with a greater faith and hope for their future. They moved back to their beautiful home in Georgetown, the middle of the month of May, 1969. In June, Gabriel would go on the planned study tour in the Middle East and meet a new friend in Christ who would become a rich blessing for the remaining years of his entire life.

Chapter Sixteen

The Travels

(1955 - 1969)

The empirical method of study was preferred by Gabriel above the academic method, if you had to decide between one or the other. It is the method, undoubtedly, that the common man and the masses have pursued the most in history. There has always been books, but not everybody has owned the book from which knowledge has indeed been passed on to others. Common sense is the unacademic learning process; academics is simply a more sophisticated method of the same but enlarged learning process. Both are ultimately in the books.

This did not indicate Gabriel had avoided the academic training of his years, but he only did it because God impressed him to do so, and it was not his own desire at all. Gabriel also knew that the academic method had the ability to teach you many things faster and in a larger epistemology. Also, many more voices would give either confirmation or rejection. However, that is a two-way street in that the error often heard could affect the heart and mind with defilement. Academic knowledge has great power. Gabriel also knew that the average person does not have the time to spend such years in fields he does not need or does not heed. Most of the people of the world, by sheer necessity, must learn life by experience alone. There are dangers in experiential knowledge, too.

Jesus and His Disciples did not magnify the academic community, nor did Jesus condemn intelligence and knowledge.

Gabriel uses the empirical method in a different way than that which has already been noted. Also, the very word "empirical" carries with it various definitions, and that could hinder life's search in that way. Two of these definitions are as follows: "that which is based entirely upon practical experience"; "a person who lacks theoretical or scientific knowledge and relies entirely on practical experience."

Gabriel preferred, however, the more balanced definition, "knowledge based on experiment and observation, whether academic or empirical."

One of Gabriel's studies of an Christian English writer proposed: "Nothing can be ultimately believed without a faith seeking to experience it." In more Christian words, a Christian's Faith must show up in his life and in his living it; what is preached must be practiced. We are indeed saved by grace through faith that works. It is the "works" that are either distorted one way or another. Works become the fruit of faith. Faith is the lifting up of empty hands to receive the Unspeakable Gift of God's promise. Reformation Christianity cleared this up; works are the fruit of true faith.

Gabriel's academic studies must take on experience: from the simplest acts of love between Gabriel and Evangeline in experiencing the Land of Evangeline to Biblical and spiritual matters. Gabriel had considered the academic studies an exercise-burden he must bear. The greater test, however, was how would it be in other lands, cultures, languages, and conditions?

The time had come for this test.

Gabriel had attended several Congresses of Fundamentalism and returned with an encouraged heart. The overseas Extension of the University had been delayed considerably, and the property purchased near Jerusalem had been interrupted by several wars in the Middle East and had changed hands now from the Arabs to the Jews. Only a legal court could save things. However, overseas teaching was now scheduled for Gabriel and from other directions as well.

Evangeline and Gabriel discuss the nearness of the overseas trip.

"Gabriel, the time has finally arrived for the overseas teaching opportunities. We should be hearing from Dr. Jonathan soon."

"Yes, my dear Evangeline. I know your own heart would desire this trip with me, but I am only a servant to the invitation of others, for not only the Extension but for a larger teaching to a number of Christians in foreign places."

"I understand, dear."

"That's fine; we shall await the time." (a time of pause)

"Gabriel, knowing your appreciation in the learning processes, academically, as well as empirically, I do not believe it has hindered your deep hunger for Christ to live in the simplicity of your life. Also, you have been a faithful and loving husband and father in your living experience of our marriage. We would never fool each other that you and I have two ways in our wills. I can say, with all my love and heart, you are still my head because of my life joined to you."

"I am aware of this, my dear Evangeline."

"Well, I wanted to share a portion of musical history with you, and if you, too, have read of it, we will enjoy the recall anyway."

"This will be interesting to me, Evangeline, and especially since it will be communicated to me by my favorite musicologist."

"Your humor and compliment are both accepted, dear. (a little laugh passes between them.) But seriously, there was a most important period in musical history in Italy from 1600 to 1750. A race of singing masters sprang up in Italy and taught the singers to produce such an artistry with their voices as had never been known before. This breed of teachers is known today as the 'Old Italian School.' By 1865 it was superseded by the modern scientific method. The 'Old Italian School' of teaching is known as the 'empirical method.' Many attempts have been made in recent years to reconstruct the 'Old Italian School' method in the light of modern scientific knowledge of the voice, but no such analysis of the empirical system of that day has ever convinced musicologists of an artistry greater than the Old Italian School. Presentations of the music and the voices of that period cannot be duplicated again. A number of the operas and oratorios have been laid aside because of the lack of the empirical, experiential discovery and the gifts of that time. Would you not say that is a plus mark for the empirical method, which you speak so respectfully about, Gabriel?"

"You have given a classical, historical illustration of what we should believe as Christians in order for God to bring a revival of the primitive, spiritual schools of the heart and mind in our time. This is exactly what Primitive Christianity brought first. The spirit of the first, original group of disciples and believers during that actual time of the bodily presence of the Lord Jesus Christ is what is needed in our own time. The principles were so simple, but within that simplicity was a greater depth than men saw even at that time. Worship and grace permeated the time. Only later would greater insight come out of that simplicity of the Gospel. Yet they had to forward their Christian life and experience with what was ahead. Once again, I tell 'thee,' dear Evangeline, you were a gift to me of simple faith, simple trust, and simple life. I thank God for that. (Evangeline was not able to respond to the personal remarks; a pause comes.) Today, you have added to my belief through your historical observation of the 'Old Italian School,' which I did not know about. Thank you." (another pause)

"Gabriel where would you go in the Bible to illustrate for me what might be a possibility of such a revival in our own time for the people of God?"

"I was thinking of a passage in the prophecy of Joel, chapter 2, verse 28. The prophet, there, speaks so wonderfully that 'your young men shall see visions:...' I do not think that the prophet is referring here to new-revelation 'visions' such as the modern Charismatics claim. If the mystical form of 'vision' is thought here, then that would mean that modern man does not have God's sufficient, final word, but rather that we are waiting for additional revelation to the Bible. But since we believe the Bible has been forever completed, we must seek the other Biblical meaning of 'visions.' Proverbs, chapter 29, verse 18 would be appropriate: 'Where there is no vision, the people perish: but he that keepeth the law, happy is he.'"

"Gabriel, what kind of 'vision' are you talking about in this?"

"I mean 'vision' like a Christian's earthly view of what he would like to do for the sake and glory of the Lord Jesus. I think you and I have a 'vision.' We have an earthly view of what we would like to do for Christ with our lives."

"Yes, I truly believe that, dear Gabriel."

"I believe that now since our hearts and lives are clear in placing our nine years at Antioch Theological Seminary behind us, that God will show us our 'vision' for our ministry. (a pause) But back to our text in Joel, I believe that we could have a revival of 'light,' as God's people in our time, in these last days. We may 'see visions,' spiritually, something like a 'revival of light' for us in these very dark days of the church in the time of the apostasy. We should be enjoying a wonderful access to true knowledge and light, to not only prepare us for the future, but bring into our testimony and evangelism Biblical light in contrast to the apostasy of false evangelism going on in our time."

"Gabriel, I see that. Please pray that I might have that in my own life. (Evangeline's face becomes radiant to the thought.) (after a pause) But what about that other verse you mentioned from Proverbs?"

"Yes, I do need to give addition to that verse, because that is quite distinctive for us. Solomon, in that verse, is really giving a warning to the people, something like, 'where there is no true authoritative vision in life, the people will become lawless.' He goes on to say 'but he that keepeth the law, happy is he.' Or, he that sees 'vision' as an authoritative influence in his life, and keepeth it, will find a happy life in every way. Of course, that underlines my first words to you concerning our need of 'vision,' like this — a revival of precious, Biblical, spiritual light in our time."

"What happens when we lose such a primitive experience or 'vision' with Christ, Gabriel?"

"The church at Ephesus, which in the New Testament, is not only one of the seven churches revealed to John, but is also the *first* of the seven churches so appropriate as an illustration of Primitive Christianity. John speaks that this church had *left* its 'first love,' Revelation, chapter 1, verse 4. Jesus revealed to John that unless that church repented, its 'candlestick' would be removed, verse 5. We think, prophetically, of these verses as indicating that since the 'first love' of Primitive Christianity failed in this matter of *love*, that it would bring about the removal of *light*. As a long-term result of this, the Dark Ages and Roman Catholic slavery would enter into church history itself."

"Gabriel, you mean that later church history was affected by this loss of Primitive Christianity?"

"Yes, my dear."

"What is the way back. Gabriel?"

"I must be careful in my answer to you. For Ephesus, while it was leaving its first love, there was a remedy, at that time, through repentance, that would have returned it to its first love and the safekeeping of its candlestick. However, that church period passed; there was no way back. Neither history nor any individual can go back or undo historical tragedy. After that, the next church period will have to take hold of greater, deeper truth from the Bible to defeat a deeper darkness of the apostasy. We must experience the deep power of God's Word since every generation takes us deeper into error. When men taste the new wine of heresy, it becomes more difficult to refrain from being the drunkard to it. In all things: first, the 'drink,' then the 'drunk.' So, that adds the burden of not only dealing with problems, under the fall, of a sober man, but the matter is compounded to the greater problem of being a drunk man, too."

"Well, my darling, we come to another time in our lives

together concerning our Lord."

Thus, another soul-searching time comes into the lives of Gabriel and Evangeline.

So, the empirical method, through a number of travels, caused Gabriel to add to his academic learning the empirical school of human experience with a large variety of other people in other lands.

Gabriel proceeded through every open door that extended itself to him as an invitation to other nations and countries. He lectured in many seminaries, a number of universities, summer camps of ministerial students, as well as family groups and children, and to a host of churches. From 1969 to the mid-1990s, Gabriel went to Greece, Asia Minor, Jerusalem, Israel, Spain, Switzerland, England, Wales, Northern Ireland, Scotland, the Philippines, Singapore, Hong Kong, Malaysia, South Africa, Japan, South Korea, Bolivia, besides at least thirty states in America. To a number of places he went back several times; to South Korea he returned seventeen times.

This unusual journey, across the globe, extended an empirical learning of peoples, places, and things he would have never known through the books. He saw the church, everything from Primitive Christianity to the depths of Reformation Christianity; and also, the apostasy was manifested in all of the very same places.

But there remained two experiences in his travels which were unmatched in his walk with the Lord. These became the two covers on the one book of his human experience. The first was in the Middle East; the second was in South Korea. The first dealt with his most personal and precious friend; the second, was with his own dear Evangeline, but as far away from the Land of Evangeline as one could possibly go to gain such a blessed experience for Gabriel and her. Gabriel met the new-found, Christian friend when he was forty-three years old; and his experience with his Evangeline was at the age of sixty-nine.

In 1969, while on a study tour to the Middle East, including the places of Greece, the Hellespont, Troy, Asia Minor (Turkey), the Island of Cyprus, then on to the Holy Lands, the good providence of God led Gabriel into a new Christian friendship with Rev. Matthew Noel Wiley. In reality, Gabriel was in at least one class with him, prior to this trip, at the Bible Christian University in his Ph.D. studies. Their acquaintance, however, really came to fruition during the overseas study tour. About a dozen persons were in the group, including Rev. Wiley's dear wife, Bettina.

It was a most unusual beginning to a lasting, close friendship. Bro. Wiley became a Christian as a very young man, back in the wild, wonderful state of Kentucky, near the border of West Virginia. He was led to Christ in a very strong fundamentalist church. He came into church leadership while he was yet young, and was even quite a businessman at that age. At his conversion he became a strong, active Christian wherever his influence was known. His testimony remained strong until the end of the days of Gabriel with him. This strong beginning was sustained by growing in the grace of the Lord Jesus into a maturity of an appreciation for the entire Body of Christ wherever he met Christ's members to that Body.

Gabriel and Rev. Wiley fell into many and varied conversations on their trip together. God began to use His Anvil, hammer, and heat with both of them. This friendship became an anchor of integrity to Gabriel, yet Gabriel was older than this Christian brother. Rev. Wiley, at the age of about twenty-seven, was commencing a southern pastorate during his graduate work at the University. Not too much later he would move to a larger church, farther south, in the greater metropolitan area of Atlanta, Georgia.

Each of these two Christians had come from opposite extremes in their denominational backgrounds, dispositions, personalities, and there were a number of other differences; yet in a respectful setting overseas they began to see a miracle of the first magnitude in their friendship. It was something that Gabriel did not really expect to see in his lifetime or, for that matter, in his generation. Gabriel, in his readings in the Bible had read of some friendships of such dimension. He had also read of a few such friendships in the times adjacent to

Primitive Christianity, Remnant Christianity, and Reformation Christianity. However, in his studies of the times since the development of the theological systems, which came into existence in the aftermath of Reformation Christianity, Gabriel had noted that those who followed the systems seemed to find it the hardest of days in history to be a part of a great friendship across the theological lines in the full Body of Christ.

Gabriel had read of the friendship of Calvin with Luther through a mutual friend, Philip Melanchthon; John Wesley with Jonathan Edwards through George Whitefield; and others. Finally, Luther told Melanchthon that Calvin's definition of the Lord's Supper was better, but Luther told that late in his own life, being about twenty-five years older than Calvin, after writing what he thought was the best rendering on the subject of the Lord's Supper. Gabriel recalled the personal differences between John and Charles Wesley, with George Whitefield mediating them back to a precious relationship. However, the difference and distance between the Heidelberg Catechism and the Westminster Confession of Faith and the Larger and Shorter Catechisms is not short or shallow. The boundary between Arminianism and either Luther or Calvin is even wider. But there remains John Wesley and his distinctive Wesleyan position away from Arminianism that, to say the least, Charles Haddon Spurgeon commended.

Fletcher of Madeley seems to have been respected in spite of theological differences more than most others to be named. When one of his elders asked Spurgeon if he thought he would see John Wesley in heaven, Spurgeon replied, "No." The elder seemed pleased to note that Spurgeon believed Wesley would not be in heaven at all. "Oh no," corrected Spurgeon, "I meant that in heaven John Wesley will be so far ahead of me towards the Throne that I probably will not see him."

So, it was in this context that Gabriel met Matthew N. Wiley in 1969, on foreign soil.

Their early conversations of the first few days of their personal acquaintance were friendly, but Gabriel learned later that the good, young pastor was fitting himself for boxing gloves in view of the fact they were to be with each other, as companions, on a large number of summer weeks. Gabriel did not know these developing thoughts at that time. However, Rev. Wiley was still quite respectful to Gabriel in spite of these differences.

One morning, early, while awaiting departure to their next study site on the agenda, Gabriel entered into his serious hope to make a friend. It concerned the uniqueness of Evangelist George Whitefield.

"Brother Wiley, I was thinking earlier this morning of the man and ministry of George Whitefield."

"Yes," responded Rev. Wiley, "Whitefield stands tall in his stand for Christ in his day. I believe he came across the Atlantic ocean about seven times, from England, in his evangelistic efforts for the Lord. He died, I believe, on that seventh trip and was buried here in America, rather than being returned to his home in England."

"That is correct, Brother Wiley. He was buried under the pulpit floor in the last church in which he preached his last message; there in the Old South Church, Newberryport, Massachusetts."

"I did not know that Dr. Parsons. Was that his very last message?"

"Yes, my brother, the last sermon in a church. After preaching that night, the congregation followed him two houses to the rear of the church itself, where he had his lodgings, and after entering the home, the people urgently requested him to preach another good Word to them."

"Well, well, well," responded Rev. Wiley.

"Mr. Whitefield, after entering the house, took a candle with him and was in the process of ascending the staircase to his room. He paused, however, turned to the crowded house, with some even standing outside the house listening as well, placed the candlestick on the staircase post, and took another step up towards his room. He responded that he would take another brief time and say a few words for his Lord. He preached until the candle was low, gave a prayer, and went up to his bed. He died late into the night towards the morning, in his bed, having had discomfort for several hours."

"Yes, I remember now that story, Dr. Parsons. He had not always enjoyed good health in later years."

"Quite true. Mr. George Whitefield, for about the last nine years of his preaching ministry, would spit up blood for some time after each sermon he preached."

"You know, I'm sure, Dr. Parsons, Whitefield knew the Wesleys, too. There were several clashes between them. Wesley either took several worship properties from Whitefield, or he requested him to do so. Whitefield gave the properties to Wesley."

"Yes, that is correct. Lady Huntingdon desired Whitefield to separate himself from Wesley and start a new denomination of his own by his own name. She did not think Wesley's manner was always good. (a pause) However, I wanted to get to another story involving John Wesley and George Whitefield. May I do so, my brother?"

"Please do, Dr. Parsons."

"As you know, the founder of Methodism, John Wesley, was not a Calvinist. George Whitefield was the Calvinist."

"Yes, Whitefield was definitely a Calvinist; that's true."

"However, Brother Wiley, George Whitefield died a member of John Wesley's Methodist Church. Why do you think that was so?"

"Well, I really had not considered such a matter between them before, Dr. Parsons."

"May I venture a resolve of this, my brother?"

"Please! Yes!"

"George Whitefield, the Calvinist, had the precious Primitive Christianity of the Spirit of Christ. I like to call this incident in history 'the George Whitefield Spirit.' I am from a Methodist background, myself, but in view of the fact that the liberals and neo-pentecostalists are taking over the Wesleyans and modern Methodism, I had to leave it. In fact, I have finalized that exodus by being fired as president of a seminary that was founded by a presbyterian pastor, a godly man, whom my father respected, and I, too. Having been in that seminary for nine years, I must now leave. However, in the case of

Whitefield, I believe he, being a Calvinist, had the better position in his time than the theological extremities which fell out in Arminian Methodism."

"I see what you mean; this is very unusual for a Calvinist, who certainly sees his Lord different than a Methodist."

"Yes, it is rare; I wish I had such a spirit, like George Whitefield, for men opposite to my own position who are genuine Christians, like George Whitefield."

"I join you in that, Dr. Parsons; I join you, my brother."

"I am glad to accept your offer, my dear friend. Whitefield did this with Wesley, and never preached another public sermon in his remaining life on 'Predestination' because he wanted to keep Wesley's friendship and he did not want to bring a division between them. In reality, Jonathan Edwards, George Whitefield, and John Wesley, who all lived at the same time, all believed in the sovereignty of God equally. Edwards and Whitefield worked out that sovereignty through predestination; Wesley worked it out through 'prevenient grace.' But it cannot be rightly said that Wesley slighted the sovereignty of God."

"Yes, I understand your observation, and I would like to gain your friendship, Dr. Parsons."

"And I, yours, Brother Wiley. It is my own personal opinion, my dear brother, that because of this spirit in George Whitefield, a definite distinction must now be drawn between Wesleyism and Methodism in church history since the Reformation. Of course, other doctrinal distinctions could be made between Wesley and Methodism, and Wesley agreed in a number of things with John Calvin. In the former, Wesley responded to the primitive distinctive of 'the burning heart'; in the latter, it is 'the mere subjective experience,' and probably sheer humanism in many places."

It was not long in the travels of that summer, in the friendship of Gabriel and Rev. Wiley, that they met each other in a unique spirit, yea, even a Christian experience, in the very geography of the Garden of Gethsemane.

From that trip, to the end of their lives, they remained the very best of Christian friends. A sovereign God did it all;

amazing grace was brought in to play upon their lives together until the end of their lives on earth. Within twenty years they would enter into a unique, Biblical ministry with each other which lasted for ten precious years of work directly together, sometimes with hardship and hard places; but through it all God brought forth a definite testimony to the glory of God, with a permanent contribution to the cause of the Lord Jesus Christ. All of this was done because the love of God embraced both of them to be friends. Once again, God's Anvil, God's hammer, and God's heat brought it about. Not just a clay vessel, but a vessel of iron. Gabriel would later mark this distinction in the Bible with two passages: Jeremiah, chapter 18, verses 1 through 3 and Isaiah 41:7.

At another extremity in Gabriel's life, at the age of sixty-nine, he had a most blessed occasion with Evangeline in Seoul, South Korea. In an audience of almost six thousand people, Evangeline gave a forty-five-minute sacred concert, as the soloist with organ accompaniment. Evangeline, too, was sixty-nine years old. She presented nine musical renderings. From the sacred classical to the great hymns of the English people, she stood there as the Holy Spirit touched her knowledge and her character within her gift.

Gabriel had already been requested to give a few words at the end of the concert, for he was on a lecture-tour in seminaries for two weeks prior to this final item on his itinerary before returning to the United States.

Gabriel, deeply moved, informed the audience that they may never again hear such singing from such a unique time in Evangeline and Gabriel's lives together. He stated it with solemnity:

"You have just heard the music of one of God's servants who is sixty-nine years old. My dear Evangeline started public singing in Yarmouth, Nova Scotia, Canada, at the age of five. She was soon launched on radio at the age of five; then as a teen-ager, a member of 'The Stars of Tomorrow"; then on to the Acadia Music Conservatory in Canada; and finally gave her public recital in which a representative from the Juilliard Music Conservatory was to give an invitation for studies there.

Her mother, who died near that time, had requested Evangeline to go to the United States to a University that loved the Word of God, so she would have a spiritual and Biblical balance in her life. I met her there; we married and have had three children. She has been in music for sixty-four years. In the good providence of God this may be one of her very last appearances to such a gracious and large audience. You may never again hear her voice like this. I love South Korea, having known you for sixteen trips in sixteen years. Now, my dear Evangeline loves you, too."

The travels of Gabriel, around the world several times, brought to his heart both burdens and blessings. It was a time now that God would move upon his heart to set forth the principles and hopes for the future of God's divine interruption of both seen and unforeseen events.

Chapter Seventeen

The Pause

(March - July, 1970)

The year is 1970 and Gabriel must make a final decision concerning the events, studies, the family, and all else for the future resolve of the purpose of his calling before the Lord. Gabriel had thought all through his ministry that the will of God, specifically, is viewed in four distinct divisions. First, to know the will of God; second, to commence the will of God; third, to proceed in the will of God; and fourth, to endure and finish the will of God. Gabriel had seen these four distinctions clearly in the Word of God, and in the lives of others. Some seem to go all their life not to know the will of God; others come to know it but cannot start it; still others cannot proceed on; and fourth, many do not endure and finish the will of God for a good "crossing" to heaven.

At this point in Gabriel's life, in the best of his prime for God, he had come to believe that he had passed through three definite places, generally, in life. He was born, from childhood to age twenty; he had pursued academic learning by the scientific method, age twenty to twenty-nine; he had pursued the empirical method, age twenty-nine to forty-three. Now, he must proceed, endure, and finish the will of God for his life.

Gabriel and Evangeline are now 43 years old; Joseph Paul, a Christian, is 21, studying for the ministry; Soma Jeanne, a Christian, is 16; and Ariel John, a Christian, is 15. All of this represented 138 years of 5 Christian individuals. If each of them were to live until 75 years old, that would be a total of 375 years of the 5 Christian individuals. This meant they had, together, 237 years of their lives for the glory of the Lord Jesus Christ. Gabriel has concluded that for the purpose of his unpretentious ministry in the past he had continued in a preparation period, but that God's good providence in leading him, including God's leading him away from the Antioch Theological Seminary, had brought him to 1970, which, in reality, was the year of the actual beginning of the larger purpose of the fruit of his ministry.

Gabriel had come to realize that God had led through all the past of his twenty-three years as a Christian. He knew God brought Evangeline into his life. Gabriel never thought he had taken too much time in the preparation for his mind and soul; he believed in the need of the trial of his soul to be as necessary as any other subject matter to fulfill a course for an academic degree. This was his distinction between the scientific method of learning and the empirical method. What we have learned must be applied to life itself.

It was necessary now for Gabriel to review the history of his lessons, his audiences, his associates, and his friends in life because until this point in life he believed he had mainly pursued truth in a state of observation and contemplation, preparation, and spiritual growth. He was constantly drawn to the true illustration of the life of a great Christian scholar, now deceased, who served in an earlier generation at Princeton Theological Seminary. The scholar, at the age of nineteen, was on his way to Atlanta, Georgia, to consider serious preparation to be a lawyer. He was traveling alone and stopped at an overnight place for lodging and breakfast. The lady who owned the house of his lodging was a Christian and after supper graciously, in her primitive Christian heart, invited him to revival services at her church just down the street. He had now noticed her actions during the brief afternoon. He was not a Christian himself. He endeavored to graciously reject her invitation, and the lady simply responded, "Well, if you change your mind, the church is just down the block." The gentleman dismissed the idea and went immediately to his room, only to find himself restless.

After a brief time, he left the boarding house presuming to take a walk. He walked down the block past the church, only to turn back to the church and enter the door. He was greeted and seated about mid-way the audience on the aisle. He then heard the sermon of the guest speaker on "The Lordship of Jesus Christ." At the end of the service, in a prayer room he accepted Jesus Christ as his Lord and Savior.

He returned to the boarding house and his room, and pulled a little scatter rug on the floor at the foot of his bed to kneel and pray. God had given him some natural gifts of intellect, and he prayed: "Lord Jesus, I can only give you, as my Lord, the gifts you have given me. I believe I should give you my gift of books and study. I will now pursue the study of the Old Testament Hebrew language, as from an Old Testament text the minister spoke tonight. I will study in the field of Hebrew and related languages for fifteen years. I will also study the New Testament Greek language, as the minister spoke tonight, in the field of Greek and related languages for fifteen years. I then will compile my Biblical studies for the profit of others, skeptics and Christians, for the next fifteen years of my life. These forty-five years, Lord, I would like to give and live before you call me home to heaven. I am kneeling in prayer on this rug before you. I had intended to go in another direction tomorrow morning, but, instead of my previous plans, I want to give this to the glory of the Lord Jesus! In Jesus' Name, Amen."

That man arose from prayer and fulfilled the forty-five years with six years beyond.

In Gabriel's case, God had set the agenda, and now he must fulfill the will of God for his life, to the end.

The question, to Gabriel, which this agenda raised, was "What shall I do with my life now, O Lord?"

When Gabriel prayerfully looked back over this agenda and his life with Evangeline; their three children; The Land of Evangeline; the Blue Ridge Mountains; Metropolitan Washington; Groveland, Georgia; Grandville, North Carolina; Memphis, Tennessee; Ocean View, North Carolina; and their beautiful Georgetown home; he saw his own small world-view of his own total life.

He saw meaning in this view. He gave himself to more prayer and the reading of the Holy Scriptures, and he sought to know what applied conclusion he should pursue for the rest of his life. Gabriel was keenly aware of the fact that he had been brought to the point in his life when he now must, with all his own heart, exact a plan to minister to others concerning the Lord Jesus Christ and the historic Gospel of Christianity.

He pondered it; He pondered it. He and Evangeline pondered it and pondered it.

Their lives had been so full, so busy, so active in their teaching life, they had really not had a vacation of any length through it all. They certainly had taken several days at a time together. One of the main problems that Gabriel had in the twentieth century was the sacrifice of a number of times with wife and children. The family must have these times; it was a definite part of the Christian life. Evangeline always observed that Gabriel gave emphasis to quality time for his family.

So, God had provided for their every need and had richly blessed them as a family. Realizing this, the Parsons took the entire family on a planned vacation. The home teacher, Miss Juliana Queens, would also take her own vacation while they were away. She had been a most valuable asset to this home, and they all considered her as a part of the family. The downstairs, first floor space for living, Mr. & Mrs. Olsen retained. However, it was agreed that in the fall they would move into their new home in the Maryland suburbs of Washington which was in progress of building at this time. They had agreed to stay in the Parsons home until they returned from their vacation.

The family trip was to Nova Scotia, landing in Yarmouth on the Bluenose from Portland, Maine. The Bluenose had full accommodations for their automobile aboard as well. Upon arrival, Evangeline took over the leading conversations as guide, as Gabriel had suggested. He wanted her to go through the wonderful story of the Land of Evangeline from Yarmouth to Grand Pré, noting each landmark and shoreline and any personal references from her childhood.

They took the route from Yarmouth east up the coastline to Halifax. This is called "The Lighthouse Route." The names start from Yarmouth to Rockville, Little River Harbour, Wedgeport, Shag Harbour. They did not go down to Cape Sable Island, but Evangeline took the time to mention that the ocean tides rise higher than anywhere else in the world, and that Sable Island tides rise more than fifty feet, there at the head of the Bay of Fundy. Sailors call Sable Island the "Graveyard of the Atlantic," but others believe the inside waters of the Bay between Yarmouth, towards Maine, are equally such a "Graveyard."

Then on to Shelburne. At Beaver Dam, near Shelburne, and in Stillwater in Guysborough County, hunting guides and lumbermen match skills during Guides' Meets which are held seasonally. Then on to Liverpool, going somewhat inland to Bridgewater, to Lunenburg, to Halifax, and then straight northwest to Wolfville. Here, Evangeline paused and the family visited the Acadian Music Conservatory in which she studied music. From Yarmouth to Halifax, "The Lighthouse Route," was marked by many small fishing villages with interesting traditions. Fishermen can catch swordfish and tuna along the coast and salmon and trout in the inland streams. Further inland, in the forests, sportsmen hunt deer, snowshoe rabbits, and grouse.

They were in time to see the profusion of "The Floral Emblem," the Trailing Arbutus. They went to museums and government buildings which appropriately set forth the "Symbols of Nova Scotia," including: "The Provincial Coat of Arms," in the center of which was the blue cross of St. Andrew and a lion that represents Nova Scotia's ties with Scotland; an

Indian, symbolizing the province's first inhabitants; and a unicorn, representing England, flanked away from the shield. Charles I of England granted this Coat of Arms to Nova Scotia in 1626. The Provincial Flag of Nova Scotia was granted by the royal charter in 1621, and also bears the cross of St. Andrew and the lion of the Scottish kings.

Evangeline extended her native continuity throughout the trip of how Nova Scotia was one of the four original Canadian provinces. In 1867, it joined with New Bruswick, Ontario, and Quebec to form the Dominion of Canada. The first British settlers in Nova Scotia had arrived from Scotland in 1629. Evangeline was very careful to declare that Nova Scotia was just about as old as the United States. She also emphasized that all of the talk about "Mayflower pedigree," if true, must include a ship landing at Chebogue, near Yarmouth, who were actually relatives of the "Cape Cod Elite." But she smiled through all of that detail. Of course, she emphasized that the Latin words, Nova Scotia, mean "New Scotland."

Evangeline also mentioned the meaning of "Bluenose." Some have thought it came from the winter windy "frosted nose" of the people themselves; or, the pride of the "blue-blood" pedigree claim. However, these all must be corrected and understood as a nickname from the "bluenose potato," which the Nova Scotians grew and shipped to New England. Evangeline admitted that the name, therefore, loses much of its romantic value, but the people still call themselves "a bluenose."

But the excitement of the trip continued to expand as the Parsons turned their motorcar down the west side of Nova Scotia from Wolfville.

This is where "The Land of Evangeline" begins. The lowlands have Nova Scotia's most valuable soils and mineral deposits. The rich farmland of the Annapolis-Cornwallis Valley is south of North Mountain. Fertile marshlands lie along the Bay of Fundy, Chignecto Bay, and the Minas Basin. Cape Blomidon, near Wolfville, overlooks Minas Basin and nearby orchards.

In this regard, after the phrase Nova Scotia, the prominent

208

word becomes Acadia. The French called the Nova Scotia region and the land around it Acadia. In 1755, British Colonial troops from New England began to drive the Acadians out of Nova Scotia for refusing to swear allegiance to Britain. Several thousand Acadians fled to Prince Edward Island, central north, above Nova Scotia, in the Gulf of Saint Lawrence; others fled to Quebec, which was the French colony of Louisiana; and others to British colonies in America. This historic event occasioned Nathaniel Hawthorne's telling the story to the American poet, Henry Wadsworth Longfellow. Longfellow then wrote the Epic Poem, "Evangeline," concerning a tale of how these French colonists, called "Acadians," were driven from their homes in Nova Scotia by British colonial troops from New England. The Acadians had remained loyal to France after Great Britain won control of Nova Scotia in the early 1700s. The poem gave part of the province the nickname "Land of Evangeline."

Grand Pré is that central place of Longfellow's poem where the poet gave the names of "Evangeline" and "Gabriel." Now at Grand Pré, where the statue of "Evangeline" stands, commemorative of Longfellow's poem, Gabriel takes over the pleasantry of voice, during their picnic there, and tells the entire story of the poem, "Evangeline." He dramatically pursues the beautiful story, having seated Evangeline in the middle space, upon the ground, with the three children seated around her in front of the monument to Evangeline. Gabriel reads directly from the poem certain passages to punctuate the highlights of the story.

When Gabriel finished the story, and the readings, he extended further paragraphs of thought centered upon his wife, their mother, Evangeline.

"We have just taken the time today to remind you of this beautiful Epic Poem by Henry Wadsworth Longfellow. It is indeed a beautiful American story, which centered itself around a sad history in a lovely country. But we must remember it is a part of a poet's imagination and fiction. God allows us to have fiction to expand our imagination and creativity in life because he wants us to think down fresh avenues of thought, as long as the fiction does not 'untruth' life and build up evil. God gave fiction because a story is important to our learning process. God gave us the privilege of poetry to have the privilege of song. God gave us non-fiction, however, to preserve that mode of literature to protect truth and truth alone. The Bible is replete with a story, a tale, as seen in some parables and proverbs; also, the Bible has poetry in the parallelism of the Psalms; but God, in the Bible, also gives us explicit truth which we must also believe in, knowing our redemption is dependent upon absolutes.

"So, today, the higher reason for this presentation is to lead us to the thoughts of Evangeline, my wife and your mother. She is not a fictitious character; she is very real, both in her very presence and beauty, as well as real in her love and character. It is imperative for us to know why we are happy: it is rooted in our Savior; it is manifested in our redemption; and, it is living in the life of our own Evangeline. Will you remember that, dear children? Will you remember your father told you this also, along with the Holy Scriptures, so that you will tell your own children about your family, in this historic story with fiction, poetry, and truth? I know you will. Tell your mother today of your love; I tell it now, openly before you all. This is a tribute to her today."

They wept and laughed and loved and had such great joy as they bundled up the remains of a "gone" picnic. Joseph Paul sang the song "Shenandoah"; Soma Jeanne accompanied him on the flute; and Ariel John saluted the monument statue of Evangeline. They spent the night here at Grand Pré.

The next morning they proceeded leisurely from Grand Pré away from the direction of Wolfville to Kentville to Middleton, on down past Annapolis Royal. At Digby, Gabriel, without introducing the subject, went straight down the land-neck of St. Mary's Bay to Long Island and the ferry to Brier Island to Westport Island and the home of Evangeline's mother, Mildred Joye. The story was reiterated again how on that island Mildred Joye Prince, daughter of Captain John Prince and wife Ellen Mae, was seen on the arm of her father as he walked with pomp and circumstance down the aisle of the First Christian Church to give her away to McArcy McGee Peters. After the story, they walked down to Gull Rock and were reminded that Dad Peters owned this land once and had a sheep ranch which did not amount to all that he had hoped.

They came on back through the cemetery where a number of relatives were buried. Once again they took to the automobile and returned from Westport Island to Brier Island and Long Island, back up the neck of land by St. Mary's Bay. They were a bit tired, somber, and sleepy as Evangeline sat close to Gabriel in the front seat. Every few seconds she would look over to Gabriel with a smile and another smile; finally, she leaned upon him in quietness.

As the neck of land extended before them, Gabriel called out loud at the top of the land mass and even yelled, "Let's go on into Digby and eat those famous 'Digby Clams!'" Everyone in the motorcar yelled back, "Yeah, let's go and eat those famous 'Digby Clams!'" Evangeline repeated it again, each word on the melodic line of 'high C'! "Yeah, for those 'Digby Clams.'" Whenever Evangeline experienced great joy, she simply expressed her delight with a phrase on "high C," and whenever it happened the children would prepare themselves for the occasion by saying in unison, "Here we go again!"

After returning on down to Yarmouth, to once again see "Joye's Yellow House," and homeplace, they proceeded, on time to the ferry dock, the next morning, to go back home. With reservations confirmed, they gave their ticket to the gateman and motored their automobile into their parking spot on the lower deck of the Bluenose, and then went up to the lounge deck to await departure across the Bay of Fundy for the docks of Portland, Maine. Evangeline once again was in charge of the conversation, noting all the familiar places of her childhood along the docks, and as the Bluenose moved on out into Yarmouth harbor she gave the exciting identification of Captain John Prince's lovely homeplace up on the hill overlooking the harbor. His last years were spent in that home, overlooking the harbor and home port of his ship which made so many trips to the West Indies. As the Bluenose receded from the harbor, Evangeline declared:

"The waves are mounting, the white-caps increase, the fog is coming, and we are in for a glorious ride through a beautiful storm."

When she said that, the children responded: "Yes mother, we know: you love these white-caps and waves; and you love the fog, but do you have to love a storm, too? You are one 'salty' lady, but we love you just the same!"

And the storm that Evangeline predicted brought them to the Portland dock that night.

Once supper and sleep and morning breakfast were past, Gabriel motored on down on a shorter time-frame for the family to proceed on to the Skyline Drive and the Blue Ridge Mountains of Virginia and North Carolina. They did not take as much time for stops and places, but nevertheless the trip was to be the postscript to the vacation.

The Blue Ridge Mountains are the eastern ranges of the Appalachian Mountains System. They extend from southern Pennsylvania across Maryland, Virginia, North Carolina, to northern Georgia. The name comes from the blue tone given these peaks by forests on their slopes, as seen at a distance.

The Skyline Drive, in Virginia, goes from Front Royal to Waynesboro, over one hundred miles north to south, but it is a part of the Blue Ridge Mountains. In 1933, President Franklin Roosevelt made an inspection tour of the first Civilian Construction Corps which came to be established in Virginia. The Corps was building the Skyline Drive in the Shenandoah National Park.

The Blue Ridge Parkway joins the Skyline Drive at Waynesboro, Virginia, at a point called Rockfish Gap and will wind its way, south, through the state of Virginia, and all of North Carolina, to northern Georgia. This Blue Ridge Parkway is about 470 miles from Waynesboro, ending at the Great Smoky Mountains National Park, Oconaluftee Visitor Center, actually located on US Route 411.

It is almost six hundred miles for this unusual Blue Ridge Mountains, Skyline, Parkway beauty.

The Blue Ridge Parkway construction began on September 11, 1935, over two years after the Skyline Drive was under way. Also, the entire Parkway was built in parts, starting near the Virginia-North Carolina border, then north in Virginia, south in North Carolina. Most of it was finished by the 1970s, and then it was finalized with the Linn Cove viaduct on the side of Grandfather Mountain, and another short length of the Parkway involving a cantilever shelf projecting off of the remaining mountain section south of Grandfather Mountain. This was completed later, on September 11, 1987. It took fifty-two years. The entire Parsons family met there for the final section dedication occasion with state officials.

The Skyline Drive and the Blue Ridge Parkway have a beautiful two-lane highway with over one hundred Park Service Trails along the Parkway itself, and dozens of Forest Service pathways which come close to its access.

Congress placed the entire Parkway system under the jurisdiction of the National Park Service in 1936. The speed limit is forty-five miles per hour; no trucks are permitted to enter the Parkway.

Gabriel spent a three-month summer on the John Felix Farm in 1936 at the age of ten. The farm was situated near the ascent to the Blue Ridge Mountains about midway between Luray in the north and Schuyler in the south. Cabin Peak is near the general area up from the Felix Farm. A road came off Route 64 up to the beautiful Shenandoah Valley from which you would turn off to the left on an old dirt road. The Felix Farm was two miles down that dirt road away from the main county road. That dirt road, now paved, would continue up the Blue Ridge Mountain about nine miles. That same dirt road was installed by the CCC Boys as an exclusive road up to the access for the construction of the Blue Ridge-Skyline Drive. For three months Gabriel followed the CCC Boys working crew, with a trusted friend, up and down that dirt road after the Skyline Drive section had been under construction for over two years. Gabriel bunked and had his daily meals with the CCC Boys in their make-shift, portable barracks as they kept ascending the Blue Ridge Mountain from the east side with materials, tools, and machine tractors. Gabriel would then go back to the Felix Farm every third day for fishing, horse riding, swimming, and exploring the farm area. Alternately, he would then return and travel with the CCC Boys again and again. The John Felix Farm was used quite often to assist the traffic and the workers with their needs for the Blue Ridge Parkway project. The Boys, of course, were young men who were suffering under the 1930 national Depression, financially, and the government provided this work. They were young men from about seventeen to twenty-one years old. These young men were considered to be an upstanding group in their daily habits of life.

After the completion of the Blue Ridge Parkway, Gabriel's father, Bishop Parsons, made many trips during the summer months of his childhood to these same mountains and planted churches where loggers cut down timber. Also, it was a place for bootleggers with illegal whiskey stills.

In the late 1950s and 1960s, Gabriel took Study Groups up on the Blue Ridge Parkway, near Green Meadows, Luray, and Cabin Peak, as shelter cabins were also being built by the government for hikers and campers. Gabriel would take as many as one hundred to camp out for morning, afternoon, and night Bible and history studies.

The vacation, now, of the Parsons family, in its final leg of the return trip from Nova Scotia, was to conclude with a three-day drive down from Front Royal, Virginia, to Grandfather Mountain, North Carolina. Of course, they had been up here before and again, but most of their previous visits had been on the Skyline Drive, distinguished from the southern Parkway system added to it in the later years. Waynesboro, Virginia, was the connecting point of the Blue Ridge Parkway with the Skyline Drive. So, they entered the Parkway at a slower manner of observation towards Grandfather Mountain. Leaving the Parkway at that exit they proceeded on down Route 52, and back over, east, to Interstate 95, and then north to Washington, D.C., and their Georgetown home.

They especially stopped and noted on the Parkway, however, the places of Humpback Rocks and the Visitor Center there; then on to the Peaks of Otter Visitor Center. On Abbot Lake Trail at the Peaks of Otter, Joseph Paul observed that the beauty of that particular spot would be a perfect place for a wedding. Gabriel remembered once again that his oldest son was now twenty-one years old. He had been dating a few girls, and his father thought he was probably still just in the dating period. No one gave any response to Joseph Paul's observation; but it was not forgotten.

Motoring on south, the Parson family also stopped at the Rocky Knob Visitor Center, Cumberland Knob Visitor Center, the Doughton Park Information Center, and then made their exit at the Linville Falls Visitor Center, turning off to Grandfather Mountain and then, gladly on to their home

The vacation had now become the final assistance needed for Gabriel to make a permanent decision for his ministry for the rest of his life.

Chapter Eighteen

The Couple

(1955 - 1970: March 28, 1974)

The years of 1960 to 1974 were the hardest years for Gabriel and Evangeline in their personal lives together in the "Land of Evangeline." It was a time when Gabriel was in his hardest schedule of travel, lectures, sermons, and writing books. He was on a very exacting and tight schedule. The burden of those days was to get the word out concerning the change in the definition of historic Christianity.

The travel ministry began when he initiated the Night Institute at the Georgeton Theological Seminary back in 1952. However, the travels were only beginning then, one or two a month. But during the year of 1957 the invitations increased from churches and seminaries to denominational conferences and workshops. This was the year of his studies of Fundamentalism in contrast to the major denominations.

In the year of 1960, because of his acceptance of the presidency of the Antioch Theological Seminary, his schedule enlarged into a wider spectrum to the independent churches and Bible Colleges which were connected with Fundamentalism as well as denominational seminaries and conferences.

Although Gabriel's writings, as an author, commenced also in 1957, when he was completing his formal studies, yet he endeavored to do this with his typewriter, and later the computer, while he traveled. He would search out the books from his library he needed for reference sources and would then take them with him on his travels. Although this was commenced for the necessity of his own studies, yet his authorship resulted from a demand for the contents of his writings.

As the fourteen years began to wind down into other demands, after he left the Antioch Theological Seminary, he settled back into Georgetown with a hopeful leading of the Lord into a ministry nearby, but his travel-load increased. More and more he sought his home and his Evangeline and his children in the years that followed. During this time of settling down in Georgetown and his travels, after the study tour in the Middle East in 1969, Gabriel became conscious of a burden that had begun to come into his heart with his dear Evangeline and himself. This burden began only after his return from the study tour in the Middle East. That trip brought Rev. Wiley into his life.

However, Gabriel was not conscious of the source of his burden until the year of 1974. The burden became clear to him of a certain pattern that began, he believed, in late 1954, when he visited the president, upon his return to the University for his Ph.D. studies. Gabriel had made two promises to Dr. Jonathan that he did not first share with Evangeline. These two promises commenced Gabriel's travels for lectures and sermons and were actually the beginning of all of his travels.

The two promises to Dr. Jonathan were: one, that Gabriel would attend and be one of the speakers at the First World Congress of Fundamentalists; and two, that Gabriel would agree to be one of the overseas professors for the University Extension in Jerusalem. Although the Extension never came to pass, yet the World Congresses did launch his travels to Scotland, the Philippines, Singapore, London, and Canada.

Other regional places were designated in-between the Quadrennial World Congresses. Evangeline did not accompany Gabriel on any of these trips, although, at the first, she was excited thinking she would go with her husband.

Gabriel remembers when he first told her about the Congresses and the travels, Evangeline assumed she would be going with him. After she did not go, Evangeline never brought up the subject again. Across the years, however, from 1954 through 1970, Gabriel had noticed a certain pattern in Evangeline. He now realized his dumbness in not seeing this before, through almost twenty years. He now saw the entire picture after so long a time of thick-headedness. Now he must, after considerable prayer, go and pour out his heart to Evangeline about this long-term failure. It had begun to affect them both in several ways.

Now, in the early spring of 1974, Gabriel, having just returned from a lecture tour, proposed a special afternoon trip to Hains Point, on the Potomac River, in the Metropolitan Washington area. The children were all away for the afternoon and evening with friends. Gabriel and Evangeline leisurely walked around the Point and Gabriel saw an isolated bench and table quite a ways from the walkway. They departed from the walkway as Gabriel once again took Evangeline's hand, which he was so famous for in their affection in public. It was about two o'clock in the afternoon and the area was empty of people. Gabriel ventured his heart to Evangeline, as he had many times before on other subjects, which always opened as follows:

"Evangeline, my beloved wife, I want to talk to you about you and me."

"Yes, my dear one, I know." This was her usual response, although not knowing the exact subject matter.

"First, I want you to forgive me for a mistake I made back in 1954."

"That was almost twenty years ago, Gabriel. Why so long? You have carried this a long time, my dear."

"Yes, and my dumbness is what delayed it, but my memory has finally caught up with me. The Lord has opened my eyes

218

of understanding and my heart of love in repentance to Him and you."

"All right, my beloved. Tell me about it."

"It goes back to the time I made two promises to Dr. Jonathan without first conferring with your heart and mine together on the promises. I know you will remember the occasion, but may not remember, exactly, our conversation. I will reiterate the matter to you. (pause) On every occasion that I can remember, my dear Evangeline, I have sought you out for your knowledge and response for a decision in my life before I made the decision."

"That is correct, Gabriel."

"However, I fear that this particular incident, although it was early in our marriage, has come to be a severe hardship on you through the years."

"In what way, Gabriel?"

"In my setting a precedent for so many times of travels. I have made some of them for several weeks at a time. I believe I have found out that it has been an extreme hardship on you for me to be away."

"In what way, my darling?"

"Unless I am wrong, my dear wife, I think I finally noticed a pattern in your reaction each time I went away. It appears to me that on such occasions when I would leave for a trip, you would be somewhat impatient with me for about two days prior to my departure, and upon my return you would be somewhat cold and impatient again. Do you think my thoughts are justified, my darling Evangeline? Have I been so dumb, so long, until now, and did not know why your attitude was so?"

"Oh, Gabriel, Gabriel, Gabriel, you have found me out, according to the Holy Scriptures, 'be sure your sins will find you out.' It is true; it is true; it is true. I never wanted you to know, and now you have arrived at your knowledge of heart through my bad attitude. It would have been better for me to have just told you all from our beginnings of this."

"But why, my darling, Evangeline? Why?"

"Because I was selfish; I selfishly loved you in this mistake. Your travels hindered my love for you. I did not mean for you to ever know. I did not realize my heart did show up so poorly before you each time you would depart and return."

"Well, Evangeline, the problem was greater than that. I have not given you the assurance as I should have done each time I left, myself. I thought, before God, I must be strong; I believed it was the will of God, of involuntary obedience that I must go. I thought, until my dumbness was revealed, I was the coward and you were the strong one. I suppose in the average marriage it is possible that there is not enough love at such times, but we have gone too far in another direction for the good of our love. I had such a burden of departure that I was determined I would telephone you, and if that failed in my schedule, I would write, send a card or flowers. The flowers were the desperate, rare expression."

"Yes, you did, my husband; yes, you did! You did always faithfully express the consistency of those things to me on every trip you made."

"I dealt with my love for you in the hope you would never know my struggle about being away from you, hoping you would know my heart while I was away, through the habits I invented as consistently as I could. But I make it clear; it was my love; it was not a hypocrisy with you. Remember my promise and use of 'always'?"

"Yes, you did, Gabriel. I am sorry I did not do something about my own feelings. I did not know it showed. I thought you would think, at the most, that I was just quiet. But in reality, my dear Gabriel, it was a deception; I am glad you brought it out. I want no secrets, even if it is painful."

"I know I did not deliberately become dumb, Evangeline; I was not conscious to cherish you in this, my Evangeline. The Bible gives husbands this word, 'cherish,' and this should have been my responsibility. I did not have an understanding heart; I am sorry; forgive me, Evangeline, forgive me." (seated at the park table, Evangeline, weeping, turns to Gabriel and embraces him)

"It was I; forgive me, my husband, forgive me. Please forgive me."

Gabriel stopped her mouth with his hand and pulled his

handkerchief from his lapel pocket and wiped away her tears as she continued to weep.

"Oh my darling, Evangeline, you are the one who has suffered from these times in our past. I am going to seek the Lord if possibly another direction could be taken in my own ministry. My ministry in the travels have been, seemingly, the most effective ministry I have had through the years. The travels, also, have been the marginal difference that God gave us financially to raise our family. Although that is practical, it is true, and I want to thank God for these opportunities given to us through the travels. I know you agree."

"Gabriel, do not try to change the will of God for me. I never dreamed that it would be something else other than the Abraham Lincoln Hotel, the Martha Washington Hotel, or Green Meadows, or the Luray Caverns, or Cabin Peak as a problem. The problem has been me. Selfishly, all I thought of was the 'Land of Evangeline,' or any land, without Gabriel. But now, with all my heart, I want the Lord to deliver me from this selfishness, for I believe it has been a deeper root than what you even saw as you endeavored to lovingly tell me. I will not ask the Lord to take away my love, and our love, but to take away the selfishness of it. To take that away might even give more room for our love to grow. I have respected you in your studies, your life, your sermons, your lectures, your writings, and now, also, in your observations of this matter. It has been true, Gabriel. Oh yes, my darling; it has been true."

"I suppose, Evangeline, my dumbness through the problem was a blessing. If I had known your need, I may have failed God in such a gigantic decision about my travels. But I do need the habit of your advice in these decisions. As it now has happened it has become a habit that grew out of my lack of talking with you from the beginning. This is the year of 1974 in our lives; we are fortunate to have come to this situation, finally, at this time. Joseph Paul is twenty-five; he marries soon. Soma Jeanne is twenty and will be finishing undergraduate school in another year. Ariel John is nineteen, a freshman in college, also. Do you know what all this means, Evangeline?"

"After the burden of this day, dear Gabriel, I cannot imagine, at all, what this means. Will you tell me, please?' (a little laughter between them)

"Yes, I will tell you, Mrs. Parsons. You and I are practically single again. In the very near future you are going with me, wherever I go: the Lincoln life? Or, the Martha Washington life? Or, the Green Meadows? Or, the Luray Caverns? Or, Cabin Peak? Or, (a long pause) the 'Land of Evangeline' and heaven!"

What a blessed conclusion and joy and peace and happiness resulted from this old problem which had existed between Gabriel and Evangeline..

From 1974 through all of the 1990s, Gabriel and Evangeline Parsons never left each other for any extended length of time. The days of the halcyon returned and Gabriel even found a scripture to prove it: "...he shall return to the days of his youth," Job, chapter 33, verse 25. Even Evangeline found scripture, as the musician in the family: "...she shall sing there, as in the days of her youth..." Hosea, chapter 2, verse 15.

They left Hains Point at about dust of day, and went back to their Georgetown home, but not without going back to the Abraham Lincoln Hotel restaurant in nearby Alexandria, Virginia. This time they viewed much more the beautiful decor there that they ignored on their first wedding night together years ago. They returned home and no one was home but them. The children had left a note saying they were staying that night in the home of Miss Juliana Queens.

So, Gabriel and Evangeline slept all night on the third floor, the "Land of Evangeline," with blankets all over the floor for their bed. He whispered to Evangeline's ear the story of the seasons of spring, summer, autumn, Indian summer, fall, and winter. He told her that, sometimes, a year goes from summer to an autumn-Indian-summer, without having a fall or winter at all. Gabriel said he hoped that they would now move into a long autumn with no winter at all. Then, they both fell asleep on the third story floor.

222

The next morning Gabriel arose early and composed the ballad "Autumn's Bridge" to joyfully forward their lives, yet in love, yea, even their first love, with each other.

Yes, the next morning Gabriel arose early and composed his ballad, "Autumn's Bridge," to joyfully forward their lives together, yet in love with each other. Some of the lines went as follows:

> "Every springtime's season hears winter's call.
> Every summer's chasm leads to a fall.
> But the bridge of autumn, the best of all,
> Brings golden red trees so tall.
> Build your bridges; build them strong.
> Raise a fortress against the wrong.
> When you build your bridges, you build the road
> For man to carry the load.
> Build for autumn, but not for fall."

Chapter Nineteen

The Separation

(May 19, 1974)

Upon their return home to Georgetown, after their beautiful vacation, Gabriel knew that it was time for a final conclusion of the past leadings of God so that he would now endeavor to obey the will of God for his permanent future ministry.

As a part of that final resolve, Gabriel knew that LeVon Gilbertson had desired for Gabriel to visit him at the state headquarters of his denomination in Memphis, Tennessee. LeVon had become state bishop of the denomination, and there was some talk about his being senior bishop of the entire denomination, headquartered in Oklahoma City. Gabriel had come to believe God desired this visit as well, and Gabriel had desired to meet this appointment graciously. However, he also knew that the appointment was either an urgent appeal of a return in LeVon's heart to historic Christianity, or he indeed would be proceeding on into the greater danger of the ecclesiastical apostasy.

Gabriel had kept up with his readings, and it was in his heart to make clear his Biblical conclusions to the contemporary

Christian times. He was thoroughly persuaded, at this point, that the neo-definition was not the historic definition of the Gospel of the Lord Jesus Christ. Gabriel must make a review for a finalization of his hopefully Biblical evidences of proof for his future presentations.

The first proposition had already been established in Gabriel's dealing with "The Doctrine." It was observed by Gabriel, and believed as being true to him, that there are only these three classical models by which to judge historic Christianity in modern time. First, there was the inspired legacy of the Holy Scriptures as revealed in Primitive Christianity; second, there was the heritage of church history as reviewed in Remnant and Reformation Christianity.

In this first Primitive time, worship and doctrine are marked clearly as the path through which that early church passed. In this first Biblical proposition, worship and doctrine were indeed the most obvious criteria in the revelation of the Bible before preaching and teaching had enlarged the understanding spectrum of Biblical truth. The doctrine of being saved by grace through faith is consistently revealed on the basis of the resurrection of the Lord Jesus Christ. Peter inaugurates the Church on the Day of Pentecost quoting from the prophet Joel of the Old Testament. This concerned the outpouring of the Holy Spirit on the Day of Pentecost, but preaching and teaching of the historic Christ Jesus and his bodily resurrection from the grave were urged as well.

The doctrine of scriptural separation and the distinction between Christians and unbelievers, further identified as rejecters and apostates, was also made clear. The incidents of Ananias and Sapphira, the Sanhedrin, Stephen, Saul, and Simon the Sorcerer, the Greek gods, the damsel with a spirit of divination, and confrontations with Jewish and Roman powers are noted almost everywhere in the same Book of Acts.

Also, there were persecutions at this time which led to the martyrdom of many of the saints of God.

All things were settled by Biblical doctrine. Anyone who identified himself as a Christian, but worshipped idols, was not a Christian. Fellowship with the unbelievers and the ungodly was not practiced. Being a Christian was strictly identified by doctrine from those who were "eye-witnesses of His majesty," the Lord Jesus Christ.

Primitive Christianity would have never implemented unchristian liberals, modernists, Roman Catholics, and idolatrous religions as partners to evangelism or as Christians based on historic Christianity.

The second proposition of the Primitive Church concerned what indeed had endured and survived down to the twentieth century as the proclaimed, fundamental, essential doctrine from that Primitive Church? Gabriel's presentation of doctrinal identity under Fundamentalism suffices for this answer.

The Fundamentals revealed in the New Testament as the core-truth of the Gospel may be outlined as follows, and identifies a Christian who:

1. Maintains an immovable allegiance to the inerrant, infallible, and verbally inspired Bible;
2. Believes that whatever the Bible says is so;
3. Judges all things by the Bible and is judged only by the Bible;
4. Affirms the foundational truths of the historic Christian Faith:

   The doctrine of the Trinity.

   The Incarnation, virgin birth, substitutionary atonement, the bodily resurrection and glorious ascension, and the Second Coming of the Lord Jesus Christ,

   The new birth through regeneration of the Holy Spirit,
   The resurrection of the ungodly to final judgment and eternal death,

   The fellowship of the saints, who are the Body of Christ;
5. Practices fidelity to that Faith and endeavors to preach it to every creature;
6. Exposes and separates from all ecclesiastical denial of that Faith,

   compromise with error, and apostasy from the Truth; and
7. Earnestly contends for the Faith once delivered.

Remnant Christianity bears the second witness to these things as historic Christianity is confirmed through dogmatic theology in the ongoing truth of Christianity in history. The historic Creeds and Councils, which confirmed and passed along historic Christianity, were brought about by Remnant Movements of Christians who stood true throughout every test of apostate Christianity against historic Christianity. There were indeed historic movements through church history that proclaimed and defended the Christian Faith. The priesthood of the Christian believers survived and, yea, triumphed with historic identifications of certain smaller groups. Some of them, both individual and group, were: The Waldensians; Wycliffism; Hussites; Moravians, associated with Bohemia; Huldreich Zwingli, of Switzerland; and Ulster Dissenters; Covenanters; Northern Ireland Reformers.

The third force is sharply set forth in the immediate manifestation in Reformation Christianity. Reformers of the major period were: Martin Luther and Philip Melanchthon; England's John Wycliffe and Thomas Cranmer; the Huguenots, the noblemen of France; the Puritans and Pilgrims of the "Biblical Commonwealth," of the Mayflower Christians, at the birth of the United States; the Revivalists of George Whitefield, John Wesley, Charles Wesley, of England and America; and the Revivalists of Torrey and Alexander, David Morgan, Richard Owens; etc., to name a few.

In our own time, we have seen both believers and unbelievers in union together, involved in evangelism, and it is not according to New Testament, historic Christianity. This evangelism is being sponsored by those who, formerly, were fundamentalists, but who have compromised their testimony and practice and theology to the fellowship of those who have rejected historic Christianity and who have not repented of their error and apostasy, such as the Roman Catholic Church and the Liberals.

The twentieth century has well marked those who are or have been departing from historic Biblical Christianity. Just as Gabriel had attended the "First Quadrennial Conference on

Evangelism," in Memphis, Tennessee, so there have been many such meetings, conventions, boards, committees, and crusades of fellowship from all of the major and minor denominations.

By 1970, the charismatic gifts and glossolalia had become evidentially experienced in the Protestant churches and the Roman Catholic Church. The fellowship through evangelism, including pentecostal healers, neo-orthodox, neo-evangelicals, earlier pentecostalists, reformed churches, Salvation Army, and others, truncated their own theological and doctrinal distinctives to become a part of the modern ecumenical movement. The implication was real: if you did not join into these neo-fellowships, you were placed out of your churches or delegated to the backwoods' churches. This latter tragedy often led to the necessity of a remnant-Christian people making an exodus from their denomination entirely to birth independent Biblical churches with pulpits for the Word of God.

Gabriel had responded to LeVon's request for him to visit, by appointment, with him. The date was set for May 19, 1974, in his administrative office in Memphis, Tennessee. This date reminded Gabriel that it had been almost twenty years since the First Quadrennial Conference on Evangelism and the meeting of LeVon in his Georgetown home as well. It was requested by LeVon that Gabriel should meet him at his state denominational headquarters.

Now Gabriel and LeVon were to meet in the foyer of an impressive building and proceed to LeVon's office. They have greeted each other and spent some time speaking of the well-being of their families. (a slight pause has come to their conversation. They take the elevator to the twelfth floor.)

"Well, Dr. Parsons, I am glad you agreed to come for this meeting, and, also, I wanted to show you our evangelism-fellowship headquarters. This is called The Evangel Building. I want to take you on a tour after our conversation. This twelve-story complex represents the central offices of the seven bishops, their secretaries, and staff of the seven historic denominations that were born at the beginning of the twentieth century. I have become Bishop of Evangelism for this denominational Fellowship. You may remember that Bishop Carl Simons Keifer was chairman of evangelism at our First Quadrennial Conference on Evangelism." (The elevator arrives quickly at the twelfth floor)

"Yes, I do remember him, LeVon.

"Tennessee is something of the central hub of pentecostalism in the United States. I now have one entire floor of the building, the top floor, overlooking all of Memphis, as we are also situated on something of a hill here.

"Yes, it is a beautiful city with a lovely view of your surroundings, including the Mississippi River, LeVon."

"Yes, Gabriel, this was born after the Quadrennial Conference you attended with me. Meetings are going on here almost daily, or some aspect of the work proceeds from here regularly throughout the world. You can see we have a gigantic program and job before us. Besides that, the investment of this building and the leasing of office groupings on several floors to other businesses give an increased revenue and prestige to our denomination as well. I am indeed excited about it all. World-Wide Evangelism is the key for the church for the future."

LeVon's office is situated back from the entrance offices, and it was obvious to Gabriel that LeVon had proceeded headlong into the presupposition and philosophy of the Charismatic movement, although he sought, in this visit, to make it a friendly one.

As LeVon approaches his office, his son, with a pleasant smile and appearance, is standing at his office door next to Levon's. Just as LeVon was introducing him as his son, saying, "Gabriel, this is my son. He is ordained to the ministry and is my personal assistant..."

His son congenially interrupts his father, "Dr. Parsons, I am Gabriel Talmadge Gilbertson. My father named me after you, and I am honored to bear your name and finally meet you. When I was born my father must have respected you very much to give me both of your first names. In my boyhood he often spoke of you, and I am glad now to become personally acquainted with you."

Gabriel was completely taken aback by the spirit of this young man, and he responded: "I am glad to meet you Gabriel Talmadge, and I am honored from your father of this namesake for such a fine son. (pause) How old are you, Talmadge?"

"I am twenty-three years old, sir," responded Talmadge.

"Gabriel Talmadge, I am going to remember you."

He responded again: "Thank you, sir."

LeVon's son quickly turns into his office. LeVon hastens Gabriel into his own office next door without another reference to his son.

"It is certainly a beautiful and impressive situation here, LeVon. I have been somewhat following you through the periodicals and papers you have been sending me, but I did not realize such an immense effort as this was being set forth now. You have, evidently, been prized highly for these new offices for your ministry. I can hardly realize that it has been almost twenty years since the Quadrennial Conference of 1954."

"I do remember, Gabriel. My immaturity at that time was obvious, I am sure, as well as at the later meeting we had in your 'Attic.' (a small laughter from LeVon is noted.) Twenty years have made a great difference for me, in many, many things and thoughts. I am not the same man you talked with so long ago, Gabriel."

"Yes, LeVon, I understand. I do appreciate your thoughtfulness of inviting me, but was there a purpose in requesting me to come back into your life at this time, my friend?"

"Oh, I did not mention it in my letter, Gabriel? I have now become senior bishop of my denomination. The facility here in Memphis is dedicated to evangelism in view of the birth of that ministry in the Quadrennial Conference. Here we train evangelists for and from all over the world."

"No, I do not recall any reference to any matter; but you said it was urgent, and so I thought I should come. I only remember our former relationship. The correspondences have been much less frequent."

"Yes. Well, I believe I understand you, too, Gabriel. (considerable pause) Of course, as I said to you in the foyer of this building when you arrived, I wanted to show you our new facility here; but also, I wanted to inquire of you, once more, about the possibility of you bringing your scholarship and influence to such an opportunity as this. (another pause) But first, I wanted to know if you were still the same man you were when we met in 'The Room' of your third floor, the Land of Evangeline, in your Georgetown home?"

"Yes, dear LeVon, and probably much more so."

(After a longer pause) "Yes, I think that you are the same man. (another pause) Many men are changing now; dynamic and thrilling things have come to the churchmen of the last half of the twentieth century. I did not know but that you may have changed your point of view by now, but I can see I should have known better. I really did not think you would change because your love for doctrine and theology and history were too strong a bond in your Christian Faith of the New Testament."

"Well, LeVon, it was really my love for Christ which started the need of doctrine, theology, and history. Yes, I am more so, and the age is more so as well. LeVon is more so, too. And all of us stand in dangerous days, my dear friend."

"Yes, but God has been sending a mighty world-wide awakening, Gabriel. Don't you see it and feel it and desire it?"

"But LeVon, the 'awakening' does not change people towards God, and it does not change the deplorable condition prevailing in our churches and pulpits across the nation, or the depraved condition in the hearts of mankind. The messages are simply filled with ecumenical cries for peace and evangelistic work — peace and more work. It reminds me of the days of Constantine when Bishop Sylvester was baptizing three and four thousand people at a time, and yet those who were baptized, generally speaking, did not personally know Jesus Christ in their hearts, their families, or their lives. It was a time when few people were really converted to the Lord Jesus Christ."

"Gabriel, the greater reason I wanted to meet you was that

I would have liked for you to have taken our leading seminary, being especially built for evangelism, to become its president and voice. We are building it now, here in Memphis. I know that other men would need to meet you and inquire of your belief in these unusual days, but my suggestion to them is respected. However, I doubt, having seen you today, that such an opportunity would even tempt you."

"Dear LeVon, your continued thoughts of me as a candidate for such a position are not received without a certain kind of love and gratitude. I do not know if you are aware of it or not, but I accepted a one hundred-year-old seminary, reputed to be conservative and Biblical. In the nine years I spent there, I realized that the power of the methodology of evangelism has brought in a floodgate of new definitions and beliefs to modern, ecumenical Christianity. I cannot accept such a request and hope to serve you and the Lord in what I believe is a different presupposition than my own Christian faith."

"Yes, I heard of your presidency at Antioch Theological Seminary and the unusual respect you commanded there. A number of that faculty there at that time speak very highly of you, your scholarship, your spirit. In fact, one or two of them might come to be members of the faculty of our new seminary here in Memphis. Even those members of the faculty would like for you to come because of the strength you would lend to our cause for evangelism. Of course, both of us know that you would have to be able to fit into our testimony for it to work. However, you believe that would be impossible, do you not?"

"Yes, my faith in Christ and His Word precludes my management of two different presuppositions of Christianity in these last days in the light of the Holy Scriptures."

" I see. I think I understand your heart and mind, but I do not understand how you can afford to reject such an opportunity. You would be given a greater audience and influence for people to respect you."

"But, my friend, LeVon, that is not what I am looking for in the ministry. I am seeking the pure will of God and His grace upon me in whatever I do." (another long pause; LeVon

paces to the spacious window overlooking Memphis. Gabriel
keeps his seat.)

"Well, Gabriel, my long-time friend. I suppose that is that."
(a long pause)

"Gabriel, I have been curious, so a follow-up question for
you brings us to full-circle in our friendship. (a pause) What
would be the plain reason why you rejected the seven messages
of the seven bishops who spoke in the First Quadrennial
Conference on Evangelism? I thought every Christian in the
world would have been thrilled in its attendance and
enthusiasm. Tell, me Gabriel."

"Well, LeVon, actually I never told you I 'rejected' the
messages." (LeVon interrupting, gently)

"When I visited your home, your conversation about the
age and the condition of the time and evangelism, Gabriel..."

"Yes, but I want you to accurately remember my spirit in
these things. If you really recall both incidents, in your
Conference and in my home, our conversation came about by
other questions you asked me. Remember, our conversation
started with your inquiring about my Night Institute, and then
you proceeded into objective questions about my lectures in
the light of Evangelism." (pause, waiting for LeVon's response.)

"You are correct, Gabriel; I stand corrected."

"Actually, LeVon, in 1954, I was simply pursuing my own
studies and then accepted your gracious invitation to be your
guest to your denominational involvement in a consideration
of a possible Fellowship of interdenominational hopes for
evangelism."

"Yes, I remember your studies were certainly at that time,
and that you did not know, fully, what the Conference was all
about."

"As your guest, I would not have ever desired to give you
my rejection that evening, and the reasons are two-fold: I had
not time to think it through, and also, and besides, you did not
ask me anything about it. Also, when you visited me in my
home, you were my guest, and did not ask me one question
directly on this subject; I was still studying the entire situation.
I believe my heart was open in those days, twenty years ago,

and that I was truly searching for truth wherever it might be in my life. As we have said, that was twenty years ago."

"Well, that is all true, Gabriel, quite commendable of you in both incidents."

"Oh no, not at all, LeVon. I should not be commended. I took in the Conference as any other study I would make, and was endeavoring, in those days, to resolve the whole picture instead of just the Conference. It was an energetic, dynamic, enthusiastic, fiery conference; it was not the kind of conference I was used to at all. I knew and still know that unless I study without prejudice and hatred and anger, I will not know the truth."

"I understand you, Gabriel; I see your heart in this. That is most unusual for our time."

"Well, that may be, but I am not encouraged by my heart; I am encouraged by the Word of God. LeVon, I have simply endeavored to get to a greater presupposition in these preliminary words to you before I yield to answer your inquiry. The fact before me then is that I must build my entire faith upon the Holy Scriptures, nothing else—that alone! Also, a secondary need is just as great: I will need the Holy Spirit to answer you well. I am not desirous to just get an enemy; everyone of us needs friends—Christian friends."

"Does the Holy Spirit also mean that much to you? about your own spirit, I mean? I thought it meant a lot to me, as a pentecostalist, but your purpose is different. I know that you are not a pentecostalist as I am."

"Well, first, the Holy Spirit does mean that much to me, and no, I am not a pentecostalist or a Charismatic. (a smile) But unless all of us come first to the prayer of hungering to know the Truth of the Spirit in the Spirit of the Truth, we will utterly fail in our Christian Witness as well as in our understanding and knowledge of the Lord Jesus."

"I see what you mean, Gabriel."

"I have been also including the facts of what Bishop Fagin and Bishop Cranwell alluded to that all of the fourteen denominational theological systems of the contemporary churches were to come together from their respective affinities and were planning similar conferences around the world. That was indeed true, what they said, and it has become clear, now, that in twenty years since those words were stated, the present contemporary protestant churches are indeed getting together as the two bishops reasonably predicted. I only say that because it was necessary for me to search that out before I could believe it. I have been utterly astounded at how many people have managed to sacrifice their own doctrine of the Lord Jesus, as revealed in historic Christianity, and even slight their own theological system and distinctive, and come together for something God's people have never been able to do before with enemies of the Word of God; and of course, will not be able to do now, although they believe their ecumenical enemies can."

"Yes, Gabriel, I have attended quite a few of these meetings since then, and wish you could have seen the love, the fellowship, the peace, the unity, the zeal, and the plans being put into place; and it was all for the sake of the methodology necessary for World-Wide Evangelism."

"That is what has disturbed me, LeVon, and what I have come to believe according to the teachings of the Bible. In every movement in history there has always been a core-theme that the movement is driven by in their own energies to their own desired end. The core-theme in the past has often been a different word than yours and theirs, but I believe that the current denominational drive is 'evangelism.' However, that is not the Core-Truth of the Word of God, LeVon."

"It is not, Gabriel? (a shocked pause) Are you sure?"

"It is not, my friend. The Core-Truth is 'that all things must be done simply for the glory of God through the glory of the Lord Jesus Christ.' This can only be realized by following Biblical doctrine—the fundamental truths of the Gospel of the Lord Jesus Christ."

"Gabriel, do you really mean to say that winning souls in evangelism is not the greatest aim of the church?"

"Yes, that is what I meant to say, LeVon. But please listen carefully: Contemporary evangelism is a human system of methodology, and modern methodology will lead to the compromise of Biblical doctrine. You cannot package the

Gospel as you do merchandise. We are not salesmen; we are ambassadors for the Lord Jesus through His Word. The Charismatic leaders, by their own declaration, believe it has been a waste of time in history to seek evangelism through doctrine. They believe it comes by the Holy Spirit alone. They would state that Martin Luther, who brought the Reformation against the false doctrine of popes and Romanism, should have adopted the presupposition of using the 'Holy Spirit' and human 'charismatic methodology' in his hope of Christianizing the world.

"You can only have true evangelism by the truth of Biblical doctrine, which gives all the glory to God in the exaltation of the Lord Jesus Christ. There is no Christianity if there is no governing definitiozn by Biblical doctrine. Otherwise, there have been many 'Christian concepts' other than the revealed, singular truth of the true Gospel. Primitive Christianity, Reformation Christianity, and Remnant Christianity are our greatest historical evidences of Biblical Christianity. Also, we are the 'salt of the earth,' as well as the 'light of the earth.'

"The greatest evangelist in the Word of God is Noah; he preached hundreds of years to the whole wide world. He spoke to more people by his six hundred years of age than any other man in history. Even archaeologists attest to this fact by their measurement of the bones, both human being and animal, stacked like cordwood in snow and ice wastes of the planet earth. Yet, however, as far as it is revealed in the Word of God, Noah led only his family to the Lord. That was eight souls. The higher work of Noah was that he found grace in the eyes of the Lord and was perfect in his generation towards the true honoring of the Lord as a 'preacher of righteousness.'"

"Oh, Gabriel, what then do you believe we have in this great awakening of our time?"

"My dear friend, this is the day you asked me; and I will now respond. (pause) From the Word of God you have to come to your own conclusion of whether this is indeed an 'awakening' from God or an 'apostasy' from error. Personally, I believe, with all my heart and mind, that this contemporary amalgamation of the protestant denominations, of which you are a participating bishop, of this ecumenical World-Wide evangelism, is a false definition of Christianity—a neo-christianity. It is not being tested by New Testament Christianity, Remnant Christianity or Reformation Christianity. What you call an 'awakening,' your Romanist bishop calls a 'renewal,' which to him is a 'renewal' of that which his sacrament gives to a Romanist believer in baptism. Is your baptism the same as his? I think not, or should not be. His comes from the papal authority, the Council of Trent, in Roman Catholicism. Rome is the most historic apostasy of all centuries; no pope has thrown down his 'Keys' in repentance. As far as I can see, LeVon,... (interruption)

"...But Gabriel, I have given so much already,..." (Gabriel gently continues)

"Excuse me, please; you have requested me to respond in this matter, my dear friend. All fourteen of the theological systems in the aftermath of the Protestant Reformation have been made void by the fellowship-testimony with Romanists. They have come together on the basis of human love, without the Scriptures, but with only human methodology. The protestants have allowed union and oneness in the quest for evangelism to be greater than the guiding of even their own doctrine and theological belief, or their knowledge of heresy and apostasy."

"I do not accept that, Gabriel." (a long pause)

"My friend, I knew that when I entered the door of this plush office in this magnificent twelve-story building that you had joined an energetic evangelistic movement for the sake of a neo-christianity that does not historically exist in the pure Word of God. But please remember my words, as your friend. You will need them one day, and hopefully see that you cannot leave revealed truth and still have truth. It was you who asked me, not I. I came here today because of my love for you, and I will, with that love, still love and pray for you. But I cannot be a part of the undoing of historic Christianity and its Biblical principles. I had hoped that you would see something of these things, by now, my dear friend."

"Oh, Gabriel, you have been an unusual friend, and I

respect you as a person and your spirit in responding to me in all of our visits and correspondences, but I must give this subject up. If I were to accept your belief, all of the investment of my life, my time, and plans in which I have sought to achieve this singular goal in my denomination would be in vain. However, that seems nothing to you. You have given your life only to a Biblical cause which will bring failure instead of success."

"Dear LeVon, before I leave from this our last meeting together, on my part, as hopefully as I desired to be a Christian gentleman with you, I must separate myself from your ministry. As I close my open heart to you for this day, I will leave with you a printed letter of my estimate, in response to your request, of the 'First Quadrennial Conference on Evangelism,' and the seven notable bishops of that Conference. I did not know what your attitude actually would be towards me today, and I was prepared only to visit with you out of our past relationship and leave these items with you alone. You have been kind to hear me, for which I am grateful. Should you ever desire to see me over these precious matters, I will cordially receive you.

"I also leave in this envelope a key to my beautiful home in Georgetown. Should the Christian testimony I have given you in these times together ever be needful for you in your life and ministry, you are cordially welcomed back into the fellowship of my heart and home. This key to my home indicates my heart remains open to be a blessing to you in any desire you may have for the historic Christ and the apostles' doctrine. Remember that, my friend. (pause) Tell your dear son I said, 'Good-bye.' He is a fine young man."

LeVon was stunned to tears, took Gabriel's envelope, the paper, and the key, but did not return with Gabriel to the first-floor foyer; he only saw him to his office door. They nodded and departed. As Gabriel turned the knob on the door of LeVon's office, he said to him, "Remember the sealed envelope, which was entitled at the top of the three-page presentation, 'An Open Letter to My Friend, LeVon Gilbertson, in Response to My Attendance to the First Quadrennial Conference on Evangelism, As His Invited Guest, August 23, 1954, in Memphis, Tennessee.' You requested this 'Response,' and don't forget

238

the key. (pause) Good-bye."

After Gabriel handed his sealed envelope to LeVon, he went down the swift elevator to the foyer, then straight to the parking lot to enter his automobile. Gabriel wept; he had lost a friend. He spent the night in a Memphis suburb motel, arose early the next morning, and returned to his beautiful Georgetown home. Every mile home the grass was gloriously green.

When he saw Evangeline he was so happy in heart to see her radiant face, her Christian charm, and laughter.

That night on their bed together, he whispered into her ear:

"My dear Evangeline, we will no longer be puritans in a decaying system of religion; we have made a full exodus, and we are now pilgrims until we get home to heaven."

"Yes, my dear Gabriel; and I will travel with you with all my heart all the way to our heavenly home."

Gabriel would remember this decision to be a pilgrim, no longer a puritan. He believed that many more would have to become pilgrims, either from false religions to historic Christianity, or leaving the apostasy in Christianity to become historic, Biblical Christians. Man must experience this exodus and teach others what they had learned from the decaying systems and denominations. A bridge must be built to teach others who would follow. Many would make this exodus before the Lord would set up His millennial kingdom.

Chapter Twenty

The Dedication

(November 3, 1970)

The separation which came in the personal lives of Gabriel and LeVon Gilbertson, as well as a number of incidents of the past that had happened in Gabriel's life were only a token of that which was to follow. Gabriel continued to love and pray for LeVon, but it was obvious that the die was cast and only a Biblical separation in their fellowship could solve God's intent for Gabriel's future. It was an age-old question in the Word of God before: "Can two walk together, except they be agreed?" The prophet Amos, chapter 3, verse 3. If agreement cannot be made or sustained, then peace comes through separation. Yes, peace comes through separation, because separation is not only difficult but it also brings precious peace. It must be remembered that religious conviction has been the strongest conviction in the history of the world. Gabriel thought, in contrast to this loss of a friend, of his dear friend, Rev. Matthew N. Wiley as being as deep in joy as LeVon's friendship was in sorrow.

Gabriel continued to see the publicity extended to LeVon in the various popular religious and denominational periodicals across the nation and even foreign reports. As the senior bishop of his denomination, still residing in Memphis, Tennessee, he commuted to his official office which was housed in another impressive building in Oklahoma City, Oklahoma. He was the most noted ecclesiastical leader in the ecumenical Charismatic movement of evangelism. He was the main speaker in the assemblies of several international ecumenical meetings in the 1980s, and in 1990 he had a personal interview, along with several other religious dignitaries and denominational leaders, with the Pope, himself. Of course, this occasion involved World-Wide Evangelism, Unity, and the charismatic teachings of the Holy Spirit, including the Glossolalia and other Church, Apostolic Succession Gifts. Gabriel heard LeVon's message from that meeting with other speakers in Rome on the television's nightly news. They spoke of how wonderful the spirit of love was manifested, prevailing upon each face as they met in the Sistine Chapel with "the Holy Father."

By the end of the 1980s the protestant leaders of the world had written many books and given many commendations to the Pope and Romanism. The mainline protestant denominations had returned to historic Rome away from historic Primitive Christianity and the Remnant Christianity of the early Creeds and Councils leading to the Reformation. Wherever there was a break-down in church history, there was the departure from historic Christianity.

Gabriel, maintaining the empirical method of furthering his accuracy of his reportings of the trends of the various ecumenical meetings, as an official observer, continued to see that the seven bishops of the seven historic pentecostal denominations in 1954 were accurate in their predictions of what they would call "prophecies." To Gabriel, this did not mean they were genuine Biblical "prophets; rather, they were simply astute discerners of their own concepts and the religious mind of the time. That "First Quadrennial Conference on Evangelism" also announced that the fourteen denominational theological systems would be dividing themselves into their affinity-group and become involved in World-Wide Evangelism.

All of the terms were coming together into a synthesis, terms such as: "renewal," "awakening," "evangelicalism," "Romanism," "crusades," "rallies," "congresses," "conferences," "workshops"; yes, and Rock Music, etc.

It had become clear they were going to "tear down the walls of separation" that heretofore had made the theological doctrine and system the distinctive of each denomination that formerly had its root in Reformation Christianity. The union of this synthesis was so great that the leaders of the larger ecumenical authorities were much greater than the bishops, superintendents, district conferences, and church pastors within their former authorities. The forerunner of the "Full Gospel," Charismatic movements of the mid-1950s was now giving way to the "Pledge Keepers" of a male movement founded by a sportscaster on the Charismatic Television Network (CTN). The denominations and local churches were being swallowed up by the impressive impact of the national and international movements and assemblies. The local church assembly was becoming extinct with less than twenty-eight percent of church membership giving Sunday attendance, and yet over fifty percent of these same members attending the large mass meetings both for evangelism and healing services with Charismatic "prophets," so-called.

The same pattern could be seen in the distinctive nations of the world which were being dominated by the United Nations Order which was bringing all people everywhere to a global, world, government, and social force. There was talk that 192 nations would soon represent all nations, including combined tribes of the world. The pattern was so much the same that you could imagine the entire political and religious world, contemporary "Christian," in name, being driven together like cattle into a final arena with a political Antichrist, and the power of a singular False Prophet giving honor, charismatism, glory, and power to that Antichrist.

The Charismatic Churches, led by the Union Presbyterian scholarship, the Charismatic Gifts, the South Baptist Convocation influence, and Methodist experiential method were all involved with the ministry of Evangelist Willie

Wheyman and his international crusades. Rock Gospel and Contemporary Music were everywhere prominent in all the gatherings of all the ecumenical public services and conventions. This meant that the Reformation Christian Ethic was dead as far as the public proclamation of the Gospel of the Lord Jesus Christ. The Westminster Confession and Catechism no longer held dominant influence; the resolutions of the huge Baptist conventions no longer presented their famous controversies; and the impressive history of the sanctified life no longer attracted the Methodists.

It was to be a world-church; a neo-world-church would rise in the earth. All of the former influences of the great Reformation Christians would die. Now was the time, according to all the church leaders, to bring peace and love and fellowship for all who would accept neo-christianity. The Church would not have to be on the battlefield anymore; the trend was to bring a doctrinal loss of mind. Many former Biblical Christians were now suffering from battle fatigue; they wanted peace and rest; they wanted to embrace everybody and eliminate the sin-question from the face of the earth. They desired the power of the Charismatic Gifts; they desired a prosperity theology and divine healing programs to replace the great Bible sermons and writings against the former greater enemies such as sin, demonism, error, and apostasy. Above all, they desired a "human Jesus" for humanitarian needs. They no longer believed that an apostasy existed in the Contemporary, Neo-Church; the world had come to believe in a "neo-universalism" for all mankind.

Yet, there remained a Bible remnant in the world.

The Lutherans, forgetting Martin Luther, with both liberal and conservative wings, were now involved in the ecumenical movement back to Rome. Luther's Reformation Christianity was bent to the breaking point as it, too, became a part of the synthesis with the Charismatics and Evangelist Wheyman and his crusades. Most everything in religious sight had begun to fall under one person, Willie Wheyman. The Glossolalia became a prominent manifestation, with musicians on drugs presenting the contemporary beat of the "gospel song," even in the large, impressive formal churches.

Yet there remained a Bible remnant in the land.

The Wesleyans and Methodists met together in their fellowships with the ecumenical forces. The Gifts began to appear in their reputed "revivals," in their larger colleges and seminaries. The Methodists now were very close to the pentecostalists with a number of the "new revelationists," with their "audible voices," reputedly from God, having joined the Methodist Church through impressive liberal bishops ordaining them. But standing in the shadow of things was Evangelist Wheyman.

The Arminians, alike, were even further involved in all the same ecumenical movements and the Wheyman crusades. "Good works" of the neo-christian now overshadowed the pure grace teachings of the New Testament. Of course, with so much energy involved in all of this union of denominations, "works" had taken its place equally with "faith," in sharp contrast to the remembrance of the greater victories, theologically, of salvation by "grace through faith" as was so preciously emphasized by Primitive Christianity and Reformation Christianity. The methodology of the ecumenical, evangelistic movement was a direct result of works and human instrumentality. Even the administration of businessmen was as necessary and prominent as the former spiritual forces of the Holy Spirit of yesteryear in the Church. Here, too, the Arminians stood in awe of Evangelist Wheyman.

Yet there remained a Bible remnant in the earth.

The Pelagians and semi-Pelagians had an upsurge of importance with their goodness of man at birth, historically rejecting the inherited depravity passed down through the human race from Adam. A large number of modern presbyterians were claiming that they had been born again in their mother's womb and therefore repentance and a personal acceptance of Jesus Christ were not necessary in their adult life. The Liberals had already revived a semi-Pelagianism in the nineteenth century, but historic Pelagianism, itself, had returned in full force among the widening group of the universalists. Pelagianism, however, had its power in its ability to creep into a stable church and somewhat unobtrusively get into any kind of people's theology. Pelagianism has had many forms back in history. It was most fitting to its purpose that it returned in this liberal ecumenical time of evangelism.

It must be remembered that Gnosticism and Pelagianism are religious forces which cannot be dealt with once and for all. These come from Tradition and are set among us in history. Also, there is no way of eradicating Sabellianism and Donatism from its influence in history. Man is simply prone to fall back into these forces unless the Bible is believed. Gnosticism comes from man's faith in his own knowledge; Pelagianism comes from man's confidence in his own goodness; Donatism is a Christian sect of North Africa that believes they alone constitute the whole and true Church; and Sabellianism, or Monarchianism, emphasizes the unity of God as One with three unifying aspects rather than belief in the Trinity. So, all of these old forces continue to return from time to time through whatever modern channel open to them.

Universalism must be added as the fifth reoccurring religion in the history of the world. Of course, with the proliferation of the religious impetus so strong in the present generation, Gabriel believed we could expect the return of these religious presuppositions to collide in a world or state religion of a one-world government. None of these old forces were involved in a religious presupposition demanding the retention of a historic testing ground.

The manifestation of all Liberal and Pelagian elements was rapidly bringing the world to believe that all were saved, ultimately, and it was easily fitting to all of the liberal interpretations of the old theologies after the Reformation. Universalism, in the minds of thinking, Biblical Christians, seems to eliminate the need of evangelism entirely since it was being uttered and espoused by Evangelist Wheyman that a person could be saved and go to heaven without a Bible and the preaching of the name of Jesus Christ as Savior. However, the reverse was true of his followers; it simply magnified his success as an evangelist to come up with such a universal acceptance of his kind of neo-gospel of evangelism.

Yet there remained and survived a remnant movement of Christians in the world.

Of course, from all of these identities enumerated, the Charismatics and the Roman Catholics and the Pentecostalists were receiving most of the converts from the Wheyman evangelistic crusades. And within this union there were some who actually rejected a trinitarian monotheism such as the "Jesus Only" pentecostal who rejected the historic trinity and believed that "only Jesus" was God. On the other hand, the Unitarians still persisted that "only the Father" was God, and therefore there was no need of the Savior, the Lord Jesus Christ. However, the mix-up of the names of "Jesus" and "Father" did not hinder the success of their ecumenism. In church history, in her councils and creeds, no doctrine had been made any clearer than the Trinity of the Godhead — Trinitarian Monotheism. Once again, the historical influence was minimized.

The outcome of much of the historic compromise ended up in Universalism, that all were either born saved or all would be saved and arrive in heaven, ultimately. Even election and predestination were used to assist the final outcome of the salvation of all men. Hell was rejected by most every fellowship in the ecumenical movement. The later ministry of Willie Wheyman was so weak in the matter of the definition of "Hell" that for all reasonable conclusions, everyone would finally survive hell anyway, and one must reject the "eternal hell," entirely. Modern belief about hell was much more life a purgatory, if anything.

Yet, there remained those of the true identity of Remnant Christianity.

We must not forget, and we will not ignore, that there were some true puritans still in the denominations, as well as many pilgrims who had made an exodus from what they believed to be the apostasy. These pilgrims planted independent churches, Christian Schools, colleges, and seminaries upon the freedom of the Primitive, Remnant, Reformation presupposition as was once led of the Holy Spirit at Antioch during the days of Barnabas and Paul.

The most prominent puritan-pilgrim principle yet remained among the fundamentalists who identified themselves openly as separatists from the ecumenical apostasy. The fundamental core-truth of the Gospel of the Lord Jesus and the teaching of scriptural separation, as revealed through the Biblical doctrine of sanctification, became the fundamentalist's battle-cry. They would not preach for or cooperate with any of the "neo-movements" who were a part of the ecumenical movement of evangelism. They identified their separatist position, however, only as "ecclesiastical separation." Personal separation was not usually a part of the fundamentalist standard. The greatest problem with fundamentalists was the inroads of contemporary music. Some of their churches were destroyed by their unseparated music in worship.

The fundamentalists agreed with separation, unanimously, in their earliest days, but because they did not agree concerning "personal separation," this opened up for some to later on discard "ecclesiastical separation" entirely. Of course, there were some fundamentalists who simply did not live consistently with their principles, so compromise brought them to be seen on preaching and assembly platforms which they had formerly condemned. Hypocrisy is in every movement throughout the history of man. The fundamentalists were being tested and reduced, but the remnant that stood became a greater influence for God.

But Fundamentalism still remained the best testimony against the ecumenical apostasy. There were definitely three different definitions among the fundamentalists on the matter of separation: one, simply meant ecclesiastical separation only; two, ecclesiastical and personal separation; and three, separation unto the Lordship of the Lord Jesus Christ, and motivated by this, separation from the apostasy and apostates in all contexts of Christianity.

Gabriel came to believe the Bible in the light of these careful, thought-through principles. He did strive to come to this objectively, not being persuaded by a person or sentiment. He believed he had come honorably to be a fundamentalist with the third definition of separation. He was able to accept any individual, in his personal fellowship, who conscientiously considered himself or herself as a fundamentalist. He went as far as he could on the road with a man who professed this — as far as he could before making a separation decision against him. He believed there had to be an honorable forum in Fundamentalism whereby a different distinction should be permitted in order to test and keep his own or another fundamentalist in the arena against the larger foe.

It was during the middle 1970s that Gabriel finalized his heart to make a complete exodus to be a pilgrim in the earth, desiring the fellowship and identity as a fundamentalist. However, he reserved the right not to be a part of the "ism" whenever his conscience saw it as an exclusive or elite entity, or one lived with hypocrisy.

After the time of Gabriel's resignation from Antioch Theological Seminary in 1969, and his move back to his Georgetown home, Mr. Broadman requested an appointment with him, privately, of an urgent matter, for November 3, 1970. So, sandwiched in-between Gabriel's requested resignation from the Antioch Seminary, and the 1974 meeting and separation from the fellowship of LeVon Gilbertson, Mr. Broadman contacted Gabriel with urgency. They met together that evening at 6:00 in the large third-floor room, "The Land of Evangeline."

They had a cordial reunion and Evangeline was there to set forth her beautiful hospitality for them from her famous, but modest, kitchenette in what she called "The Room," her nickname for the third floor of her lovely home. After the refreshment was received, Evangeline graciously excused herself, having told Mr. Broadman of their delight to see him once again. Mr. Broadman responded, and then, seated with Gabriel, he spoke of the beauty and uniqueness of Evangeline's "The Room." Gabriel spent several moments explaining its historic importance to him and his family.

Mr. Broadman then commences the expressions of his heart to the heart of Gabriel.

"Dr. Parsons, your nine years at the Antioch Seminary were

especially for me. I profited much from every sermon, lecture, and all Friday sessions that I was able to hear from your heart and mind. I shall never forget those years."

Gabriel acknowledges to him and the Lord that this had blest Mr. Broadman. Mr. Broadman continues.

"Dr. Parsons, all of the former conversations we have had together brings me to my personal need of God at this time. I have, for years, been in attendance of many religious meetings, in churches, crusades, banquets dedicated to some great speaker involved in Ecumenical Evangelism. I attended, with my wife and family, a number of the Willie Wheyman crusades. I have gone forward down the aisles on some occasions, hoping and thinking I would come to know God. Probably, others have found something in it all; I did not. My wife has attended a number of the Healing Crusades of Rev. Bobby Lynn and left so disappointed, only thinking she did not have enough faith. On one occasion, Rev. Lynn said she was healed, but for some reason she was not. She would return from time to time, leaving with the same condition. She does not know a great deal about the Bible, but I sincerely believe she is a Christian. Also, because of our being an administrative leader in the old, revered Antioch Seminary, we have met quite a number of individuals from all religious walks of life. As you probably have suspected, I have come to believe that I am a Christian agnostic, whatever that means.

"In other words, I am in a Christian church, and considered to be a Christian administrator, and am identified as a Christian. However, this is not a lie entirely, since my church is so liberal that the need of my heart or spiritual condition is not that important where the Gospel is not preached. In all truth, I had not heard the Gospel until you preached and taught it in the seminary. I was called into the Board because of my administrative ability, without knowing what you taught and believed. If I had known, I am sure I would not have taken on the administrative chairmanship of the seminary. I have, through the years, been identified with a liberal presbyterian church.

"My children all go to church with us; they have not been

'born again and converted to Jesus Christ,' as you would say. We are just a nice family, I suppose; but I am sure we are not 'born again.' It is something we did not know. I have tried to believe in God, not knowing what to believe to know Him. Every member of my family has either tried to obey a healer or an evangelist or a pastor, but we have nothing in our hearts and lives to indicate we are Christians. With all of these words, I still think my dear wife is a simple Christian woman without much knowledge of the Bible at all.

"My dear friend, Dr. Parsons, do you really believe there is anything to that which I have heard about Christianity? I think you call it 'neo-christianity.'"

With great soberness and care, Gabriel replies:

"My friend, Mr. Broadman, there is really not much to it. There has been a change in the definition of Christianity in our lifetime. I believe you are an example of many people in our world who have heard the 'new' and found nothing for your soul. You are most accurate, I believe. You have sincerely come to believe you are a Christian agnostic, and now you must begin anew with the Gospel of the Holy Scriptures. I agree with what you say because you have gone to Christian churches and occasions, and yet you are an agnostic because you do not know; you are not sure there is a God, and therefore you have no Savior."

"Well, what does all this mean for me at this time in my life, Dr. Parsons?"

"It means the Holy Scriptures must be presented to you where you are, spiritually, at this time in your life. Someone must teach you a 'word in season,' appropriate to your spiritual condition, or need."

"What is that condition, my friend?"

"I believe, Mr. Broadman, that we must commence with gaining the foothold of that which is plausible and credible to you with the early essentials of believing in God. You have experienced doubts of Christianity because of the false concept of Christianity in our time; we must find out if you will welcome even that which is credible and plausible and reasonable to your agnostic condition. It may well be that your not being a

Christian does not mean you are an atheist who denies the very existence of God Himself."

"Dr. Parsons, I would welcome even an illustration of what you mean that I must come to know God, first."

"Well, an agnostic must be given a plausible understanding of the bare possibility of God to get out of the agnostic condition and frame of mind in his lost soul.

"I would like to set this forth in two examples: first, a passage in the Bible; and second, an illustration in nature.

"First, the Apostle Paul spoke to the philosophers on Mars Hill years ago, as recorded in the Book of Acts, chapter 17. Keep in mind, these men had run out of gods, too. They no longer knew if there was a god, and so they erected a religious idol to 'the unknown god.' This could mean either that they had sought after so many gods, in their idolatry, that they were seeking a new one who would truly answer their longings and prayers. Or, it might be that some of them had been thoroughly convinced that they no longer knew, at all, if there was indeed a god at all.

"At this point, Paul did not preach the wonder of saving grace through faith in the Lord Jesus; he did not mention His Name in the entire discourse. He started with natural theology simply to bring their minds to a plausible, credible belief in the Creator and Providence of the true God. It should be thoroughly understood that there is God's prevenient grace or common grace that is available to enable the sinner to see this credibility of the existence of God. This enablement does not save them but enables them to want God if they want Him. Of course, there is also the Holy Spirit in conviction for sin and His illumination of the Word of God to the human heart. Saving grace would follow through the Gospel if the person accepts Jesus as his Savior, too. We believe that when the Apostle Paul left Mars Hill, the philosophers came to believe in the true God, or at least God was now credible and plausible to their minds through natural theology. He concluded then that God 'had appointed a day, in which he will judge the world in righteousness by that man whom he had ordained,...in that he hath raised him from the dead.' With both common grace and specific saving grace, we would see the reason for such a verse as 'Let not your heart be troubled: ye believe in God, believe also in me.' The Gospel of John, chapter fourteen, verse one.

"That is as far as Paul went with the Gospel of the Lord Jesus to that audience. I believe the Holy Spirit led Paul in this sermon appropriate to his audience. Paul continued with just one word after presenting God the Creator. That was the word 'man' and he concluded the entire implication with the 'resurrection.' After that brief close to his sermon, Paul stopped preaching further. (a pause) My friend, I believe it is also appropriate for you as well at this time in your life and hunger to know God."

"I will certainly read that chapter more intensely after I leave you today as well as the verse in John's Gospel."

"Mr. Broadman, I would like to support this need with a second witness in possibly two illustrations.

"Our modern neo-christianity is something like a counterfeit one-hundred-dollar bill. The counterfeit bill is not worth one penny. It may look real; it may feel real; but it is not real. Yet it represents value to the viewer. A person may try to spend it, and somebody may accept and pass it and believe it, but it is not genuine at all. No matter how well it is printed, it is not genuine. No matter how many people are fooled by it, it is a counterfeit. There will always be at least one feature that the counterfeit does not have, but that the genuine does have, and that one very small feature marks it to be genuine."

"Dr. Parsons, is that one very small thing that important?"

"Yes, it is my friend, because that one little secret is a huge truth. Only the completely genuine bill has the legal tender and power of its worth."

"What could possibly be that one little thing?"

"That one little secret power is the secret of a certain minute marking that only the engraver knows; that marking is the mark of living truth."

"Living truth? What's that?"

"The living truth of the incarnate engraver who lives, alive to make a true monetary bill. (a pause)

"But allow me to give another illustration. The vegetable cabbage has two chemical elements identified by biologists. Both of these chemical elements are known by man. A synthetic seed may be put together in the exact proportion of chemicals and shape, and all else, but when that cabbage seed is planted in the ground, it will not grow."

"Yes, I've heard that, but why not?"

"Why? (pause) Because the man-made seed does not have the secret of invisible life. Therefore, once again, the cabbage seed, like the counterfeit one-hundred-dollar bill, is worthless without the invisible, non-physical life that every seed in the vegetable kingdom must have. We call it *zoei*."

"Cannot man give a synthetic life to the two chemical visible elements?"

"No. At this point in history, man has not been able to do that. We believe that God, our Creator, placed that life in that first seed so effectively that it has continued down through history only through the direct providence of Almighty God in the continuance of that species-seed line."

"I have now been hearing you about the subject of a counterfeit bill and a lifeless seed. Dr. Parsons, how can we receive the genuine bill and life-giving seed?"

"Listen carefully to this answer: 'He that hath the Son hath life; and he that hath not the Son of God hath not life.' First John, chapter 5, verse 12."

"You mean, Gabriel, that the secret to the truth of life is in actually and personally accepting Jesus Christ?"

"Yes, the living truth of Christ in our heart brings the genuine, living Seed. What we are generally watching, at this point in history, is a seed called Christianity, but without the historic, revealed Christ and His promise of life in the Seed of the Word of God. My friend, why don't you accept Him right now? Is not this plausible? Is not this reasonable? Is not this credible? (a considerable pause)

"In spite of all that is false today, with an understanding of my concern for your agnosticism, you must come now and reason with God anyway. Isaiah, the prophet, has an appropriate word for you: 'Come now, and let us reason together, saith the Lord: though your sins be as scarlet, they shall be as white as snow; though they be red like crimson, they shall be as wool.' Chapter 1, verse 18. (Mr. Broadman drops his head in thought.) No amount of error and misunderstanding of it all must keep you, personally, from becoming a genuine Christian. Boaz, what will you do with Jesus Christ of Nazareth, in history? This question does not at all concern modern neo-christianity. It concerns you, my friend." (a long pause)

"Gabriel, I will accept that living Lord Jesus Christ and His life-giving power into my own life at this time." (pause)

Gabriel responds in prayer: "Dear God, here is your creature, Mr. Boaz A. Broadman; he wants the eternal life that Jesus died to give him. Save him now, Oh Lord, for Jesus' sake..."

"Yes, God; I repent of all my filthy sins; forgive me of my agnostic delays in life that have hindered me from accepting you. Most of all, give me this eternal life in your Son, the Lord Jesus." (a pause of weeping) "Lord, I believe; Lord, I believe!"

"Amen! And Lord Jesus, I, Gabriel Parsons, want to rededicate all that I am to make credible your holy Name, Thy Word, and Thy life for men just like Brother Boaz A. Broadman. In Jesus' Name, Amen!"

"Brother Parsons: I have become a Christian tonight (pause), and forever. This is my spiritual birthday, November 3, 1970."

"My dear Brother Broadman, let us go to heaven together. Let us maintain our faith and look to God for this new-found friendship together as long as we live on earth, too."

Thus, a Christian friendship was born in Christ, and only God would know the future of this friendship of ten years, from 1960 to November 3, 1970.

Gabriel walked with Mr. Broadman downstairs from "The Room" and to his parked automobile with a quiet joy and rest in heart and mind. Evangeline met them there and rejoiced with both of them for God's salvation, through faith in Jesus Christ, for Boaz A. Broadman. Gabriel and Mr. Broadman clasped both hands and promised to pray for each other in the days ahead, and see each other again before too long.

Gabriel returned with Evangeline into their home and shared with her all of the happenings of that evening. Brother Broadman's conversion and Gabriel's own rededication to Christ were fixed in their hearts.

Gabriel concluded his remarks to Evangeline, "I believe tonight the Lord has revealed His direction for my future."

Evangeline responded: "And I will follow you, Gabriel, wherever that might be."

"Evangeline, my dear, we will see Brother Boaz A. Broadman again, and soon. He has become a pilgrim, too."

Chapter Twenty-one

The Friends

(Christmas, 1970 & January 5, 1971 & June 29, 1974)

The Christmas of 1970 was a great blessing to Gabriel. This was the overflow of their summer vacation. Gabriel knew that a minister must first have a Christian home with Christian principles, Christian love, and Christian discipline.

This 1970 Christmas was to break forth into blessing upon every member of the family. He and Evangeline were now forty-four years old; Joseph Paul was still twenty-one; Soma Jeanne, sixteen; and Ariel John, fifteen. Joseph Paul was having the Christmas break from college; and he was still fervent about his call into the ministry. Miss Juliana Queens was still teaching in Gabriel's home school her remaining favorite students, Soma Jeanne and Ariel John. She was a genuine blessing to everyone.

On Christmas Eve, the Parsons family gathered together around the fireplace for the reading of the Christmas Story from the Bible, and then each member of the family, as was the practice of their regular Family Altar, would lead out in prayer. The order was: Evangeline, then Joseph Paul, then Soma Jeanne, Ariel John, with Gabriel finishing the prayer period for the evening. Their prayers were filled with

thanksgiving to God for His goodness and the gift of earthly
friends.

After the prayer Gabriel suggested that a list of friends be
written out by Evangeline, and that a letter be sent
acknowledging their friendship by the first of the new year.

It became time for sleep but not before an immediate list of
names and addresses collected of close friends, numbering
about 200, that would initiate a larger list to send the New
Year's letter.

Gabriel was too excited to sleep that Christmas Eve night,
and Evangeline sensed his longing heart in-between her own
sleeps.

In January, 1971, before the letter was sent out to their
friends, Dad Peters died. Gabriel and Evangeline, and their
children proceeded to Westport Island with the rest of the
family to the First Christian Church, the cemetery, and Gull
Rock. Mr. McArcy McGee Peters was buried beside his first
wife, Mildred Joye Prince Peters, daughter of Captain John
Prince and his wife, Ellen Mae Prince, who had both preceded
Dad Peters in death. Gabriel had been there to preach the
funeral of Captain and Mrs. Prince in 1962. Both had died at
sea from a plague received from the West Indies. It was to
have been Captain Prince's last voyage and he wanted Mildred
Joye to be with him. Now the second time had come to be
there again in the sorrow of death.

Mr. and Mrs. Carl Vernon Louisia were there for the funeral
and interment. It was good to see Louise Louisia again. She
had followed the life and ministry of Gabriel through the
earnest testimony of Evangeline; but Louise did not know Jesus,
as her personal Savior. And now, once again, Gabriel had
been called upon to preach the funeral in the Christian Church
for Dad Peters. He loved Gabriel; and Gabriel, him, too. The
title of Gabriel's sermon was, "A Pilgrim Christian Goes Home,"
the text was taken from First Peter, chapter 2, verses 11 and
12. A eulogy concluded the service in the church.

After the worship and sermon service, the entire
congregation walked the usual half-mile down to the cemetery

where Gabriel gave the interment of the body. Gabriel always used the thought of his funeral sermon again in the benediction of the graveside remarks. His words in the opening prayer were: "Our Heavenly Father, we thank you for the life and testimony of our Dad, McArcy McGee Peters. He was a refreshing pilgrim in the earth to us; he enjoyed, by your grace, Primitive Christianity, through his great, simple faith. Thank you again for this pilgrim in a modern world. In Jesus' Name, Amen!" Then, immediately after the benediction, Gabriel gave his own poem for the actual interment. He did not prefer the older English funeral form, in the phrase "ashes to ashes, dust to dust..." He wrote this in its place for the committal.

> **"And now upon his casket,**
> **We lay these flowers fair,**
> **In tokens of sweet mem'ries**
> **We trust beyond compare.**
> **Loose is the cord of silver;**
> **Broken the golden bowl;**
> **These flowers, in faith, immortal,**
> **At home with God is his soul.**
> **Through the bodily resurrection of the Lord Jesus Christ,**
> **Amen!"**

After the interment of Dad Peters, Louise Louisia came to Gabriel and thanked him for the sermon and service. She also requested that he walk privately with her down the road farther to Gull Rock, the piece of land Dad Peters purchased when he married his wife, Mildred Joye, there at Westport Island.

Louise Louisia stopped and sat with Gabriel on the remaining wood foundations of Dad Peters' house of long ago. She said to Gabriel,

"I have not always understood your Christian life and ministry. It seemed too separated for me. I made a mistake and thought of it as too much religion. However, Evangeline has taught it through the years in her many conversations and correspondences to me, in her beautiful and simple way. Today,

I see it clearly, and as dear Evangeline would say, 'the Holy Spirit can open a person's eyes to see what is in the Gospel of the Bible, even after a person has been taught truth they could not understand.' I believe that has happened to me today as you preached the sermon about 'A Christian Pilgrim in the Earth.' Gabriel, I have already confessed my many sins of selfishness and pride. I have accepted Jesus as my personal Savior, during the sermon, and believe Him to be the Son of God. I wanted to tell you straight out about this in the privacy of this old homeplace of my father. Will you forgive me for disliking and misunderstanding you for so long?"

Gabriel immediately responded in the affirmative with Christian delight and tears.

"Yes, my dear Louise, I forgive you, and most of all, Jesus does. Also, I do not really know why, from our first meeting, I have always thought of you by the two names of Louise Louisia. But as from this day, and from now on, I will call you only Louise. Sometimes we read in the Bible, whenever a person accepts Christ as Savior, the Bible gives him or her a new name or a changed name. Jesus did this with some of his disciples. Today, you and I are both in the very same Christian family of God, our Father. Louise, I want us to both go to heaven together. It is my hope that you will lead your husband to Jesus, too."

They embraced, which had never happened before, and they returned to Evangeline, arm in arm, as Evangeline ran towards them with her radiant smile. Louise had already told Evangeline as they walked together the half-mile from the church service down to the cemetery.

The Parsons family returned to their home in Georgetown with peace in their hearts about Dad Peters being in heaven with Jesus, and the added joy about Louise becoming a pilgrim on earth, too.

The rest of the year of 1971 was filled with Gabriel's agenda of travel lectures, which he had limited to only five different places in America and one in South Korea, his regular annual return.

The main burden of the year was to finalize a location for a ministry in historic Georgetown, the place of his marriage home into which Gabriel and Evangeline moved in 1949. Gabriel was now considering the actual name for the ministry laid upon his heart by the Lord.

The return of Gabriel and his family to Georgetown, after his resignation from the Antioch Theological Seminary in Ocean View, North Carolina, in the year of 1969, led to a series of special events. He and his family sought God on their long-awaited vacation to the Land of Evangeline and the Blue Ridge Parkway, only to return home with four urgent appointments ahead in the providence of God. These four appointments are placed in the narrative at this point, including several to actually come later in time.

The first appointment was made with Mr. Boaz A. Broadman, the former chairman of the Board of Trustees of the Antioch Theological Seminary. He had, also, resigned from the Board because of the request-resignation made by the Board upon Gabriel as the president of the seminary. The appointment of Mr. Broadman in Gabriel's home, in "The Room" on the third floor, brought the wonder of God's grace unto the saving of Brother Broadman's soul, November 3, 1970.

The second appointment from the Lord came as a surprise to Gabriel and Evangeline as it concerned Mrs. Louise Louisia, who became a born-again believer, converted to historic Christianity during the funeral sermon of Gabriel for Dad Peters, January 5, 1971, in the First Christian Church on Westport Island. This was indeed an unusual "grace through faith" reality for Evangeline's sister, Louise.

The third appointment from the Lord came through a visit of Rev. Matthew N. Wiley and his wife, Bettina, to Gabriel's home in Georgetown, March 26, 1973. God opened up the hearts of Gabriel and Rev. Wiley to such an extent that Gabriel saw that he would be a faithful friend in his forthcoming ministry which was to be announced in a gathering of twenty-four persons, including the Wileys, June 29, 1974.

The fourth appointment from the Lord came through the final appointment Bishop LeVon Gilbertson requested of

Gabriel to come to his office in the Evangel Building in Memphis, Tennessee, May 19, 1974. Gabriel was constrained to meet LeVon, but the appointment that day definitely brought about an honorable separation in the heart of Gabriel because of the change of their past fellowship. LeVon was on the road to the apostasy, and Gabriel endeavored to warn him as a friend. Although they both knew they did not agree concerning Contemporary Christianity, yet LeVon wanted to maintain their meetings together, so he could monitor the ongoing mind-set of the heart of Gabriel whom he believed to be a scholar.

From these four appointments, believed as from the Lord in the life of Gabriel, he could see something of the leading of God for the remaining period of his life. Gabriel had been greatly blest of the Lord in his travels, his lectures, his sermons, and teaching, but now since God had made it clear to his heart about the apostasy, he must proceed with the clarity and strength of his convictions to exalt the Lord Jesus in historic Christianity.

In the case of Mr. Broadman, Gabriel thought he might be used of God to lead agnostics, skeptics, atheists, and others who had become disillusioned concerning contemporary Christianity in its departure from the Word of God. This indicated to Gabriel that it was not his own respectability that won Mr. Broadman, but respect for the consistency of the pure Word of God.

In the case of the conversion of Louise, Evangeline's sister, there was a deep work of the Holy Spirit involved because Louise was deeply rooted in the tradition of the Anglican Church in Canada. This was a rich blessing to Gabriel and Evangeline, personally, for after all of their many conversations with her, and lack of wisdom for her, they thought they had turned her against them.

In the case of Rev. Wiley, Gabriel was simply overwhelmed by the grace of God that had brought about in his own life a friend of such a proportion of fellowship, yet from such a different background and natural temperament. This brought Gabriel to believe that God could indeed reach the lost and bring strong friendships to bear upon the need of strength and blessing to one another in the warfare and the apostasy, where many friends were being divided.

In the case of LeVon Gilbertson, here was a person known to Gabriel before his being saved by grace through faith. They began from similar places in life in the Metropolitan Washington area, and yet Christ separated them because they took two different roads. Gabriel had no hatred nor bitterness in his heart about this matter; his walk and knowledge of the Lord Jesus simply separated them in life. However, Gabriel continued to have a burden of prayer for LeVon. Gabriel had great reservations and longings for LeVon and yet he did not fully know why.

Both the separation and the sealing of friendships were a part of the confirmation to Gabriel of a number of scriptures God had given him to guide him into his future ministry. Gabriel realized, throughout his life, that there was not only a separation unto the Lord against the apostasy, but there must be a personal dedication to the ministry "for such a time as this." The Book of Esther, chapter 4, verse 14. There were many ministries, in variety, God needed. Not all was pastoring, evangelizing, administrating, teaching a classroom, ministering in the prisons, on the streets, etc.

Every door everywhere called for a ministry. There was a need of a ministry in art, in music, for families, for broken homes, and for the elderly. The current apostasy, in the name of Christianity, was affecting everyone in every walk of life. Gabriel believed there was no ministry anywhere that did not need to include the presupposition of historic Christianity. The word "Christian," of the contemporary time, was insufficient in presenting Christ; most people only understood the Bible in the light of the modern preacher of neo-christianity. In every ministry the definition of Christianity must be re-taught; the Gospel must be made clear as it had been made clear in Primitive Christianity.

After months of searching and praying, a piece of property was located near the home of Gabriel and his family. All of the property could be viewed from his own home. An appraisal of the property was made in light of the asking price for its purchase. He had already contacted a list of names that he desired to share his ministerial vision with, who had already encouraged him, on a number of occasions in the past, to commence a ministry of his own. These persons had followed his message through the years, and although they were seriously involved in their own ministry or a ministry of another people who followed historic Christianity, they desired to be a friend to his longings of heart as well. It was not necessary that a denominational identity be involved; these people were basically a part of the Fundamentalist movement in the earth.

The names of these friends were now to be contacted and invited to meet Gabriel at the address of the piece of property in Georgetown. A previous letter of Gabriel's intent had been sent and these friends were excited in response. Gabriel would show them around the nine-acre plot of historic ground, on which was a beautiful antebellum home contemporary to the Civil War that had been preserved with care. However, the long-term family name that had built the home, originally, and their succeeding children who had maintained its care, did not want it to be sold to the Historical Society of Washington D.C., or nearby Virginia, who did desire it. The family had fallen on hard times and needed to sell, but they desired for it to be preserved outside of state influence. The family desired that some honorable institution purchase it with a meaningful purpose to the public and their own hearts and minds.

When Gabriel and Evangeline visited the Georgetown family who owned it, and gave explanation of his desire for a ministry there, they were pleased with its purpose. The family were relatives of the Georgeton family of wealth who had endowed both Georgeton University and Georgeton Theological Seminary. Dr. Beauchamp Paulson knew the family and responded to Gabriel's confidence of what he had on his mind for a ministry. God used Dr. Paulson to substantiate the integrity of Gabriel. In fact, one of their married granddaughters had attended the introductory session in the Night Institute of Gabriel at the Georgeton Seminary.

Gabriel and Evangeline presented the scale-drawings of plans for a new learning center facility to be built on the proposed acreage. The stately antebellum home was to the front right as you entered the beautiful estate, rising up at some small distance from the Potomac River in the western section of historic Georgetown, a western suburb of Washington, D.C.

A new facility was proposed to be built to the left side of the front of the property and back in the beautiful trees of magnolias and Virginia firs. On that side of the property there was a knoll situated just right for the new facility to be built in the midst of the trees. There were three winding roadways to the property: one, to the front of the present historic house; two, another loop around the front of the large area for the house; but three, there was a circumferential winding drive around the entire estate, but back far enough to lend privacy, as well as at a proper distance from the front property road of entrance.

It was indeed an expensive area of Georgetown, and across the front property and state road there was a large public park area leading down to the Potomac River. Because of the slope of the land, the Potomac could be seen from almost any position of the nine acres except from the trees themselves. The historic river was less than a mile away. All of it was an authentic, historical spot from the days of George Washington, America's first president. This entire area, up the Potomac, would lead to Mount Vernon, the home of Washington, less than an hour away. Gabriel considered it to be compatible to his hope for historic Christianity.

The twelve guests, besides their wives, arrived and the owners had opened the pre-Civil War Mansion House entirely for this day, June 29, 1974. This was Gabriel's forty-eighth birthday. After ascending the six steps to the Colonial Front Porch, Evangeline led them all into the large Drawing Room. After further greetings from both Gabriel and Evangeline, Gabriel requested Dr. Jonathan to give the first, leading prayer for the purpose to which they had come. He proceeded seeking the true God of heaven to meet them in that Room and that God would give Gabriel wisdom for the day, and that God would give discernment to those who were gathered together to know the will of God for this place.

They were all seated appropriately in the surrounding decor of the colonial furnishings so replete in the Mansion House.

Gabriel acknowledged all of his friends and read the entire chapter of Isaiah, chapter 54, verses 11 through 17.

O thou afflicted, tossed with tempest, and not comforted, behold, I will lay thy stones with fair colours, and lay thy foundations with sapphires. And I will make thy windows of agates, and thy gates of carbuncles, and all thy borders of pleasant stones. And all thy children shall be taught of the Lord; and great shall be the peace of thy children. In righteousness shalt thou be established: thou shalt be far from oppression; for thou shalt not fear: and from terror; for it shall not come near thee. Behold, they shall surely gather together, but not by me: whosoever shall gather together against thee shall fall for thy sake. Behold, I have created the smith that bloweth the coals in the fire, and that bringeth forth an instrument for his work; and I have created the waster to destroy. No weapon that is formed against thee shall prosper; and every tongue that shall rise against thee in judgment thou shalt condemn. This is the heritage of the servants of the Lord, and their righteousness is of me, saith the Lord.

Gabriel commenced the words of his heart with deliberate expressions for the sake of special clarity.

"There is not a foregone conclusion in my heart today concerning all that I would like to express to you. Without any further meetings that we might ever have, your presence today, within itself, is overwhelming to my soul. I must take the time to make that so clear to your hearts. You are the closest people Evangeline and I know in the whole earth. I do not need to go to another place or another person to improve it. I have desired that my dear Evangeline call everyone of your names, because we believe this is a very historic day for us, both in that it is my birthday, and if God leads, it could be a far-reaching day in a ministry for the Lord Jesus. (a pause) You may signal your presence by simply raising your hand. Will you call the list of names, Evangeline?"

Dr. and Mrs. Robert J. Jonathan, Jr.
Dr. and Mrs. Beauchamp Paulson
Senator and Mrs. Charles Baker
Rev. and Mrs. Matthew N. Wiley
Mr. and Mrs. Boaz A. Broadman
Mr. and Mrs. Carl Vernon Louisia
Mr. and Mrs. Michael & Michelle Olsen
Mr. and Mrs. Kenneth G. Dean
Mr. and Mrs. John Felix
Miss Juliana Queens
Mr. and Mrs. Joseph Paul Parsons
Miss Soma Jeanne Parsons
Mr. Ariel John Parsons
Dr. & Mrs. Gabriel T. Parsons

"Thank you Evangeline. (pause) We are delighted to welcome twenty-four individuals present, besides myself, for this unpretentious occasion, all of you whose names have been called, including Evangeline, and our three children, Joseph Paul, Soma Jeanne, and Ariel John. (a pause) I simply wanted to definitely record this brief acknowledgment of your presence with us. I should distinctively acknowledge Drs. Jonathan and Paulson, as well as our notable, conservative member of the United States Senate, Senator Charles Baker, as well as his wife. (a pause) Now, without any further words from me at this time, I want to have a prayer and then take you on a tour of this lovely colonial Mansion House, as well as a walking tour around the property area. We can easily see the extension of the property lines by driving our automobiles around the three different driveways. (a pause) I believe Evangeline has an announcement."

"Yes. I wanted to mention that you may stop off, at anytime of the House Tour, at the Dining Room for refreshments, to the hallway on my right, and you may also note the Restrooms on each side of the entrance hallway off from this room to my left. Thank you."

Gabriel prayed: "Dear Father, we would rather die than miss Thy will today. Our hearts are dedicated for the Gospel's Cure in the hearts of mankind in our time, rather than to add to the Sinful Plague already among us in this world. May the Lord Jesus be honored by our gathering in His name today. Amen!"

Twenty-four people disbursed as Gabriel led the way throughout Mansion House. He commented upon the decor, the art pieces, the other furnishings, and the furniture. He also gave a general history of the place and that the original Georgeton family father was a member of George Washington's Continental Army; later family generations served on both sides in the Civil War.

Within one hour, the entire group were in their automobiles with Gabriel leading the motorcade through the three roadways on the property. He would stop at particular spots and speak, informationally, of various scenes, settings, and landmarks. Within forty more minutes they would be back in the Mansion House Drawing Room.

Gabriel was about to speak, when Dr. Jonathan arose to request the opportunity to speak, to which Gabriel gave way.

"Dr. Parsons, everyone of us are acquainted with you through our years. We have been informed of this meeting with as much information as you could have possibly provided. A number of us have talked privately; some others have corresponded concerning this occasion. I do not believe you should be duty-bound to a further gracious presentation of this day. Senator Baker and Dr. Paulson have mentioned to me of their heart, and I would like to request that you simply present to us what you believe the Lord would have you do. Everyone here, I am sure, will be praying for it from this time on, and a number of us will desire to assist more tangibly. You have shared so many things with us before, including a number of details, and we have come today, I believe, to resolve a decision about this matter. You have not made any request, pointedly, of anyone of us, but we long to hear your conclusion at this time. Your own integrity and care for our understanding should no longer be burden to you to assure us of the decision needed for this historic occasion."

There resounded a hearty "Amen" to hear Gabriel's presentation of "The Ministry."

"My dear friends, you are so kind in this matter. I shall go straight from my heart to what I believe the Lord might have for us to do, either directly or indirectly, but in a Christian way, all of us. Prayer is my greatest need and blessing.

"In view of this response, my brother, I am simply going to express my heart and mind.

"I believe that the Lord would be pleased, at this time in history and the growing Christian apostasy, for me to humbly lead in the purchasing of a piece of historic property, such as this, to bring together a learning center for historical studies. It does not have to be a college or seminary, but certainly a conservatory center to evangelize people and strengthen saints, using Biblical studies and historical testimony together. The emphasis upon a conservatory brings in historical relationships with music, art, and oratory. As all of you know, I have been concerned about the loss of historical studies in both the scientific historical method of academic areas, as well as the empirical method of practical studies in the Christian life and history. Historic Christianity is no longer in the precincts of public pulpits in the churches, or in the university and seminary classrooms as they should be. Historic Christianity is becoming extinct in the public arena.

"There are really four histories which have been divided from the one continent of knowledge. Man does not choose to study with a world-view in mind, more particularly thought of in the classical world, and therefore, so much knowledge is now only a specialty within itself. The Christian World-View of History includes: World Civilization, Church History, Remnant Christian History, and revealed Biblical History. In this time of apostasy, our children must learn about history in all of its relationships with historic Christianity. I want you to realize that I am seeking a ministry of evangelism and revivalism which is contrary to our time, involving a return to the truth of history and its relationship with the Word of God.

"This piece of property, which you have visited with me today, is a very historic colonial place in America. All around this property in every direction is almost sacred with God's planting of the United States of America. I never dreamed such a property would be here, possibly for such a ministry as this. Washington, D.C. is my homeplace; I have studied this great property involved here having lived on Capitol Hill as a child.

"I would like to purchase this property, this nine-acre place, and use it with the building of a new learning center on the knoll of the wooded area here. This building would not be an art gallery or a museum. Rather, it would be a learning center for special studies, to raise a testimony through Bible preaching and teaching, implementing the four shorter quarters of the year in deliberate classrooms in the rooms of the new learning center where all decor would give a representational picture of the times and people God honored in the past, such as the Remnant Movements to which I have called attention so often before. Christianity is a historical fact, and it is that Christian reality of the facts that is necessary to Christian doctrine.

"The building itself would use early twelfth and thirteenth-century gothic architecture with eight surrounding towers, quite often appropriate to those times in past history, besides the eight divinity halls within the main structure. Even children might accompany their parent or parents on special days to see, through the art forms, what their father and mother believed about historic Christianity.

"With this summary once again given to you, as I have previously given in writing and classroom lectures, I believe the Lord would be pleased for me to contact my dearest friends to be the witness of my honesty and records by commencing such an institution. My dear Evangeline and I will be continuing in our present residence, which as you know, adjoins this famous property. We have already placed pledge-money on the contract for the property for its purchase. I have sought advice from several of you in the background of this occasion. I will soon finalize the purchase of this property.

However, I have waited until this day, on my forty-eighth birthday, to air this decision, and already some of you have given me your voluntary response that you would serve on my Board of Trustees for this venture. I intend to forward tangible evidences to you of our resolve to proceed. I will be taking the liberty of placing in writing my request for you to serve in some way with us in the very near future as you have privately informed me before. My dear Evangeline and I have formed a mailing list of at least five thousand names and addresses which have come to us across all of our first travels and lecture years since 1955."

Senator Charles Baker arises for a point of order:

"Dr. Parsons, I would like to make a motion, on this historic occasion, that you proceed to forward your ministry upon this property as you have previously announced to us in detail and rehearse again today. I readily realize that this motion is only a preliminary expression, but I do not desire to see this day pass without some kind of expression and encouragement to you for this hope. When I first heard of you, it was from our mutual friend, Dr. Jonathan, but since then, having heard a number of your lectures and sermons, here in the Washington, D.C. area, I understand your desire and pray for its fulfillment."

Immediately, Dr. Jonathan seconded the resolve, with Dr. Paulson making it the third. The entire group of twenty-four persons arose from their seats and said, "Amen!" Even Evangeline and their three children arose, contributing their "Amen" to it all.

Gabriel concluded the meeting with the fact that it was the first time in his life that he had witnessed a parliamentary action of people before the fact of a parliamentary order of the organization itself. However, he, with great Christian delight, responded to the three brethren who made the resolution. Although it was only a resolve for resolution, awaiting the actual ratification by the Board of Trustees, yet the resolve was forwarded with complete unanimity.

"You will be hearing from me very soon, responded Dr. Parsons."

Evangeline gave the benediction, called upon to do so by

her husband.

The twenty-four individuals left that afternoon somewhat reluctant, believing the property had already been given to them by the Lord.

Now, Gabriel would leave dedicated to proceed with his charter, constitution and by-laws, through the immediate effectiveness of a Board of Trustees confirmed. A tentative staff of workers had already been contacted to commence the work.

They would be seeking to start with a Fall Quarter of this year of 1974 to begin their temporary classes in the Mansion House. However, Gabriel presented the plans for a new learning center, called Anvil House, which he had received from an architect, and a contract was ready for the forthcoming Board of Trustees to consider a resolution for adoption. Having secured the purchased property, a contract for the building of the new learning center was being readied.

Gabriel was careful to say to Evangeline back in their home that night, in bed,

"Evangeline, the seed is planted so be on the look-out; next we must expect 'the blade, then the ear, after that the full corn in the ear.' The Gospel of Mark, chapter 4, verse 28. To God be the glory!"

Then Evangeline responded: "Gabriel?"

"Yes, Evangeline."

"It appears to Evangeline that we will not fulfill the Abraham Lincoln Hotel luxurious place of ministry, or the Martha Washington proposal, or Green Meadows, or Luray, or Cabin Peak. God has ordained Washington, D. C., the sixth night, Christmas night after the day of our marriage, for the place of our future ministry. (a considerable pause) Good-night, my darling!"

"Yes, good-night, Evangeline. And welcome to our Nation's Capital, my homeplace."

Chapter Twenty-two

The Foe

(July 15, 1974)

The friends of Jesus Christ on earth are in contrast to His foes. If one man has the genuine right, liberty, and freedom to take a position on a subject, then every person of the teeming millions of people on earth have the very same right. Every person has the right unless his right interferes with the right of another person. This is what is meant as the privilege of a pluralistic society in a fallen world.

There is no conviction of earth stronger than a religious conviction; it deals with the highest Person in the universe, God, or what is believed to be a god. This conviction also speaks of the most eternal subject of all of man's responses and expressions.

Gabriel Parsons is only one unpretentious man, saved by grace through faith, in Primitive, historic Christianity. Because of so many religions back in history, to say nothing of the many faces and changes in the meaning of Christianity in the twentieth century to many different people, it becomes quite necessary for Gabriel to advance his studies and prayers as far as Reformation Christianity. Every Christian is responsible to

271

"Search the scriptures," The Gospel of John, chapter 5, verse 39. Yea, according to the Bible, "the price of wisdom is above rubies," which man must not only search but dig for as well. The Book of Job, chapter 28, verse 18; and, Proverbs, chapter 8, verse 11. There is length and depth to truth. Every man is called upon by God to search and dig for the truth.

If the historical accuracy of Christianity cannot be found in the Word of God concerning Primitive Christianity, and then vouchsafed through Remnant Christian Movements, including the orthodox creeds and councils of dogmatic theology, then we have no hope that Reformation Christianity will confirm the true theological faith of Christians through history. The modern proliferation of neo-christianity has veered away from these historical moorings and is now adrift in new waters, foreign to historic Christianity itself.

From every consideration by Gabriel, he cannot believe that the Dark Ages and the building of Roman Catholicism in the aftermath of the Reformation in the Council of Trent which led to "the infallibility of the pope," "mariolatry," "purgatory," and all of the other dark errors of Romanism could be once again invited back into the protestant fellowships. The pope would need to throw down his reputed "keys to the kingdom," and repent of all false beliefs. However, it was clear that the protestants were indeed going to discard their historic beliefs in favor of the neo-christianity and ecumenical unions going on now in the ecumenical movement and would ultimately return to Rome.

Evangelist Willie Wheyman, in his new book, presents himself with an approach that is open and warm to everyone — Roman Catholic, Orthodox, Liberal. Everyone, that is, but fundamentalists. His unswerving commitment to ecumenical inclusivism is a central theme. So his theological blood brothers, the fundamentalists, won't follow him. It is disingenuous to say that they are alienated from Wheyman because Fundamentalism, as a movement in the earth, is separated from Wheyman. For the fundamentalists it is not methodology but doctrine that must be believed. The fundamentalists believe it is disobedient to the Lord Jesus to cooperate with apostates in a spiritual, Biblical ministry. Willie Wheyman studiously disregards many Bible doctrines that divide the unbelievers from the believers. Wheyman majors, only, on what unites; his emphasis is on the unity of modern Christianity and other religions instead of on the purity of the Bible and historic Christianity.

A most recent example of this is also found in the "Pledge Keepers," a male organization originated by ecumenical and charismatic Christians of the athletic and sports world, both collegiate and professional. These unleashed ecumenical forces are leading contemporary Christianity into the belief of universalism-evangelism. Another astounding acknowledgment Gabriel must make concerns the fact that it does not seem important at all to the general denominations and pastors that the larger ecumenical, charismatic, and Roman Catholic movements are stealing their congregations away from the churches and reducing the pastors to be a puppet for the personalities of the mass movements.

Because of the emphasis upon a total methodology towards World-Wide Evangelism, the New Testament definition of historic Christianity has changed. This is true, however, not only of the old established Christian institutions, but also of political governments, secular, social, democratic, as well as scientific, medical, and psychological entities in sociology. "Neo" (new) is in the vogue for all things, even for the New-Age Movement with the return of a new-occult, as well as a one, new-world, global government.

The fever persists: everything must change; all old presuppositions of history must fall down into the new entities and essences of the post-modernity days, and a new (neo) presupposition must be inserted. The time is urged to keep science, religion, technology, art, astronomy, and mathematics, but insert a new (neo) presupposition into each specialty, as a science, with a dedication to change and the "new."

Never has there been so much world-wide activity with a contemporary form of Christianity. Generally speaking, in this six-billion world population, almost everybody is involved in some relationship with contemporary Christianity. Rooted in the West, predominantly from England and America, so suddenly, some crusade, movement, or personality has been involved, attending, viewing, associating, or interested in "making a commitment to Christ," or something similar to such an identity. Some small or larger missionary group has some time or money investment in a mission area, or a six-week trip for the purpose to witness or just get involved in the name of some kind of Christianity. Restaurants have received some Christian tract for a waiter, waitress, or cashier, given by some kind of movement or cult or sect of contemporary Christianity. Airports and airlines have had the Christian witness, of a kind, or word from some emphasis on modern Christianity.

In times past Christian belief had to respond to the extreme right or the extreme left in Biblical positions. Belief, then, was simply true or false. However, now the situation has actually the "extreme middle" that is devouring the majority of those professing Christianity. The other two extremes were considered unloving or inappropriate for the times. Truth and error have both been drawn into the dangerous middle—a place to be called by the Biblicists "apostate Christendom," the most deceptive of all. The synthesis of existentialism has done its sorry work; syncretism abounds.

When great personalities of neo-christianity fail, sin, embezzle funds, get involved in adultery or other kinds of fornication, the failures, now, do not usually destroy their 'ministry." Like the proverbial "Wanda," the prostitute, who was invited back to the city again and again, so the false preacher or pastor who does such things is requested to come back to his same ministry, church, or one nearby, again and again.

Never has the holiness of God been so hurt, or the purity of the Christian so rare. Christian character has all but gone from the life of its people—that character being a grace-saved soul living a life that is dominated by Biblical principles. Christian integrity in a man of God is so absent in our time, and the word of a Christian has fallen to the ground. These are still other effects that neo-christianity is having in the earth.

Gabriel, however, sees a different kind of foe than these

most obvious ones. Not even a person, by name, is the greater foe. Sin, the Satanic, false doctrine, compromise, Christian hypocrisy, selfishness, weakness, inconsistency, pride, demonic power, ignorance, lukewarmness, apathy, immorality, all the so-called Christian manners and methods of a person born in sin have reached dark fullness, but the individual continues to claim Christianity. These are the greater profanities, and sacrileges. Man's will may choose any or all of these things in our day, and yet such a false Christian may administer to thousands of people in the name of religion.

Only true doctrine, free grace, through faith makes the difference.

True Christianity must begin at the right theological center and carry that throughout the entire life of the Christian from the new birth to death. If any claim of Christianity is off-center from these great doctrines, then the rest is off, too. If a person starts right, he need never change.

The year is 1974. Gabriel is in the midst of prayerfully planning the beginning of a permanent ministry for the Lord. He believes the time has come to begin the building of a learning center for historic Christianity. Back in his mind and heart has been the vision of a purposeful study of history in relationship to historic Christianity. He seeks a ministry that will bring more than just a controversy between two or more people in aggressive and passionate words of human argument. He believes that the current, contemporary apostasy has grown acute, and that this war must be fought with wisdom rather than anger and recklessness. His earlier words of being both "militant and magnificent" still ring in his heart. He has established a mailing list of upward to five thousand names which has resulted across his ministry of almost twenty-five years. The burden of these things started in his heart on July 10, 1949, in his burden with God over his own need of dedication and consecration before the Lord in a crisis time in his own unpretentious history. He is forty-eight years old now and believes that all that has happened to him has been the result of the good providence of God, in mercy, and that he endeavored to be led of God through all of his studies.

Now, after five years of prayer and seeking God, Gabriel will enter into his own personal purpose and ministry for life. He believes it has been absolutely necessary to go through the entire schedule and agenda of his past if he is to even remotely touch others with his ministry of what he believes is for "the last days." Gabriel has come to understand more and more why Noah was six hundred years old when he entered the Ark in the days of the universal flood, and why Moses was eighty years old before he led Israel forth from Egypt. The Christian today needs such deliberate heart and mind preparation for these days. Yes, Gabriel believed every man must be a mighty man of God for these mighty days in the earth.

Gabriel had been continuing his lecture tours which started back in 1952. This had been the resource for his mailing list and growth of friends across the years. He had been circulating his quarterly periodical paper entitled "The Divine Interlude." This particular presentation was always expressing, in as good a format as Gabriel could arrange, the basic presupposition of his thoughts towards the contemporary times which were so unhistorical in their own presentations of Christianity. But most importantly, Gabriel preached and taught and lectured the Word of God and its narratives in history as well as the great doctrinal benefits received from God's people through church history. Gabriel always endeavored to make his articles as objective as possible with the hope that his audience would respect the truth of the subject rather than merely the contemporary personalities involved in the contemporary new definition of Christianity itself or even the great errors of the time. Gabriel had, with great experience, learned that you cannot build on that which is false; you can only build on that which is true.

A final catalyst came for the entrance into his ministry by a very special invitation from Dr. Beauchamp Paulson, who had continued to call upon Gabriel to share special lectures at the Georgeton Theological Seminary. Dr. Paulson knew that the days were short for his historic conservative seminary to continue in a modern society with their past tradition in the national Capital of the United States. Dr. Gabriel Parsons had occupied a place of esteem at the Georgeton Seminary since his first Night Institute lectures over 20 years ago. He also gained his graduate theological studies there and later became one of the leading professors as well.

Dr. Paulson had set a special conference for "The Young Fundamentalists," for July 15 through 17, 1974, at the Seminary. He had set this agenda as he had done before in setting conferences for the benefit of a clearer understanding of contemporary religious movements. This was done to reveal the total spectrum of contemporary religious thought for all students and faculty members to be aware of for the century in which Fundamentalism was born and proliferated into their Biblical message. He desired for the fundamentalists to be included for a more accurate understanding of their Biblical purpose. The mutual love and respect between Dr. Paulson and Gabriel continued in fellowship and strength. The format procedure was to have Dr. Paulson, as he had done previously in other conferences, to interview a younger man giving him certain questions which he had selected to bring out of the younger man responses appropriate for the representation; in this case that of a third or fourth generation of Fundamentalism.

Of course, a number of other professors in the Seminary saw this to be an outstanding format for the future because the contemporary apostasy was mutating on into a deeper error. In reality, there was a more artistic deception and heresy now coming into their own third and fourth generations of other conservative theological belief. There would be other professors interviewing other leading fundamentalists, as well, in this three-day Conference. Dr. Paulson considered this, possibly, to be their last opportunity of witness to the attacks made in this generation against the Word of God and the Christian Faith which could affect the Seminary. Dr. Paulson chose to be the questioner of Gabriel, and Gabriel considered this opportunity to be a special privilege which he did not think he was worthy to receive. Also, the questions delicately move to the center of certain personalities and positions of some against historic Christianity.

The time had come for the first day of the Conference to begin and Dr. Paulson and Gabriel had met for prayer. After going over the interview agenda, they readied themselves for Gabriel's second session which was set for 1:30 PM, on July 15. Dr. Paulson was to introduce the interview as well as speak a few words about Gabriel again in his opening remarks.

"We welcome this large attendance on the day of our 'Conference of the Young Fundamentalists.' We believe this particular Congress should have a lasting effect upon our understanding of historic Fundamentalism. Some of us are getting older, but our hearts are encouraged to meet such a young man who is our guest for today. He is no stranger to his Alma Mater here at Georgeton. His morning session gave a clear history of Fundamentalism and vindicated the fact that 'Fundamentalism Is Not a Cult,' the title of his 10:00 morning lecture.

"I am especially gratified to introduce, once again, our esteemed Dr. Gabriel T. Parsons, a young man I have watched since the day he entered the Seminary here. He came to the Lord Jesus at the age of twenty, and in a few years he gained his graduate theological studies honors. Amazingly, he is a Washingtonian of this very city which is very rare in our time. His lecture this afternoon concerns the subject of 'Contemporary Voices and Fundamentalism.' (a pause) Dr. Parsons."

"Thank you, esteemed dean and friend. It is a distinct privilege for me to be with you again today."

"Dr. Parsons, no fundamentalist would desire to be accused of being a charismatic 'prophet' in our time, and knowing you and your writings, it would be a gross falsehood to accuse you of such. However, as a hopeful fundamentalist who has watched the past, and seen the trends, there are legitimate forecasts which result from history past and the contemporary present. The uniqueness of your emphasis has been from Biblical studies and history; therefore, all of my questions will be centered around these areas in the light of the contemporary voices surrounding Fundamentalism.

"What do you believe represents the most urgent truth that is being swept away by the apostasy of our time; that is, what is the very first thing we need to address in the Biblical definition of historic Christianity?"

"There is a great error in the modern public presentation of the Trinity. There is a great confusion concerning God the Father in relationship to God the Son. For example: it is being said in the post-modern Christian world, in view of so much preaching with a false definition of the Gospel, that the Mohammedans and the Jews and the Liberals and the Christians, all, believe in the very same God. However, the New Testament reveals that it is impossible to preach God as our Father if Jesus, the Son, is not our Savior. It is this divorce between God the Father and God the Son which has caused the cheap grace and easy believism of the time."

"Dr. Parsons, what should be our presentation in this need to get the average person to see this truth and its necessary principle in order to correct this fallacy?"

"Certainly we should go back and call attention to an old enemy which broke forth in the second century of the discovery of America and continues to be the most popular contemporary gospel of our time. And that is Liberalism."

"In what way should we go back to remind our generation of this error?"

"Well, you will ably recall that Liberalism, or the Romanist's Modernism, gravitated to the fallacy of 'The Universal Fatherhood of God and the Universal Brotherhood of Man,' while actually rejecting the deity of the Lord Jesus Christ. In this matter, the liberals exalted the worth of man, but lowered the dignity and deity of Jesus Christ. In other words, for the sake of interpreting the New Testament with a different presupposition, they inverted and perverted a fundamental truth. Instead of man's being depraved and lost, he is good; instead of Jesus Christ, being God, He is simply the best model of man ever known in history. This strikes down the basic tenet of the entire Bible, and especially the clarity of the infallible doctrine in the New Testament."

"Dr. Parsons, how do you apply that principle to the modern neo-christian view in the field of evangelism?"

"Modern neo-evangelism, as espoused by the new evangelicals, has simply come back to full circle in the popular voices of the neo-evangelical personalities who occupy the preaching in the popular crusades. Since the modern methodology of evangelism has exploded around the world, it has gradually come to the time of believing in 'universalism' through another door other than that of old Liberalism. Evangelist William Henry Wheyman has finally put forth, in his own words, things he only implied earlier."

"Give us those earlier implications, Dr. Parsons."

"Well, as you know, he has advocated in his first article on the subject, in the *McPhal* magazine, January, 1972, on the peculiar and personal subject that he did not want to play God any more. The subject itself is quite a subjective springboard into his own position. He explained what he meant in this statement by giving the following examples: first, the Jews are a special people of God, and God can reveal salvation to them in another way than through the Gospel; second, the heathen have the light of nature, and God could possibly use that light for their salvation. He also included that the doctrine of the Roman Catholic Church was agreeable to his own doctrine except for a few minor points. Therefore, he did not want to play God in judging the souls of these different religious groups. Of course, the fundamentalist simply resolves this matter by the Word of God. All are sinners; every man needs the Savior. Even some of the men that were associated with him in those days were surprised to hear this idea."

"Where would you say that Evangelist Wheyman is at this point?"

"His most recent presentation, in an off-moment conversation with America's most avowed liberal, Dr. Ronald Shullman, on a television interview, was that he personally believed he would see some people in heaven saved who never saw a Bible and never heard the name of Jesus but simply loved God and wanted to live right in the earth. This presupposition is the very same as the old Liberals. It is false in two regards: first, it makes the death of the Lord Jesus Christ at Calvary unnecessary; and second, it makes man, in his own humanity, thus denying depravity, able to know God without God's revelation through the Bible, and able to save himself by his living right and loving God in his own human way."

"Dr. Parsons, why do you think this falsehood about the Trinity arises here at this point in history once again?"

"It is obvious that more of religious history, apart from God's true people, has always relied somewhat upon a kind of fatherhood concept as a way to gain mercy in their misery and judgment of their own, personal fear. The old, ancient paganism constantly switched back and forth on these two ideas. Old Sabellianism and Monarchianism believed only in a unity-god without the trinity. Pantheism came out with God in everything, including man; Animism came out with demons in everything, including man. The earliest paganism thought of their gods as fathers, too, in a similar manner. There remains great respect in the Orient for male elders, beside ancestral worship after their death.

Nebuchadnezzar, as 'the head of gold,' sets forth something of that kind of assumption. He presents himself as a fatherly head of his own kingdom. The 'fatherhood' concept comes out not only in the time of Nebuchadnezzar, but also Darius, and in the time of Cyrus. The Egyptians, as 'pharaohs,' or 'great heads of houses,' presented themselves in the same way as fathers. The very symbol in Daniel's dream gave Nebuchadnezzar the position of the 'head' of his people. The pope has gained the title of 'Pontifex Maximus,' being presented as 'Papa,' or 'Pope,' as 'the divine father.' Attalus, the Second, is given the praise of being the first priest to have this claim in a crown as 'Pontifex Maximus.' This actual crown was taken from Attalus at Pergamus by the armies of Rome and given to the Caesars as they proliferated in history. History has it that Pope Hormisdas, in his papal reign from 514 to 523, AD, wore this very crown. This would indicate that the popes of Rome are actually identified with paganism in their claim of headship.

"The male and female find the oldest idea in the sun and the moon gods. They are indirectly the father-mother concept, and this is just another kind of the same thing."

"So, what must we preach and teach in these awesome days of such an apostasy in the light of these truths?"

"We must first see the importance of Bible doctrine, and we must turn to it once again, very seriously. It is necessary to say that there must be a return to a serious and intelligent study of the pure Word of God, especially given by teachers, pastors, and fathers of Christian families. We have lost the Saviorship of the Lord Jesus by magnifying the Father above the Son. The Trinity remains true: *one substantia, three personas* — never to be separated at any time in history.

"No religion, according to the very Word of God, may choose to believe in God without belief in His Son. A denial of the Lord Jesus Christ as Savior is also a denial of God the Father, because Jesus' death on the Cross was to reconcile the sinner back to the Father. As long as there is no acceptance of the Savior, Jesus, there can be no peace with God. Jesus revealed that the singular 'sin of the world' was 'because they believe not on me,' the Gospel of John, chapter sixteen, verse nine. In verse eight, it is also revealed that the Holy Spirit, the third Person of the Trinity, is that Person of Deity Who 'reproves' or 'convicts' the world of that 'sin,' thus revealing the need of the entire Trinity for anyone to be saved by grace through faith. The Trinitarian Monotheism of the Bible is indivisible."

"Dr. Parsons, I know that the time for these unusual sessions of this day in this 'Conference of Young Fundamentalists' must be limited for the sake of time and audience as well as the remaining agenda. However, I would like to superimpose a final question in several parts. (a pause) In the matter of evangelism, what do you believe is an area of neglect, which has not been addressed, that has contributed to the underlying weakness of this present time?"

"I believe this could be one of the most important questions before us in this interview. (a pause) There are two great areas of learning from the total epistemology of the world-view of life as it is related to mankind. The smaller part of the population of the world has had access to the scientific, historical method of academic learning; the larger part of the population has had access to knowledge only through the empirical method of study and learning. Everything we know is through books, or teachers who taught books, or people who wrote and taught books. Since most of the world is illiterate to books, it falls upon those who read and teach books to become more responsible to teaching, in every way, for the learning process from the books. The empirical method of the learning process is a learning from observation of that which has been passed on from generation to generation. This could be either in a very practical, or common sense way. This often assists the illiterate to learn to read better as well as increases their understanding of what they read. We must remain steadfast: we know nothing but by books.
"God, evidently, gave man this inner hunger for books for all legitimate knowledge. Adam wrote a book or was a part of the book, the Bible; Genesis, chapter five, verse one. Of course, the greater purpose for the ingrained love and knowledge of books, directly or indirectly, was that man would already be adjusted to the reading and knowledge of books so that God

might give His own infallible, inerrant, and inspired Word, the Bible, The Book."

"Dr. Parsons, that is an excellent point in all the knowledge of things. Explain more about God's Book or books. We need to nail this down in our knowledge of total life, or as you refer to it, the world-view of all things."

"Yes, God has His infallible Book here on earth, complete, sufficient for all that we need to know about Creation and Redemption. But, also, in heaven there are books. Daniel, chapter ten, verse twenty-one, reveals 'the scripture of truth,' which we believe is in heaven, from which all truth on earth comes. Now, we do not have to think of a book, every time, as a calf-cover or hard-back, hand-size, with pages. There are books in antiquity written on stone, metal, clay vessels, architecture, as well as vellum parchment and regular paper. David, the Sweet Singer of Israel, Psalm 139, verse 16, reveals that the identity of every person born of woman, all the 'members' of that identity of soul and body 'were written' in God's 'book.' Of course, all the deeds done in that human body, after birth, are also written in 'books,' Revelation, chapter 20, verses 11 through 15."

"Yes, now that this has been understood by our audience, Dr. Parsons, continue with my original question of what is the area of the greatest neglect in modern evangelism?"

"There is clear evidence that modern evangelism has dealt, almost exclusively, with reducing the preaching and teaching of the Gospel of the Word of God to its easiest explanation and proclamation. This is underlined by the proliferation of translations of the Bible in our time in order 'to relate' the Gospel to the language of the slob-culture of our time. Some of these are not only translated without the faithful sanctified scholarship of literal translation from Biblical languages, but also by insulting the Christian mind and heart with some kind of loose jargon in so-called 'thought translation.'

"A companion area of deficiency in modern evangelism is that the average intellectual mind in the professorial realm of the academic world concludes that one has to be ignorant to be a Christian. They may not bugle out this criticism against Christianity as such, every time, but there are things happening in some so-called Christian writings which are quite ludicrous and our foes will always catch it. Now, I want to be careful as I bring this answer to a close; I am not advocating 'academic scholarship,' per se, as the deficit of modern evangelism. I am stating that there has been a decline of a reasonable, sanctified intelligence to either the academic or empirical methods of the learning processes of many things in Christianity. This is a particular and prominent danger and problem in evangelism and its popular use of 'Rock Music' and the drug mentality in communicating the Gospel."

"Dr. Parsons, right there: what is the answer to this deficit?"

"I believe that since we have witnessed a great and alarming bending down of the noble Gospel to the street and unthinking gutter, we must urge evangelism to lift the street, the sinner, and all else to the high nobility of the Gospel of the Lord Jesus Christ.

"The statistics, for whatever value they may have, speak of the fact that the denominational attendance to local churches, in the United States, concerns only twenty-four percent of the membership. However, we are told that fifty-six percent of the attendance of the mass meeting crusades, whether evangelism or healing, comes from the very same people who are not attending their own church. It is time to consider the possibility of the fact that many church members are simply being spread around to mass meetings, or to a different denomination or church, and therefore it should not be understood that there is a large group of sinners outside the churches, being actually saved by grace through faith. We have not begun to penetrate the 'field' of the world that is clearly mentioned in the New Testament. Matthew, chapter 13. I believe that this 'field' is what is being neglected in evangelism. Modern evangelism is dedicated to the church-going people; the great majority, the 'field,' has not actually heard historic Christianity."

"Are you implying, Dr. Parsons, that we are not reaching the unreached, but are rather only spreading the 'neo-gospel' to the modern Christian world, itself?"

"Well, certainly we have touched some, but the greater majority are untouched. I believe one of the great reasons why we have not seen a conversion of souls come to our own country and to other countries is because the 'neo-evangelism' does not radically change the heart and lives of those who profess it. We have forsaken the sound intellect and reasonableness of the Gospel, and a great host of people who think about life in at least one category or more remain unevangelized."

"What categories would you name, Dr. Parsons."

"Those who make a living or serve in the thinking, intellectual areas of life. They are: scientists, mathematicians, philosophers, artists, professors and teachers dominated by the false theory of evolution in the university system, and those who have come from the various disciplines of learning, as students going into businesses who mark the intellectual needs for a profession. Historic Christianity, as marked later in its history, found men of great learning involved. Now, the intellectual communities do not see Christianity as a viable, plausible, or credible Faith. Therefore, they do not know Biblical terminology, doctrine, theology, and the valid defenses of the apologetic and preaching pulpits of the past years. Now, once again, I am not seeking mere academic scholarship; I am simply speaking of the loss of a valid, intelligent medium through which the Bible and true history, in days gone by, made strong historic Christianity. The Gospel reached Caesar's palace and staff.

"Unless there is a return to the definitive expressions of

the Word of God that produce the truth of God's Word in the strength of the Bible, we will not be able to return to historic Christianity. That is the testimony of Reformation Christianity: the power of a proclaimed truth that draws lost man out of spiritual ignorance and lifts him to the nobility of the truth of the Gospel as it is in Christ Jesus."

"Amen! (a pause) Thank you, our esteemed young fundamentalist, Dr. Parsons. Thank you for your wisdom that has given an 'understanding of the times,' so Bible-believers might know what the Church ought to do, not only in our age of the Apostasy, but in our evangelism awaiting the coming of the Lord Jesus Christ back to the earth. (another pause)

"This closes this session of the afternoon. In fifteen-minutes, there will be a buffet in the adjoining room where you may speak to Dr. Parsons or even extend a question. Let us stand for prayer."

Thus, the session of Gabriel comes to an end in the "Conference of The Young Fundamentalists." "The Foe" includes false voices, persons, and the teachings which oppose historic Christianity. They must identified; it must be done to honor the Lord Jesus Christ and His Word.

Chapter Twenty-three

A Brother

(March 26, 1973)

The difference between a brother and the entire Body of Christ, in Primitive Christianity, is simply that the Body of Christ is more so. However, in a time of the apostasy of the institutional church, knowing a true brother in Christ is of an urgent need and a rare experience.

Wherever Primitive Christianity is not believed and lived, a brother becomes even more unique. Therefore, historic Christianity affects everyone who possesses or professes Christianity at all. The Lord Jesus revealed something special that we would not have known had He not stated it: "By this shall all men know that ye are my disciples, if ye have love one to another." The Gospel of John, chapter 13, verse 35. This was given lovingly by Jesus as a commandment. To this very day, the world marvels when Christians love each other, not in the romantic way, or evil way, but in a distinctive way in the bond of brotherhood or sisterhood, respectively. In an age of apostasy we need to know more about a biblical "brother."

Rev. Matthew N. Wiley became such a friend to Gabriel in 1969. They had shared some graduate studies together, previously, at the Bible Christian University. Although Rev. Wiley was sixteen years younger than Gabriel, yet it did not matter at all. In another way, Dr. Jonathan was sixteen years older than Gabriel. Rev. Wiley respected Gabriel far above what he thought he deserved, yet undoubtedly, their friendship was rooted in something far greater than all of this. Gabriel believed they were brought together by the sovereignty of God, alone, and that their relationship was to be a testimony throughout their respective influences and separate acquaintances in both the mutual friends of Fundamentalism, as well as in areas unknown each to the other.

Brother Wiley was simply a unique and different individual member of the Body of Christ in Gabriel's acquaintances. Gabriel saw in him an extremely honest man, a characteristic which was sharply contrasted by the age in which they lived.

Gabriel had already observed that far too many professing Christians had a religious manner that most people thought of as spirituality, which in reality, amounted to a facade somewhat different than they really were, naturally. Gabriel saw this refreshing Christian quality in Brother Wiley which transcended the surface of life; understood aright Gabriel thought of him as a natural Christian with a deeper spirituality than an age desired. These were two different individuals, Gabriel and Brother Wiley, born on the scale of two entirely different backgrounds, theological distinctives, who would not have come together apart from the pure grace of God and the Holy Spirit working through Primitive Christianity.

Their unique friendship really started in the crucible of Gabriel's suffering in the time of his making a complete, radical change in his ministry from his own former background to an exodus from the Antioch Theological Seminary of 1969. Gabriel's decision was to enter into an independent, fundamental ministry of establishing a conservatory ministry of Biblical Studies. Gabriel would lose and leave a thousand family acquaintances of the past, and the friendships of several thousand students he had loved and taught in the seminary. Gabriel's exodus was to be a complete break with the religious background and theological system of families on both sides of Gabriel and Evangeline. His was a departure from the charismatic influences; Evangeline's departure would be from liberal influences. They had been puritans in a decaying neo-christianity; they would now be pilgrims outside those systems.

It was in this crucible that Gabriel simply poured out his heart to his younger friend, Rev. Matthew Wiley, who also was pastoring an independent, fundamental church. This experience initiated a laboratory and bond in which their lives would be drawn into relationships they never dreamed possible. Gabriel could only account for this through the great sovereignty and good providence of Almighty God.

Yet, neither one was aware of the extent to which their friendship would be taken. However, almost immediately, Gabriel was aware of a distinction between them. It was quite different, yet it did not impede a strong, growing Christian friendship, unprecedented in their lives. Dispositional differences did not destroy it; theological backgrounds did not controvert it; age differences did not dim it; and differing gifts in each other only adorned it. Gabriel appealed to literature to define it along with the Holy Scriptures. He finalized his thoughts with the two distinctions between prose and poetry; and then as the days enriched it more, he saw the wonder of poetry and song between them. This illustrated that some people are as distinguished from each other as prose is from poetry. Prose is often dedicated to non-fiction with an emphasis upon truth and fact. On the other hand, poetry would preserve the place of the purpose of fiction in life, to be a cushion in things, like humor and simplicity. But both shared the song of life, the love of home, wife, and child.

Gabriel constantly reminded himself that this would have never happened without God in it and grace around it. They did not, at first, know the potential of what this friendship would yield. If there was indeed a direct catalyst of Christian concepts, it was founded upon their affinities with the fundamentals without the "ist" and the "ism" of a human movement. There was a distinctive definition of scriptural separation which each interpreted straight out of his own soul rather than the soul of the other. From each, individual, distinct color of the definition of scriptural separation, there arose a complement to the larger meaning and purpose of it all. That definition of separation was linked to Gabriel's favorite presentation: "first, a separation unto the Lordship and glory of Jesus Christ; and second, because of that, a separation from apostasy and apostates." They did not, at first, know the potential of this friendship.

Brother Wiley, and his ministry, had been blest early in his life; God had led him to a large metropolitan area and church with its Christian Day School. His integrity and love for the Holy Scriptures did forbid his being just a personable personality, although he had a deep love for people, compassionately understanding their sins and their problems. His heart simply drew a straight line in his life and ministry, and he walked it before others. He had Biblical, legitimate enemies as Gabriel did; and they respected him. But Gabriel's and Rev. Wiley's enemies were in different arenas. Gabriel had strong affinities for these matters and sought the Lord, also, to imbibe them into his life.

Gabriel believed God brought them together to set forth an example in the Body of Christ for each other, as a Jonathan-David friendship for two different places in life: one, in the Court of Saul; the other, in the open field of life.

From these paradoxical affinities two large hearts were opened into a common bond in the Lord Jesus that simply amazed Gabriel. Every day, month, and year opened up new avenues of expression. All the way through their friendship, Gabriel believed he was in greater debt to Brother Wiley's acquaintance; but in all personal things, Brother Wiley was always paying the personal bills and awarding all the gratitudes to Gabriel. Gabriel realized, after some length of time, that he would have to get Rev. Wiley clear out of his home state and house in order to finally have a rare opportunity to pay a gratitude debt. But even then it was hard to accomplish. There were also a few times when it seemed Gabriel would be able to catch some incidental restaurant check from the waiter, only to lose it again to Brother Wiley before reaching the cashier. But this was typical of larger benefits as well—a larger spirit indeed.

However, this generosity and hospitality were not a cheap joke; they symbolized larger hearts. They were underlined by the fact that Pastor Wiley was a very thrifty man and very unusual in business affairs. Gabriel had never known, so personally, a man of astute business practices who was so generous in kindness and thoughtfulness. This revealed the secret of how he could go to a pulpit and preach the honorable truth about any subject the Lord led him, and also give personal, plain, but extremely loving advice from the pastor's study and private call when addressing the troubles and problems of others. Gabriel and Evangeline thought of visits to Matthew and Bettina Wiley as a special event in their lives, sharing everything from shopping to antiques, from the finest of dining rooms to the most casual hamburger joint, from a private trip to a public auditing of a neo-christian convention. Their friendship was more like the developing of a picture in the darkroom than the display of the picture in a place of prominence.

The meeting on the overseas study tour to Greece, Asia Minor, Cyprus, and the Holy Lands ended in the Garden of Gethsemane and a sudden, but quiet, evidence that a lifetime friendship would come. It was what Gabriel and Brother Wiley did not do on purpose to each other that gave purpose to a life-long friendship. There was never show; there was only openness There was never a seeking to win a controversy; there was, instead, a hunger to understand each other, and yet both of them were strong in their belief, contributing a different presentation of spirit in each experience. It was believed, but never explained, that the Lord Jesus was in this unusual experiment. Gabriel often said in other places, "Why are the brothers against the brothers? Brother Wiley is my brother."

This experience with Rev. Wiley revealed an answer to the question in many blessings learned and cherished. In later years, when Gabriel would enter into a deep personal suffering, which was not theological as was the first suffering of 1969, Rev. Wiley and his dear wife, Bettina, were always there in help and prayer.

This second suffering concerned the illness of Evangeline in later years. Brother Wiley and his wife, Bettina, were brought together to the heart of Gabriel. There were times they could just sit, not speak, and realize Christian love. A tangible gift was never necessary, but when expressed it was a unique gift. In all humor, on one occasion, an excellent discussion arose about "pheasant under glass." At the next meal of Pastor Wiley in Gabriel's home, Evangeline brought to the oriental dining table an impressive server which we thought pretentious for the occasion. But when Evangeline took away the cover it revealed only a bird-chicken or something or other. We found out that both sobriety and humor were holy.

On one visiting occasion, planned in a hotel-meeting, a discussion arose in the heart of Brother Wiley about desiring his ministry to grow and flourish in the Lord along with his own spiritual life, upon which Gabriel said with care: "one of the teachings on sanctification in the Holy Scriptures is: 'thou shalt not be perfect.'"

Both Gabriel and Pastor Wiley were deeply refreshed by this true observation. On still another occasion, later in their friendship, Rev. Wiley dealt with his son about a needed matter, which would not have been the normal way in most homes. That incident fell out for the future blessings and dealings of God upon that young man, changing his entire attitude about some very important things for his own life.

But the time came during the year prior to the meeting of the twenty-four persons, including the Wileys, at the Mansion House in Georgetown, June 29, 1974, that Gabriel invited Brother Wiley and his wife to make a visit to their beautiful home in Georgetown. The date was set for Thursday, March 26, 1973, at the end of the first quarter of the Night Institute at the Georgeton Seminary. The Wileys were encouraged to arrive in the early afternoon so that Brother Wiley and Gabriel could meet in "The Room" for a discussion of a precious matter, while Evangeline and Bettina would go to the shops at Georgetown Park as well as a special antique place called Kelsey's

Kupboard. Later, all four of them would meet for supper at the Japan Inn promptly at 8:00 PM.

The Wileys arrived at about 2:00 PM, and after a pleasant greeting with the entire Parsons family, the children went to other responsibilities, the ladies to the shops, and Gabriel and Brother Wiley went to "The Room." Brother Wiley took some time to view The Land of Evangeline and a few additional pieces Evangeline had added. Among the gifts of Pastor Wiley was the fact that he was an unusual interior decorator. He commenced this artistic gift on the ground floor of experience, during his days as a teenager, in the efforts of wallpapering and painting on the practical ladder of success. From that start and study, along with many other contributions of art, he became an unusual artist as an interior decorator. This was only a hobby for him after entering the pastorate, but nevertheless, that hobby had become an in-depth study with attendance to art shows, auctions, and personal involvement in the ministries of the university-college-art gallery decor. "The Room" in which both sat on this occasion bore evidence of gifts Rev. Wiley and his wife had given to the Parsons. Bettina was a painter in her own right, and Gabriel thought she was most unusual in water-color.

After a pause from admiring "The Room," both sat down with a quiet delight in seeing each other again.

"Brother Wiley, I am glad to see you for a special occasion this time, rather than just a refreshing visit of our usual times."

"Well, as usual, I am the recipient of the delight of being here, my brother."

"Yes, I know well your heart along that line of thought. (a pause) It has been a Christian joy for us always to be together."

"Yes," responded Brother Wiley.

"I am sure, Brother Wiley, that back in our many conversations you have gleaned something of my thoughts or at least avenues of thought related to what I wanted to discuss with you today. My ministry has now become a pilgrim-ministry in the earth. My exodus from the past systems has marked a fresh path for my heart. My studies and past ministry have brought me to a desire to set forth an educational ministry with a little different presupposition. It is somewhere in a conservatory direction in order to set forth what I believe pertinent to our time as well as Biblical in its purpose."

"Yes, I am aware of these things and appreciate your heart and mind in these things, Dr. Parsons."

"It is the firm conviction of my heart that the apostasy attacks two vital paths of truth in our time. There are only two divisions of understanding we have from God. One is Natural Theology, through which God speaks to man in a providential way through nature and all of its blessings and resources, providing prevenient grace enablement to understand it. Also, there is Revealed Theology, through which God speaks to man in an infallible way revealing redemption and the purpose of Christ's coming into the world to die on the Cross, providing specific, saving grace so that we might understand it through the Holy Scriptures.

"In the former, God gets everybody's attention through the natural resources and circumstances of human need. However, in the latter, God must call workers to evangelize, preach and teach the Gospel of salvation for the lost.

"It is through the history of mankind and the history of the Bible that all of the past is preserved. The Old Testament history and the New Testament history center around the teachings of the First and Second Advents of the comings of Christ; and, secular and church history reveals all history within a singular world-view."

"Yes, Brother Parsons, we have discussed a number of these things before, among other subjects related to them."

"Yes, my brother. It boils down to four histories in all: the History of World Civilization, Church History, Remnant History, and Bible History. We have also discussed the conditions of the world in these areas, distinguishing the secular, the political, the social, the religious, and the Christian. As fundamentalists, we are also aware of remnants of Christians back through history who suffered and yet took a bold stand for the Lord Jesus. As you know, we call this section Remnant Christianity."

"Yes, including the martyrs. I believe I have heard you

also speak of the distinctives of the church fathers versus the papists, the scholastics, the reformers, the theologians, the churchmen, and the divines of church history."

"Yes, my brother, as well as the seven revivals since the Reformation until the twentieth century in which we are beginning to see false revivals."

"Yes, Dr. Parsons. I have often reflected upon those things and as you have agreed before, a similar agenda could be outlined in the history of art, music, architecture, and other similar areas."

"Yes, my brother, and that brings me to the heart of this discussion. If your heart would be clear, and you may take time to pray about it, I would like for you to consider a precious project with me. I have come to believe that I see your gifts in a perspective that seems so appropriate to my hope, and I would like for you to consider assisting me in this matter. I have only seen this before at a distance, never really knowing if God was leading in it all.

"I have already designed a building according to scale in which we might use various art forms, such as gothic architecture, the pointed arch, stained glass windows, stone, and stucco, which all came together in the same century, and build a facility according to the representative times of the late eleventh and twelfth centuries; and yet, have rooms within the exterior walls that would be furnished with paintings, murals, molding, statuary, tapestries, etc., representative of the actual time of the Remnant Christians of the past."

"Such as the reformers, the puritans, and the pilgrims?"

"Exactly! The Moravians, the Hussites, the Huguenots, the Swiss Brethren, the Colonial Puritans, Pilgrims, the English, and others. From the ceiling to the floor and on all the walls would be a representative presentation of their times. This would not be a prestigious art gallery or a museum, but rather a learning center for adults, for families, for people of all walks of life, in an apostate time, to view the story and facts of these respective histories."

"Yes, Dr. Parsons, we are all seeing in many areas of life, the reinterpretation of history, some outright lies perpetrated in changing history, whether it be the change in the lives and character of the Puritan-Pilgrim Ethic or Shakespeare's integrity or even that it was a mistake of Columbus to start his voyage for a new world."

"Our past conversations have been heavily freighted with our mutual concern about these fragile attacks upon the integrity of historical fact."

"So, Brother Parsons, what is really on your mind with me."

"Well, Brother Wiley, I simply believe you are the person who could bring all of these ingredients together for the interior decor, arrangement, and purchases and guide my hopeful vision to a conclusion. You know more about the places where these things would be, the warehouses, the auctions, the businesses, and the contacts otherwise."

"What does this mean about the sources?" Dr. Parsons.

"Well, you have spoken about auctions you have attended where stained glass is available. On several occasions I have gone with you to different places where these items would be available. In our modern time we would have to assume a more modest investment towards present available decor. With the prices of the time, I am sure it would be hard to gain much in the area of genuine antiques at shop prices. Your business ability, your choices, your honorable search for prices could be most helpful, God willing and going before us. I am praying for a window of available resources exactly as we need them. My heart speaks of what I know of you and your God-given gifts. Had I not met you and your heart and character, I do not know if I would have really pursued this as I believe I should. Of course, I know of other individuals who could help us in other things because of this same necessity. This is a simple vision of some things in my heart for many years.

"In the narrative of all of this, I find my heart more bold to you than I have otherwise been. However, I simply lay it before you; nothing is lost in the depth of our relationship if nothing is forthcoming, my beloved brother."

"Dr. Parsons, I will enter into my contacts for these things soon; you may be assured of that. The vision of your heart is a valid one. This will be a new dimension for us, and I only want to serve you and do exactly what you tell me to do. By the way, what do you intend to call this building?"

"You are the first person to whom I will share the name for this facility. It is to be called 'Anvil House.' I think I have mentioned something of this before. God has an anvil upon which He uses His hammer, while extending his control of the heat for His people. Nothing of spiritual worth has come from anyone who does not yield to an anvil house experience with God which is centered in the theology of the Cross of Jesus and His sufferings."

"Well, Dr. Parsons, it seems to me that it will be the most beautiful Blacksmith's Shop I have ever known. I will be in touch with you, soon. There are several auctions going on at this time. We will see what the Lord will bring into this experience with Him."

The discussion ended with prayer; the evening spoke no more of it; the supper at the Japan Inn was excellent. The Wileys returned home on Friday, and Gabriel heard from Brother Wiley, Saturday afternoon, late, wanting to know how much money he thought he should bid for stained glass windows at the auction that evening. Gabriel set the modest figure of $600 for each. Pastor Wiley, although usually a more bold businessman, with his respect for Gabriel caused him to restrain his opinion about the small amount he gave him for the stained glass. Pastor Wiley quietly gulped down air, Gabriel believed, and only weeks later shared that he thought it would take far more money. But Pastor Wiley purchased it within the financial amount Gabriel had hoped. That became both a pattern and a providence of the way the project would proceed to the very end.

Thus, under the direction of Pastor Wiley, commenced the tedious process of gathering and transporting furnishings by truck to Gabriel for warehouse storage against the day of the building of Anvil House.

Gabriel, on that night, informed his dear friend, Pastor Wiley, that he would be calling a meeting June 29, 1974, in

Georgetown, to consider the announcement of this vision, and he urged Rev. Wiley to be present if at all possible.

Gabriel does not remember whether Pastor Wiley ever really said, "I will take your project as the interior decorator." All he remembers was that Pastor Wiley began the job and finished it according to the vision of his friend, Gabriel. Gabriel has no other frame of reference of such a friendship, and even in their diversity of taste, viewpoint, or temperament, Gabriel recalls no breach or break in their Christian friendship.

Later that evening, in bed, Gabriel spoke to Evangeline concerning the subject of "Friendships." He reminded her of the Christmas of 1970 when their family spent a part of the evening remembering friends. He said he had thought much on the words of the prophet Micah, chapter 7, and how he spoke of friends as a cluster of grapes. However, Micah lived in bad times, and he declares that when he looked for friends as a cluster of grapes, he could not even find a friend as looking for only one grape on the vine. He then revealed that a friend, the best of them, was like a "brier," and the prophet declared "Trust ye not in a friend," chapter 7, verse 5. But Gabriel said he had found a "whole cluster of friends," and not merely one grape or a brier.

"Evangeline, you are my first and best friend, the greatest human gift God ever gave me. Joseph Paul is the best, youngest Christian brother I ever had; Soma Jeanne is the most beautiful servant I have known; Ariel John is my most precious soul-winner; and Brother Jonathan, the finest 'encourager' I have had. Brother Thomas Lee, a few years older than me, is a friend that appreciates and respects me beyond measure. We have a great, deep bond together in Christ. But Brother Wiley is my closest and most versatile brother of all my seasons and sufferings." (a long-enough pause) "Did you hear me talking, my beloved wife?"

"Yes, I did, Gabriel, and especially the first person you mentioned. The other six just underlined it all. (pause) I love you, too, Gabriel. Good night."

"A good night to you, too, Evangeline, my friend."

Chapter Twenty-four

The Internet

(1976-1977 & 1989 & 1992)

The origin of the Internet is actually much earlier than most people think. The Internet and World Wide Web have become more and more popular in contemporary society, establishing their presence every time a consumer turns around. From television commercials, to web addresses in every ad, commercial, and display, as well as universities, colleges, seminaries, churches, and other ministries, there is no question that people today are constantly bombarded with talk of the Internet.

The Internet actually originated decades ago as a military project. Due to cold war issues and the threat of nuclear attacks, there was a need for a communication system that had no central location or head, but instead had an integrated, revolving, adaptable communications channel that could flow and change at a moment's notice. The solution: the Internet.

Anybody who uses the web for business, pleasure or profit, educational, charitable, or religious purposes may be grateful for the need during the Cold War between the United States and the former Soviet Union. Without it, the Internet might never have existed, or might have a totally different shape than presently exists.

In 1957, in response to the Soviets' launch of Sputnik, the first artificial satellite, the United States created the Advanced Research Projects Agency. The mission for ARPA, a part of the Department of Defense, was to guarantee U. S. technological supremacy over the Soviets on the battlefield.

Between 1957 and 1969 ARPA and other researchers developed the basic theories behind the Internet: how to send and receive computerized information using the telephone system, how properly to address that information, etc. They envisioned a giant network of computers around the world in which information could be physically transmitted through any of several routes, in the event that a route was destroyed during an attack.

In 1969 ARPA officially created the "Internet," connecting and passing information between three host computers at separate locations. At first the Internet grew slowly, with new host computers coming on line one-by-one.

Not much changed for the next ten years. By 1984, there were only one thousand host computers on the Internet, used by a few thousand people. But by the late 1980s, colleges, universities, and some businesses had tapped into the net and planted the seeds of a giant infomart. While the complex commands and addressing schemes needed to navigate the Internet were beyond the average person, comparatively large numbers of people were exchanging e-mail and surfing from web-site to web-site on their computer from the comfortable confines of libraries and offices.

Gabriel was persuaded that the coming of the Internet could either be a terrible tragedy of harm to millions of people or a blessed triumph of evangelism for the whole world. He intended to enter that arena with his ministry.

Gabriel Parsons had come to a time in his life and ministry that he was constrained, by God, he believed, to do everything in his resources to set forth the message of the Holy Scriptures and historical studies. The Liberal Critics of the Bible were indeed using "scientific historical research," as they called it, in interpreting the Bible in the presupposition that it must be demythologized. This, of course, placed the narratives of the Bible as a non-historical fact in time, space, and history. They believed that the Bible is to be interpreted just as any other piece of literature, and especially with regard to historical data, so-called.

The most ancient manuscripts, archaeologically speaking, in regard to history, were indeed written as a saga, a legend, or a myth. This was the ancient way of writing history. As Gabriel had mentioned before, it was not until the days of Herodotus, of the Greek period, that history was then known as dealing with literal, historical facts. Previous to Josephus, the Jews had also used the mythological form in their historical records. This is not true, however, of the history as in the Old Testament; it followed factual history. The Herodotus form of historical recordings of facts is the only form the Bible would use.

Gabriel came to the opinion that some great erroneous influence was involved in this ancient manner of writing history, and that it would be a great mistake to think that the Word of God followed such a mythological method in dealing with historic Creation, continuing historical Providence, the nation of Israel, or the necessity of historical accuracy in the coming of the Lord Jesus into this world other than through God entering actual history. Gabriel believed that the Incarnation and Virgin Birth of the Lord Jesus should be believed because it was indeed an accurate historical event. The same consistency must be maintained concerning the Bodily Resurrection and Bodily Ascension of the Lord Jesus from the earth in time, space, and history.

The ministry of Gabriel Parsons was built upon the presupposition that all history, secular, political, religious, and Christian had to get back to valid, truthful, literal history. This was that which had motivated him in his studies, and these are the conclusions he drew from those studies along with his empirical method involved in the twentieth century. As the liberal critics of the Bible used the extant "scientific historical studies," as used in ancient literature, Gabriel must use the "grammatico historical exposition," involving the literal exegesis of the Text of the Bible in both the Old and New Testaments.

Anvil House was to be the artistic learning center to teach people about these histories, as Biblical history was to be proclaimed from the central sanctuary, Whitefield Sanctuary, of one thousand seats for a community church. Surrounding the Whitefield Sanctuary would be the Gothic Walk of 46 niches with 111 art pieces arranged in chronological order to show the history of World Civilization along with the appropriate chronology of church history. Outside the Gothic Walk, surrounding it on two floors, would be eight Divinity Halls dedicated as an artistic representation of the time of the Remnant Christian Groups in history. There was the French Divinity Room, reflecting through all of the furnishings and art pieces, the Huguenot Movement; there was the Bohemian Divinity Hall, depicting the Moravians, the Hussites, the Waldenses, their time and decor; there was the Colonial Divinity Hall, setting forth the Puritans, the Pilgrims; the English Divinity Hall, presenting the times of the Anglican church and political leaders during the times of the exodus of the Puritans and the Pilgrims from England and Europe. On the second floor there were the representation of the times of the German Reformers in the German Divinity Hall; the Ulster Divinity Hall, presenting the times of Northern Ireland Protestantism, of covenanters, separatists, and non-conformers; the Swiss Divinity Hall, presenting the Zwingli, Swiss Brethren movement; and the Welsh Divinity Hall, presenting the Welsh revivals which came from the influence of George Whitefield, the Torrey-Alexander meetings and several other revivalists.

This entire facility of 30,300 square feet was placed with a balcony and a colonnade immediately surrounding the Whitefield Sanctuary as well as a gallery separating the balcony from the hallways.

There was an exterior Gothic Walkway that gave access to Calvin Pavilion in the north, at the South end of Anvil House, the Wesley Tower, and six other three-story towers with chapels situated on the ground floors of six other Remnant Christian groups.

The entire facility had 866 gothic pointed arches. All of the various historical rooms would be used to seat about 100 students in each room for the study of history, and the preaching and teaching of Biblical History through expository and Biblical theological sermons and messages.

This would be a facility of about 45,000 square feet, altogether, including the seven outside towers, and Calvin Pavilion. All rooms were wired for tape and video coverage of all lectures and presentations. Conferences and congresses would be held in the main Sanctuary and workshops held in the rooms. Credit could be gained for a college education through the classes of the conservatory purpose if desired.

The Board of Trustees was formed, a Board of Visitors was established, deans and faculty were selected, and the first semester was set for September 30, 1974. The classes of that first semester were held in the Mansion House where the twelve couples met on June 29, 1974, just weeks before the classes began. Mansion House would be used, primarily, until the new facility for the learning center was completed.

Gabriel finished his last Night Institute quarter-session, June 22, 1974, and entered the Mansion House classes that fall. Approximately two hundred students were present for that first fall semester, and the format continued similarly to the Night Institute while Anvil House was being built. However, the germ-seed that was sown in the Night Institute at the Georgeton Theological Seminary was to be greatly embellished and would reach academic maturity in the learning center in Anvil House. Most of the furnishings had been gathered from Gabriel's friend, Pastor Wiley, and the in-wall, stained-glass windows were being installed as the building progressed to that point. Over 1,800 art pieces, furnishings, and furniture were gathered within the year.

The contractor had stated that if all of the furnishings were on time, Anvil House would be completed by summer or early fall of 1975. God had opened a window of providences as

Pastor Wiley and Gabriel began to see the furnishings and art pieces and furniture and decor come from England, Europe, and the United States. They came from old historic churches and appropriate buildings that were being destroyed and replaced by new condominiums and parking lots.

Most all of the pieces were upwards to one hundred years old, and several exceeded four hundred years old. Dr. Jonathan, gave the largest painting, approximately twelve feet by fourteen feet, a Benjamin West painting of Joseph introducing his brethren before Pharaoh.

Gabriel wept before Evangelizne several times in thanksgiving to God. He made it clear: "God is giving our history-laboratory historical evidences from actual places."

While Anvil House was proceeding on time, Gabriel knew the matter of securing a firm Internet window would involve a great deal of hard work.

It would not be until 1989 that the number of host computers would top 100,000.

It would not be until 1991 that a European think-tank, CERN, would find a way to make all the information on the Internet available to anyone. This was an information—transfer procedure known as Hypertext Transmission Protocol, or HTTP. That procedure automatically opened the information, whether text, pictures, audio or video, using the correct program.

It would not be until mid-1992 that the National Center for Supercomputing Applications (NCSA) developed a browser that allowed users to see that information in one environment. It also allowed users to access information without knowing the exact location of the information file.

These two developments, which coincided with the number of host computers on the Internet topping one million, signaled the explosive birth of the Web. It was that Web that Gabriel sought through every avenue possible.

Gabriel was fortunate to gain pre-date membership to the earlier organization of Internet in 1976, but did not materialize until the early days of 1989 to become a participating member.

This opportunity was the best of the first privileges since the Internet was in its public infancy. Senator Charles Baker, a member of the Board of Trustees of Gabriel's ministries, assisted greatly in this hope of the Internet membership.

Finally, the electronic lab throughout the facility was put in place to use the Internet channel to set forth a library and lectures to be picked up by peoples around the world. This was a twenty-thousand-volume Anvil House library, with thousands of lectures printed for The InterNet files according to the historical period desired. All of this was for a testimony, an evangelistic learning center providing another side of history for modern historians to include in their studies and account for in the twentieth century. Too many people had formerly thought that a minister was only a pastor in a dark suit and tie or an evangelist in his modern-colored suit of casual attire.

These two kinds of Christian recognitions were not to be limited; the testimony of the Lord Jesus needs to enter greater channels to the "field" that Jesus spoke about. (Matthew, chapter 13.) But Gabriel saw that the study of the four histories was actually a part of "His Story," the story of the Creator, Providence, the Trinity, and the greatness of the sinner's Redeemer who saves men from sin and righteously does it through the Sacrifice of the Lord Jesus Christ at Calvary.

Anvil House, in Georgetown, as the home base, and the InterNet as the larger base would set forth the great fundamental doctrines of the Holy Scripture. These doctrines would be announced once again as being true, and they must be preached as truth. Starting with the subject of "sin," man must look back to the Cross and the historic Bodily Resurrection and Ascension of the Lord Jesus Christ. Also, with history reconfirmed, prophecy would be credible and hopeful to the human heart again.

The God of Creation, Who often sent his prophets, priests, and kings in the Old Testament and Who also sent the apostles and writers of the New Testament, had fully entered into history, time, space, event in the Incarnation and Virgin Birth of the Lord Jesus. He lived 33½ years on earth, in history. He died in history; He arose, bodily, from the dead in His resurrection power and ascended from the earth in true, historic fact. This same Jesus Who had been seen as He went, into heaven, and Who had been handled by human hands, would return in like manner as He was seen going into heaven (The Book of Acts, chapter 1, verse 11.) Jesus now resides in heaven, over the earth, and will return to the earth, in history, for a historical one-thousand-year reign, extending peace through all the earth.

It was Gabriel's prayer and effort that other places in the earth would break out with an anvil house, and that people would once again return to historic Christianity. Of course, this included an emphasis upon Primitive Christianity, Reformation Christianity, and Remnant Christianity with the longing for a revival in the earth as the saints of God occupied and waited for "the Son from heaven" to return. But in the meantime, Gabriel prayed and preached that "young men would see visions" of what they would like to do for the Lord Jesus throughout their own generation. The "visions seen" would be the only revival for the difficult time of the apostasy.

In talking with Evangeline, from time to time, Gabriel emphasized that the word "Internet" must be understood with an emphasis upon the word, itself, "InterNet," in his ministry. God was using the Internet as a "Net" to catch the fish through God's "fishers of men," for the truth of those seeking historic Christianity during the time of the neo-christian apostasy.

For the future they would proceed in the Mansion House with all studies of courses and pray for the Dedication of Anvil House in proper time.

Mansion House, the place on the original property, and on the original "Threlkeld's Addition," was fully used for the first quarter of the classes with over two hundred students who came and registered the latter part of the year of 1974. Dr. Paulson closed Gabriel's Night Institute, officially, June 22, 1974, and graciously cooperated with Gabriel's move to the new property they had purchased, closing the contract July 7, 1974. Work began immediately in the building of Anvil House. The following officers, deans, faculty, and staff were named:

Board of Trustees: Dr. & Mrs. Gabriel T. Parsons, Dr.

Parsons, chairman; Mr. Boaz A. Broadman, vice-chairman; Mr. & Mrs. Carl Vernon Louisia, trustees; Mr. Kenneth G. Dean, Business Manager; Mrs. Kenneth G. Dean, Trustee; Mr. John Felix, trustee; and, Mr. & Mrs. Joseph Paul Parsons, trustees. Ten members.

Board of Visitors: Dr. Robert J. Jonathan, Jr.; Dr. Beauchamp Paulson; Rev. Matthew N. Wiley; Senator Charles Baker; Senator Robert A. Tafton, Jr.; Mrs. Mary Slocum; Miss Nina Holcombs; Dr. David Lawtell; Mr. Everett "Sonny" Alberts; Mr. Bruce A. Spinson; and Mr. Ron R. Ryan. The Board of Visitors, following the old Oxford Educational System, is a group of very responsible and respected individuals who are capable of business responsibilities and knowledge of affairs. Twelve members, including Chairman Parsons.

The Presidents and Deans: Dr. Gabriel T. Parsons, Chairman of the Deans; Dr. Kenly G. Grayham, Dean of the School of English Bible; Dr. J. Lee Davidson, Dean of the School of Education; Dr. Daniel T. Ussher, Dean of the School of Biblical Languages; Dr. Donald D. Dawson, Dean of the School of Special Christian Care; Dr. Evangeline Marguerite Parsons, Dean of the School of Fine Arts. Everyone of these deans came with Gabriel when he resigned from the Antioch Theological Seminary, along with Mr. Boaz A. Broadman. All of the deans, by virtue of their offices, were members of the faculty as well. There were seven deans, including Dr. Parsons.

Other faculty members were: Miss Juliana Queens, English; Miss Nina Holcombs, History; Mrs. Elsa Felix, Geography and Literature; Mr. Joseph Paul Parsons, Church History; Miss Soma Jeanne Parsons, Music, Art, Speech. This gave five more members to the faculty.

The Staff: Mr. Kenneth G. Dean, business manager; Mr. Austin M. Moore, business, maintenance engineer; Mr. Marcus Wendall Wilshire, Jr., electrical engineer; Mr. Joseph Paul Parsons, administrative assistant; Mrs. Alicia Whitstone, personal secretary to the president; Mrs. Dorothy Dawson, nurse; Mr. Murray L. Edwards, bursar; Mr. and Mrs. Robertson M. Wilmore, members of the faculty and host and hostess of Mansion House; and Edward S. Deanson, security engineer.

There were ten staff members.

Mr. & Mrs. Michael Olsen were to assist as host and hostess for special events, as well as Mr. & Mrs. Marcus W. Wilshire, Sr.

The three children of Gabriel and Evangeline were now adults, and all were working in the various ministries of the work of Gabriel, their father. By 1977 their personal status was as follows:

Joseph Paul was twenty-seven years old now and had married a fine lady, Catherine Rachel Keats, from the west, who attended some of the lectures of Gabriel when Joseph Paul accompanied his father to Oklahoma City, Oklahoma. It should also be noted that Dr. Parsons officiated in the wedding, and his wife, Evangeline, guided the schedule of the service. This wedding was lovingly conducted on an extremely beautiful day on Abbot Lake Trail at the Peaks of Otter in the first change of summer to autumn, August 27, 1972. The foliage was still gloriously green, but color changes of the forest was beginning to appear among the prolific evergreens. At the wedding, the Parsons remembered Joseph Paul's words when they were on their vacation in 1970 to the Blue Ridge Mountain Parkway. Joseph Paul married at the age of twenty-three. He had completed his Master's Degree in English Bible; he was ordained by his father.

Soma Jeanne, at the time of the opening of classes, was twenty-one years old and unmarried. She completed her undergraduate degree in musicology. On May 29, 1975, she married a fine young man, Dr. William K. Wilmore, from South Africa.

Ariel John was twenty years old at the time of the opening of classes. He received an Associate of Religious Education degree. He married a lovely young lady during his college days, Janina Gloria Kenly, from the state of Connecticut. They married in 1977 on the wedding anniversary of his parents, December 20, at the age of twenty-two.

The total number involved in the work of the ministry of

Gabriel was almost fifty. Each had been acquainted with Dr. Parsons through the years, rather directly, extending encouragement and support, since the year of 1955.

Dr. Robert J. Jonathan, dedicated Anvil House, May 15, 1976, 3:00 PM. The new learning facility had been completed in the summer instead of early fall. The Dedicatory Sermon was "The Biblical Trumpets of Christ."

Rev. Matthew N. Wiley gave the first baccalaureate sermon of the first graduating class of the "Conservatory of Historic Christian Studies." His sermon was entitled, "Take Heed How You Build." His message was like a hot branding iron being placed upon Anvil House for its future purpose and ministry. Appropriate awards were rendered in art, music, oratory, and comparative Biblical histories. A number of students from his last lectures from the Night Institute transferred to the Conservatory with academic credits accompanying them. On May 18, 1976, 11:00 AM, after Pastor Wiley's sermon, twenty-five students, with Christian delight, followed the academic processional from the Whitefield Sanctuary balcony around the colonnade, descending the staircase down under the large podium to the chancel area under the pulpit to receive their academic acknowledgments.

By the year of 1989 the InterNet Ministry did come into existence when, at that time, there were 100,000 host computers functioning towards greater days ahead for an international voice.

By 1992 the international electronic medium of the international Internet was in full operation. Gabriel's ministry had now been fully set under the title of "World Wide Web Lodebar" (www.lodebar).

In retrospect, however, Gabriel's esteemed mentor and personal friend, Dr. Robert J. Jonathan, Jr., died within a matter of weeks after the Dedication of Anvil House. His sermon in Anvil House was next to the last sermon he preached. God's "Trumpet" called him home, a reminder to all of his sermon preached on Dedication Day.

Gabriel attended the funeral of Dr. Jonathan with great

joy and sorrow. It was the largest funeral, personally, he had ever attended. Dr. Jonathan had given his life with a multiplicity of gifts given him by God. He was now in heaven. Gabriel would not pretend about his Christian heart; he sorrowed over the departure of this unusual man of God. The historical year of 1976 closed with the death of a friend that, to Gabriel, seemed to be an ominous prelude to the coming of dark days for the world.

Gabriel simply used that sorrow to bring everything in place for a greater historical interruption as the sounds of the twenty-first century seemed ominously near. The key-phrase would be whether it would be an "interruption" or an "interlude?"

Chapter Twenty-five

The Interlude

(2000 A.D.)

New Year's Day, January 1, 2000, brought the Parsons family together for the noon meal, but it was agreed that Ariel John and his family would have to proceed back to Pennsylvania immediately because of his duties at the Grace Memorial Base of "The Divine Interlude" fellowship ministries. Ariel must be there for a round of sermons he must deliver to the elderly in the domicile homes of his area. Joseph Paul, Catherine, Ken, and Soma Jeanne had planned a day down on the Mall between the Capitol Building and the Lincoln Memorial. A special New Year's Day program was scheduled for that afternoon, also, at the Smithsonian Institute. Their families were all to be together and pursue a mutual interest and then proceed to one of the fish restaurants down at the river in the southeast area of Washington, an area famous for seafood.

Gabriel and Evangeline would be spending the rest of the day in "The Room," which Evangeline had so named. There in The Land of Evangeline they would be together for a few hours, away from "all things," which had been a habit in their lives for many years now. Gabriel and Evangeline needed to be together and just enjoy themselves. Also, Gabriel needed the time of contemplation and perusal of several things in retrospect of the soon-to-be twenty-five years at The Lodebar Base. Thus, thoughts commenced for the afternoon of January 1, 2000.

Gabriel and Evangeline, as they started out in their marriage together, were definitely a contrast between prose and poetry. Most acquaintances of this couple would probably have identified Gabriel as being prosaic; Evangeline as poetic. More accurately, it was the other way around. Gabriel married a musician because of his poetic heart; and he was a musician, too. Evangeline loved Gabriel because of his didactic teaching gift as well as his love for her and music. Therefore the observation stands: Gabriel's heart was poetry; Evangeline's heart was for prose.

In the final analysis of these precious acknowledgments, however, a step further might be taken. Gabriel, in his conversion to Christianity, had, of necessity, followed a non-fiction principle for his studies so that he would teach fact and truth. That signified more the non-fiction prose. His faith, therefore, was built upon truth. However, in Evangeline, he saw the aesthetic, the poetic, the literature upon which fiction had been built: more accurately a sanctified appreciation for the story, the narrative, and the creativity of both fiction and the preciousness of the Christian life. However, their marriage had blended several of these things together, and once their Christian lives had been established and was growing, the literary characteristic distinction became the delicate relationship between poetry and song, with Evangeline leading the "song" and Gabriel leading the poetry.

It is with these distinctives their Christian lives had matured. This musical journey in their lives together had already heard the Prelude. Just as all history since the days of Adam and Eve has had its Prelude and then did move on towards the Postlude, so the lives of Gabriel and Evangeline were to await the Postlude in the more modest and shorter history of their own lives later. Under the wonderful influence of the grace of the Lord Jesus Christ in history, Gabriel believed that he should use the metaphorical symbol of music in history and in each history in the lives of God's people in what he would call "The Divine Interlude."

A prelude is known as a musical piece, like an overture, which precedes a more important series of musical movements which carry with them the main theme which is the purpose of the oratorio, opera, symphony, or other song form.

A postlude is known as a musical piece in the concluding passage of music for the various song forms sometimes identified in the "finale" at the very end of the concert itself.

In the plainer language of history, whether for the planet earth or individual persons, man has had his Prelude because the Gospel promise of Genesis, chapter 3, verse 15, has been fulfilled in the Incarnation and Virgin Birth of the Lord Jesus Christ in His First Advent, fulfilling the "seed of the woman." Man is now awaiting the Postlude in the Second Advent of the Lord Jesus Christ of Nazareth and His return to earth.

Man has now been given an Interlude, a parenthesis in the opportunity of grace, before the final curtain falls in the drama of the ages. The individual drama in the history of the life of a person has this privilege as well. It was through this Divine Interlude that Gabriel's ministry had built its hope of leading others to Christ and His Gospel.

There is a great deal of difference between an interruption, an intermission, and an interlude.

The interruption marks a breaking into and upon the talk, work, rest, or speaking of a person. This breaking into a person's actions or privacies in life is not conducive to setting forth the Spirit of the Lord Jesus in our hope of winning the soul of man. The only soul-winner at Jacob's Well the day the holy Stranger met the Woman of Samaria was the Lord Jesus. His Spirit and insight revealed the appropriate aspect of the Gospel of Grace that was explicitly needed for her.

The intermission of a person's life is a better word than interruption, offering a better way of reaching into the life and soul of a man. This speaks of a time between periods of activity or a pause in the agenda of the life of a person.   Church attendance and worship, two of the Christian's greatest assets, are the fulfillments in church history of the most excellent opportunity of how to reach the soul of a sinner as well as the saint of God with the ongoing message of the Gospel, through a distinct intermission between their days of occupational work. The true success of such a privilege lies in the Biblical presentation of historic Christianity by the minister in the pulpit. This intermission between the daily work, the weekly duties, and the delights of family is marked on the calendar as Sunday, the Lord's Day.

The word, "intermission," is a better word than "interruption" as a means of reaching souls with the Gospel. In addition to the church, Primitive Christianity reveals that the Christians went from house to house in fellowships, prayers, breaking of bread, and the apostolic doctrine, which places the intermission of people with home visitation being the next best avenue for evangelism to the church worship itself. Of course, the New Testament marks the marketplace, down at the river, over in the cities, the synagogues, and the church in the private house of a Christian brother, as becoming places for the saving of the souls of men.

However, it is to the word "interlude" that Gabriel turned in the hope of reaching all men with Christ in a day when historic Christianity was not known. The "interlude" carries with it the more excellent way of reaching souls through "the filling up" of the time between at least "two artistic things," like work and pleasure, with "a beautiful piece of music played between parts of a song," or church service, or other. From the interlude came the "intermezzo," a "short musical piece between acts in a drama," or in Gabriel's case, between the regular history of a person's life and death. This is the kind of heart the Christian should have in his personal evangelism. He believes God is the Soul-Winner; He has already gone ahead of the Christian. The Holy Spirit is leading the Christian wisely so as to best find this interlude in the life of a person for the best receptivity of the Gospel.

Companion words follow: intercede, intercession, interim, interplay, interpose, intervene, interview, etc. All of these words could follow the initial blessing of the "interlude."

Gabriel believed that instead of a search for human methodology in evangelism, there was the need of wisdom's search for the leading of the Holy Spirit in evangelism, as well as for revival of the saints. A human method is merely a human method. Soul-winning, to Gabriel, must be more like Jesus' Discourse at night with Nicodemus, or the unusual meeting of Jesus with the Woman of Samaria at Jacob's Well. These were interludes of life. Of course, there were incidents of Jesus with individuals like Zacchaeus, a short man of stature who climbed a tree to see Jesus. Jesus passed by and invited Zacchaeus to come down from the tree because he wanted to go home with him and talk with him concerning his soul. Of course, and probably somewhere between the limb of the tree and the ground, Zacchaeus was indeed redeemed and saved by grace through faith. This, too, was an interlude.

Jesus, in dealing with the souls of men, carried with Him the blessedness of the event with the prospective convert, and the proper occasion was always sought to deal with the soul of a person. It is true that he that winneth souls is wise, but it also stands that a Christian must wisely win souls. Jesus was perfect in reading the heart of a person as easily as men can read human books. Gabriel never believed that human instrumentality was perfect, but man had the Holy Spirit to guide him and give him wisdom as much as a human being could have.

It was this "Divine Interlude" with the souls of men that Gabriel sought with people. He was not the kind of evangelist that ran down the street yelling for people to be saved. The button-hole scream to a soul going to hell was not an interlude for Gabriel. However, he was sure there was, somewhere, a need for a "scream" like that. Gabriel cried in prayer for the Holy Spirit to lead him to a soul each day, and he did it not as a cop-out but rather as a more excellent way in which to win souls and edify the saints of God. Gabriel believed that the Christian must reason with men, seeking their questions, giving a Biblical answer, causing the sinner to think. Gabriel believed that the greatest apostasy of all was in thinking of the man, personally, rather than in the system or choice of religion he followed. Gabriel's ministry was more a matter of getting the individual to think. He saw this in Paul's preaching to Felix and Agrippa on their thrones, as well as to those who met him on Mars' Hill.

Therefore, Gabriel selected purposeful themes and identities for his ministry. He remembers well the First Quadrennial Conference on Evangelism of August 23, 1954. The methodology of that Conference, and that which was adopted by the other denominational conferences, was mainly a humanistic effort on the part of people seeking mass-conversion and whole church-planting concepts on an instant happening and experience. Evangelist Willie Wheyman was a master in this form of methodology in his world-wide crusades. The Gospel that was preached, the prayers prayed by the convert, the singular moment of the religious euphoria were to capture the emotional moment, to seize the enthusiastic time which was often a call to a person of cheap grace and easy believism of the moment. The Charismatic Healers dealt with their candidates for healing exactly the same way. It was subjective and existential.

Historic Christianity was not established upon the basis of merely an invitation down the aisle to make a decision and set forth a commitment. To Gabriel it was often the "aisle experience" that limited the view and understanding of what should happen to the entire life of the Christian. Men could become "aisle-hardened." Gabriel longed for the winning of a soul if it took a number of interludes, a year, or even a lifetime, to set the feet of the convert on the Rock of Ages. Yes, Gabriel desired "godly sorrow that worked repentance" that led to a complete conversion of the soul to the Lordship of Jesus Christ. Yes, conversion was a key word to Gabriel. This would hopefully bring Primitive Christianity to the full fruition of the test of Reformation Christianity.

Gabriel also believed that the world was living in the Last Days of history. All the trends of history, all the driftings of history, all the catastrophes of history were coming together for the climax of history. But God was giving man a "Divine Interlude," a last season to hear and see the beautiful grace of God doing a thorough work before man entered into the dark time of Jacob's Trouble and Daniel's Last Week of prophecy, the Great Tribulation Period. This was a true "Interlude" time for the souls of men. It was a time of the freeness of grace and the manifested presence of the Holy Spirit. After the catching away of the saints to the clouds to meet Jesus in His Second Advent, such privileges could be harder as the Judgment of God commences its work on earth.

Gabriel must proclaim, at this time of God's "Divine Interlude," an opportunity through Anvil House of the summaries of histories needed for man to find out where he was in such a time as this. A library was assembled, teachers were made available, times for the interludes of men were cordially requested. Whitefield Sanctuary would give the Divine Interlude on the Lord's Day; courses would be provided by competent teachers to set forth the heart of historic Christianity. The completion of the availability of the international Internet in 1992 brought an open forum in which man's individual needs were identified and addressed. Gabriel continued to believe there were souls who had rejected religion but were with sincere questions seeking answers about historic and apostolic Christianity. This ministry was not presenting prophecy as its emphasis; it was rather that the conditions of mankind, the sins, and the desperate conditions were demanding spiritual help through the Gospel in these dark days. It would be a mistake to think of this as some cult or sect involved in an isolation project. "The Divine Interlude" was to be an open help and hope to the souls of mankind everywhere!

This was the first time in history that Gabriel could see from his readings that Christians, so-called, were also seeking help to get back to God in their sins and sorrows. The apostate definitions of neo-christianity had so harmed the church that there was only a remnant identified with Christianity who sought the Christ of historic Christianity. In history, past, no one who sought a personal relationship with the Lord Jesus

Christ as a personal Savior had to deny a false Christianity first. In Primitive Christianity, the converts to the Gospel fled Judaism, Gnosticism, Stoicism, and a host of other false beliefs in order to come to the Savior, the Lord Jesus Christ.

There was preached in the early days "another gospel of another kind," but it was not the perversion-inversion of the genuine Gospel falsified within its own definition. But there was one thing helpful to those seeking to be saved in those days: They did not have to be confused by a neo-christianity of a weak Christ for their souls. Never had it been known before that such a wholesale number of so-called Christians were fleeing neo-christianity, endeavoring to know the historic Christianity of the Lord Jesus Christ.

As contacts were made to Gabriel's ministry over the InterNet, their questions were categorized under subjects ranging from Agnosticism to Zoroastrianism. The simplicity of this ministry was that it desired to extend the Interlude to meet the people at the very place in life they lived and no matter what status in life they possessed. This was identified with something of a "presuppositional" approach to evangelism. Gabriel had come to identify his ministry as "Remnant-One," endeavoring to contact small groups of people, even one person. "The Divine Interlude" was what Gabriel was seeking—an Interlude for a person, not an interruption, to what he or she thought was life. Sometimes, Gabriel had to accept an intermission of the individual's life, but everything must lead to "The Divine Interlude" if the ministry was to be effective through historic Christianity.

The international Internet was becoming a historic Christian Net, with listings of modern groups under "www.lodebar":

1. Abortionists
2. Agnostics
3. Animists
4. Astronomers
5. Atheists
6. Baptists
7. Biologists
8. Cavillers
9. Charismatics
10. Confucionists
11. Congregationalists
12. Denominationalists

13. Doubters
14. Drug Addicts
15. Drunkards
16. Episcopalians
17. Evolutionists
18. Fornicators
19. Gainsayers
20. Humanists
21. Hypocrites
22. Infidels
23. Invalids
24. Jesuits
25. Lampooners
26. Lutherans
27. Liberals
28. Mathematicians
29. Methodists
30. Modernists
31. Moonies
32. Murderers
33. Nationalists
34. Naturalists
35. New-Agers
36. Occultists
37. Pantheists
38. Paranormalists
39. Parapsychologists
40. Parseeists
41. Pentecostalists
42. Physicists
43. Post-Tribulation
     Period Saints
44. Presbyterians
45. Pre-Tribulation
     Period Saints
46. Prisoners
47. Psychiatrists
48. Psychologists
49. Quakers
50. Religionists
51. Revolutionists
52. Roman Catholics
53. Satanists
54. Scientists
55. Secularists
56. Shintoists
57. Skeptics
58. Sociologists
59. Sodomites
60. Suicidals
61. Taoists
62. Traitors
63. Under-privileged
64. Zoroastrianists

The InterNet List was growing in number and in the various kinds of people, from many religions and basic backgrounds, inquiring concerning a need of God. Yes, they were seeking answers in their severe troubles. The world was internationally in trouble in the hearts of the people.

Gabriel intended to encourage other home bases in other parts of the world for those who had come to know the Lord Jesus through the New Testament "apostles' doctrine" of Historic Christianity. All three of his children had been actively engaged in the Home Base in Georgetown. Joseph Paul was now vice president of his father's ministry, along with his wife, Catherine Rachel, who assisted him. Soma Jeanne and her husband, Dr. William K. Wilmore, were making contacts for other bases in the United States; and Rev. and Mrs. Ariel John Parsons were seeking bases for the hardship cases in the United States. At times, every member of his family became available for public speaking in behalf of "The Divine Interlude."

Gabriel and Evangeline were traveling all over the world together, but it must be kept in mind that this was not a big-business operation with unlimited funds. Evangeline's health had been greatly restored. This ministry was in contrast with big-business attitudes of the Charismatics who had taught "Prosperity Theology." Most all of the travels were at the request of different peoples, organizations, and institutions who provided the air-travel monies in advance desiring strongly for them to come. The salaries of all of the workers at the Lodebar Base were modestly rendered because of the sacrificial hearts of those who served the Lord in their respective ministries.

However, it was never believed that it was a sacrifice at all by any of the workers. God had revealed to Gabriel through the Books of Ezra and Nehemiah that his ministry must be one of trust and faith and thrift and hard work with a little style. That is the way in which Anvil House was built, with Rev. Wiley being so faithful in serving Gabriel through those days and saving considerable finances through his natural gift given by God. Many answers to prayer came as a result of the kind of purchases and how well God honored this hope. Anvil House cost about one-third of its appraised value when it was completed. But it must also be said that God had met every need, supplying large sums of money as the ministry enlarged around the various Bases. Some Bases had monies to assist other Bases; it was amazing how God was working through "The Interludes."

The home ministry at Georgetown was called "The Lodebar Base." "Lodebar" is a rather obscure place in the Bible, unless it is also to be identified with "Debir." It was a place in Gilead, north of the brook Jabbok, not far from Mahanaim. The man

Mahanaim had a son, Machir, who entertained Mephibosheth, the lame surviving son of Jonathan, King Saul's son and friend of David. That surviving lame son was living there in Lodebar, which means "a place without a pasture," when David found him. The Book of Second Samuel, chapter 9, verses 1 through 11. King David took Mephibosheth from "a place without a pasture" and brought him to the King's Table where he put his lame feet under that Table all the days of his earthly life. Gabriel saw in this historic narrative that God desired to give that spiritual victory to many now who had come to a time of spiritual lameness in "a place without a spiritual pasture" for their souls.

This narrative revealed a very important insight to Gabriel. In Primitive Christianity, of the first century, that Christian experience was originally connected with one particular view or interpretation of the Gospel; and where that particular interpretation was abandoned or substituted by another interpretation, the actual experience ceased. In other words, no one in history would ever be able to be "saved by grace through faith" without that particular, singular, explicit interpretation of the New Testament teaching and doctrine. God would not allow nor make a case of grace in any soul where the teaching of this doctrine was not interpreted according to the revelation of the Gospel as presented in the New Testament. That was indeed the problem with the popular preaching of Willie Wheyman and the entire concept of neo-christianity. This indicated another proof that evangelism must be preached on the base of historic Christianity according to the "apostles' doctrine."

So, the "Lodebar Base" was the first base of presentation of that historic Christianity in the full view of Gabriel's ministry. It should also be understood that there were indeed other ministries around the world which truly held to the truth of the historic Christianity but had never met or known the Georgetown call of "The Divine Interlude" of the "Remnant-One" ministry of Gabriel T. Parsons. His was not the only true ministry in the world; he believed he was one of the least pretentious one. He believed there were many Christians who had not compromised their historic birthright with the Word of God. Gabriel was simply presenting the Gospel of historic Christianity in the open reality of what he had come to understand from the Holy Scriptures of the Bible. That ministry started in Georgetown, formally, May 15, 1976. The "Remnant-One" ministry at the Lodebar Base had continued now for twenty-five years directly under Gabriel's leadership.

It was now the year of 2000 AD Gabriel and Evangeline, still always together, traveled to the lectures, the sermons, the speaking engagements. In fact, Evangeline was almost always giving a lecture at everyone of the places Gabriel's ministry extended. It was encouraging to see them together. Evangeline, by her natural gift as a human being, but more importantly, her spiritual growth through the years in her Primitive Christianity, brought a blessing to Gabriel's ministry wherever they went. Their lives were becoming more fruitful unto the Lord, but it should be understood they were building remnant groups.

The definition of neo-christianity had become world-wide, and greater antagonism was everywhere against the Remnant-Voice of Christian believers of historic Christianity. To the Parsons, Georgetown was the permanent place of their lives. God had placed them there, strategically, in the nation's Capital, near airports, transportations, and communications. A remnant of congressmen, senators, governmental workers had become Christian friends to the Lodebar Base, and souls were being gloriously saved "by grace through faith."

Evangeline was not always sure whether their ministry was like Cabin Peak or Green Meadows or Luray Caverns or Martha Washington. It certainly was not like the luxurious Abraham Lincoln Hotel. "Possibly," Evangeline would sometimes say, "our lives and our travels are mainly between the 'peaks,' the 'meadows,' the 'caverns' and 'Washington.' And it is all good!" But personally and humanly, she liked Georgetown and that was where God had planted them and their ministry.

Georgetown has been a favorite destination of

Washingtonians and visitors alike for almost three hundred years. Once it was a busy port that hummed with factories and mills; it is where George Washington planned the nation's capital. Coal, grain, and lumber were transported into Georgetown by mule-drawn barges on the C. & O. Canal, identified with the Chesapeake and Ohio railroad company. Francis Scott Key, who penned "The Star Spangled Banner," lived and practiced law here. Several former presidents lived here as student or senator.

Georgetown is a National Historic District in recognition of its treasure of fine old homes and renowned historic attractions. A visitor may stroll the boardwalk of Washington Harbor to view the sculling teams on the Potomac River.

Modern-day Georgetown is a place for culture, shopping, and dining. Park in any convenient parking lot, and you may embark on a stroll, hop on a trolley, motor on an electric bus, or cruise the Potomac River on a dinner-cruise ship. Georgetown Park and the surrounding retail area are a fashion and shoppers' paradise with hundreds of unique shops, boutiques, art and antique galleries everywhere. World-class cuisine is found among the community's scores of restaurants. Georgetown is also a charming place to stay overnight with its distinctive luxury and competitively-priced hotels.

Georgetown offers an open invitation to explore the past, glimpse the future, and live in the present time.

One of the most historical areas of Georgetown will enlarge itself beside the Potomac River. The C. & O. Canal stretches from the mouth of Rock Creek in Georgetown to Cumberland, Maryland. Its 74 lift locks raise the canal from near sea level to an elevation of 605 feet at Cumberland, Maryland. Its towpath, which used to tow or pull the barges by horses on the canal of yesterday, provides a nearly level byway for hikers, equestrians, and bicyclists now.

Hike-Biker overnight campsites for tent camping occur approximately every five miles. Camping supplies, ice, food, and beverages can be bought at most stores along access roads. The first camp site is Marsdon Tract, which is Milepost (MP) #11. Free permits may be picked up at the visitors' center. If you enter C & O towpath at approximately 28th Street, N.W. and L Street N.W., Milepost (MP) 0 is actually 0.3 miles south at Potomac River. This is the closest point on the trail to downtown Washington. From that point, using one of the free map-outlines, there are points south and north to Milepost 167 at Old Town, where the ADT crosses the Potomac River into West Virginia to a privately-owned, covered wooden bridge. At last report the bridge was closed to vehicular traffic for safety reasons; however, it remains open for pedestrians and bicycles.

From every consideration, the Georgetown home, in northwest Washington, D.C., has now been the permanent home of the Parsons Family for about fifty years.

Fortunately, the private home of Gabriel and Evangeline in Georgetown was located in the adjacent area of the property which had been purchased for "The Lodebar Base" Mansion House and the property upon which Anvil House was built. Gabriel did not plan this mutual proximity of his own home and that of Lodebar. However, while living in his own private home, Gabriel had spoken about the availability and beauty of the surrounding property. The home of Gabriel and Evangeline had been purchased with sacrifice, and they had hoped to save it if it were possible. Now, it had become possible, and Gabriel believed, once again, it was the good providence of God that did it. The history behind both of these properties was quite significant.

In the late eighteenth century a subdivision was made of the western portion of Georgetown called "Threlkeld's Addition." The original mid-eighteenth-century Town of Georgetown had been centered on land near the Potomac River waterfront and M Street, but as the need for expansion arose in the bustling port, several nearby additions were laid out by land merchants eager to sell individual lots to willing buyers.

One of these additions was "Threlkeld's." Lot 135 of the new addition referred to 60 feet of Fayette Street frontage below Fourth Street. The south half of lot 135 was the land upon which Gabriel's house was built, number 84 Fayette Street.

This three-story town house, besides a complete basement, was built and completed in 1856, before the beginning of the Civil War. It was exactly the year that James G. Buchanan was elected as the fifteenth President, almost five years before the country's greatest internal conflict, the Civil War. Ann O'Neale, after her husband's death, as she had been living at 88 Fayette Street, purchased a vacant lot just to the south of her corner house, in August 1855, and arranged the construction of this Victorian House which Gabriel had purchased. This was an Italianate-style, flat-front, brick house of three stories besides the full basement area. Her new house would be numbered as 84 Fayette Street. It would have a total of 5,000 square feet to its floors.

Of course, the story would be incomplete if its history were not traced back to the Alexander Graham Bell family and relatives. With the fifty thousand francs awarded him as the Volta Prize for his invention of the telephone, Alexander Graham Bell established the Volta Laboratory at the Georgetown compound which included some of the property owned now by Gabriel and Evangeline. Other members of the Bell family, including his scholarly uncle, finally lived on the proximity of Gabriel's property.

The main building retains much of its original exterior appearance. Its heavy- bracketed cornice is perhaps the most notable feature and clue to its Italianate design. The scrollwork, modillions, and dentrils define its mid-nineteenth-century origins. Also significant are the floor-to-ceiling first-story windows of six over nine lights. One can easily imagine a member of the Bell family relatives seated before a tall mullioned window of the sumptuous double-drawing room as he conversed and described his latest invention, a phonograph record.

The facade of the house is enhanced by the classical and restrained frame of the slightly-recessed front door. The old wrought-iron fence and gate delineate the boundaries and contribute to the property's distinctively Victorian, nineteenth-century flavor. Of course, the other interior rooms, through all these many years, have suffered one renovation after another, but always with taste.

The house of Gabriel and Evangeline was plotted upon the old "Threlkeld's Addition," as well as the newly-purchased property for The Lodebar Base of the Interlude Schools. The Potomac River could be seen from the "Threlkeld's Addition," but not the details of the waterfront itself. The entire Fayette Street down to the Potomac was most historic in its day. Gabriel was not interested in the pomp and boast of it all, but the emphasis upon its local history would be used as an introduction to history itself to those students who had very little history in this geographical background. It would also educate them to the area for their shopping necessities.

That first quarter the classes in Mansion House, the place on the original property, and on the original "Threlkeld's Addition, were fully used for the over two hundred students who came and registered September 30, 1974, twenty-six years ago. The schedule of the classes were staggered from 7:30 in the morning to 9:30 at night. That first year, everyone was awaiting the completion of Anvil House.

Almost twenty-five years had passed, and much activity had taken place not only in Gabriel's home, Mansion House, Anvil House, and the beautiful nine-acre plot, but from that Lodebar Base, ministries had been contacted and established in some thirty-one other places of the world. The InterNet had effectively rendered a real service to the Interlude Ministries. Gabriel believed that it had taken away the sales-pitch pressure of earlier methods of mass crusades as well as some of the earlier extreme methods of personal soul-winning.

The InterNet brought out the Interlude more, the privacy of the contact, by individuals who would, themselves, be searching first the credibility and plausibility of God and then the truth about historic Christianity all around the world. Also, the InterNet took the message to the international places quickly, efficiently, and economically. Gabriel had all of the studies presented in a multi-lingual form. For more than any other part of the Interlude Schools, the greatest expenditures had been for the processing of all the materials for InterNet.

The reservoir of historical research at the Lodebar Base should be understood with clarity. The twenty-thousand-volume library was now housed in a new annex to Anvil House, beautifully rendered with adequate room for a five-hundred-member student body. Gabriel never desired to have a larger student body than that because he believed he would lose the personal testimony with the individual student of the Interlude Schools of the Conservatory. Should they outgrow that, then another new Base would be formed.

Of course, most of the library was stored from a computer base that gave access to those constantly inquiring through the InterNet.

The Machen Library was screened and selected to serve the greatest needs in the process of establishing historic Christianity. It also served the Conservatory's demands for art, music, and oratory, which were a part of the avenues through which the message of the Lodebar Base served the need in this contemporary time. It was firmly believed by Gabriel that evangelism must include definitions of Biblical doctrine and historical accuracy if the Remnant-One ministries were to lead a soul to the Lord Jesus according to the definition of Primitive Christianity in the New Testament. However, it should not be understood that the evangelism was sticky and technical; rather, it simply was Biblical and clear.

The Main sections of the Library were as follows:

History of the Ancient Hebrews
History of the Six World Empires
History of First-Century Palestine
History of First-Century Judaism
History of First-Century Rome
World History of the 21 Civilizations
Church History
History of the Creeds and Councils in Dogmatic Theology
History of Christian Remnants
History of Christian Doctrine
History of the Caesars

History of the Popes of Rome
History of Roman Catholicism
History of the Reformation
History of Protestantism
History of All the Reformers
History of Evangelism
History of Revivals
History of the Great Theologians
History of the Early Church Fathers
History of the Scholastics
History of the Dark Ages
History of the Ecclesiastical Divines
History of Denominationalism
History of the Contemporary Ecumenical Movement
History of the Languages of the World
History of the 192 Nations in the World Today

Gabriel was still dedicated to the "grammatico historical exposition" of the Holy Scriptures although there was an increasing interpretation of all literary works, including the Bible, through scientific historical research as espoused by anthropologist and archaeologist from the presupposition of history as told through the myth, the legend, or the saga.

Gabriel continued to follow the historical method as the record of historical fact, as given by the "Fathers of History," Herodotus and Josephus. This was contrary to the modern and post-modern "scientific historical method" of the neo-christian and liberal world as they used studies of ancient literary interpretation as a basis for interpreting the Bible. They had adopted a world-history with a world-form of interpretation as was necessary for an understanding of the historical record of peoples and nations of the past. They saw the Bible, the Holy Scriptures, simply as another human book as other books were understood. Gabriel persisted that the Bible was a supernatural Book, and inerrant, infallible, and inspired directly from God rather than man.

The trilogy of history did lie in the honorable distinctions of non-fiction, fiction, and poetry. The first was the literary form dedicated to the historical preservation of truth; the second was the literary form dedicated to the historical preservation of the story-narrative; and the third was the literary form dedicated to the historical preservation of the song.

Dr. Gabriel T. Parsons was completely convinced by the Holy Scriptures, through its revelation of Law, History, Poetry, Epistle, Gospels, and Prophecy, that God had given in His time this open window for man with the privilege of a Divine Interlude before the coming of the Lord Jesus in clouds of glory! This Divine Interlude, however, should be understood as a divine calm in-between an intensely busy life of busy people in a last Interlude before the Great Storm of Jacob's Trouble and Daniel's Last Week in prophecy. This in-between privilege, this "divine interlude," at the end of all history, would be tested by a Christianity that is both historically true and prophetically true.

Thus, the January 1, 2000 "interlude" of Gabriel and Evangeline ended at midnight as they both retired to rest for another day. However, they spoke of their love for each other and went to sleep holding hands.

Chapter Twenty-six

The Forum

(May 15, 2000)

For twenty-five years, May 15 had always been a very special day in Anvil House at the Conservatory for Historic Christian Studies. It was commemorative of the dedication of Anvil House, as well as remembering the first Baccalaureate service.

This quarter-of-a-century Christian celebration was at hand, and it was to be a milestone in the work of God through Gabriel's ministry. Representatives of the thirty-one other Remnant-One Bases had come for the occasion in Anvil House. Most of them had come with great financial sacrifice, but the hearts of Gabriel and Evangeline were filled to over flow. Evangeline spoke again of her husband's "cup" and her "saucer" in "over flow" as the week of activities began on Monday, May 11. All activities were working for the special Friday, May 15. They were especially glad to see the delegation from the other thirty-one Bases.

Dr. Parsons would hold one of his last Question Forums for the academic year with his Deans, which included eight Deans, the fifth being Dr. Joseph Paul Parsons, Dean of the

Machen Library of History. Of course, Evangeline was included to be present among the deans, too. Since her increased travels with her husband, in which they were always together, her daughter, Dr. Soma Jeanne Wilmore, had become the sixth dean at the Conservatory as the Dean of Fine Arts. Her husband, Dr. Kenneth W. Wilmore, the seventh dean, had become the Dean of the Divinity School. All of the other deans since the founding of Gabriel's ministry in 1974 were still alive and active in his ministry. Several of them had been serving over forty years as either teacher or dean. The date of the Question Forum was May 15, 2000 AD. It was presented in the Whitefield Sanctuary. Dr. Gabriel Parsons is still the president and Academic Dean at the Lodebar Base. His wife, Evangeline, is the Academic Dean-at-large. They are 74 years old.

Rev. and Mrs. Ariel John Parsons came from their own Interlude, "Grace Memorial Base," located in the humble area of Clarksdown, Pennsylvania. They came just for this occasion.

The time for the Question Forum was set for 2:00 PM.

The eight deans, the faculty and all students, and a large number of guests were gathered in the Whitefield Sanctuary with a total audience of about nine hundred.

Dr. Gabriel Parsons is standing in the center of the Chancel under the Podium with the eight deans seated somewhat surrounding the president with four on each side within the Chancel. The front pews, all across the circumferential Sanctuary have been reserved for the honored governmental guests, including the leaders from the other thirty-one Remnant-One Base ministries. This is to be a teaching-worship service.

As has been the usual custom in the Question Forums, each Friday, Dr. Parsons would set forth a series of statements on a particular trend of thought which would act as a catalyst for questions from the deans.

Since the very beginning of these Friday Forums here at The Conservatory of Historic Christian Studies, the entire student body was required to be present, including a number of guests and visitors. At other times, the president had invited speakers in the Monday through Thursday Chapel services, each morning at 11:00. But the Question Forum was always scheduled for Fridays at that time. However, on this special day it was scheduled for 2:00 PM.

It should be recalled that Dr. Parsons initiated this Forum of teaching in the first year of his presidency at the Antioch Theological Seminary. However, here in the Conservatory, the audience had widened including the student body and outside visitors. Today, Senators Charles Baker and Robert A. Tafton, Jr., two new senators, and four congressmen had joined the occasion from their Capitol Hill offices. This was a special Question Forum where only Dr. Parsons would respond to the questions. Usually, there was a joint-participation of the deans with the president in the questions posed by Dr. Parsons.

So, the time had come for the 25th Anniversary commemoration of Anvil House. This entire week had been dedicated to various programs in the Conservatory in the areas of art, music, oratory, and orals in theology and history.

Dr. Parsons has just opened the session with prayer and the audience is now comfortably seated.

"Greetings to each of you today: our beloved and respected Senators Baker and Tafton with their guests, our deans, faculty, students, and friends. We are especially glad to see a representation of our dear workers from 31 other 'Remnant-One' bases from around the world. They have sacrificed much to be with us today. (a pause)

"I well remember my first "Question Forum" in 1960. That was forty years ago. It was entitled 'The Distinctive of Time With Consideration of our Creator, His Creatures, and History.' Even that early in my own walk with the Lord Jesus, history was important to me. If God had not created time along with 'all things,' there could have been no possibility of history or an avenue for Jesus Christ, the Son of God, to enter into a time, space history, as Jesus of Nazareth, to save fallen man.

"I also remember another Forum, the last one in that same series in a nine-year ministry in that same place. That was thirty-one years ago. It was entitled 'The Contemporary Voices of Neo-Christianity in Our World Today.' (another pause) I trust that you can see the connection between these two former titles. One deals with time versus eternity as set forth in history; the other deals with a period, some six thousand years later, in our twentieth-century contemporary history. (a pause)

"But today, we must deal with the climax of these two forums: Creation and the Contemporary Times lead to that point of history which must be joined to prophecy future. Of course, there are many views concerning the 'order of events' at the Second Advent of the Lord Jesus, but that is not the area in which we desire to set forth our 'Question Forum' this afternoon at all. The subject will be entitled 'What Relationships, If Any, Are There Between the Contemporary Times and Prophecy?' Simply stated, we have viewed Creation and Time; we have viewed our Contemporary and the Present; but, we must still inquire of the Contemporary and the Future.

"I will not be treating this subject as 'a prophet,' in the predictive state; I am no prognosticator of 'spiritualism,' such as a 'new-ager.' I will only speak as one who respects very highly, history, and as one who respects and endeavors to obey the Bible as the infallible Word of God. We have discussed history many times before concerning the distinctions between the human trends, driftings, catastrophes, and climaxes of man, as happening under the sovereignty and providence of Almighty God. I will speak of 'trends' and 'driftings' in our contemporary as they tend to meet prophecy as revealed in the Word of God.

"I will be speaking from the great departments of history past as they are indeed related to The World-View of 'things' today. Behind 'all things' is some principal 'thing' or law, or order, or design, or purpose. Behind 'all things' lies 'the thing,' 'The Thinker,' God. We must read concerning 'these things,' explicitly, from the Bible, as follows:

For by him (God) were all things created, that are in heaven, and that are in earth, visible and invisible, whether they be thrones, or dominions, or principalities, or powers: all things were created by

**him, and for him: And he is before all things, and by
him all things consist.** Paul's letter to the Colossians,
chapter 1, verses 16 and 17.

"We are assured from the word studies of the Greek New
Testament that we may understand, from the Bible, God's
Creation, His universe, and 'all things' of that original creation.
These 'rudiments,' from the Greek word *stoicheion*, indicate
that the 'things' are from the 'elements' — 'one of a row or
series' — in the material substance of which God created the
world — the universe. As Creator, in Him, 'all things' — 'all
elements' — 'consist,' or 'cohere.' Nothing could be revealed
more explicitly than these words of Paul. The Greek word for
'consist' is *sunesteiken*. This simply means everything in the
entire universe consisted and cohered in God under His control
and providence.

"Presupposing God as Creator of All Things cohering in
Him, this reveals that we are indeed talking about a universe,
under God's providence, directly 'cohering' through His
immediate providential purposes and actions. It is truly a
'universe,' a singular harmony under God, but wherein Satan
and sin are allowed for this time. Yes, chaos does exist at times,
as man thinks of disorder, or more properly, enigmas and
puzzles. However, the definition of a universe must be
sustained, and its definition is made clear, as follows: 'the
totality of known or supposed objects and phenomena; all
existing things, including the earth and its creatures, the
heavenly bodies, and all else throughout space; the cosmos,
the macrocosm.'

"With this in mind, we propose a number of statements
today to introduce our 'Question Forum.'

"First, we believe that the revealed God of the Bible is
capable of pre-existing, forever, in eternity; but that He is also
capable, and did come into the fallen history of time at the
Incarnation and Virgin Birth of the Lord Jesus Christ. This
truth is absolutely necessary for the human race to survive in
our time as well as for the salvation of the individual soul 'by
grace through faith.'

"Second, the desecration of the arts, and especially music, has caused an addiction to evil so powerful that God's natural gift to man of the aesthetic capacity has been damaged beyond repair unless a miracle of grace intervenes. This has been mainly because of advertisements and television where immorality, nudity, lust, and 'Rock and Roll' music are packaged with rampant damage upon the viewing audience of the people.

"Third, the field of Literature has entered into a major destruction to the definitions of man's vocabulary; therefore, instruction and understanding are being destroyed to such an extent that human communication is in a state of confusion rather than a state of truth. This deplorable condition was first mentioned by Bertrand Russell years ago, but his solution was unsatisfactory. However, at this point in history, it is being used deliberately, in some areas, like the media and the government, to deceive the people.

"Fourth, the mass contemporary religious movements have destroyed the denominational identities both in their theological and numerical influence in the world. This was necessary in order to bring the world to one religious concept and belief which certainly was chosen by those involved.

"Fifth, the combined leadership of world influence has been reduced to a political and a religious authority. The hope of merely a secular world is not possible because of the religious nature of man. There is no longer a separation between state and church in the world; all religion is dominated by the state. In fact, the church, too, now honors the one world government. A Global World is now in the offing with the coming of a singular political power, with all religious influences giving impetus to that one political force.

"Sixth, a singular educational pool has gained control of world-wide educational acknowledgments through the United Nations with a unanimous resolution undefeated. This educational process is necessary in order to prepare future generations to accept the one-world political government and religious authority.

"Seventh, because of the ecumenical union of the 1990s,

all religious fellowships of all religions are to be known under the title of 'Christendom.' The only two distinctions within this 'Christendom' are the 'liberals' and the 'moderates.' This presupposition is acceptable to the mass because they see no natural way to survive, otherwise.

"Eighth, there are no more 'correctional institutions' for any kind of prisoner throughout the world. They are out-of-date and have served their purpose for the past. There are, in their place, 'control institutions' which maintain state 'legislative abortions,' 'euthanasia,' 'parental planning,' 'genocide,' 'sterilization,' 'capital-death injections,' 'and forced labor camps' as a way to control the populace.

"Ninth, forced universal peace is everywhere, and the only uprisings in the world concern small, sporadic religious groups identified as 'historic Christians,' who still speak of a conscience and conviction about the Bible. The answer from the state to them is 'martyrdom.' The entire governmental state is a force of greed and graft.

"Tenth, there is no more public, Biblical evangelism going on in the world because it has been theologically acclaimed and concluded that no one is lost in sin. Pelagianism is the presupposition, one way or another, and the word 'Gospel' is only used to announce to everyone that they are all already saved. All of this is espoused from a world-wide force of spiritualism under Satanic influence. The occult is most prominent. A delusion has been embraced and enforced that the world has produced 'peace and prosperity,' and a universal salvation has been wrought by the same program.

"Eleventh, historic Christianity has come to a time of preparation only for an underground church, while in the Middle East, the former Jewish Problem is being thoroughly solved. The shift of commerce from the East Coast to the 'Pacific Rim' has now moved, as a result of many settlements, at least temporarily, with China. However, international trade has moved to the Middle East with an international Common Market in control of the total flow of monies in the world.

"Twelfth, although the political powers of all the 192 nations formerly known in the 1990s have been absorbed in the Middle East political center, yet a powerful political leader is rising in the United States, and a religious leader is rising out of Roman Catholicism. These two personalities dominate the media publicity and the propaganda notoriety. (a pause) Now, our Deans may stand before their microphones and announce their questions."

Dr. Grayham gives the first question.

"Dr. Parsons, in your very first statement you alluded to the sovereignty of Almighty God and the entrance of His Son, the Lord Jesus, as coming into human history for the redemption of man and the survival of mankind itself. To strengthen our understanding of this, give us a response concerning our knowledge of His sovereign ways among mankind for this time."

"As you know, my dear Doctor, the sovereignty of God has always been a deep truth. As finite creatures we struggle with this subject. However, the Bible reveals such a sovereign Lord, and we must defend it. (a pause)

"It is our understanding from the Holy Scriptures that we may divide God's sovereignty into several steps of reasonableness for our own finite knowledge. First, God has indwelling thoughts. He does not do or create anything apart from His indwelling thoughts. Second, from God's indwelling thoughts He sets forth in His mind certain purposes. We must not assume that all of His indwelling thoughts always come to purpose. Third, once God has set forth His thoughts into His purpose, He then will act upon that purpose and it will come to pass. Fourth, after God has purposed His actions, then we might understand this as a decree; but His decrees are distinct from His execution of those decrees. I would prefer the phrase 'fulfilled purpose' over the word 'decree,' but both are applicable, I suppose. Finally, when those purposes come to pass, they come to pass predestinated immediately. Whatever it takes to say these things, we must say them.

"In the Bible, all of these matters are basically reduced to a certain order of 'foreknowledge,' 'election,' and 'predestination,' and it is within those words tzhat we have set forth our explanation. We know of no other way to give a response. Companion to predestination we must acknowledge God's prevenient grace which gives man the proper and necessary enablement to want to want God, thus bringing into history human responsibility.

"Two other things must be included in what we have said. We live in time and not eternity at this point. Whatever the Eternal God purposes from His thoughts must be placed into acts immediately. In our own problem of time, we become easily confused as our human reasoning is not able to go as far as eternal thought. But God's purposes must become God's acts immediately and eternally. When His actions fall upon us, they do so in some order of time and events, or else we would not be able to see them or be accountable to them.

"With a full faith in this, we are not talking about fatalism. Fatalism comes from Fate and our God is not Fate. We should be very thankful that He is our God; otherwise all of our lives would be destroyed if it were possible for a false god to be in control. After removing that impediment, we must move on to the truth that all of God's purposes and acts include all of man's will and responsibilities and ways. Nothing is left out of God's knowledge of all things through Creation, Providence, Redemption, and His enablement for man through His prevenient grace. All things were included in His indwelling thoughts, and then His purposes, and then His acts. We regret in one way, and it is only a human regret, that because God must finalize through His foreknowledge, election, and predestination the salvation of the saints in a way that seems difficult for man to fully understand. Also, in this regret, this purpose, inherently, demands God's reaction to the unredeemed. They must go to hell. However, our regret only lies in the fact that they are lost, not because God purposed them by His sovereignty to hell as the only other alternative."
(pause)

Dean Soma Jeanne Wilmore stands to give the second question.

"Esteemed President, I will combine two of your statements together for one, longer question. I am sure you will need more time for the answer, but I believe they should be kept together.

"You have mentioned the current trend and drifting towards the desecration of the arts as well as the damage and destruction of human language which is going on in the field of literature. (a pause) What do you mean by God's natural gift to man of the aesthetic capacity, and what directly is the cause of the state of confusion in literature and human communication in our time?"

"It is a delight for me to welcome you, as my daughter, to the Forum today. (a chuckle from the audience). It is appropriate for you to bring together in one question the matters of both art and literature. And you are correct; I will need more time. (another chuckle from the audience.)

"In Creation, the Holy Spirit gave man an aesthetic capacity just as He did other capacities such as conscience, intellect, emotion, will, and all physical desires. None of them are evil of themselves. Jesus had the lust of the flesh, the pride of life, and the lust of the eyes. That is clearly revealed in the three temptations He experienced in the Wilderness recorded in the Bible, The Gospel of Matthew, chapter 4, verses 3, 6, and 9. Adam and Eve, prior to the fall, were created with these same three avenues of desire, Genesis, chapter 3, verse 6. The desires are not sinful; the unlawful use of them is.

"However, there were other capacities of a more sensitive and refined nature which, even after the fall, man continued to enjoy.

"The capacity for the aesthetic is a companion gift to man's faculty for the arts. Originally, Adam was commanded by God the privilege to have 'dominion' in the earth, to 'subdue' or domesticate the animals, and 'dress' or beautify the Garden of Eden. Of course, God, creating man in the 'image' of Himself, gave the spiritual capacities of 'knowledge,' Colossians, chapter 3, verse 10; and 'righteousness and true holiness,' Ephesians, chapter 4, verse 24. However, these spiritual capacities were completely lost in the fall, and only 'grace through faith' can restore them in the righteousness of Jesus Christ.

"The natural gifts, although fallen, remained in God's purpose for man. Amidst man's depravity the stamp of creation was there. Man still has the human faculty for art and the aesthetic capacity to behold beauty through the art in nature and human life. Every person is born to this faculty and capacity. It may be that in most people it is manifested in the practical arts more than the fine arts, but nevertheless they are there. This would be true because the practical arts are more necessary in the occupations and professional service man must maintain for his livelihood. Nevertheless, that is a part of the art and the aesthetic relationships.

"But man, by certain sins, can permanently damage and even destroy the faculty of art as well as the aesthetic capacity. In other words, the aesthetic functions in a wholesome way whenever we see something as beautiful, distinguished from something sinful. Fine Arts came along in history for the purpose of man's actual observation of art, such as viewing it in an art gallery. Fine arts also resulted when man began to sign his name on the actual art form itself, like a painting. In the true sense, this art should only be viewed aesthetically. If and when man views art with sinful lust, fornication, and immorality, the basic aesthetic is interrupted and will be ultimately destroyed by immoral eyes and the mind. In other words, an apostasy occurs: the mixture of the true aesthetic with false uncleanness. Just as in religious apostasy, the individual is comforted by the truth he has but is not able to escape an apostasy when he mixes error with that truth. At the appropriate time, afterwards, God ordains a delusion in the person.

"It was the Greeks that gave the Western World Civilization the awakened instruction and exercised capacity of the aesthetic view. For example, the Greek drama was written and presented deliberately to awaken the human capacity of the aesthetic view. Although some of the dramas portrayed characters who had sin, murder, rape, fornication, and sinful lust in their lives, yet they would not parade the actual happening on the stage. Our English word 'obscene' comes to us from this Greek principle. The word 'obscene' means 'off stage.' This indicated that what happened 'off stage,' such as murder, immorality, etc., would take place 'off stage,' in-between the acts and scenes. It was considered 'obscene.' They believed this violated the aesthetic view and that view must be protected for the stage audience. Otherwise, it was 'obscene.' The risqué and the immoral would spoil the aesthetic view. I do not mean to imply that the Greek drama did not have its 'bawdy' language at the edge of the open curtain of the stage, but I do mean to strike a difference between that and the 'immoral' and 'violent' acts of the drama. The Greeks were definitely dealing with the hope of being good dramatists, cultivating the aesthetic view of life.

"So, we have observed, in our time, that the aesthetic capacity has been damaged and/or destroyed in the public, contemporary man. Man's desires for sinful lust, the risqué, and the immoral have been so indulged that he cannot easily distinguish between his aesthetic and his lust. Man is not able to manage both of these forces of desire, simultaneously, without morally damaging himself. This explains why, in modern drama, you might read of a sodomite 'stage manager,' or a contemporary playwright, who takes an old classic drama and gives it a risqué, modern interpretation. This is spoken of in our popular time as 'the interpretation of the stage manager' of the play itself.

"An example of this may be seen in the difference between one of Franz Schubert's *lieder* ('art songs') as presented in his day versus the way it would be presented in the contemporary risqué performances of our time. The 'Art Song,' called *chanson* in French and *lied* in German, is a setting of a poetic text for solo singer with piano accompaniment. Franz Schubert was born in 1797 and died in 1828. He wrote *Der Erlkönig,* or "The Erl King," at the age of eighteen. Much of the music composed in the nineteenth century was intended to be performed in the intimacy of a salon rather than in a large concert hall. The composer gave us the beautiful sorrow of a father and son in conversation as the son sees death riding on a horse towards him to take him away. His dear father's hope of life for his son precludes his ability to see death taking the fair life of the child away. The fast tempo reflects a sense of haste; the rapid, repeated notes in the accompaniment that sound like galloping hoofbeats; the sharp harp-like figure that accompanies the Erl King's alluring manner of taking the son; and the pair of abrupt chords that terminate the song suggest the finality of death itself.

"The modern interpretation of this Art Song, on the "Old Broadway" stage of a few years ago, presented this as a rape scene in a violent and passionate death of morality itself. The aesthetic view is completely lost in the neo-interpretation of Schubert's old *lied*. To many people the original composition, in meaning, is lost forever.

"Of course, the aesthetic was never intended by God to be a cure for sin. It has no power for that. Only the power of Christian redemption, through the blood of Jesus Christ has that power. However, God gave the aesthetic capacity for man to enjoy God's creation and nature to the glory of God and the good of man himself.

"The same thing is happening in another way in the field of literature. (a pause)

"There has always been the legitimate matters of denotation versus connotation, the definitions versus semantics, speech versus rhetoric, and grammatical rules versus 'the exception to the rule.' All of these things reveal the finiteness and frailty of the human race. However, we are now living in a time when there is a deliberate attempt to destroy meaning in literature and conversation in communication and pervert it to other ends. At the root of the literature and communication apostasy is the loss of the belief in 'absolutes' of any kind, whether in the Bible or other literature. Truth comes to each person differently in modern time; the Constitution of the United States does not mean today what it meant to its framers when it was written. This has happened in many, many fields of literature and human communication. Man is holding back more truth than he tells; he is also rewriting the literature of history believing in an entirely different motive and interpretation than were present when it was first written.

"In this climate of things Christian apologetics stands at a crucial crossroads. The current polls indicate that only fourteen percent of Americans have a strong belief in *absolute truth,* and that a corresponding *relativism* is on the rise. This simply means that men hold the belief that the criteria of judgment are relative, varying with individuals and their environments rather than with any source or standard of 'absolute truth.' We are being urged from many quarters, as a Christian, to set forth a 'rational defense of Christianity.' This has been a demand before in other times of history. However, we must underline again that seldom do we win a soul to the Lord Jesus Christ through this kind of apologetic witness. Probably Apologetics' greatest asset is that it could stop the mouths of skeptics and critics as far as argument is concerned.

"The same polls mentioned above say ninety-one percent of Americans believe there is no such thing as absolute truth. This poll was taken of those eighteen to twenty-five years of age. Even more sad is that seventy-seven percent of those who call themselves evangelical Christians believe that there are no absolutes.

"It is the firm conviction of this speaker that the great doubts and denials being placed against Christianity at this time are more because of the presence of the neo-christian apostasy in the land rather than the accusation that Christianity, inherently, has passed its day of credibility and faith. That this credibility is now found in the balance of the scales of reason alone, indicates the Bible is no longer considered to be the Scales to measure Christianity and authoritative truth. Wanting to help, then, as historic Christian believers, we must endeavor to give to others some plausibility for the Christian Faith, because of damages religious faith, while we rely solely on the power of the Word of God and the Holy Spirit to do the work in their hearts. The following passage from the Bible is our guide and strength:

But sanctify the Lord God in your hearts: and be ready always to give an answer to every man that asketh

you a reason of the hope that is in you with meekness and fear: Having a good conscience; that, whereas they speak evil of you, as of evildoers, they may be ashamed that falsely accuse your good conversation in Christ. First Peter, chapter 3, verses 15 and 16.

"As I have presented in my writings and lectures before, we are experiencing an 'Eclipse of Hope' in our world. If we are only seeking the 'relevance' of the visible church for its institutional survival in the earth, there is probably a permanence in our 'eclipse of hope' in the public arena of life yet before us. The institutional church is a church that has learned to function without the power of the Holy Spirit and the Holy Scriptures, but simply survives through a working of 'relevance' with an evil age in an antichrist time. This is an apostasy which yet uses Christian symbolism.

"All the way back to our most ancient literature, the 'myth' form of literature has been recorded in many books, monuments, and scrolls. The world has returned to the propaganda 'myth' again. However, this time, we must face some questions of concern about two 'final frontiers.'

"Will the final frontier of 'doubts' be words themselves? Are there any words from any of the books and minds of the men of the world, from all history, believable? If not believable, credible? If not credible, plausible? If not plausible, erroneous? Is there a book of words, anywhere in the world, in its entirety, believable? If believable, are the words refutable or irrefutable? If irrefutable, are they infallible? And inerrant? Were they written by man? or by God?

"Is there a second final frontier of Reason itself? The greatest loss to human reason is the rejection of any absolutes and objective truth. Are words merely floating islands, drifting aimlessly? If the very presupposition upon which man builds his platform for such a fatalism about reason, is invalid and fallacious, then the superstructure, so-called, is also only unreasonable chaos. It is this chaos, every time, that destroys the elements of law, order, design, purpose, and beauty, without which there is no reason at all. A human, so-called paradox, will contradict itself every time because it all stands within itself—a state of immanence. So, the above statements negate and contradict themselves. A revealed paradox, as in the Holy Scriptures, can maintain validity where immanence and transcendence exist with Almighty God. Without God there is only the sleep or death of reason.

"There was a story told in old Oxford town, when I was a student there, about three men who were considered to be very honest. Notwithstanding, they had met, along with a fourth friend, at the Bodleian Library. The urgency of their conversation concerned a missing Porter of the University. The three honorable friends said they saw the Porter earlier that day. Witness One said he saw the Porter standing before Carfax Church as the clock struck 1 PM. Witness Two said he had seen him passing before St. Mary's Church, blocks away, as the clock struck 1 PM. Witness Three said he had seen the same man on the steps of Christ Cathedral, more blocks away, as the hour was striking 1 PM. A fifth man had been listening and began to question the three witnesses in doubt. The fourth man responded: 'No, my three friends speak the truth; it must be the clocks which are off.' Yes, we live, once again, in a day when the clocks are off, but no one wants to question them, only honest men.

"A final word must be said in conclusion to these two questions on which I have taken so much time in our Forum. (a pause)

"There is a word now being expressed and studied by some writers identified as 'antilogocentricity.' That very word strikes hopelessness for all books, all communications, and all other expressions of man. The word itself should be translated as 'against words as being central to meaning.' Is this the place we desire to be, against the centrality of words themselves? This simply indicates the destruction of all words. Will man end his own existence giving a final encomium only to despair? As one unpretentious individual, I do not want to live without the lifting of 'the eclipse of hope' from my own life. Only God's infallible Word promises such a lifting power for hope. Man's encomium, through his own thoughts and practices, should be to the glory of God and not to his own despair in the loss of a valid literature." (Although the audience, in response to this presentation, did not clap their hands, yet there was a united chorus of 'Amens' and 'Yeas' for Gabriel's extended answer. The deans and many in the audience stood to their feet. A general pause ensued.)

Dean Ussher stood to pose his question.

"Dr. Parsons, I also would like to bring two of your statements together for one consideration. Give us your appraisal in your words concerning the demise of denominational identities and the loss of the separation of state and church.

"My beloved Dean, both of your questions should be placed together as you have indicated so well, but I certainly trust that I will not take the amount of time I did before. (a general chuckle from the audience.)

"The great, popular success of the mass religious movements of the 1980s and 1990s brought religious man to a greater enjoyment of the mass meetings than his own church attendance. Gradually, it reversed to such a degree that presently seventy-eight percent of professing Christians, whether Charismatic or Ecumenical or Roman Catholic, attend the mass crusades and healing services, while only nine percent attend, with any regularity, their own church services. This statistic is an increase from previous years. The ecumenical spirit has overtaken the theological and denominational ear and audience. We must acknowledge that the fault lies in the surrender of the historic denominational Protestant Reformation Bible doctrine and pulpit to the easier believism of the mass crusades. Every evidence indicates that this change was not a deepening of the New Testament 'apostles doctrine' of salvation 'by grace through faith.' A general apostate condition has prevailed through the mass meetings, and it has effectively brought its people to the ecumenical identity.

"Of course, when this condition all started with the neo-evangelicals at the helm, and the neo-pentecostal Charismatics following, no one ever dreamed that it would come to this—to be an ecumenical move back to Roman Catholicism. It has been a gradual departure from the historic Christian Faith. The neo-evangelicals, at their beginning, only desired to dialogue evangelical truth with the academic liberals and neo-orthodox scholars. However, the neo-evangelicals could not keep their dialogue from becoming a fellowship with their enemy. Then, after the neo-evangelicals realized what they lost in the rejection of the 'inerrancy' of the Holy Scriptures, the landslide could not be brooked and they realized it had gone too far. Now, the neo-evangelicals still do not call themselves 'liberals,' but with a little compromise from both sides they have united under the tag of ecumenists. Evangelist Willie Wheyman is presently identified fully by his own colleagues as an 'ecumenical evangelist.' Of course, his admittance of belief in universalism with Dr. Ronald Shullman underlined the matter back in 1997. He had already made many concessions, substantially, back in the 1990s.

"While this has been going on, especially and gradually since the early 1950s, the political and economical world has been festering for a global world. They believed so much would be accomplished through international trade and politics. Instead of fighting 'hot' and 'cold' wars, the politicians believed that 'political peace' could be achieved by uniting together through international trade. The United Nations Order has been for a long time supporters of the environmentalists and the control of the family through a parental-planning legislature, along with other civil and human rights. Civil and human rights no longer are racial in their benefits; they have become weapons to whip the world into slavery under a singular political power. The powers that be, both ecclesiastically and politically, are also given over to the popular ecumenism of the time.

"In reality, therefore, the governments of the 192 nations which were in the earth in the twentieth century had to give way to the greater purposes of the whole world. The separation of state and church had to be changed to a church dominated by the political state.

Dr. J. Lee Davidson, one of the deans, raises his hand for a proper interruption addressed to Dr. Parsons.

"Yes, Dean Davidson."

"Pardon me, Dr. Parsons. I thought that the two questions which I desired to raise were most appropriate right here at this juncture, and I did not want it to pass without a very definite address from you in resolving all of these things together."

"Of course, Dr. Davidson. Please proceed."

"Thank you. (a pause) In your opening statements you mentioned the 'underground church,' the 'Jewish Problem in the Middle East,' 'the shift of commerce' from the Pacific Rim to the Middle East, as well as the 192 nations and a personality rising in America as well as Romanism. Would you bring those aspects into your remarks at this time?"

"Yes, Dr. Davidson. (a slight pause) I will commence with the presence of the 192 nations which existed in our twentieth century as identified in the United Nations Order roster.

"We speak in history of the decline and fall, but not the death, of the Roman Empire, which commenced in 410 AD when Rome was sacked by the Goths under Alaric. However, there survived in that fall, something like broken pieces, certain nations in the world which continued down to our twentieth century; approximately 192 of them have been recognized to date. Until the end of the twentieth century, the United States had been known as the most economical yet wealthiest nation in the entire group of nations. Internationalism has changed America's centrality to a great degree, and it started when England and Europe lost their economic position with America, and the East Coast seaports shifted in their importance to the Pacific Rim by the end of the century. All of the Orient and China were now open for the international trade markets.

"However, because of the Persian Gulf, leading up to the

Tigris and Euphrates rivers, the Red Sea, the Suez Canal, the Mediterranean Sea, the Aegean Sea, etc., the accessibility of international trade, as well as the common markets of the world, was joined in Europe. The Middle East is where the forces are concentrated.

"Therefore, with the longest tension of nations, in modern time existing between the Jews and the Arabs, the Middle East is also the center of 'The Jewish Problem' and the Arabs. This struggle is on the verge of being solved because of the influence of a singular man who is rising, politically, in the United States. Also, there are undertones of unity between this individual and a leader rising out of Roman Catholicism. The propaganda of the media is thoroughly supportive to these two personalities, and they are being pushed forward with much hope in the solving of many, many horizontal problems of the world powers and the populace of the world. As Christians, we need to keep our eyes on these matters and give ourselves much to prayer for the world. It is our deepest conviction of the time that these matters are a part of Biblical prophecy and its connection with the Second Advent of the Lord Jesus Christ back to the earth.

"These two personalities, one from the West and the other from the proximity of the Middle East, could be understood as either a fulfillment of the return of Biblical 'Babylon' and 'Rome,' or two personality-powers, political and religious, in the process of educating the world to two others who will come as the last two world leaders before the coming of the Lord Jesus Christ. In view of the fact that my interpretation of the 'trends' and 'driftings' of history are not at all intended to name the personalities of Biblical Babylon and Rome, more familiarly known as Commercial Babylon and 'Mystery Babylon,' I am only alerting us to the educational principles we need to recognize at this time by which prophecy might proceed even for another day. I do not announce dates and explicit personalities, but rather certain Biblical conditions of the times and prophetical personalities.

"This may be illustrated in the example of the prenatal period of the child. Just as the mother knows there is a child in her womb, without actually seeing the child, so there are evidences in the world, as prophetically exampled in the days *before* the flood, that a judgment time must come from God. Many circumstances are shaping up in the nations of the world today that fit some of the likenesses of the prophecies of the Bible. It was the days *in* and *after* the flood that were so devastatingly visible and judgmental to the work of the Lord. We are at least realizing the prenatal period of that coming judgment which marks the 'times and seasons' which are revealed, First Thessalonians, chapter 5, verse 1; and which are familiarly known to be involved with the Antichrist and the False Prophet in prophecy. Revelation, chapter thirteen, verses one and eleven, respectively. And yet, no one knows the 'day or the hour,' Mark's Gospel, chapter 13, verse 32. There will be other Biblically-revealed signs of the actual beginning of 'the Day of the Lord,' such as God's Christian *restrainers* before those days, Second Thessalonians, chapter 2, verse 7, being taken away to the clouds. First Thessalonians, chapter 4, verses 16 and 17. Then, after that, 'the man of sin' will be revealed to the world, also known as 'the antichrist,' Second Thessalonians chapter 2, verses 3, 4, and 8.

"The later action and influence of the Antichrist will be revealed as 'a beast from the sea' of the multitudes of peoples, Revelation, chapter 13, verse 1; then, there follows, 'the beast from the earth,' possibly the religious section of the earth, which is a little more stable than the 'sea,' and he will give glory and honor unto the 'beast from the sea." These two 'beasts' should be understood as The Political Antichrist and The False Prophet, undoubtedly related to 'Babylon' and 'Mystery Babylon,' respectively."

Dean Dawson stands to give the next question.

"Dr. Parsons, our Christian hearts have been strengthened through this Question Forum today. We thank God for the clarity of this session to our hearts and minds. You have given us safe and sound words from your heart, and most of all you have carefully underlined it all with the Word of God. (a pause; Gabriel nods his head in acknowledgment of him.)

"Being the only psychologist among our beloved deans, I wanted to ask the question concerning your expression 'controlled world-wide education.' What exactly do you mean by this phrase and also give us a background history to our modern social studies so prominent in our time."

"As you well know, Dr. Dawson, modern sociology is not as scientific as our studies in mathematics or physics. Mathematics and physics are exact sciences, and wherever they are studied we see quite a precise and perfect universe. We keep in mind, however, that there is chaos here as well, yet physics with computers brings us to the ability of dropping a spaceship into the target of a three-foot square.

"In the social studies, or sociology, we are dealing with man and his behavior, and the perfection is not quite that simple. Man is a fallen creature. If physics tells us that the universe, for all practical purposes, may be worked out according to law, order, design, purpose, and beauty, then sociology clearly tells us that man is something less than a perfect masterpiece. In sociology we are only using the study of human behaviorism as a solution for human behaviorism. That will not stand as a viable solution. It is like the sick healing the sick. Of course, we Christians would immediately say that man's imperfection is the result of a positive and total fall into sin and rebellion away from God. In the sciences, we are encouraged to believe all is well in the universe; in the social studies, there are no perfections.

"There was a time under the old Oxford learning process that the studies of man demanded the classics as received from the Greeks, in which all studies were held accountable to law, order, design, purpose, and beauty. Matthew Arnold is remembered in our time as one of the first spokesmen in the Oxford system, after he became first chair in English literature in 1857, to speak of the demise of former classical days. However, it was in 1882 that his boldness of venture launched a powerful commentary of the times when he delivered a famous lecture from his chair at Oxford, in which he stated that 'a hundred years hence there will only be a few eccentrics reading letters and almost everyone will be studying the natural sciences.' His word 'letters' referred to 'a study of the classics,' which he said would be no longer a part of the academic learning process of education. This became the watershed which ushered in the 'neo-education' of the social studies, and made the academic world more secular. He was substantially saying again that reading, writing, and arithmetic were to no longer be the frame of reference for our studies. This would include that the McGuffey Reader influence was to cease. Or, that the day for the application to learning was to no longer be through the classics.

"There followed men like Horace Mann, John Dewey, and William James who brought us deep into the application of the studies of Freud, Jung, Roger, and a host of others in the new fields of sociology, genetics, and evolution. Instead of raising students to the level of the tested and proved classics, the system would lower an education around the individual and his level of learning and then grant him "a social promotion' in his academics to enter into society as an adult.

"Sociology has failed in that it extends no permanent ability to lift man from his sinful state, and it accepts only a secular world for mankind. The old system did at least reason the need of ethics, morality, character, and certain absolutes in life.

"The failure has become so great that society can no longer bear sufficiently the responsibilities of even the horizontal life and family. Therefore, the governments of the world have inherited the liabilities of the problems of mankind and are forced to provide at least a crawling form of socialism in some parts of the world, and even a galloping condition would be found in communism as demanded in other parts of the world. No wonder the Bible reveals the coming of 'the mark of the beast' for man's need to 'buy and sell.' But for the citizen that takes that 'mark' he will have surrendered his soul to the incarnate Satan in the human body of Antichrist. Revelation, chapter 13, verses 16 through 18; and, chapter 14, verse 11.

"As a result of these unleashed irresponsibilities, a global condition would damage the environment as well as the social strata of man. This insufficiency would bring an unbalanced work-load to others which, in turn, would bring many other problems which would result in the need for the world powers, politically and religiously, to pay the bills for the human race. In view of the fact that it is impossible for man to perform such a task, and because man has left God out of his world, the world powers must become world forces to control man in all things. Of course, the direct judgments of God will be brought to the earth during those days.

"We are in desperate need of our sovereign Lord, who created the world and gave us His precious, merciful providence. However, until sin is dealt with by grace through faith, the problems will continue, as will crime, poverty, selfishness, disease and drugs."

Dr. Wilmore rises with the next question.

"Dr. Parsons, esteemed president, I have two questions which follow the previous question dealing with 'Social Studies' as well. (pause) You mentioned in your opening statements, numbers 8 and 9, concerning a 'forced universal peace' in our time as well as the need of 'correctional institutions' and 'control institutions.' Give us a further explanation of these seemingly contrary situations prevailing simultaneously in our modern world."

"Yes, thank you, Dr. Wilmore. (a pause) The prophet Daniel speaks of the final antichrist person to appear at the end of history, the Book of Daniel, chapters 8 through 11, with certain characteristics of his political power easily identified. Among them are the following: he will be 'a king of fierce countenance, and understanding dark sentences, shall stand up.' Chapter 8, verse 23b. Also, 'he shall destroy wonderfully and shall prosper, and practise, and shall destroy the mighty and the holy people. And through his policy also he shall cause craft to prosper in his hand; and he shall magnify himself in his heart, and by peace shall destroy many: he shall also stand up against the Prince of princes; but he shall be broken without hand.' Chapter 8, verses 24b through 25.

"Although there are other passages in the remaining chapters of Daniel about this coming antichrist, to answer Dr. Wilmore's question, the passages we quoted are most appropriate.

"Let us enumerate them again: first, he will destroy wonderfully; second, he shall destroy the mighty and the holy temple; third, he will cause craft to prosper; and fourth, he will use peace to destroy many.

"This is a claim of a world-wide personality who will use destruction 'wonderfully'; he will use destruction of the 'holy'; he will cause the craft of 'deceit' to prosper'; and he will use 'peace,' falsely, to bring destruction. These are wicked actions made by antichrist against the world. These words 'craft,' 'destroy wonderfully,' the 'holy,' and false 'peace,' are good words, but for bad things. This is how he will 'control' the world; this is how he will speak of 'peace,' or false peace. These words will be received by the populace believing them to be good for them. We have seen some of these things under communism in earlier days of the twentieth century in America. The Korean War brought 'brain washing,' which was a weapon against the people. The implementation of only that which is apparent, such as 'wonderfully' and 'holy' and 'peace,' is uncovered to be deceit and lies. This is false peace, false wonder; this is most deceitful to the people. This has already been initiated; it will proceed to greater destruction for the people."

Dean Joseph Paul Parsons stands for the next question.

"Dr. Parsons, in your statement concerning the ecumenical union of all religious fellowships in the 1990s, you made special emphasis of the title of a universal 'Christendom,' designated as 'liberals' and 'moderates.' Give us the definitions of these words and the implications of this observation you have faithfully presented of our immediate time before us."

"Thank you, my son and respected colleague. (pause) The word 'Christendom' has several superficial renderings such as 'Christians collectively,' or the 'Christian world,' or even

Christianity, per se. However, the most historic representation is realized by taking the final syllable of 'Kingdom' and placing it at the end of the word 'Christ' — 'Christendom.' It has also been associated with the word 'dom,' the title of a monk in the Benedictine, Carthusian, Cistercian, and certain other monastic orders. As an English suffix it refers to 'domain,' 'kingdom,' 'collection of persons as officialdom,' 'rank' or 'station,' etc.

"In its most historical situation with historic Christianity, it becomes associated with Roman Catholicism's finally appropriating the claim that the Pope possesses the 'Keys of the Kingdom of Heaven.' It is this meaning that has finally brought the word, 'Christendom,' to be the final title of all Christianity to the final ecumenical union of the apostasy against historic Christianity — 'Christendom.'

"The final form is appearing in the earth: historic Christianity became a neo-christianity in the twentieth century. After the historic theological denominations from the influence of Reformation Christianity came under the modern ecumenical movements through the Charismatics, or neo-pentecostalists, they changed and joined the liberals of the Council of Christian Churches. This resulted in a return to fellowship and union with Roman Catholicism.

"Now, in the twenty-first century, the total amalgamation has resulted in 'Christendom,' the only religion acknowledged by the world system of politics and the parliament of religions. With this one religion in the earth, 'Christendom,' they hold the 'Keys,' and all other religions must bow to this international state-religion authority. Remnant Christianity is being reborn in the earth, and every Biblical Christian must take his stand for the Lord Jesus Christ. Within 'Christendom' itself, one may be a 'liberal' in his theological interpretation of it, or even a 'moderate,' but in either of the two positions one must abide under the authoritative powers of the state-religion and its definition of the same. Once again, we are reminded of the days of Pharaoh and Nebuchadnezzar and Darius. Their decrees became the total authority of the religion of their time. The underground church is being born; another remnant movement in the earth."

Dr. Parsons concludes this response to the question of his own son with deep sobriety. The audience senses that soberness with a short atmosphere of prayerfulness, as Gabriel leads them to "The Throne of Grace."

The "Amen" returns the audience back to the fulfillment of the purpose of the occasion.

Dr. Evangeline Parsons rises from her seat among the deans and goes to the microphone which was designated for her for the final question of the Forum.

However, as she comes forward, the audience being alerted through the program bulletin of which Evangeline was deliberately not given a copy, stands to their feet as two ushers come quickly down the central aisle toward the area of the chancel where Evangeline is to speak. She, of course, waits because of the approaching surprise which originated by the faculty, staff, and students for the academic year, 2000. The two ushers are carrying two large sprays of 'white day lilies.' These were the kind of flowers Evangeline walked another aisle with to marry Gabriel.

Evangeline, in her gracious way, received the flowers and responded with a tearful gratitude to the ushers and the audience. Without explanation, she knew the meaning of the flowers and why they were presented to her that day. She indicated to the audience to be seated. All the while, Gabriel stood by his microphone, knowing that this presentation would take place. Before Evangeline could speak further, Gabriel spoke.

"Dr. Evangeline, you are the only dean that received flowers today."

"Yes, Dr. Parsons," Evangeline responded, "I am the only dean that married the president."

The audience once again erupted, but this time with an outburst of joyous laughter.

"Did you have a question for the Forum today, my dear?" continued Dr. Parsons to his wife.

"Yes, dear. I have a question of a kind to make. Your tenth statement at the beginning of the Forum concerned the sad plight that has come to the meaning of 'evangelism' and the loss of its historic meaning in our time. The name that was given to me by my beloved parents was 'Evangeline.' Since the age of thirteen, when I was saved by grace through faith, this namesake has often encouraged me in my Christian life. We rarely hear, any more, in the public assemblies of the modern religious crusades, anything said about the words 'evangelism' or 'evangelical.' These two words, just a few years ago, were often mentioned in many contexts of daily life from professing Christians to the public media. Through the eyes of my own heart of primitive Christianity, I do not see and hear the Gospel of my childhood in the public arena of the new-religion any more. As a simple soul, at the age of thirteen, I wept my way through to the salvation and conversion of my soul to Jesus Christ. I confessed my sins that day, repented, and accepted the Savior. I am so glad the Lord laid this ministry upon my dear husband's heart to pray for the whole world and endeavor to bring people back to the historic Cross of Calvary.

"It was a genuine blessing for me, today, as I saw my beloved husband greet each one of our individual friends from the thirty-one other Interlude Bases around the world in our early morning prayer meeting. I heard with my own ears of the souls being led to Christ, individually. The words 'evangelism' and 'evangelical' are still among us in their New Testament meaning and faith. I hope that my own little name, 'Evangeline,' will always remind me of these precious truths.

"And to the inquiry of my beloved husband, Dr. Parsons, my question today resounds to you who are present in this Sanctuary: 'Is everyone of you in this audience a genuine historic Bible Christian? It is my prayer that you are indeed. (a pause) Thank you for being with us for this triumphant occasion for Christ in the first year of the twenty-first century."

Dr. Parsons extends a prayer with Evangeline's question prominently made to all. (a pause) Gabriel gives an invitation for sinners to come to Christ. The two new senators, recently elected to the United States Senate, as well as four new congressmen, come forward to the chancel altar to accept the Lord Jesus Christ. The congregation remained standing as twenty-three others come forward to repent of sin and accept the Savior. (a pause of the new converts to Christ before they return to their seats)

Dr. Parsons then gives a request for the delegation from the thirty-one Interlude Bases to stand and come forward to the chancel altar and face the audience in the Whitefield Sanctuary. There were about seventy-eight in the delegation. Another prayer was given in their behalf by Dr. Parsons' son, Joseph Paul.

The congregation, with hearty voices sing joyfully, "Jesus Saves."

Dr. Parsons called for Senator Charles Baker, a member of the Board of Trustees, to come forward to the pulpit above the chancel and give the benediction.

His prayer resonated to the hearts present in a brief acknowledgment to God, as follows:

"Our Heavenly Father, we serve you today being keenly conscious of two great privileges in this life. First, we serve you because you are our Lord and Savior Jesus Christ. What a privilege. Secondly, we serve our fellowman through serving the government of our beloved, historic country of the United States of America. This is a privilege as well. We have sung and prayed, since our Christian childhood, 'God Bless America,' and you have graciously done that over and over again through our over two hundred and fifty years in existence. We now enlarge our prayer, O Lord, and add this plea: 'God Save America.' May you, in these dark days, give us Thy goodness and mercy and wisdom until we see Thee face to face. May hope spring up in our hearts and in the earth, as the joy which makes full our cup of life against any hardship ahead. (a pause) In Jesus' Name. Amen."

The audience disbursed with reverence, but not without friendship and Christian delight.

Gabriel, that evening, late, in his beautiful home, wrote

the following national hymn in the Key of F and 4/4 time.

God Save America

God save America; God save us we pray;
    God save America; we humble ourselves today.
There can be no real blessing now,
    While in our sins we live.
God save America;
    Thy pardon and grace to give.

God bless America; we prayed this before.
    God save America To worship Thy Name the more.
There can be no real blessing now,
    While in our sins we live.
God save America;
    Thy pardon and grace to give.

I love America, and God I obey.
    God calls America 'Repent now without delay.'
There can be no real blessing now,
    While in our sins we live.
God save America;
    Thy pardon and grace to give.

In future days ahead, may God give us peace.
    In truth may we be led to know mercy will not cease.
There can be no real blessing now,
    While in our sins we live.
God save America;
    Thy pardon and grace to give.

Chapter Twenty-seven

The Wilderness

(2007 AD)

The twenty-first century arrived in an extremely busy, prosperous world. Global proportions were eminent; all human activities were ubiquitously rendered. The initial international upsurge of the economy of the world brought a great optimism for a long-term wealth in the earth. If you had taken a spaceship for a personal vacation or occupational need in technology, which was now possible, and were away for seven years around the moon, you would have returned to a strange world. You would have easily realized a great difference in the word and spirit of the people, their immoral pleasures, their expensive entertainments, their new professions, and the loss of the old-fashion family.

It was a world more psychic with less emphasis upon physics; it was a world of increased impatience towards one another, and less respect for character and sympathy with human beings and natural things. True Christian spirituality, as once evidenced in some public affairs of the past, was all but gone. Many of these former benefits to mankind were now replaced with forms of Nimrodian idolatry and spiritualism. Visible signs of the occult were everywhere present in the public—at the airport terminals, down in the subways of the metro-media, as well as in book and department stores, and anywhere literature was sold.

Dr. Gabriel Talmadge Parsons had just returned to his Georgetown home from the organized "Sinai Base" of his ministry, which was the newest Base to be born to the present number of 128 Bases in the world. Many of them were small. Times had become exceedingly desperate for Christians. More and more political pressure was being brought about by international forces as a result of the liberals and moderates of Christendom—the state religion. Biblical Christians were being considered as radicals and revolutionists to the international government, but at this point they were still in their infancy in size and number. The old religionists, who sometimes called the Remnant Christians "bigots," did not remember that the etymological dictionary described a bigot as a "by-godder." This term was rooted in the days of the reformers who, often on the verge of martyrdom, would respond, "by God's grace I will endure"—thus, "by-godder." In view of the fact that the word "cult" carried with it a better meaning in the occult of the time, yet "sect" or "lunatic fringe" still lingered in the vocabulary of the day when referring to historic Christianity and the Remnant.

Gabriel had been to the Sinai Peninsula, in the wilderness area, where he had delivered 107 lectures and sermons in 28 days to 11 gatherings, averaging 1,000 Jews in each group. Once again, Gabriel was witnessing to historic Christianity, and this time it was to the Jews. A large number of them were "saved by grace through faith" during those days. Most of them had never read of the New Testament Scriptures, but were now being instructed in the New Testament through Gabriel's messages. Gabriel went expecting "a firstfruit" from the Jewish people to accept the Lord Jesus Christ as their Lord and Savior. But Gabriel knew that this sheaf of "firstfruits" would undergo a great test, and it meant everything that they would endure with the Holy Scriptures in their hearts and minds.

Dr. Elijah Goldstein, professor of Old Testament history in the University at Jerusalem, invited Gabriel to come. He, with a number of his associates from several areas around Jerusalem, had become genuine Christians from Gabriel's outreach witness for Christ through the InterNet. They had labored long and hard for the gathering of these groups of Israel to hear Dr. Parsons. The lectures were to be delivered in three particular areas of the Sinai Peninsula, where available assembly warehouses were used for the various congregations to come.

Dr. Goldstein is now a revered Christian from an orthodox-Jewish background, a scholar in the Holy Scriptures, in his seventy-eighth year of age, strong in mind and body. He had been a distinguished Rabbi over an orthodox synagogue, but recently was excommunicated because of his Christian conversion. A young Christian Jewish boy of sixteen, from Ramallah, three days' journey from Jerusalem, told Dr. Goldstein about Gabriel's InterNet Christian witness. Dr. Goldstein was amazed by the boy's knowledge of the Old Testament, from which he had memorized all of the Old Testament prophets. The young boy, whose name was Samuel, used only the Old Testament to persuade Dr. Goldstein to contact Dr. Gabriel Parsons through International InterNet. Dr. Goldstein did just that, and Gabriel led him to a genuine conversion through the Lord Jesus Christ. Dr. Elijah Goldstein had become a primitive New Testament Christian.

Dr. Goldstein had such an influence throughout the state of Israel that there were Jews who heard Gabriel's messages from various religious interpretations of Judaism. They included the Reform Jew, who does not believe in a coming messiah, and probably not God; the Conservative Jew, who does believe in God, but some of them do not believe in the coming of a personal messiah, but interpreted the messianic passages of the Old Testament as a religious renaissance in the world through the Jews. Of course, the orthodox Jew, who believes in the coming of messiah and that the Old Testament is inerrant, inspired, and infallible in its revelation and authority. Some Zionists attended the meetings of Gabriel at The Sinai Base, too. The Zionists are those who serve the land

and property of Israel and reflect a larger segment than the Jews themselves. They share responsibility to the *kibbutzim*, designated communities, chiefly agricultural, but including even artist communities, etc., organized under collectivist principles.

These were a refreshing blessing to Gabriel because he remembered back in the mid-1990s that a public declaration had been made by the orthodox Rabbinical authorities that it should be understood that only the orthodox Jews are the real Jews of the nation of Israel and the Old Testament. There had been some controversy over the pronouncements, but Gabriel thought it was necessary for this distinction to be made in Israel. As far as theology is concerned, the orthodox Jew is from the only group of Jews that stands on good ground to see the messianic hope. Of course, the Word of God can still do its work, as Gabriel saw in the lecture services in the Sinai Peninsula responses. Wherever the Old Testament is believed, man stands on a better ground of accepting the Lord Jesus as his Savior than any other present religious position other than historic Christianity.

So, at this time the orthodox Jew was drawing opposition, but it remained fertile ground for the Gospel to be preached. More and more orthodox Jews, because of the distress of their own nation and problem in the world, were seeing more clearly that their hope of a messiah to come might be superimposed upon the historic Christian's faith in the Lord Jesus Christ of Nazareth, a Jew. It was the "Six-Day War," of 1967, that placed the orthodox Jew in religious charge of the city of Jerusalem itself. The Reform Jew, however, controlled the University system of Jerusalem.

Back in 1969 Gabriel remembered a story told by a Reform Jewish professor of the Hebrew University in Jerusalem. During the "Six Day War," of 1967, he was a captain in the Jewish army. He said he did not believe in God at that time. However, the young army soldiers under him were assigned to take the city of Jerusalem in that war and particularly the Holy Mount of Moriah. These young orthodox soldiers met for a prayer meeting the night before the war was to commence. Early the next morning the captain met with them for last-minute details concerning the taking of the Holy Mount in Jerusalem. The captain was dismayed that there was no secret way in which to approach the Mount. One of the young soldiers spoke-up and informed the Captain that during the prayer meeting the night before, he remembered that there was indeed a tunnel that he had played in as a little child. The captain inquired the location and the size if possibly a small jeep could get in there. The young man said it was brought to his mind during the prayer meeting where the tunnel entrance was located and that it was big enough for jeeps to go through. The captain acknowledged to his men that formerly he did not believe in God. However, this incident made him consider that this could not be an accident for a soldier to just casually remember this in a prayer meeting; it was no accident either to remember it that particular night in prayers; and, that this remembrance was the only means they had to actually take the Holy Mount. That captain believed in God from that day on and was now witnessing it to Gabriel and others two years after the war was won. He reasoned that this could not be luck or fate, but it must have been of God.

Gabriel rejoiced in the Lord to see that the Gospel of the Lord Jesus Christ, the Messiah of Israel, was reaching the Jews directly at this time. There had been a few Jews in the world who had accepted Jesus Christ in the twentieth-century, but never in this number before. Of course, the orthodox Jews had always believed in the coming of their messiah, but down through church history it was very rare to meet a Jew who believed that Jesus of Nazareth was the fulfillment of their hope of their messiah. But now, "The Jewish Problem" in Israel, was to be solved in a hopeful settlement of "peace" with the Arabs through the human instrumentality of the American world leader. This American Political Leader had come to the conclusion that the problem in the Middle East and around the world was religion. To him religion had always been the entire problem of human history. So, now that there was a one-world government, that power of religion must be stopped simply by legislating one state religion, from the political state itself, and bringing into a union all the religions of the world. This American Political Leader had a great insight into the religious moods and teachings at this time in history. He saw that religion was already universally ecumenical in desiring certain goals in life anyway.

Evangelist Willie Wheyman had, as the singular most important individual in the world, brought this ecumenical force together. His message included Christian, Jew, Pagan, Heathen, Moslem, Roman Catholic, Greek Orthodox, Russian Orthodox — all. The American political force was also in place for a World Empire, and it was thought that this was a golden time for a state-religion to be born. Both Egypt and Babylon had accomplished religion dominated by state before in history. Heretofore, it was not known that such an ecumenical possibility was available. This was the greatest historical moment in all the times of world civilizations. The religious impetus of the twentieth century had pursued presidents, kings, popes, dictators — all political entities and geographies. The religious doctrine espoused by the ecumenists was universalism, and so the American Political Leader would advise the United Nations Order and the Global World Powers to adopt the religion of universalism and give it the name of "Christendom," which should be adequate in the union of all religions. As a result of this stroke of genius he was made Secretary General of the United Nations Order, retaining his presidency of the United States, and afterwards he was given an international title: "The American Political Presidium Leader of World Order." The nickname would be "APPL," commemorative of the "apple" which tradition had given to the name of the forbidden fruit of the Garden of Eden. The "APPL" had brought the world to one religion — it was now believed. Of course, "apple" is not the actual fruit mentioned in the Bible of "the tree of the knowledge of good and evil," but only an ancient tradition. Back in the twentieth century, all nations had progressed to certain statutes of limitation concerning the ordination of ministers and other church policies and charters for existence. "APPL" simply desired to extend these authorities and their respective powers of the past into the Global World Government. The APPL was the nearest step towards the coming of the final Antichrist.

The Moslem world was so much involved in international trade that they, too, would adopt this expediency for the business and commercial world. Their own religion would be tolerant and bear the strain of the religious clauses for the sake of their own enterprises. Of course, all the twentieth century religions that had been talking for the last 50 years of a hopeful coming of a "Christ," among their own kinds of "prophets," were a part of the present belief of a world leader. Some of the stronger religions that joined the state-religion simply believed that when it was necessary, they would rise up to defend their own religious survival in the future. However, the American Political Leader also knew that the Islamic world also had used Islam merely as a state fixture rather than its being religious within itself. At least this was true in some of the Islamic nations. The pantheists and the animists were already involved in kinds of religions and many gods and did not mind adding another god or other gods. They were adaptable to universalism even if they did not believe in it. "Christendom" also omitted "Jesus of Nazareth" as the "Christ."

The historic "Jesus Christ" was not the touchstone of "Christendom." All religions were looking for "Christ," a Savior, a deliverer, a leader, for their political, social, and economic survival. The American Political Presidium Leader was able to devise this seemingly compatible idea of religion into a workable resolve of "The Problem of the Jews" in the Middle East and the world. Adherents to the state-religion, with its new laws and powers, knew that there would be remnant groups still persisting in their own "orthodoxy" of religious things. This was particularly true of the orthodox Jew and the orthodox Christian. However, as the Christian ecumenists, so the Jewish nation: they both did not object to compromise if it brought them to their own desired end and purpose. The word "Christendom" would satisfy the greater influences of the world, for the word "Christ" stood for more than a human messianic leader, which could include him as a political leader. The American Political Presidium Leader would simply advise that the "remnant" groups be dealt with by a more patient, gradual control or genocide.

Because of the state-religion there was an increased reverent study of the Old Testament being pursued more now by the Jewish people and Gentile Christian influence. This solution to the "Problem" of the Middle East was not the usual talk of a mere "accord." The problem had to be solved through the genius instrumentality of the American political world leader whose aim was to destroy all religions except the state-religion itself. Gabriel was beginning to believe that the Jews' "veil" of judicial blindness of interpretation of their Scriptures was being lifted for them to see the Messiah, the Lord Jesus. Second Corinthians, chapter 3, verses 13 through 16. They were not only back in their Homeland; they were seeking their Biblical God. Back in the late 1990s it had become law that proselytizing or evangelizing the Jewish citizen was forbidden in the state of Israel.

However, now, with the World Government being a state-religion, the laws of all groups were brought under the religion of the state. If any group accepted some distinctive religious concept, it must serve the state through Christendom, either as a liberal or a moderate. The new global state brought all religions under the state. This placed both the historic Christian as well as the orthodox Jew in jeopardy. That was another reason why Dr. Goldstein desired the lectures from Gabriel for the Sinai Peninsula areas.

Before Gabriel left Sinai to return home, there was a dedication service of "The Sinai Interlude Base," with the ordination of Dr. Elijah Goldstein to that ministry as a pastor for this his new fledgling flock by Dr. Gabriel Parsons. With the new laws of the state, no Jew could be ordained as a rabbi without a registered organization through the government, and neither could anyone now be ordained to the Christian

Faith by any person who did not have authority to do so from some government department of authority. When Gabriel organized "The Lodebar Base," in Georgetown, back in 1974, Senator Charles Baker was instrumental in gaining a charter and government privilege in Washington, D.C., which was twenty-six years before the year 2000 and international law.

After the World Government was organized in the year 2000, all previous authorities and commitments were accepted in World Parliamentary Law. The new law, however, was not retroactive in spite of the state. That was included in the new law, but all had to fit their religious concept into the state-religion. Pastor Goldstein knew the burden now placed upon him in accepting Christ as his Savior, but he and his dear wife, Ruth, who had also become a Christian, were determined to fulfill the will of God before the Lord Jesus returned. From this ordination and organization through Gabriel, Dr. Goldstein had an open window to be the legal pastor of a circuit of these three congregations in the three areas in the Sinai Peninsula where the lectures and services were arranged. They did not have to have a permit from the government at this time because of the legal guardianship of Gabriel's ministry recognized in America. The new World Government accepted these previous regulations, but would deal with the religious problems later if they arose. Also, Dr. Goldstein would now be able to ordain other Christian ministers for the evangelism of Israel.

In each of the three areas in the Sinai Peninsula about 300 to 350 Jewish people had accepted Christ and thereby a congregation was formed under Pastor Goldstein. This circuit of congregations would represent almost one thousand Jewish Christians. All were to be baptized as soon as possible by Pastor Goldstein and his pastor-associates. All three of the congregations would be known as "The Sinai Base" of "The Divine Interlude Ministries," yet each of the three areas was identified as The Enoch Church, The Mosaic Church, and The Elijah Church, respectively. Yes, it was agreed that the word "church" would continue in the language of Jesus as Gabriel had required.

Gabriel was clear, however, that some time in the future,

at the second coming of Jesus Christ, the word "church" would be dropped in New Testament prophecy, because after the saints depart, the state-religion will have institutionalized the new Christendom to a completely false religion of the Antichrist, and therefore the word "church" would be no longer authentic for New Testament believers. Also, Gabriel emphasized that after the first stage of the second coming of Jesus Christ, it will be clear concerning the actual and final religion of the Antichrist. Gabriel noted this with clarity, and continued to maintain that the present state-religion was only the beginning to which the final religion would be made manifest. The quotation was as follows:

> ...Neither shall he (Antichrist) regard the God of his fathers, nor the desire of women, nor regard any god: for he shall magnify himself above all. But in his estate shall he honour the God of forces: and a god whom his fathers knew not shall he honour with gold, and silver, and with precious stones, and pleasant things. Thus shall he do in the most strong holds with a strange god, whom he shall acknowledge and increase with glory: and he shall cause them to rule over many, and shall divide the land for gain... The Book of Daniel, chapter 11, verses 37 through 39.

Dr. Goldstein was deeply impressed in reading the Book of Matthew, chapter 11, verse 17, that Jesus spoke of the Jerusalem Temple as being "a house of prayer for all people." Could it be possible that the Jewish Christians and Gentile Christians were to be a part of that? Also, Dr. Goldstein mentioned the scripture about the coming of the New Jerusalem down from heaven, the Beautiful City, after the Millennial Reign of the Lord Jesus, that there was "no temple" there. The reason being: "the Lord God Almighty and the Lamb are the temple of it," Revelation, chapter 21, verse 22.

The Gentile concepts and traditions were to now give way to "The Nazareth Call" of Jesus back to the Jews as well as all Gentiles. In the New Testament it was the Jewish Christians who had to give way to the Gentile Antioch Christians at the first point in historic Christianity. This was the benefit of knowing Primitive Christianity in the light, also, of the controversies of Reformation Christianity. The Body of Christ was more important in its identifications than denominations now. Theological Systems would not be the beginning basis of Christian identification; the necessary "badge of courage" would be a call for the "fundamentals" of the Gospel of the Lord Jesus. Scriptural separation was now a very necessary doctrine in view of the Biblical revelation of the final empire prophesied as the Antichrist powers and the "mark of the beast" as espoused by the False Prophet. This separation from this apostate condition of the world demanded such a position.

The teaching and the larger view of theology would come later in the pastors and the teachers under the leadership of Dr. Goldstein and his Elders. Gabriel would not hold any further burden upon The Sinai Base. However, it was made clear that orthodox, historic Christianity was the identity of this spiritual birth and movement in Israel. Gabriel had already, through the lecture days, been sending appropriate information through the InterNet ministries, and would continue to do so. Gabriel, before he arrived at Sinai, had already worked out "The Base Workbook" for such possible ministries around the world. Gabriel's ministry clearly presupposed that there was no going back to any earlier understanding of the Holy Scriptures; the entire Bible was now the full revelation by which the Christian was to be known. The Jew was not to retreat to the Old Testament alone. The New Testament fundamentals were to take precedent over all orthodox earlier theological systems. As Gabriel's language interpreter, Dr. Goldstein carefully conversed with him at length so as to be accurately understood in the Hebrew language. Dr. Goldstein could speak fluently both Hebrew and English.

It was at this very juncture that Gabriel and Dr. Goldstein earnestly discussed Fundamentalism. Very graciously, Dr. Goldstein desired to have Gabriel reiterate, carefully, the Fundamentalist Movement. Although the state was particularly monitoring anyone or any groups identified as fundamentalists, yet, at this time, it was only extending warnings and regulations against any public belief of religions against the state-religion.

Gabriel informed Dr. Goldstein carefully that Fundamentalism was born across denominational lines through the very Body of Christ in the late nineteenth century. This movement, historically, transcended denominational theological systems and polities and policies. Dr. Goldstein was greatly relieved by Gabriel's words because he had labored under the impression that Fundamentalism was believed by some in Israel as being denominationally oriented if not a sect with problems. Dr. Goldstein made it clear; he never thought of the movement as a cult. He did, however, think of it as being too denominationally oriented for these desperate times. He told Gabriel that since he had become a Christian he had wondered if he was correct in the strong denominational bias of Fundamentalism he had detected in his readings.

It was at this point that Gabriel shared "the burden" he had had in Fundamentalism which he had sworn to himself he would not tell unless God revealed it to another Christian heart as witness of the truth of it. It was at this point in time, Gabriel confirmed to Dr. Goldstein the singular "burden" he had about Fundamentalism back in 1957. Gabriel had prayed back in those days that God would reveal it to all fundamentalists because he believed they must see this themselves, or the burden would destroy the honorable movement. Much of Fundamentalism had already fallen away to the press of the government. But the Fundamentalism that did remain — a very small remnant — was stronger than it had been. In that emphasis there were customs and manners that had been brought into Fundamentalism, since its first generation, by the denominations; and those who observed Fundamentalism naturally thought these were a part of Fundamentalism itself. Some fundamentalists did not see these customs and manners as a denominational distinctive alone but as a necessary Biblical pattern for the Body of Christ. Some of the differences dealt with church polity and government; other differences concerned doctrine. That was indeed most unfortunate to Gabriel and Dr. Goldstein. Gabriel believed that denominational tags would finally give way for a more primitive Christianity because of the coming of Antichrist, "Christendom," and the return to the underground church of the End-time. Therefore, Fundamentalism would be committed, ultimately, to martyrdom. Gabriel marked well the prophetical light which would become more clear from the Holy Scriptures at this time. The "wilderness" of prophecy, Revelation chapter 12, verses 6 and 17 was to be understood literally. Gabriel believed that this prophesied "wilderness" was the Sinai Peninsula.

The two most important items which denominationalism brought to Fundamentalism were as follows: first, by the second generation of fundamentalists, some began to be against the intellect, art, and honorable scholarship; and second, they had brought the wrong kind of music into Fundamentalism. Also, Fundamentalism was sometimes more militant than magnificent, but both were in great jeopardy. He knew that the war before them could only be won with God's wisdom. The situation was that acute. Much of Fundamentalism as it had been known was now destroyed. The tag continued to have some meaning, but the actual remnant was exceedingly small. This explained to Gabriel why fundamentalists, formerly, had little Biblical or spiritual position concerning church and family contemporary music, or even art in a family's life. Gabriel remembered that the catacombs had primitive art upon its walls during the time of the flight of Christians underground. That is really where Christian art began and it reveals how important art was even in the days of persecution and martyrdom.

Gabriel believed that it was necessary for God's people to study the history of music in the Holy Scriptures. In his lectures he would present it something like this. The Old Testament reveals two golden periods of music, and during these two golden periods God's people lost it with great sorrow.

The first golden period was in the time of the exodus from Egypt, during the days of Moses, when Israel went to the wilderness with "borrowed" gifts from her friends, the midwives, as well as the borrowed knowledge of music and other fields of learning from "the wisdom of Egypt" itself. The first manifestation of music was undoubtedly a result of the Egyptian teachings of music. That began to change, however, as God revealed to Moses, Miriam, Joshua, Barak, and Deborah concerning the use of musical instruments and songs. It becomes clear by the time of King David that, in addition to the rudiments of Egyptian earlier music received from their "wisdom," God would now reveal to Israel, through His own spiritual wisdom, a concept of music unprecedented anywhere among the peoples of the earth. It would come by revelation and Israel's natural gifts granted through creation and the immediate work of the Holy Spirit in the birth of Israelite children and the birth of Israel's true song. God would also salvage something from the "wisdom of Egypt" as well.

The second golden period was in the time of the Psalter which reveals the Golden Age of King David and his Son, Solomon. Musical instruments, musical notation, musical nuances, musical superscriptions of interpretations, all consorted to a beautiful and prolific time for Israel. Large choirs and orchestras were linked with at least three composers and/or conductors. We are talking about thousands directly involved in the voices and instruments of music. This influence continued on down through Israel's history until the time of the Babylonian Captivity. In the time of the Captivity a great tragedy came into Israel's history of music from which there has never been a recovery to this day of some aspects of music which were lost. The Biblical record should be noted here:

> By the rivers of Babylon, there we sat down, yea, we wept, when we remembered Zion. We hanged our harps upon the willows in the midst thereof: For there they that carried us away captive required of us a song; and they that wasted us required of us mirth, saying, Sing us one of the songs of Zion. How

shall we sing the Lord's song in a strange land? Psalm, chapter 137, verse 14.

In these words we find "The Lord's Song" distinguished. It is very obvious that "this song" was lost because Jerusalem was no longer the home of Israel geographically and spiritually. That spiritual environment had ceased to be. When the judgment of God came upon Israel and they were sent away to Babylon, they lost "the Lord's song" because of their spiritual backslidings away from God. Gabriel believed the very same thing would happen over and over again in history whenever God's people were spiritually fallen back from God. Note the Record again:

If I forget thee, O Jerusalem, let my right hand forget her cunning. If I do not remember thee, let my tongue cleave to the roof of my mouth; if I prefer not Jerusalem above my chief joy. Psalm, chapter 137, verses 5 and 6."

Gabriel interpreted this with care, as he would say:
"It is clear: if God's people lose the spiritual place of Jerusalem, they lose 'the Lord's song'; if they 'forget' Jerusalem, 'the right hand' will 'forget her cunning' use of the harp; and the 'tongue' of 'the Lord's song' will 'cleave to the roof of' the mouth; and the 'chief joy' of music and worship will be destroyed."

He would continue:
"Whenever we see God's people, or those who profess to be God's people, singing other songs than 'the Lord's song,' then we know they have lost their own spiritual Jerusalem and their spiritual privilege of communion and fellowship in the worship of God. Bad music in the sanctuary is an index to both the singer and the place in which they sing their own worldly, carnal songs. Rock and Roll music, with all of its fallen rhythm forms, along with the contemporary craze for similar forms, whether 'contemporary Christian' or the 'Gospel

Song,' are all a part of a lost sanctuary and 'the Lord's song.'"

Gabriel continues:

"So, the great loss of music, historically, was made manifest after the Babylonian Captivity. By the time of the writing of the Septuagint, the Hebrew scholars could no longer really know the musical meaning and interpretation of the musical instruments or the musical terms, and especially the superscriptions before the Psalms themselves, as were kept in the Septuagint translation. These superscriptions, formerly, had great meaning to the overall musical abilities and spiritualities of Judah before the captivity from the times of David. The words of the terms may be known only slightly by the very value of the root-meaning of the unusual Hebrew spellings, but the musical meaning passed away with the loss of Jerusalem to their daily spiritual lives.

"However, God preserved in His Word the superscription words before a number of the Psalms, even down into the time of the translation of the King James Version, as a mute testimony of the loss of the great music of the days of King David. In this, God reveals what will happen in the loss of the treasury of great church music when God's people get away from true worship in the place of the true House of God, the Church. The very word 'Selah' witnesses against us, along with other terms, as we linger around only the echo of what was fully meant in its use for Judah.

"We, too, in our generation, are in danger of losing our own great legacy of English, American, and other hymns if and when the congregation and special singers of God's people lose their spiritual relationship with God and His Word. No wonder we now hear and follow such 'dinky,' 'worldly,' 'charismatic' songs; we have lost our way with God.

Gabriel continues:

"The present musical distress in our time, with church entertainment instead of worship, is once again a repeat of the loss of 'the Lord's song' in our churches. We are not only suffering loss from Israel's lost song, but the second historical loss also stems from the Reformation-Renaissance-Classical ethic and its law, order, and design which flowed out of the classical form into the great English hymnology which has been translated into the tongue of wherever a missionary has gone. In the Reformation, Martin Luther brought congregational music back to the people of the church. Though grieved in the destruction of art in the church by some who went too far in their protests against Rome, yet Luther took all religious idols out of the House of God."

With the assistance of Dr. Goldstein in translating the words of the old, traditional English and American hymns, Gabriel arranged for the publishing of a Christian hymnbook for the Jews.

Gabriel did believe back in the 1980s and 1990s that a great change would come to Fundamentalism — changing from its early militancy to a more suave position towards those some had formerly and dogmatically condemned. Yet he heard no one who repented of their earlier positions. Gabriel believed that if a brother changed publicly from what he had formerly and publicly identified himself, he was obligated to give the reasons for his changes in public.

Gabriel continued to emphasize to Dr. Goldstein that he knew of no other remnant movement in the earth who had a basis of unity of doctrine other than the fundamentalists. Gabriel repeated his often-mentioned observation that he believed with all his heart in the fundamentals as well as a number of the fundamentalists. However, when it came to the "ism" of Fundamentalism, he saw many weaknesses. Gabriel believed that it was necessary for Dr. Goldstein to observe this matter and that Gabriel must reiterate his own "burden" in Fundamentalism. Good men, even with their peculiar personal weaknesses, may be in fellowship with each other, but never must they betray the Biblical orthodoxy of historic Christianity.

However, the denominations in the United States had left the doctrinal emphasis in their theological system, whether Calvinism, or Wesleyism, or Arminianism, or Lutheranism. They did not retain their historical Reformation Christianity.

Reformation theology was necessary, but at this early point in the evangelism of the Jews, Gabriel thought they had enough to overcome and would leave the greater doctrinal emphasis for later teachings after they had been established.

It should be understood, however, that the early persecution of the twenty-first century was arising from the old enemies, who used to be friends of neo-christianity, who use to be friends of Fundamentalism as well, against those who believed in historic Christianity. They were Charismatics and members of the former Council of Churches of the liberal constituency rather than the political state religion of the government itself. Controversy was high from the old neo-christian ecclesiasticism, even at the time before the World Government had formed, but now had become fully identified as the liberals and moderates of Christendom. They had even compromised their own original compromises, but now openly against the individuals of Fundamentalism standing true to the historic Christ.

Gabriel believed that this, when it was to be ultimately fulfilled, was the "woman" prophesied as the institutional church, rooted in Christendom, that had entered into the apostasy and would ultimately ride on the back of the scarlet-colored beast. Compare Revelation, chapter 12, verses 1 through 6, and chapter 17, verses 1 through 7, which was also identified as "Mystery Babylon the Great, the Mother of Harlots and Abominations of the Earth." Of course, at this point, this was only the preliminary preparations to be fulfilled at the coming of the Lord Jesus both in the clouds and to the earth. The present World Government was the scaffolding for the stage; when the stage was ready, the scaffolding would be taken away, and then the prophecy of the "woman" and the "beast" would be fulfilled.

The state had adopted the use of Christendom, but was, at this point, simply ignoring the remnants still remaining at that time, but the United Nations Order resolution for World Government would ultimately be enforced. However, martyrdom had already commenced for many Christians. Gabriel did not know, nor did he predict, the length of time left. He desired to take advantage of his remaining "last days" and set forth his Bases in the world for the salvation of Gentiles and Jews before Jesus came. The Sinai Base was a real break through to the Jews for Gabriel, and he, from the very beginning, believed that God desired that small groups come together in the form of primitive and historic Christianity. This was God's strategy, using small groups, as He had before — remnants. If they had been great in number, then the World Government would be more anxious to dispose of their influence in the world, and more would be martyred. The "Apostles' doctrine," from house to house, breaking of bread, unselfish giving, preaching and prayers — that was God's primitive plan then, and for this time as well. Christianity began that way, and Christianity, seemingly, would end that way.

Just as the Sadducees and the Judaizers were the first to bring persecution for the fledgling New Testament church, so it was the same now in God's plan for the remnant-bases, brought about by Christendom upon the Jews and the Gentiles. The Jewish enemies were first, before Rome, in persecution and martyrdom of Christian believers in the New Testament. So, now Jewish Christian believers would first be persecuted by their national brothers, the Jews, and the Gentile Christians by the former neo-church world. There had been 80 Caesars; there was now the 265th Roman Pope. Roman Catholicism was the apostasy in history that adopted the pagan, Babylonian apostasy which began with Nimrod, who was the first Anti-Messiah Pope, or Head, after the flood. His father, Cush, was the first Anti-Messiah political leader of the world. Roman Catholicism was simply a Christian counterfeit of the Old Testament paganism mixed together with a perverted form of Old Testament and New Testament Christianity. Christendom was a part of the false state-religion, as Nimrodian religion was a counterfeit of the Abrahamic Faith that came through the messianic line of Shem to Abraham. But God always had a remnant.

The historic summary was most revealing: Roman Catholicism was conceived in Babylon; Rome was born in Italy;

Rome was reared in the Medieval Church; Rome was refuted by the Reformers; Rome was renewed by the Neo-Ecumenists; Rome was to be restored by the Apostates and the Antichrist; but Rome would finally be refused at the Advent of the King of Kings, the Lord Jesus Christ, at His second coming back to the earth. The Battle of Armageddon would settle all political and religious conflicts and affairs in all the world. Then, Christ Jesus would renew the earth for His Millennial Kingdom.

Since the complete compromise had been finalized in the year of 2001, of all the neo-christian groups to become identified with the state under Roman Catholic influence, only remnants of historic Christianity pled against the merger. The remnant also pled for the complete freedom of their Christian Faith, just as Moses pled with Pharaoh to let God's people go to the wilderness to have a feast and worship with their own God, Jehovah.

Pope John Paul II, the 265th pope, as claimed by Romanism, had died in the year of 1999. The pope that succeeded him died shortly after that in late 2004. He was the 266th pope. The present pope, named "Pope Peter the Second," became pope in early 2005, after a long, heated, debated struggle for a successor from The College of Cardinals. It took seven months to select the new pope. He is the 267th pope identified by Romanists.

Only the first pope identified by the Roman Catholic Church was named Peter. No other pope had taken that name until this 267th pope. Of course, the Reformers declared that there was no true history that identified the Apostle Peter as a pope. Pope Peter the Second was head not only of the members of the Roman Catholic Church, but was also appointed by the World Government, through the original resolution of the United Nations Order, to have religious leadership over all Christendom. Rome had now learned to translate their old history into the casuistry of their blending themselves into the state religion of the time. This they had done many times in their history of the past.

This, evidently, was the first stage in the direction of simply bringing all religions under a single religious leader while pacifying the "die-hards" about giving up their historic distinctive of Romanism. But the situation was exactly the same, on a smaller scale, as illustrated in history past between the Archbishop of the Anglican Church, in the 1990s, in desiring to resolve their historic breach by returning the Anglican Church back to the Roman Catholic Church under Pope John Paul II. Even the Queen of England desired this reconciliation then. So, Gabriel expected, in the near future, that an amalgamation would come between the Roman Catholic Church and Christendom, under the new political World Government, and the world leader, who was yet standing in the political wings of power, from America. The Romanist group simply became a part of the moderates and liberals of Christendom, but with their large influence building the Antichrist religion of the time.

This would be true of any other groups or religions, whether animist, pantheist, Eastern Orthodox, Western Orthodox, or sect or cult of any other religion in the world. The desperation of the times as well as the political pressure being placed upon the multitudes on the earth brought an advantage to the political state and brought out the genius of the American Political Presidium Leader.

Gabriel was a distinct part of Remnant Christianity of the time, identified with historic Christianity in the twenty-first century. There were indeed other remnant movements even larger than those in the ministry of Gabriel in the world, and it was his hope that an underground InterNet would be achieved to link up these forces in such a manner as to be strengthened by God to be a "Watch" for their evangelism and survival, according to the precious will of God. Gabriel had become acquainted with a growing number of them. There was now a world population of ten billion people. Gabriel often prayed for his InterNet Ministry because he feared the World Government would ultimately shut down access of any religion in this international opportunity.

Centuries ago a Roman Catholic priest had divined a

382

prophecy of a complete list of future popes, giving their names
with an attending claim of insight to each of them. His name
was Malachy. Roman Catholic history gave him a place of
prominence, and it was in the twentieth century that once
again his so-called "prophecies" surfaced and were made
known. He designated that there would be only 267 popes in
history, and that the last pope would be named Peter. His
"prophecy" also identified that the 264th pope, John Paul I,
would only be pope for about 80 days, which was the exact
length of days between John Paul I and John Paul II before
John Paul II took the papal throne.

Maol Maedoc Malachy (1094-1148) was archbishop of
Armagh. His so-called prophecies, a series of symbolical titles
of popes from 1143 until the supposed end of the world, are
thought to be a late sixteenth-century compilation published
by Dom Arnold de Wyon in 1595. The choice of Malachy as
their supposed author is evidence for his fame in Renaissance
Rome.

Gabriel did not accept this as a genuine Biblical prophecy,
but rather the result of an apostate Magician as described
several times in the Bible, such as in the days of Daniel, chapter
2, verse 2. This is also identified in the Bible as one of the seven
forms of divination called "wizardry." The list is as follows:
an observer of times, enchanter, witch, charmer, consulter with
familiar spirits, wizard, and necromancer. The Book of
Deuteronomy, chapter 18, verses 10 and 11. Several suggestions
of interpretation concerning this "prophecy" have been offered
by Romanists in the present state-religion powers and other
contemporary voices.

First, some of those who saw the genius of the American
Political Presidium Leader would have interpreted such
possibilities that the coming of a World Empire, of a global
government, potentially under the leadership of the American
political personality of global political insight, might greatly
ease "The Jewish Problem" with the Arabs by outlawing their
religions. Then the office of the Roman pope might be dissolved
into the greater political state to keep other religions down

and the one state-religion in force. This interpretation calls for the termination of the need of a Roman Catholic pope just for the Roman Catholic Church, alone, and instead, a greater need in the global world for a state religion. This would lead to the rise of a "Prophet" of a higher order over all religions to assist in bringing about one religion by the political powers of the American political genius. There would no longer be simply a Roman Catholic Church; there would be a World-Wide Catholic, or universal Church, using the pope of Rome, because of the ecumenical unity that had come through methodological evangelism; and all religions would have found this unity also through a political solution rather than creeds, councils, reformation, pope, and charismatic revelations which finally emptied themselves into the doctrine of universalism.

Second, another political interpretation of the time, however, is posed by a more literal belief that the 267th Pope, Peter the Second, will be assassinated. This would be a political ploy by the American Political Presidium Leader for another political selection as one who would be the religious "Prophet." This in turn would be a leader for a more successful work directed by the American Political Presidium Leader throughout the world, thus removing the mere organization of the Medieval Roman Catholic Church from history as any future threat to the Global World Government. It was necessary to think that the political power was supreme; the religious power would serve and magnify that political power. However, even in that political theory, there was the desire to salvage Rome and popery as an instrument for the political cause, which would survive in the leadership of the World Leader, the coming Antichrist.

A third interpretation by others, as a corollary to the second, was that upon an assassination of the American Political Presidium Leader, history would be at the very time in actual fulfillment of the Book of Revelation, chapter 13, verse 3, and that his "deadly wound would be healed," or, more literally, he would be raised from the dead back to life and given honor and glory and religious support by the 267th Pope, Peter the Second. This supernatural event, not a resurrection, but rather a raising back to human life, would be a tremendous wonder to the fact of the power of that "Prophet," Peter the Second, who would adorn the wonderment and popularity of the political leader, and could be a Satanic power behind the raising from the dead of the "beast out of the sea" of the political multitudes. Thus, the last pope in history would aggrandize himself as equal in power by his support to the American Political Presidium Leader of the World Government, raised from the dead, as the final human world empire. Pope Peter the Second would then simply be the last pope in history because he lived at the time of "Day of the Lord" and the return of Christ back to the world.

Although Gabriel did not believe the third interpretation to be true at all, yet he firmly believed no matter how the interpretations were made, that the world was on the verge of receiving a man like the American, a greater, final Antichrist to lead the world government and dominate a universal religion that would be even more effective than Christendom. Therefore, through the genius-force of a political Antichrist, supported by a religious "Prophet," there would come together a great "New Age" movement across the entire earth. The final religion would be identified as Spiritualism—Satan's final counterfeit religion of historic Christianity.

The interpretations were so flexible that it was possible to hear the voices declare that the American Political Presidium Leader would be the fulfillment of the Holy Scriptures of the actual arrival of the last Antichrist, or possibly, more time was needed to generate through these events that this brilliant American politician could be only paving the way for the final Antichrist, another Person. Either there would be a lengthening of days for a more wicked political leader, with the American Presidium Leader only bringing an educational value for the world to be prepared, or the world was yet in need of another religious leader to be the fulfillment of the Holy Scriptures concerning "the False Prophet." Gabriel refused to finalize the actual identification of either one of the two international personalities — political or religious. Gabriel believed the time was very near, but possibly, yet another short time was ahead in the sovereign will of Almighty God. Here again, Gabriel saw that the first man or second man ahead of the Antichrist fulfillment of the Bible would have such a wicked way of deception that the series of leaders which led up to the actual Antichrist would be of little difference from the Antichrist himself. In fact, they did set the stage for him, as the False Prophet would, too.

Here again, Gabriel saw a number of international actions that could either be the actual fulfillment of the Bible, or, the proximity of two international personalities converging earlier in time for the benefit of both the Antichrist and the False Prophet. It was often in history you could see the pattern in the Bible of a good Pharaoh to a Joseph, preceding, and yet in a very fragile condition, leading to a wicked Pharaoh. The same thing occurred in the days of Daniel. Nebuchadnezzar was favorable to him, yet his grandson, Belshazzar, was most wicked, by whom Daniel was called upon to interpret the Hand Writing on the Wall. All of these observations could also be a part of the reason why the Lord Jesus refused to give any information of the "day and the hour" of His coming in two possible stages of that coming—first to "clouds" and then to "earth"—the Mount of Olives, Zechariah, chapter 14, verse 4. In the latter, Jesus would reign from Jerusalem for one thousand years in a renewed earth.

These presentations became the focal point of Gabriel's entering into the prophetical teachings of Christ. He was particularly desirous to use Matthew, chapter 24; Mark, chapter 13; Luke, chapter 21; I John, chapter 2; II Thessalonians, chapter 2; Revelation, chapters 1 through 6; chapter 12 and 13; and others. Gabriel believed there could possibly be certain prophetical personalities standing either on the stage or in the wings, readying themselves for the drama on the stage in a subsequent scene or act that would then, and only then, lead to the final Biblical Antichrist. One man only would finally fulfill the person of Antichrist, but there could be others who would participate strongly in his preparation. The same could be possible for the "False Prophet" as well.

But Gabriel was very clear that no one, but no one, was to know who he was before the "catching away of the saints" at the first stage of the Second Coming of the Lord Jesus to meet the saints in the clouds. He warned his audiences, everywhere, not to be anxious to interpret prophetical events on earth conclusively at this time. Following the Lord Jesus Christ and His Word was very important now as they drew very near to the coming of Christ. He especially warned of two things: first, Jesus had not returned to the clouds for His saints yet; the saints were still on earth, and second, Antichrist would not be clearly revealed until the saints left. Their presence in the earth restrained him from his open, "revealed" manifestation to the world.

Second, Gabriel warned his hearers to not be deceived by false prophets who may claim to know the actual time of the Antichrist and the False Prophet, or by others who would completely doubt any relationship with the days and the End-Time prophecies at all. Either position could deceive a person. Gabriel told his audiences that they should not accept a name for these two false ones; they were not to identify a known name with Biblical prophecies of Daniel's Last Week yet. It was dangerous to follow anyone except the Lord Jesus Christ. The answer was in the Word not in the voices around the Christian, or being sounded by the news media. Gabriel believed that his InterNet ministry was a God-given liberty for these fatal days, and seriously suspected that after the saints had been transported to the clouds to meet the Lord Jesus that the international electronic Internet might be closed to religious movements except for the state religion. Gabriel did not desire to emphasize but two events in a specific order concerning Christ: first, Jesus must come to the "clouds" *for* His saints, first, not to earth; second, Christ will only come to the Mount of Olives *with* His saints, when He comes for the Battle of Armageddon and to set up His Kingdom on earth for one thousand years.

Gabriel saw a distinctive dignity in the fact that Jesus, in His first stage, would not come to earth for the saints with the Antichrist on the verge of being revealed to that earth, or at least alive on the earth then. Jesus would not dignify Antichrist's day of self-revelation by being on the earth when Antichrist comes forth. Jesus would only come to the "clouds" in the "air" at that time.

Gabriel emphasized that the Christian was not waiting for the "sign" from Jerusalem, or the Jews, or the False Prophet, or the Antichrist. The saints of God would be waiting for the "shout" from heaven and the descent of the Lord Jesus to meet His saints in the air. Emphasis should also be made upon the "voice of the archangel" in the air, as well as the "trump" of God within the heart of each saint of God on earth. These three sounds would be exactly simultaneously rendered. They were not primarily interested in the long claims of the "order of all of the events" of the second coming of Christ; they simply must follow Jesus Christ through these dark and ominous days. Gabriel would only say he was a pre-millennialist, without giving any exact order of the details of the apocalypse.

Also, too many preachers were drawing upon their contemporary studies and reading certain things into their preaching and teaching of the time, and it was either misleading or false. Their contemporary studies were obscuring the Biblical clarity of the Biblical truth. Too much claim of the order of events could bring confusion. Besides, no one had enough light or revelation to distinguish between the outline of the Book of Revelation and what was to be revealed, through Revelation, at each seal, thunder, trumpet, or vial of wrath when the time exactly arrived for their fulfillment. Gabriel believed the saints of God were to have a "spirit of expectancy" just like the Primitive Christians had in the first century, A.D. It was called the "maranatha spirit" — "the Lord is coming again spirit!" This "expectancy" would come to each Christian who has the "Watch of Prayer" in his life. But God's reason for leaving the understanding of these things to only come at the point of their arrival of fulfillment was simply because every Christian must simply follow the Lord, obediently, day by day in order to be ready for the actual coming of Christ.

The thing that impressed Gabriel was that the distance between the last of the Gentile Church saints who could suddenly be "caught up to meet the Lord in the clouds" was to be close enough to the unsaved sinners who will enter the time of "Jacob's Trouble" that a personal evangelistic testimony could be given directly to the "left ones" ahead of the time of God's Judgment period. Gabriel believed that "Jacob's Trouble," Jeremiah, chapter 30, verse 7; and "The Great Tribulation Period," Revelation, chapter 7, verse 14; and "Daniel's Last Week of Years," Daniel, chapter 9, verse 27 were passages all indicative of the very same time in prophecy. The first may be measuring the longest of the Judgment Period, and the last measuring the shortest of the time at the end of the Judgment Period, and Jacob's Trouble with the Tribulation Period reaching back from the end to the center of the prophecy itself.

Too many, earlier, in a reasonable distance back from the year of 2007, might have thought that there was some clear line of demarcation between the "catching away" of the saints to meet the Lord in the air and the people afterwards, on earth, in the Tribulation when it began. No one is able to know who is saved, who is lost, or what is their motive, and exactly what is the line to draw for readiness for the catching away of the saints. God alone must judge this delicate matter, Himself.

Gabriel was even comforted by what he thought was an insight that the saints "caught up to meet the Lord in the air" would participate, indirectly, having personally known some of the "left ones." Having been given a personal "call of evangelism," they would be reminded by the Holy Spirit, when the breaking of the seals began, of what they had heard. This truth was implied when one of the living creatures said "Come and see." The Book of Revelation, chapter 6, verses 1, 3, 5, and 7. Thus, the testimony left by the saints in heaven, given while they were yet on earth, could speak through the memory of those left ones who would be saved in the Great Tribulation Period, "Come and see."

In other words, Gabriel saw the possibility of "The Divine Interlude" being applied for not only sinners to be saved before the living saints would be translated to meet the Lord Jesus in clouds, but also Gabriel's ministries could be reaching others who would become Christians later in The Great Tribulation Period after the translation of the saints. In other words, "The Remnant-One Ministries" of the "Divine Interlude" could reach the lives of sinners both before and after the departure of the ready-saints to meet the Lord in the air.

Gabriel gave one series of messages about the ministry of Noah: he preached, actually on both sides of the flood. He mentioned fathers and mothers who had prayed and taught their children before the parents died, but afterwards the children became Christians. Then, they met each other in heaven, later. However, Gabriel seriously pondered a grave problem. If those who were saved would be caught away to meet the Lord Jesus in the clouds, who would God choose to carry on the Interlude Ministries in the time of "Jacob's Trouble"? He prayerfully pondered this for a solution, hopefully, later to find an answer. He knew that only a sovereign God was able to give wisdom and take care of that time of need.

The second Sinai Base meeting was also scheduled for Gabriel and several of his own staff at the Lodebar Base to meet with Dr. Goldstein again, on another trip, for the purpose of seeking out and pooling all information of where the greatest persecution areas existed presently. It was now known that there were a number of other Remnant Movements earnestly serving God in the earth who were being led of the Holy Spirit and the Word of God in the same understanding as Gabriel and his ministries. The other ministries were not under the efforts of Gabriel, but they, too, had met similar individuals, as Gabriel had met Dr. Goldstein. God had established their own unique ministries as well as those of Gabriel. In fact, these other ministries, less pretentious, were meeting more people than the ministry of Gabriel.

Gabriel originally sought out Dr. Goldstein after he read of his persecution from the unchristian orthodox Jews. It was obvious that God had been dealing with Dr. Goldstein and some of his Jewish acquaintances before Gabriel led him to Christ through the contact on the Internet suggested by the

Jewish boy, Samuel, from Ramallah.   Gabriel read a short announcement of the conflict in a back-page of *The Jerusalem Times*. At that very same time, through the InterNet, Dr. Goldstein was endeavoring to get in touch with Gabriel. Gabriel rejoiced with him of his own acceptance of the Lord Jesus Christ of historic Christianity from the witness of Gabriel.   Dr. Goldstein experienced his own Christian conversion from personal sin and modern Judaism.

Gabriel also read, afterwards, of Dr. Goldstein's excommunication and religious death as enunciated by his Jewish peers. He was fired from his professorial chair at the University of Jerusalem as well as defrocked from his ordination as a Rabbi of his orthodox synagogue. They were orthodox Jews who had taught at the Reform Jewish University in Jerusalem. Gabriel took him into his own ministry afterwards. Dr. Goldstein was most grateful.

Although all international events implied the nearness of the End-Time, yet the physical persecution had not reached the full brunt of international law and enforcement at this point. However, martyrdom had become an obvious conclusion in the minds and hearts of Christians, and in certain places of the earth, where martyrdom was necessary for the political purposes, it was done. This observation, to Gabriel, necessitated sessions with Dr. Goldstein urging that they must search out information and print maps where the greatest and most serious catalysts were present in the world so that Christian missionaries might be sent to those hard-pressed religious areas. Also, the InterNet would be helpful to dispense the information. Gabriel could hardly believe that the InterNet was still an open avenue for the liberty of the Gospel. Undoubtedly, the present global government chose to keep the Internet open so that they might monitor, or try to monitor dissidents. It should be recalled that back in the 1950s and the 1960s the United States was endeavoring to monitor Russia for the similar reasons.

The Gospel was urgent in the places where martyrdom might break out. Already reports of martyrdom were being made in the more remote and crucial areas, too, as in those places around the location of the Global World Government in the Middle East.

If a person was to take a globe and stretch it out flat so that it would show the Western World on the left side of the map, the Near East and Far East on the right side, then one would clearly see Palestine and the Middle East in the center. That particular spot on the earth was where the religious persecution was most prominent. Gabriel believed the Holy Scriptures implied that in The Great Tribulation Period, actually, some of the godly Christians would flee to the Sinai Peninsula while others would flee to the remote areas of the world away from the Middle East. It was with this perspective that Dr. Goldstein and Gabriel would increase their contacts through the InterNet to set forth the geographies of the greatest persecutions. The orthodox Jews were already beginning to flee to the Sinai Peninsula, whereas the Reform, Zionist, and Conservative Jews were submitting to the state religion. Also, the Internet continued to serve any Christian or group of Christians desiring the message of historic Christianity in the light of the times.

The heaviest concentration of geographies where Christians were persecuted at this time, moving on the map from the Far East to the West, included: China, Tibet, Laos, Myanmar, North Korea, Mongolia, Pakistan, Afghanistan, Tajikistan, Kyrgyzstan, Uzbekistan, Kazakhstan, Russia, Iran, Oman, Saudi Arabia, Iraq, Turkey, Somalia, Sudan, Egypt, Libya, Nigeria, Angola, Libya, Algeria, Mauritania, Estonia, Latvia, Lithuania, Belarus, Ukraine, Moldova, Romania, Bulgaria, Hungary, Poland, Indonesia, Brunel, Vietnam, Bangladesh. Bhutan, Angola, Mozambique, Cuba, parts of South America, and North America. Propaganda declares otherwise, because state-religion prevails, and this is especially true in the Middle East as well.

There were Interlude Bases of Gabriel's ministry in the following locations: Northern Ireland, Spain, Switzerland, Singapore, Canada, Philippines, South Africa, Guam, California, Oklahoma, Maine, Georgia, Arkansas, Pennsylvania, and the Cotswolds in England. This was a very small portion of the need of the world. However, Gabriel was greatly encouraged as he heard of other ministries, much larger than his own, who served the very darkest areas of the world. It was Gabriel's desire to link all of these places together through the InterNet. He believed that Dr. Goldstein would bring great spiritual success to the divine Interludes. The Jewish Christians were acquainted with all kinds of persecutions; the Gentile Christians must also come to age in suffering and sacrifice for the Lord Jesus Christ.

After the second trip to the Sinai Peninsula of the ministry of Gabriel, along with several of his ministers, the Global World-Wide Government announced a very clear and strong resolution. There would be no more public preaching and teaching and evangelizing by the so-called historic Gospel of the fundamentalists or similar groups. The law specified the matter of "public proclamation" of the Gospel. The government, however, still preferred to give more time for the absolute enforcement against any religion except state-religion. They undoubtedly wanted to continue to monitor the Internet to know just where the Christian fanatics were located. This was the political psychology simply because ten billion people were in the world, and enforcement of law was a tremendous task.

The individual Christian groups were permitted to serve their own people through local congregations on their own property, but they would not be able to do missionary work away from their base to proselyte others. It was evident that the governmental police had been monitoring the flow of ministers and ministries across the world and that they desired to control religion without open uprisings and violence. However, there were any number of local spots where there were martyrs, but the news media effectively quelled any information by ignoring such matters.

This indicated to Gabriel that his own ministry would be circumscribed, basically, to the Lodebar Base, as would be true of all the 128 Bases identified with his ministry. It was clear that the smaller groups were the most effective because they did not call attention of the governmental powers. The other ministries, which Gabriel believed were larger and greater than his own, would be confined to the very same stipulations. However, InterNet remained open, and now Gabriel must direct that ministry more from his home and Anvil House.

Gabriel intended to use every remaining open-door to further his work, and he was encouraging all of his Bases, including the Sinai Base, which was legally under his ministry, to prayerfully perform a ministry as much as possible in accordance to law. It may be that it would keep open a channel for the ministry more, at least until the law increased its action against historic Christianity. Gabriel knew that all Christians in the world were at the very crossroads of the greatest change of laws against them as well as the greatest persecution ever in the history of Christianity and fallen man. He and Dr. Goldstein were in constant daily contact with these thoughts, and were endeavoring to send messages with a kind of codification or simplicity that would seem to soften the strength of their message; or, in other words, to speak and send messages over the InterNet with wisdom and cautious care. They prayed, every day, that God would give them more time to proclaim the Gospel. That was their singular purpose in life.

As the year of 2007 was closing, Gabriel and Evangeline became much burdened for LeVon Gilbertson. In following his success in World-Wide Evangelism before the Global World Government was established, he had become senior bishop of his denomination and had been seen on many mission fields of the world in his church capacity. He had had a private audience with the pope the year before the inauguration of the Global World Government. However, suddenly, Senior Bishop LeVon Gilbertson had dropped clear out of public sight. His regular daily newspaper syndicated column and monthly report and agenda of his travels around the world had been suddenly dropped. Gabriel had been extremely burdened for him and had endeavored to reach him through various communication resources.

While pondering and praying over these things, and in view

of the new advances by the government, Gabriel and Evangeline were having a personal burden for LeVon's family, his wife, his son, Gabriel Talmadge, and his wife. LeVon's son and wife did not have other children, and Gabriel Talmadge was LeVon's only child. At least, this was Gabriel's information, formerly rendered through LeVon's regular newspaper column. Sometime after a prayer session for LeVon, Gabriel was returning from a trip to California to finalize several details concerning the new religious regulations from the government, and had to make a change of planes in the Chicago airport. He went quickly into one of the restaurants there, and just as he was seated with his sandwich and hot tea, he heard a familiar voice. It was that of Gabriel Talmadge. He ran up to Gabriel Parsons and embraced him with anxious esteem. At first, Gabriel could hardly recognize him. He was somewhat haggard in appearance. This was the first time he had seen him since the quick acquaintance in Memphis in 1974. Gabriel quickly calculated the years; LeVon's son was about fifty-five years old. He wept for joy when he saw Dr. Parsons. He said:

"I only have a few minutes to catch my plane, but I believe God brought about our meeting here today. I want to beg you to contact my dear father. Write him, write him; I wish you could visit with him. He has resigned from all offices and duties this past year in both his denominational affiliation under the new laws of Christendom, and from the government state-religion conferences in Christendom, of which he had attended many. He has given up religion and God. He mainly stays at home, greatly depressed. He does not speak in any public function any more. Of course, I had to resign my own positions with him and the past denomination as well. I know what my problem is; I am not a Christian. It is as you taught my father. We knew something was wrong in Christendom, but we did not have a genuine conversion to historic Christianity as you called it. My dear father and I are both lost creatures from God. Dr. Parsons, I give you this address where he now lives. He just stays alone; he refuses even to own a telephone. Will you please write him for me? Will you promise me that? I must leave and catch my plane now. I believe God sent you to me today. My father and I have heard and read behind the scenes of your ministry of 'The Divine Interlude'. Thank God! I must leave now." (He quickly gave the written address to Gabriel.)

"I will do that, my son. I assure you, I will do that." (LeVon's son quickly embraced him again and proceeded on to his flight.)

Gabriel marked the time and date of this incident to thank God for now lifting his burden to a great degree concerning LeVon. It was 1:02 PM, December 16, 2007. They had parted as quickly as they had met.

At the 60th wedding anniversary of Gabriel and Evangeline, December 20, 2007, Gabriel and his family prayed earnestly for LeVon Gilbertson. After a season of prayer together for the Interludes around the world, Gabriel poured out his prayer for LeVon. All of his family were taking the burden to the Throne of Grace as well. When the prayer was ended, Gabriel told his family that he was going to write a letter on that day, using the address given him by LeVon's son, inviting LeVon to come and visit them at their home in Georgetown and see Anvil House and the Lodebar Base Ministries. Gabriel also invited LeVon's son and their wives to come with him.

After the letter was written Gabriel went to Anvil House to prepare another letter of instruction for the future of his ministry before the Lord. He left a copy of it in the secured pulpit drawer in Whitefield Sanctuary. He would also leave another letter on the hallway vestibule table of his home addressed to Rev. LeVon Gilbertson in case he might come one day soon and the Parsons be not home at the time of his arrival. He did not know if LeVon would notify him of his coming, or if he might just suddenly drop in to see Gabriel unexpectedly. In fact, Gabriel was not even sure LeVon would come to see him at all. Possibly, only his son, Gabriel Talmadge, might make the visit without his father and also see the letter if he had the key to Gabriel's home.

Then Gabriel returned home from Whitefield Sanctuary and mailed the third letter of invitation to LeVon, from the nearby public mailbox, using the address his son had given him. He told Evangeline and his family about the letter of invitation to LeVon as well as the two other letters: one in the pulpit drawer of Whitefield Sanctuary; the other on the vestibule table in the vestibule hallway of Gabriel's home.

That night, he told his entire family once again to pray for LeVon Gilbertson. Gabriel was eighty-one years old; LeVon was seventy-nine, almost eighty; and, Gabriel mentioned that he thought Gabriel Talmadge Gilbertson was about fifty-five.

Gabriel's family would have to leave for their respective ministries the following morning, very early.

In bed that night, with Evangeline, Gabriel took her hand and said,

"I love you, Evangeline, with all of my heart. You are the finest earthly thing that ever happened to me."

Evangeline responded:

"Thank you for loving me for so many years. I have asked you a certain question many times before, my dear Gabriel. I ask it again. 'How much more time do you think we now have left to love each other some more, Gabriel?'"

Gabriel said:

"As you know I used to measure it in years, then I changed to thousands of days, but then, my dear Evangeline, I measured it in hours. So, I answer tonight, darling, we have 'thousands and thousands and thousands of minutes' left, my dear Evangeline."

They both ended their 60th anniversary day by saying in unison, "Good-night, my darling."

Chapter Twenty-eight

The Shulamite

(Time: Unknown)

The last time Gabriel saw LeVon Gilbertson was May 19, 1974. At that time Gabriel was forty-eight years old; LeVon was forty-six. Over thirty years had passed in their separated lives from each other. The First Quadrennial Conference on Evangelism in the presentation of the seven bishops of the seven historical pentecostal denominations took place in 1954. Over fifty years had passed since that first session. The Fourteenth Quadrennial Conference was now receiving World-Wide acclaim as well as the other conferences by other denominational groups. However, these Quadrennial Conferences were now only something of a religious reunion because with the state-religion under Christendom, the only thing the denominations brought into the state-religion was a choice of being a liberal or a moderate. Of course, behind the scenes of some of these conferences was the hope of governmental change granting greater freedom of personal religious choice. But nothing on the horizon indicated such a liberty would return. Rather to the contrary, the laws were indeed increasing against any other exercise of such religious freedom.

Also, the large denominational influence through their various theological systems did not have any public showing to measure as an influence of taking a stand for historic Christianity and the Word of God. The former denominational churches gave liturgy notices in their church services which only amounted to an increase of symbolism of Christianity which was their strongest expression without receiving persecution. Otherwise, the message of Christ's coming into the world was merely to announce that His Sacrifice saved all the world and that everyone would enter heaven at the end of life. This is what all forms of Christendom were setting forth, but it should be understood that there were numbers of people who were still witnessing for the historic Christ in whatever statute of limitation they could. Some Christians were very bold in their testimony, too.

The original roots of universalism, per se, in America go back to the days of Unitarianism, a movement of liberalism. However, it should be remembered that Roman Catholicism had always believed in universalism. But in modern time, in Europe, at the beginning of the twentieth-century, neo-orthodoxy was a part of that heresy also. Karl Barth had brought to the front of neo-orthodoxy a theology that when Christ died, in the mind of God, He actually kept mankind from the fall itself in the Garden of Eden. In reality, according to Barth, there was only a shadow of a fall there; there was never an actual fall in the history of man. To Barth, a fall would have completely destroyed man and the world. It could be reasoned that neo-orthodoxy was a theology of "reverse universalism"; Unitarian liberalism, "historical universalism"; and Willie Wheyman's viewpoint, "ultimate universalism." Wheyman's view grew out of an international experience that brought out his "Gospel" in the source of God's love rather than God's grace. Therefore, the centrality of the Christian Cross of Jesus was to ultimately bring the souls of men to heaven by love, and it was not necessary to hear the Gospel from the Bible or even have the name of Jesus to go to heaven. The Cross was only a remaining symbol that all mankind was saved.

Of course, all public religion of the state had discarded the old Biblical and theological concepts of the Reformation period because it was believed that man had progressed either evolutionarily or intellectually or morally, beyond the old forms of former religions. This was simply because of the natural steps in the maturation of the human race. Although the government was a state-religion, the secular and the political powers were the essentials for its religious identity. Universalism was the necessary outgrowth of a long-time departure of the historic Gospel of the Lord Jesus Christ. Many compromises had made it so.

Everywhere in the world there was an expectancy that a "Christ,' considered as the height of evolved man, was in the world, either by preparatory resolutions of love and peace, or possibly, the man was actually present in the world, ready to enter politics or already involved in government. As it has already been acknowledged, some believed that the American Political Presidium Leader, APPL, with his world-wide popularity, had been suspected as such a man—a messiah, if you please. Evangelist Willie Wheyman had popularized all presidents, even those presidents who were known for their great immoralities and unbelief of the historic Gospel. Willie Wheyman actually expressed forgiveness for the immoralities of world leaders whether they repented and received God's grace or not.

Man was more and more being dominated by the occult of spiritualism, of which the New-Age Movement had been the forerunner back in the early 1950s. Both by a woman, Lena Nixon, as well as a man named Bengala Kremel, they had proposed through their own "illuminati" and "prophecies," so-called, that the "Christ" was already in the earth and had been living in a Pakistani community somewhere in Europe awaiting the time of the "unveiling," or "apocalypse" of himself to the whole world. It had been prophesied by Lena Nixon that he was born in 1963 and would be made manifest in 1999, but that date had been changed several times.

In those early days of the 1950s there was still enough Christian influence left in the world that books were written openly opposing the New-Agers from a Biblical viewpoint. However, by the end of the century, New-Agers were appearing even in the Charismatic Movement as well.

All of these earlier things had passed and, therefore, in the twenty-first century only Christendom remained in the public limelight. If there were any left among the liberals and the moderates who were still struggling for the truth of historic Christianity, it was not made known or proclaimed openly. However, the Christian remnants were at work for the Lord Jesus Christ. Christendom had become the religion of the world-wide, global populace, and the true Christians were going underground.

Gabriel, in more recent sermons and lectures in his travels to the various Interlude Bases, as well as on the InterNet Ministries, was emphasizing the New Testament identifications of Biblical doctrine of the centrality of Christ along with the coming of a final empire with its political leader and false prophet. He was also sounding forth the truth of the Second Coming of the Lord Jesus Christ.

He particularly distinguished John and Paul in the matter of the "Antichrist" and the "False Christ." Gabriel indicated that the coming world leader will be both "antichrist" and "false christ." He will be a schizophrenic world-deceiver in the earth and with his genius be able to be both antichrist and false christ. In other words, as antichrist he will be able to be against the historic Christ, or place himself "in the stead of" the Christ. At the same time, however, he will present himself as the historic Christ of the New Testament, with many claims of characteristics of that true Christ, and yet be actually false to that true Christ. He will present himself in opposition to the true Christ, and yet present himself as a form of the true Christ. Of course, this would be a counterfeit of Christ. This means that he will be all things to all men in all kinds of political and religious belief in all their various human environments. He will appear as Christ to some and as Antichrist to others — peculiar to the context in which different religions, formerly, might have believed. He did not ignore Christianity; but he did not endorse it, per se. He would be capable of thoroughly presenting himself as a protestant Christian, a Roman Catholic, a denominational Christian, a pantheist, an animist, etc.

This challenge to him is what will bring the world to wonder after him. There will have been no genius or brilliance in personality in history compared to him. He is the very height and embodiment of the highest fallen, satanic creature man will have ever known. This time Satan would be embodied in man, and as a beastly incarnate Serpent.

It had been the ecumenical hope of the past to be able to bring all religious bodies together, to include: the fire of the pentecostalist, the zeal of a baptist, the form of an anglican, the authority of a Romanist, the methodical life of the methodist, the reform of a Lutheran, the scholarship of the presbyterian, the transcendentalism of the pantheist, the fear of the animist, and all else into an ecumenical amalgamation of a world religion. They were never able before to do that. However, this coming political world leader would be able to achieve this resolve of mankind, both politically and religiously, at least for awhile until Daniel's Last Week of prophecy was finished.

Gabriel also distinguished the New Testament teachings of "the man of sin," "that wicked one," "the son of perdition," and "the beast out of the sea." The Man of Sin reveals that the personal Antichrist would be a perversion and a counterfeit of the incarnation of Satan in the flesh of a man, in complete possession of this Man chosen from the human race. Many believed him to be the reincarnation of a past evil world leader like Nimrod, Augustus Caesar, Nero, Hitler, or other, etc. In this, Satan hopes to counterfeit the incarnation and virgin birth of the Lord Jesus as well as the resurrection. This Man of Sin would also endeavor to justify his counterfeit through the misapplied teachings of the death and resurrection of Jesus through the prophecy of the "deadly wound that was healed" of himself.

"That Wicked One" has reference in the New Testament to "wicked Cain"—the sins of Cain against his brother Abel. The exegesis of First John, chapter 3, verse 12, is a bold statement in its literal rendering, "Not as Cain, who was out of the evil one, and slew his brother." The preposition, "out of" or "from," suggests an involvement with, or of Satan, directly, in the birth of Cain, as Eve had a temptation from the serpent that involved a deception. Some have even gone so far as to suggest that this is akin to what happened before the Flood, Genesis, chapter 6, verses 2 and 4. Gabriel would also note that this language of First John is the similar exegesis of Matthew, chapter 1, verse 20, except First John concerns the "Wicked One" instead of the Lord Jesus Christ in Matthew.

Others believed that "The Beast out of the Sea" was a prophecy revealing that the coming Antichrist of the future is a contemporary personality, as a particular, special person rising out of the sea of political forces and peoples as a singular wonder in the modern world. This prophecy is a Satanic attack upon Jesus as King of Kings. Of course, this will be a counterfeit of the power and authority of Satan becoming earth-bound through the forces and wickednesses of his time, but only for this short time.

Gabriel made it clear that this coming Antichrist was to be a man with a 7-year political plan, which could be announced in two 3½ year parts. The first part of the 7-year plan was to bring the final and complete solution of "The Problem of the Jew" in the Middle East, and win the world to his greatness as the Antichrist. Gabriel did not believe that the crisis of the Middle East would be settled until after the catching of the living saints away to meet the Lord Jesus in the clouds. In the aftermath of that The Jewish Problem was to be solved by the wicked greatness of the Antichrist. Besides that first priority there would be many other solutions extended by Antichrist powers in solutions for many, many parts of the world. He would extend a complete overthrow of all other religions and all other political forces. Yet, Gabriel made it clear that no solution granted by the Antichrist carried with it the kind of settlement that would come only when Jesus reigns for one thousand years from Jerusalem at the end of the leadership of the Antichrist and the False Prophet.

Gabriel indicated that Daniel's prophecy revealed that the powers of the north, the south, and the east would all converge upon the Holy Land. He understood, from the prophecies in the Book of Revelation, that those forces would be overthrown by the Antichrist with great power and authority. Gabriel requested a comparative study from Daniel, chapter 11, verses 5 through 9 as well as Revelation, chapter 16, verse 12. This would also harmonize with the fact that prophecy declares that the nations would be reduced to ten in number, like the 10 toes in Daniel, which were prophetically the same as the 10 horns in Revelation which would be reduced to seven by the powers of the Antichrist. Revelation, chapter 17, verses 9 through 12. Gabriel did not specify by the name of the modern nations, but we could think in the direction of Russia, the United Arab Republic of nations, and China as examples in our day. Daniel's prophetical geographies of "north" and "south" are revealed, chapter 11; and John's Book of Revelation of the "east," revealed in chapter 16, verse 12. These three directions should be interpreted from the position of Palestine. Any person who was able to subdue such geographical areas would certainly be considered to be a powerful political force as a world leader.

The 7-year plan might be understood with what is known as "Daniel's Last Week" of a 7-year length. That is what the "Week" refers to: a week or 7 years. Daniel, chapter 9, verse 27. In the "midst of the week," or after the first 3½ years, the Antichrist will go into the Holy of Holies of a Temple in Jerusalem, which he probably will build to satisfy the Jews earlier, and there deceive them as he proclaims himself as God. This, of course, will have a great effect upon the orthodox Jews, especially, who possibly believed, prior to that abomination, that the Antichrist was their true Messiah. Prior to that "abomination," they will have thought that the Antichrist was their friend since he solved "The Jewish Problem" in the Middle East. It may be at that time that these Jews, who had followed a "false christ," the Antichrist, will turn in desperation to God and accept the Lord Jesus Christ as their Messiah and look upon Him at His Second Coming back to the earth for the Millennial Reign.

There were three expectancies among the peoples of earth

at this time, but most of the expectancies concerned the horizontal events involving an immediate world leader who would bring victory and prosperity to the global world.

The first expectancy involves all of the preliminary personalities of the twenty-first century which only paved the way for this singular man. They had paved the way for a time of great optimism, and especially for the solution to the Middle East and the Problem of the Jew. This had become the central problem of the postmodern world. Many contributions had been made by the American Political Presidium Leader and his associates as being both the president of the United States and of the United Nations Order. However, although he had brought something greater than the usual "Accord" to the Middle East, there yet remained the need of a complete resolve of peace by the working out the effective laws for its implementation. Yes, it had gone beyond "Accord," but the people were restless with anxiety. They needed another confidence; possibly needed another leader. Their expectancy of such a man made them ready for such a man to come.

The second expectancy did lie in a smaller group of the citizens of the World Government who hoped for a change for a better individual religious choice. They continued in a memory as a result of the past echo of the better days of Christianity in the world. They remembered the earlier days of the evangelistic preaching of Willie Wheyman as well as the great Charismatic gatherings of the past. They sought the return of their Christianity of the twentieth-century. This still lingered in the nostalgia of the past. However, this same expectant group did not yet realize that their own ecumenical fellowships brought about by default of convictions linked with historic Christianity the downfall of the only opportunity that could preserve their freedom. This second group actually paved the way for a one-world political system and religion.

The third expectancy did reside in all the hearts of the true Biblical remnants of grace around the world, persisting in their proclamation and defense of historic Christianity, like the ministries of Gabriel Parsons. The "Call" back to Primitive Christianity as tested by Reformation Christianity was indeed being heard through the Bases strategically located, and still resounding through InterNet. The other remnant groups were still reaching even more souls than Gabriel's Ministries. Also, the underground church contacts and links together were being made with great unity and fellowship. The maps designating the heavy persecution spots of the world had helped Christians to see the power of prayer for others. Jewish Christians were still being brought to Jesus of Nazareth, the Messiah, in the old warehouses and brush arbor groves in the Sinai Peninsula. Word had reached Gabriel that Christians were fleeing to the Catacombs near Rome as the persecution was on the increase. However, it should be understood that the laws against the true Christians had not rippled to all the shores of the world in their intensity yet.

There were other Catacombs at Syracuse, Alexandria, Naples, and Paris besides the ones outside Rome. Yet, the Catacombs at Rome have exceeded all others for centuries. Before the birth of Christ the Jews used the Catacombs there in flight from the Romans; after the birth of Christ the Christians sought refuge there. Many of them lived and died there. Originally, they were simply underground burial places for the poor, who were not allowed to bury their families in the cities. "Catacomb" means literally "a subterraneous excavation," limited in its application to excavated places of burials. Primitive Christian art started in the Catacombs of Rome. These underground places of Rome could be entered *Via Flaminia; Via Ostiensis;* and *Via Appia.*

The main corridors of these excavations have niches carved out of the soft stone of the underground quarries. These cut-out niches are from eight feet to ten feet high, and four feet to six feet wide. They are called "galleries." Some galleries extend two to three miles. The St. Sebastian gallery is about twenty miles long. The period of the early flights to this underground refuge extended especially from the days of Nero to the Edict of Galerius, 311 AD. He died of great disease, frightfully rendered, and he gave the Edict of freedom as he requested the Christians to pray for him. In the days of Constantine the remaining Christians began to come out of the Catacombs. Later generations returned to the Catacombs to venerate the martyrs. Unfortunately, the Goths began to ransack the memorabilia.

The *Via Appia* entrance is about fifteen miles from Rome in the direction of the Appian Way. It finally became a violation of the law of Rome to use the Catacombs. Paul's second imprisonment at Rome is believed to be the time of his beheading under Nero. From that time on the Christians fled to the Catacombs. For three hundred years these underground corridors were used. There are reputedly 587 miles of these underground sections with several stories above each other. This mileage is equal to the entire length of the country of Italy; there are forty-two subterranean sections; there are seventy thousand inscriptions; there are four million graves, and some historical sources give seven million graves.

It is believed that on Paul's first Roman imprisonment, at the end of his journey by ship and foot, the last places he met with his brethren were at the near entrance of the Catacombs, "when the brethren heard of us, they came to meet us as far as Appii forum, and The Three taverns: whom when Paul saw, he thanked God, and took courage." The Book of Acts, chapter 28, verse 15. That was the last known contact Paul had with Christians. Immediately the Divine Record says, "And when we came to Rome,.."

Thus, the three "expectancies" abounded, but Gabriel saw the greater expectancy in the world for a human leader who would be, finally, the Antichrist.

Gabriel believed that the Antichrist had not actually been revealed to the earth yet, but he did not remove the possibility that he was alive on the earth and that his coming was timed immediately after the first stage of the second coming of the Lord Jesus Christ in clouds for His saints. Gabriel believed that as long as the saints were in the earth, they must be true to their stand for historic Christianity. Gabriel continued to preach and teach that the Antichrist, when it was his time, would suddenly come on the scene immediately after the saints rise to the clouds to meet the Lord. All of the political stage of the world would have already been set for his quick "unveiling" in the earth.

Gabriel emphasized that the very same word that was used for the coming of Christ, "revealed," was also used for the coming of the Antichrist, too—"revealed." II Thessalonians, chapter 2, verses 3, 6, and 8—*apokaluphthei*. Also, the same Greek word, *parousias,* for the "moment" of the sudden coming of Jesus Christ in the clouds, is used for the sudden coming of the Antichrist—*parousias.* II Thessalonians, chapter 2, verse 9. A third word, *epiphaneia,* is also used for the historic Christ and the prophetical Antichrist. II Thessalonians, chapter 2, verse 9. In one verse alone, verse 8, all three words are used in relationship to the Antichrist and the Lord Jesus Christ—*apokaluphtheisetai, epiphaneia, parousias.* II Thessalonians, chapter 2, verse 8. The three words defined are: first, the "unveiling," or "revelation" of Antichrist; second, the "coming" or "shining" of Jesus Christ; and third, the "presence" or "moment" of the coming of Jesus Christ.

Gabriel had finally received word from LeVon Gilbertson that he, his wife, his son, and his wife would like to visit Gabriel January 5th, next, 6:00 PM. Gabriel noted that the date was the historical "Twelfth-night," the evening before the day of "Twelfth-day," or the twelfth day after Christmas, January 6th. The Christian festival of the Epiphany is celebrated on this day. It also marks the last day of the Christian Christmas celebration when the Wise Men came to view the Baby Jesus in a house. It was believed to be the time of the reappearance of the Evening Star that these Wise Men had seen earlier back in their own country in the East.

Evangeline, once again, brought fresh decor to the two rooms in their beautiful Georgetown home where the two Gilbertson couples would spend the night. Miss Juliana Queens, who never married, was still a member of the faculty in The Conservatory of Historic Christian Studies. She was also hostess at Mansion House, on campus. She resided there in an upstairs apartment. Mansion House was now used only for the hospitality accommodations for guests and a few students. Anvil House provided all classrooms as well as the Whitefield Sanctuary for worship. The students would not be back for the spring semester until January 11, so all of the other nine apartments for nine couples were available for occupancy. Each apartment was composed of two rooms. This twenty-room Mansion House, with a private bath in each apartment, could easily take care of anyone who might be coming for a few days to inquire of the ministries of The Lodebar Base of Gabriel's ministries. However, most students lived in the Georgetown area. Gabriel desired them to live among the people of the community so that they could be known and respected.

Also, the three children of Gabriel and Evangeline, with their children, were coming for the occasion of the new year and would see the Gilbertsons. When you add up the families of Joseph Paul, Soma Jeanne, and Ariel John, with Gabriel and Evangeline, it would be sixteen including eight grandchildren as well. Brother and Sister Wiley were to be present with them, too. All were Christians. So, Gabriel's family would stay with Miss Queens in the Mansion House, and the Parsons and the Gilbertsons would reside for the night in Gabriel's home.

There would be a total of twenty-three persons, including Miss Queens, who were to have supper that night in the Parsons home in the large dining room. The Wileys had arrived about 2:30. It was about 4:05 in the afternoon of the expected visit of the Gilbertsons: all of the ladies were working in the kitchen and the dining room, and all of the men were in the drawing room gathered around the piano with Gabriel at the piano keys. He did set the agenda as follows, and said with a happy heart.

"We will sing until things are ready for supper, dear ones; and every song each one of us selects must have the name of Jesus and the noun of grace in it. Joseph Paul, please tell my dear Evangeline that as soon as the ladies finish preparing supper to come in and join us on the songs. (pause) And now, let us start the song time with 'Jesus, the Gracious Name of Grace.' It is a new song that I have written and there are copies for all of us here on the piano. Then, we will sing your song, too."

An unusual gladness of the heart and the joy of Jesus Christ prevailed throughout the entire house. The ladies finally joined in song, too. Evangeline and Gabriel sang a duet; and, then Evangeline concluded the song service with Bach's beautiful song form, "Jesus, Joy of Man's Desiring." She sang with strength and beauty; she was in her eighties in age, but in song she was still young.

Evangeline then gave her usual beautiful words to all assembled and declared that supper would be on the table in a little while. They were all seated and relaxed, in the drawing room, speaking of their ministries and God's mercies upon them, waiting for the supper and the evening. Gabriel led in prayer and prayed for the Gilbertsons as they longed to see all of them in a few moments. It was 5:15 PM. Evangeline announced, "All I need to do is bring glasses of water and place the hot tea on the table."

Promptly, at 6:00 PM, the Gilbertsons came to the front porch and door of Gabriel's home and LeVon rang the bell. After a pause, he rang again. No one came to the door. LeVon rang still another time. No one came to the door. He remembered the key Gabriel gave him in the envelope with Gabriel's letter of response to him of the Conference on Evangelism, and thought to take it from his purse pocket. However, he first tried the knob and the door opened. LeVon ventured into the vestibule and called out, "Is anybody home?" The Gilbertsons held one more pause, and Gabriel Talmadge went past his father to try the door which led to the dining room. He opened it. The entire table was set for food — for twenty-one persons, including the Gilbertsons. The glasses of water and tea cups were by each plate. No one yet answered; no one appeared.

While LeVon was standing in the vestibule he noticed an envelope on the small table there addressed to Rev. LeVon Gilbertson. He spoke out: "Wait a minute; there is a letter here addressed to me." The letter had been written by Gabriel back on their Wedding Anniversary, December 20, 2007. It had stayed in that spot on the table since then. LeVon anxiously opened and read it quickly in silence as the others waited anxiously, too.

LeVon then read it aloud for all.

"Dear LeVon, I am reluctant to inconvenience you, but please proceed across our front yard on over to Anvil House and enter the main front entrance. Go on inside and go directly down the main aisle. Ascend the stairs on either side of the pulpit. In the pulpit there is a letter of instruction and intent concerning your present visit with us. I wanted to be sure that if I were absent when you came, you would still get my letter of Christian love, because I had also left you my house key in our last visit together. That key fits Anvil House as well. Upon entering Anvil House, proceed directly to the pulpit on the podium above the chancel area. On the shelf immediately under the pulpit top, in a box, you will find another letter and further information identified for you. Please hurry on over there as soon as you read this letter, and the other correspondence will be waiting for you.

"Respectfully Rendered,
"In the Gracious Name of Jesus,

"Gabriel"

LeVon was somewhat puzzled, as the others were, by this reception, but LeVon voiced, "Gabriel has a surprise for us. This is his way for us in his precious Christian love. Let us go as he has requested us to do."

Gabriel Talmadge agreed and assured his father, "Yes, Dr. Parsons has a proper, blessed purpose in this request. Let us follow his instructions." All agreed and departed from Gabriel's house.

Although LeVon had never been on the adjoining property of Anvil House, he had seen pictures of it, and he recognized the building across the way as he drove his automobile to the house upon their arrival. Of course, he had made a former visit here, prior to the building of Anvil House, to Gabriel's house one time before.

They anxiously proceeded across the property to Anvil House, and the key to the main front door was the same key Gabriel had spoken of in the letter, but the door was unlocked. They noticed no one on the grounds or in the building when they entered it. Gabriel entered the front door, went through the Sanctuary, ascended the steps from the chancel to the podium, and found the large envelope addressed to Rev. LeVon Gilbertson in the appointed place on the shelf in the pulpit. The packet was filled with several items with a letter on the top of the information. He immediately read it all out loud; no other persons were in the Whitefield Sanctuary or the building itself.

The letter read:

"To My Dear Friend, LeVon: December 20, 2007

"Christian Greetings!

"Having met your dear son, Gabriel Talmadge, in the Chicago airport back on December 16, 2007, I was impressed in my heart to write you a letter to come and visit us. Although I did not know then if you would come or what might be ahead for all of us, I do know we live in extremely difficult times for historic Christianity. Besides that, I have come to an age in life when Jesus may call me home in death any day.

"If you have come back to visit me for the purpose I proposed in my last conversation and letter to you, I believe it must be because you desire to identify with a historic Biblical Christian heart. Therefore, I have a deep and responsible request to make of you, impressed in my soul that you have come to believe the Biblical basic presupposition of my last conversation to you in Memphis. If you receive and read this letter, I believe it means you have come to believe in historic Biblical Christianity, and personally in the Lord Jesus Christ. I know, by now, you have become aware of our ministry. I am now in need of a 'Lodebar Base' associate to help me extend this work. I believe you are the person to do so, along with your dear son, Gabriel Talmadge — especially the younger Gabriel Talmadge.

"I have already arranged with my attorney for you and your son to be associate directors of this ministry if you will accept it. The Board of Trustees agreed unanimously as well. Everything is ready for you to take the enclosed papers to an attorney who is designated by the government in international papers. I do not have to be present. If you will sign the enclosed papers in an attorney's presence and with your son, Gabriel Talmadge, as witness to your identity, and with your own credentials of identity, according to law the papers will indeed be legal. Then you and your son will be able to continue in a ministry together here with us. As you know, there are attorney's offices open day and night in Washington because life has become so heavy with the regulations of the government. We do not know how much longer we will be able to comply with the government, but we shall endeavor to be wise unto death.

"All of the property here at the Lodebar Base, including my personal home, now has a singular deed, paid-off, in full, and should anything happen to me, you or your son could continue it on. Both my

Board and Evangeline know of these things. You and your son could continue this ministry with you as the international director of our other Bases which are listed in these papers. My three children and families have their own ministries at different Bases. They must stay in their places. You will need to do all that you can to salvage every connection with these Bases to see if God is leading others to serve with you. I believe God has led me to you through your own dear son. All the keys and other assistances to this property are here in the box from which you have drawn this letter. I believe I have covered all the information you need to proceed to carry on this work in my absence or disability.

"Of course, 'The Present Distress' of the Global World Government will undoubtedly bring great loss to this ministry and these vital matters, but God will sovereignly guide you, my dear brother, as others come to realize the little space of time that might be left in 'The Divine Interlude.'

"I believe the Lord is in this 'Present Event of Distress,' and you are the only person I knew whose heart the Lord might save, along with your own son, to lead this ministry forward to help the greatest need of a time period in the entire history of the world. What you have learned from neo-christianity in the past might now help you in dealing with others for Christ's sake. This includes your need of your son, whom I love as I love you.

"There are two passages in the Bible that I offer for your exhortation and then your comfort for this awesome day in your lives together.

"First is an exhortation for you:

*Behold, I come as a thief. Blessed is he that
watcheth, and keepeth his garments, lest he walk
naked, and they see his shame.* Revelation, chapter
16, verse 15.

**"LeVon, be no longer ashamed. I invite you to
read the life of Thomas Cranmer at this time, if you
have not before.**

"Second, and for your comfort, read rejoicingly:

*Fear none of those things which thou shalt suffer:
behold the devil shall cast some of you into prison,
that ye may be tried; and ye shall have tribulation
ten days: be thou faithful unto death, and I will give
thee a crown of life,....He that overcometh shall not
be hurt of the second death.* Revelation, chapter
2, verses 10 and 11.

"Brother LeVon, be faithful unto death."

**"Good-bye, Brothers LeVon Gilbertson and
Gabriel Talmadge Gilbertson, and may God keep you
unto life everlasting, through Jesus Christ our Lord.**

"I will meet you in the morning."

"Gabriel."

Without a word, Rev. and Mrs. LeVon Gilbertson and Rev.
and Mrs. Gabriel Talmadge Gilbertson took the set of keys, the
legal papers, the informational sheets, and the letter just read,
and all else from the pulpit box, and proceeded directly to the
nearest international attorney and signed the papers as Gabriel
had outlined. These four persons were most prayerful through
it all; God gave them a calmness for the hour.

As they left the attorney's office in downtown Washington,
D.C., they heard much commotion and disturbance under the

cry of a nearby newspaper boy on the street, shouting out

"Extra, extra! Read all about it! Extra, extra! Read all about it!"

LeVon hurriedly purchased a copy of the newspaper. He had not heard the voice of a news boy crying out "Extra" since he was a young boy many years ago. He read the huge headlines and several bylines:

"Thousands and thousands and thousands and hundreds of thousands of people are missing in the earth." — "They were reported missing about 5:40 PM Eastern Standard Time, today." – "Many more have not been estimated." – "Some say the missing ones are Christians." – "Reports include Christian Gentiles and Christian Jews."

The four Gilbertsons trembled and prayed and obeyed. Each one of them bowed down on the sidewalk and confessed their sins and accepted the Lord Jesus Christ as Savior.

Gabriel Talmadge Gilbertson, standing near the attorney's office, ascended the stone steps of a monument pedestal near the corner, opened his Bible and read out loud to the top of his voice for all the people passing by to hear. He read with a stentorian, slow voice from the Song of Solomon, chapter 6, verse 13 and chapter 7, verse 1.

Return, return, O Shulamite; return, return, that we may look upon thee. What will ye see in the Shulamite? As it were the company of two armies. How beautiful are thy feet with shoes, O prince's daughter!

Then Rev. LeVon Gilbertson, without any outward promptings except his heart, ascended the pedestal a step higher than his son and called out loud, enunciating every word with extreme care and power.

The time was now 7:35 PM.

LeVon Gilbertson cried out with a loud voice:

"The Shulamite Bridal Saints of the Lord Jesus Christ have,

416

this evening, about 5:40 PM, been transported to meet the Lord Jesus Christ in the clouds...(a brief pause)...This prophecy of the Second Coming of Jesus has become a historic event at last..."

Then Rev. LeVon Gilbertson, with the other three Gilbertsons standing shoulder to shoulder, as LeVon proclaimed the unsearchable riches of the grace of the Gospel of the Lord Jesus Christ and preached of the Judgment prophecies of the judgments to come to man on earth, as rooted in the historic Christianity of the Bible!

When the sermon was finished it was midnight!

Several thousands of people had gathered from the crowded, troubled souls on all the streets! They listened to every word LeVon Gilbertson preached. They stood only with awesome fear and trembling souls! Some were sorrowingly saved by grace through faith in the Lord Jesus Christ.

There was no sleep that night! The whole world was shrouded with great trouble and anxiety.

The Gilbertsons read for their own hearts that night...

I tell you, in that night there shall be two men in one bed; the one shall be taken, and the other shall be left. Two women shall be grinding together; the one shall be taken, and the other left. Two men shall be in the field: the one shall be taken, and the other left. And the disciples answered and unto him, Where, Lord? And Jesus said unto them, Wheresoever the body is, thither will the eagles be gathered together. The Gospel of Luke, chapter 17, verses 34 through 36.

Thus, it had finally happened: for those who did sleep in the night; those around the world who did work in the day; and for those who may be seeking food at the mealtimes of the world, one would be snatched and transported away to meet the glorified Body of the Lord Jesus Christ in the clouds just as Jesus had said.